Opera Lively The Interviews Volume 2

Luiz Gazzola

Headquartered in Chapel Hill, NC, USA

Offices in Auckland, New Zealand; São Paulo, Brazil; Champaign, IL, USA; and Cincinnati, OH, USA

www.operalively.com

Cover Picture Ann Lander (the roof of Palais Garnier, Paris, France)

Publisher: - Opera Lively Press
ISBN-13: 978-0692285121
ISBN-10: 0692285121

Printed in the United States of America

See also volume 1 of the Interviews series, and Volume 1 of the new Opera Lively Guides series, by the same author:
"The Opera Lively Guides – Les Troyens"
Coming shortly: "The Opera Lively Guides – Written on Skin"

DEDICATION

This writer's family has been very patient with the fact that their husband and father spent countless hours online at Opera Lively, or on the phone and Skype with artists, conducting interviews and transcribing them from a digital voice recorder. This, in addition to spending several days absent from home while traveling all over the United States and Europe to attend opera and meet singers, conductors, scholars, directors, administrators, and composers. Wife Marta and children Luciana and Mario have this writer's eternal gratitude, and this book is not only for all opera lovers out there, but also for them.

Table of Contents

ACKNOWLEDGMENTS

Our thanks go first to our interviewees. Without their brilliant musical and academic minds, this book would not be a worthy enterprise. We are profoundly honored with having received their generosity and their attention. Each one of our interviewees is a uniquely talented individual, and talking with them was a pleasure and a privilege. The main motivation for putting this book together was to divulge to more readers their fabulous insights about the operatic art form.

Second, we are thankful to the staff at Opera Lively Press. News Coordinator Mary Auer was the most instrumental contributor in brainstorming for questions. Natalie Greenly was extremely helpful with extensive proofreading, and also contributed with questions. Ann Lander, Media Consultant, helped with proofreading and the cover picture.

Special thanks go to the Press Departments of several opera companies and festivals that have facilitated many of the interviews in this book, including, allowing Opera Lively to use their premises to interview their artists, opening up backstage access, and providing production pictures for the online version of these interviews. This list is not all-inclusive; other companies have also helped, but these were particularly generous with Opera Lively, therefore deserve to be individually acknowledged: The Metropolitan Opera House in New York City (Mr. Sam Neuman, Mr. Brent Ness); the Santa Fe Opera in Santa Fe, NM (Ms. Joyce Idema, Ms. Cindy Layman, Ms. Dolores McElroy); Opera Carolina in Charlotte, NC (Maestro James Meena, Mr. Brandon Stanley, Ms. Kathy Rowan); Glimmerglass Opera Company in Coopertown, NY (Ms. Francesca Zambello, Ms. Brittany Lesavoy, Ms. June Dzialo); Greek National Opera in Athens (Vasilis Louras); UNC Memorial Hall in Chapel Hill, NC (Mr. George Flanagan); UNC Dept of Music (Dr. Louise Toppin); North Carolina Opera in Raleigh, NC (Mr. Eric Mitchko, Ms. Beth Johnson); Piedmont Opera in Winston-Salem, NC (Maestro James Allbritten, Ms. Mariedith Appanaitis, Mr. Frank Dickerson); and Asheville Lyric Opera, Asheville, NC (Mr. David Starkey).

Several PR firms and artist management firms were instrumental in taking to completion these interview projects and are too numerous to inclusively acknowledge, but some of them were particularly attentive to our journalists: KKN Enterprises (Ms. Karen Kriendler Nelson) and 21C Media Group (Mr. Albert Imperato, Mr. Sean Michael Gross) both in New York City were outstanding, and honorable mentions go to IMG Artists and Columbia Artists in America (several agents), CSAM and Rausch Communications both in Germany, Askonas Holt, Albion Media, and International Classical Artists in the UK; Joni Hurst, Ernesto Palacio, Kim Correro, and Tim Weiler.

PREFACE

CONTENT

This book contains the best of approximately seventeen months of operatic journalism at Opera Lively, selected from our approximately one hundred twenty-five interviews with various artists, directors, scholars, and thinkers from late October 2012 through March 2014. It continues the Volume 1 of our interview series, which contained our 2011-12 interviews.

First, we introduce those artists who usually most attract the public's curiosity: the singers. They are the divas and divos of opera, and it is natural to start with them. Just like we did for Volume 1, our first four chapters feature the complete interviews with twelve established and famous or veteran singers: Susan Graham, Frederica von Stade, Magdalena Kožená, Juan Diego Flórez, Jay Hunter Morris, Lawrence Brownlee, Giuseppe Filianoti, Diana Damrau, Eva-Maria Westbroek, Barbara Hannigan, Greer Grimsley, and Ildar Abdrazakov. Of particular interest is grande dame of opera Frederica von Stade, given that she treats us to her rich memories of her great career spanning several decades.

Two chapters follow with our conversations with twelve other either less well-known, emerging, or younger singers (some of them also already quite famous), who have opinions just as interesting as those of their more experienced counterparts. These include Lisette Oropesa, Isabel Leonard, Olga Peretyatko, Jessica Pratt, Melody Moore, Ginger Costa-Jackson, Jill Gardner, Elizabeth Bishop, Michael Spyres, Paul Appleby, Massimo Giordano, and Ryan McKinny.

While singers are fascinating, they are far from being the only operatic artists who can be extremely educational and deep in their views. Next we have three interviews with conductors: Maestros Marco Armiliato, Yannick Nézet-Séguin, and Myron Michaidilis; all three with impressive views on the operatic environment and the intricate details of working with scores and of leading orchestras. Maestro Michaidilis is also the director of the Greek National Opera in Athens, Greece, and he talks about the challenges of directing a major national company. This is followed by three more talks with those professionals who can teach us about the ins and outs of operatic production: stage directors Laurent Pelly, Francesca Zambello (who also directs two opera companies), and Christian Räth.

Next section, which is not to be missed thanks to its educational content, is where we learn from educators delivering Master Classes: Lawrence Brownlee, Frederica von Stade, and pianist James Meredith address in detail young student singers. If you, reader, have never attended a Master Class, this is your opportunity to learn how it goes.

Finally we interview two composers of contemporary opera: George Benjamin, whose opera *Written on Skin* has been considered the first real masterpiece of the 21st century and arguably one of the best operas of the last forty years, and Pulitzer Prize-winning composer Kevin Puts whose opera *Silent Night* took this prestigious prize for music.

OPERA LIVELY ONLINE

If this book is your first contact with Opera Lively, we invite you to explore our online operations at www.operalively.com. Not only you will be able to see numerous pictures of the artists interviewed here (there are online versions of these interviews), but also covers for their discs (audio and video) and clips of their singing. You will also find literally hundreds of original articles; exciting online opera-themed novels being published chapter by chapter; in-depth analyses of great operas including musical structure, discography, stagings, and trivia; a singer's section; reviews of CDs, DVDs, and Blu-ray discs; reviews of live performances and broadcasts; operatic news; classifieds; a very active discussion forum, and much more. It is a friendly and accessible place that welcomes beginners, but also includes comprehensive and expert-driven content that is informative and educational. In addition to the majority of articles and posts in English, there are small sections in Spanish, Italian, French, German, and Portuguese. The entirety of our content is made available to readers free of charge, as is registration as a member (necessary to post your own comments).

WHY OPERA?

The writer is a physician by weekday and an opera journalist by night and weekends. Why would someone want to get this involved with the art form, to the point of making it a second and demanding career, on top of an equally demanding first one? Is opera still this important, today?

When opera first appeared, it wasn't popular at all. It was an elitist exercise, created in a think-tank of intellectuals, and presented to nobility in the courts. It became popular later, when in Venice some impresarios built the first opera houses open to the general public, instead of just presenting the works at the royal palaces and private auditoriums.

At that point in history, opera was wildly popular, and the castrati were the rock stars of their era. Verdi's funeral brought millions to the streets of Milan. The opera houses in Venice were what the cinema multiplexes are today in terms of mass entertainment. But this was when opera was the only game in town.

Now, opera competes with a huge number of other entertainment genres - pop music, Hollywood and independent movies, TV shows, and more recently the Internet and social media. So it has naturally enough retreated into a smaller niche, as have other art forms such as printed literature.

We opera enthusiasts ask ourselves constantly how to keep opera relevant. Some artists interviewed by Opera Lively (for example Joyce DiDonato and Jessica Cates) have said that they believe nothing needs to be done because opera is already relevant and will continue to be so. We think it is a nice way to put it.

Does opera actually need to be wildy popular? Maybe not. It may be a niche art form, but it is a strong, stubborn, enduring niche that has remained in existence for 416 years, which makes it the most enduring continuously evolving musical genre in humankind's history. Opera must have been doing something right - otherwise it would have disappeared. This is something to behold and respect.

And why is this so? Because opera touches the very core of the human condition. It has a force of truth, or "*Satyagraha*", a very appropriate name for a contemporary opera. Opera is sublime music that expresses and illustrates love, desire, duty, friendship, loyalty, jealousy, power, greed, death, murder, war, religion, mythology… what makes us human. And it does so by way of the ultimate art form that encompasses the musical, theatrical and visual arts, including instrumental playing, singing, acting, scenery, costumes, props, lighting, prose, poetry…

In fact, in many ways, opera is doing just fine, with at least 5,547 performances worldwide in 2011 (just taking into account the largest organizations).[1] At time of writing there is admittedly some temporary decrease in budgets and number of productions, arguably related to the global economic crisis, rather than to the art form itself. Once the economy rebounds, opera will likely rebound with it as well, and will continue to endure. It will hopefully continue to be necessary and relevant for the foreseeable future.

Opera is sometimes accused of being "formulaic, patently unrealistic, often poorly versified, frequently convoluted in plot and, in parts, undeniably boring,"[2] except for the works of "some five unassailable composers" whose classic operas are repeated over and over around the world. We instead believe that there are many dozens of other worthy opera composers. Out of the thousands of operas written since 1599, naturally not all of them, or not even a large proportion of them are masterpieces, which is true of any art form. But there are enough high-quality operas out there to last a lifetime of exploration and enjoyment. We keep constantly discovering new ones (new for us, as well as new contemporary works) that are outstanding, fresh, surprising, and exhilarating.

So, if you are a beginner, don't be afraid of opera. Listen to a CD. Watch a DVD or Blu-ray. Read about it. And most importantly, attend a live performance! You won't regret it. It is a thriving art form; it is both traditional and modern, it is avant-garde theater and exciting creative new productions, side-by-side with spectacular music that hails from as far back as four centuries ago, or is as contemporary as today.

Opera is alive. Opera is... lively.

Let the opera bug bite you, and you'll be in for a lifetime of pleasure. We hope that this book will be a step in the direction of convincing you to give

---

[1] Reference: http://www.bachtrack.com/concert-opera-league-tables-2011

[2] These were the words of a journalist from The Telegraph, Igor Toronyi-Lalic, reviewing the book *A History of Opera* by Carolyn Abbate and Roger Parker; Allen Lane, 2012, 604 p. While the comment is said to be according to the authors, we are not positive that the authors have intended it this way, from our reading of the source. Reference:
http://www.telegraph.co.uk/culture/books/artsandentertainmentbooksreview/9635950/Opera-by-Carolyn-Abbate-and-Roger-Parker-review.html

opera a try. But if you have this book in your hands, chances are that you are already an aficionado. In this case, well, enjoy the show!

PS - If you like our interviews, look up Volume 1 as well. It contains the words of singers Anna Netrebko, Anna Caterina Antonacci, Danielle de Niese, Deborah Voigt, Erwin Schrott, Joyce DiDonato, Luca Pisaroni, Matthew Polenzani, Piotr Beczala, Saimir Pirgu, Thomas Hampson, Vivica Genaux, Amanda Echalaz, Anthony Roth Costanzo, Bryan Hymel, Dawn Pierce, Dina Kuznetsova, Jessica Cates, Jill Gardner, Leah Crocetto, Liam Bonner, Paulo Szot; maestros Daniele Gatti, Frédéric Chaslin, Leon Botstein, and Sir John Eliot Gardiner; stage director Thaddeus Strassberger, video director François Roussillon (FRA Musica), singer and director Yvonne Fontane; opera company administrators James Meena, Eric Mitchko, and James Allbritten; opera scholar Dr. Philip Gossett (the great Rossini specialist), opera professor Dr. Marilyn Taylor and her student Richard Ollarsaba; veteran singer, book author, and painter Sylvia Sass; contemporary opera composers Robert Ward of *The Crucible* fame, avant-garde Czech composer Martin Smolka, and young composer and conductor Marko Ivanović, whose opera for children *Enchantia* is a perennial sold-out favorite in Prague.

Luiz Gazzola, MD, PhD
Senior Editor, Opera Lively
August 2014

DIVISION ONE - INTERNATIONALLY ESTABLISHED SINGERS

CHAPTER ONE – THE MEZZO-SOPRANOS

Susan Graham

We've rarely enjoyed so much an interview as the one you are about to read, with the great American mezzo Susan Graham. I'm sure you are all familiar with her phenomenal voice and exquisite acting ability - but in addition to these great qualities as a performer, Susan Graham is also very intelligent and articulate, genuine and outspoken, which makes her so delightful. Enjoy! (July 2013)

Opera Lively - Let's start by talking about *La Grande-Duchesse de Gérolstein* which you are doing right now at Santa Fe Opera. I love it; it is zany and funny, varied, fast paced, and lively, but also with lyric moments. I do feel that the third act loses steam a little bit. Please tell me about your opinion of this piece.

Susan Graham – I think it's fun, and there's some very beautiful music. Nobody does this genre better than Offenbach. He has a way of maintaining a level of humanity within the buffo construct. The music is typical Offenbach, it goes around in circles [laughs] but that's part of its charm. He very much employs a sort of leitmotif technique as well because the different themes keep coming back and remind the audience of what happened before. We took a comic turn with that. There is for example this "voici le sabre" that keeps coming back – it's very exciting to the Duchess but all of the soldiers find it very tiresome so that's kind of a little funny take on it. It's something the director has worked into the staging, which is cute.

It's light-hearted, it's one of those happy-ending, we are up and up with a bow, and we have some nice Can-Can music to go out on. It's not terribly emotionally gut-wrenching, I'll say that. [laughs] But the music is very jolly and the audience loves it. It's a lot of fun. It's nice, for a change for me, to be able to do a role where I get to smile a lot. [laughs] Because in things like Iphigénie and Didon, there is so much tragedy, there is not an awful lot of light-hearted moments. In fact, in *Iphigénie en Tauride*, I don't even get to smile one time the entire night, I recall, during one of my many performances of that.

OL - I got to know this delightful operetta through the DVD with Felicity Lott in the title role, at the Châtelet with the excellent Marc Minkowski conducting and Laurent Pelly directing – a great team, and a pretty high bar to meet.. So please tell me how this Santa Fe production is coming around. What kind of concept is Lee Blakeley bringing to us?

SG – Well, Lee Blakeley believes that operetta should be presented with a cultural frame of reference of the location and the audience that it's done for. So, in our case, since it's an American audience Lee has chosen to set the action in an American military academy, like West Point maybe, but in the first decade of the 1900's, so early 20th century. That lends itself to young men in athletic uniforms running around the track, and training for their battles or their games or whatever they are going to do, and the girls come in in there in sort of 1920's cheerleader outfits, and they've got bows in their hairs, and little stripped shirts. The costuming is absolutely gorgeous. Lee has adapted the dialogue to reflect that. The characters, he has made them very familiar American types.

OL – It is in French, right?

SG – The singing is in French and the dialogue is in English.

OL – Oh, OK. How do you feel about that? Does it get disruptive?

SG – No, I think it's perfect. Of course we have the titles on the back of the seats here, just like at the Metropolitan Opera. That technology was actually invented here at Santa Fe Opera. So the audience has the translation of what we are singing. We did *La Belle Hélène* the same way here in 2003. We did the singing in French and the dialogue in English and it worked perfectly. This audience needs to have the dialogue in English, but we didn't want to sing it in English. I wanted to sing it in French, because of course I love singing in French and so does Paul Appebly, and Emmanuel Villaume, our conductor, is French. We've maintained that part of the original composition, to keep the singing in French. It worked just fine. The audience after two seconds, they completely go with it.

OL – The standard-bearer recording conducted by Plasson with Régine Crespin, had lots of cuts. Minkowski's version had a lot more music, for instance, including "Le Carrillon de Ma Grand-Mère" at the end of the second act which seems really essential, as it is hallmark Offenbach, accelerating more and more to get to a galop.

SG – As do we; we're doing the critical edition by Jean-Christophe Keck, which also does include the "Carrillon."

OL – Oh, OK, it's always nice when people employ critical editions, it's becoming more frequent.

SG – Yes, we do, we use that critical edition and so we've got the "Carrillon," and we've also got the men's chorus at the beginning of the third act. If you are not familiar with that, it's very amusing.

OL – And you've got all the ballet, or rather, dance music?

SG – There are many scenes with dancing. I'm not that familiar with the other versions you are talking about, so I can't really compare. We do have a dedicated ballet. There is one big dance number at the end of the second act. When you see it, you'll be able to compare it with the version you are referring to.

My friend Peggy Hickey, our choreographer, told me that to her knowledge there is no ballet music that was cut. Wait until you see the choreography! What she has done is nothing short of Broadway brilliant. She has turned this into a Broadway show, and it is unbelievable. We have eight professional dancers who are Broadway dancers, and one who is a Radio City Rockette. When we do the can-can, it will be very obvious! [laughs] She's amazing. We have professional dancers who are doing the flips, they are doing some of the gymnastics, and they are doing lifts, and it's all extremely athletic. Peggy has taught the chorus men who are our soldiers, very specific military drills, riffle tossing, and twirling of riffles, and we have tap dancing, we have can-can, it's just amazing! You are going to be thrilled with the choreography!

OL – Great, I'm getting very excited!

SG – Yes, yes, it is very exciting!

OL – Your opening aria, "Ah, que j'aime les militaries" – is it exposed? Does this role include any vocal challenge?

SG – Well, there are a couple of brazen high B flats, but they are not a problem, really. It's not a difficult sing, not at all. It's fun, because there are a couple of opportunities with these B flats for emotional outbursts with virtuosity. They are not just stand-alone vocal moments; they come out of the staging, and the choreography is very cute, very amusing.

OL – Have you listened to your predecessors in this role? Is this something you typically do?

SG – Sometimes, yes. Yes, I do, I listen to them for stylistic tips. I watched part of the DVD with Minkowski and Felicity Lott, not all of it, but I watched parts of it before I even got into rehearsals at all, just to get an idea. Our production is completely different from theirs. That production was a little on the dark side and ours is very jolly and has a lot of fun informality. My character is completely different than Lott's, just because of the production. My character is completely different from Régine Crespin's. I saw some YouTube videos of Régine Crespin, and she is brilliant, she is one of my great idols. But ours is just a very different take.

OL – Well, it's opéra-bouffe, so we won't expect huge psychological depth, but anyway, your character is engaged in a rivalry with the younger woman Wanda for the love of Fritz. Santa Fe Opera is advertising your take as "Far from being 'a lady of a certain age,' this Grand Duchess is a sexy, spoiled aristocrat." How do you read your character, psychologically, and how do you plan to tackle the role?

SG – That's where we are going, yes. Well, I play her as a woman of a certain level of maturity who has a taste for younger men. I've been in her shoes before [we both laugh hard]. It comes very easily to me, I might just say [laughs]. It's just a lot of fun! I mean, the thing is, she is having so much fun with it! She knows that she is in a position of power and she can just walk along and flirt with all of these beautiful young soldiers! She is having a great time with it! The situation with Fritz starts to get a little out of hand.

I think that if she didn't know that she had such competition he wouldn't be quite so appealing. But it's the competition with Wanda that accelerates her affection for Fritz.

OL – We'll be interviewing Paul Appleby as well; I think he is great. What can you tell us about the chemistry with your colleagues?

SG – Paul Appleby, first of all, I've told him that I would be happy if I could just hear him sing French all day long, every day. His voice was made to sing lyrical French music. That's not to say he doesn't sing everything else beautifully, he does, but I just love hearing him sing French. He has a beautiful way with the language. He speaks French fluently. The timbre of his voice is just absolutely beautiful with this music. I don't know if you saw *Les Troyens* from the Met.

OL – I did, he sang Hylas.

SG – Oh, so beautiful!

OL – Yes, it was beautiful!

SG – I was in that show with him, but I never saw him at the theater because Hylas is on stage when Didon is not and vice-versa, so I really didn't see him except in the dress rehearsals a couple of times, so I didn't really know him, coming into this. He is absolutely charming, completely down to Earth, hilariously funny, but in a very subtle way. His humor is very dry, and he is very creative, and kind of fearless, in a way. I've really enjoyed getting to know him.

OL – What about your comic relief character, the General Boum?

SG – Kevin Burdette on the other hand is the Jim Carrey of opera! He is completely over-the-top and hilarious, both on stage and off. He will stop at nothing, talk about fearless! That guy is hysterical! He is one of the funniest guys I've ever met in opera. And also our Baron Puck, Aaron Pegram is an amazing actor.

OL – Now, I'd like to address your role in one of my favorite operas – actually my third favorite opera of all time, after the *Ring* and after *Tristan und Isolde*: Berlioz's *Les Troyens* – I actually did write a little book about it. My preferred version is the Châtelet production with you, and two of our former Opera Lively interviewees, Sir John Eliot Gardiner, and Anna Caterina Antonacci.

SG – Oh, how lovely. Musically, or scenically, or everything?

OL – I do love it musically with the period instruments and you all great singers, and the sets were great with the mirrors. I loved that production, it is simply phenomenal.

SG – Oh, I loved it too.

OL – So, I would like to ask you to share with our readers, memories you may have of it.

SG – Oh! Well, it was a very important milestone in my career, certainly, to do your first Didon, and to do it in Paris, and to do it in that year. Wasn't it the anniversary of Berlioz's birth?

OL – Was it? I don't remember. [She is right; it was his bicentennial of birth, in 2003]

SG – Yes, it was! You wrote a book about it!

OL – I haven't read my own book in a while! [laughs]

SG – [Laughs hard]. Anyway, it was the anniversary year of Berlioz, and it was a great honor to do it in Paris at the Châtelet. And what John Eliot Gardiner brought to it was this amazing, as you knew, texturing and clarity of the piece, because often times it is done with a sort of Wagnerian sweep, but John Eliot brought those original Berlioz instruments, these textures, these clarities, these transparencies, that made the storytelling that much more poignant, because you could hear the plaintiveness of certain instruments that sometimes you don't hear in a big modern orchestra. For starts, that was amazing.

Now, Yannis Kokkos [stage director] who – we all know – is a brilliant designer, made this gorgeous set, which I thought was kind of abstract but – him being Greek – had real references to that whole part of the world, in the starkness, and the blues and whites. And also, the darkness of the war, and Aeneas and his army who are coming into this land of beauty and light [Carthage]. I thought it was beautiful, the giant mirror reflecting what was going on the stage. The tilted mirror was brilliant. I loved the tenderness of that production. With this orchestration, Gregory Kunde and I could sing with our lyric voices, pianissimo and so tenderly in those love duets, and it was so thrilling to be able to really just sort of live it, and not have to scream it.

OL – Yes, by the way I interviewed Anna Caterina Antonacci as well and she said similar things. What an actress she is, isn't she?

SG – She is amazing!

OL – You repeated the role for the Met – what can you tell us about that production? How do you compare the two?

SG – Well, by the very nature of the house, the Met production is going to be much bigger, and the Metropolitan Opera Orchestra is much fuller, and we get to fill a much larger space. Francesca Zambello as we all know is quite brilliant at managing big epic storytelling with big choruses, and she did a beautiful job of that. The stage was full of people when it needed to be. There was a real sense of a real culture happening, both in Troy and in Carthage. And you got a sense of what life was like for those people. The colors that she uses, the designs, the different physical levels of the stage set, I think kept the eye very involved and interested throughout the piece – it's a five-hour piece; you got to keep the eye busy [laughs] and I think it's something she does beautifully.

The interaction of the principal characters, the relationship I was able to build with Karen Cargill as Anna, I thought was very special, and I loved that. That was one of my favorite things about it. I had two Aeneases, Marcello Giordani and Bryan Hymel, and I have to say, I loved working with both of them.

OL – Do you feel that with the full Met Orchestra and the 4,000-seat house, it was harder to sing it than in Paris?

SG – In the end of the day, you're just doing your performance. I will say that in the fifth act, with Didon's hysterical breakdown when Aeneas is leaving, I probably had to have more meat in it at the Met than I did in Paris, simply because in Paris it was played down front over the pit and the orchestra was much smaller. In New York you can't do that, so by necessity I had to beef it up a little bit, vocally. But I don't mind doing that, because it all serves the character and it serves the drama and it serves the moment. There were times when I was almost belting it, sort of shouting it in my chest voice those lower notes, which I think fits, because she is at the end of her rope! She doesn't care about making a beautiful sound all the time [laughs], she is intense! What I mean to say is that in the end of the day you are not really worrying so much about – "Am I going to be heard?" The conductor can help you, hopefully keeping the orchestra down at the times when it is really difficult. The real goal is to serve that moment in the drama, and the character.

OL – I see. Great answer! La Grande-Duchesse and Didon couldn't be more different as characters. The latter has an astonishing tragic depth. Would you tell me a bit how you relate to the character Didon and to her music?

SG – Oh, what a complete character! She is great. I mean, the completeness of beloved woman sovereign, who starts the Carthage portion of the opera celebrating triumph for her people and how their young culture has flourished under her reign, and she is so beloved! It's so wonderful to come out and just sing that beautiful opening scene and have the adoring faces of my people, as Didon! The chorus members are the Carthaginians, and they are peaceful, loving people, and they adore their queen! It's so confidence-giving, because you know that you have this big journey ahead of you, as a performer, but to start it that way is very comforting.

Then, the culture becomes threatened and she has to make some very hard decisions, but Aeneas comes to her rescue, and of course there is that big love story in the fourth act. And that's one beautiful tune after the other! That fourth act is just a joy to sing, because it's just beauty, beauty, beauty.

And then… it all goes wrong in the fifth act, and she turns into a woman scorned, and she basically has a mad scene. And then she gets to kill herself! So, it's the greatest character, [laughs] because she's got everything!

OL – I'll bring a copy of my little book to offer to you.

SG – Oh, I would love that!

OL – You know, not that it is that good, but there are some fun things; I've included an interview with Anna Caterina Antonacci and one with Bryan Hymel about their roles in the Covent Garden Les Troyens, so you may like it.

SG – Oh, wonderful! Goodness, I'm sitting outside in my deck and there is a huge rain storm coming up, I'll have to get inside, sorry, I'm sure there is a wind blowing over the telephone, it wasn't making it easy to hear me.

OL – Yes, there was a little wind noise. So, do you have more fun portraying women like Didon and Sister Helen Prejean, or comic characters like la Grande-Duchesse, Octavian, and Cherubino?

SG – I do love these characters with a lot of depth. I always say that a character like Didon, a character like Charlotte in *Werther*, these are the characters that allow you to go into the places of your soul and of your own psyche that you may not be able to access so easily in everyday life – for me, anyway. I'm not a person who is very, very dramatic. I'm not a drama queen in my personal life. My boyfriend mighty argue with that statement! [laughs] But I'm pretty even keel. So, these rather tragic characters – Iphigénie is another great example – allow me to access the part of every human being, me included, that has pain, has suffering, has loss. I do enjoy that.

And I have to say, I saw that you've included Octavian in the list of comic characters and he does certainly have great comedy, but he also suffers. That was always something that I've loved very much about Octavian: he also feels pain, he is hurt by some of the things that have gone on.

OL – That entire opera is a mix of tragedy and comedy, right?

SG – Absolutely.

OL – Are trouser roles a lot of fun? Do they take especial acting abilities for a woman to act like a man on stage?

SG – Oh, I love them. I've done so many of them, and everyone says, "How do you become a boy?" But for me it wasn't so much becoming a boy, as it was becoming just a kid. It was more about accessing the physical freedom and spontaneity that a young boy would have. I grew up with a brother and a lot of nephews. I've been around a lot of athletics and sports in my family. I was kind of a tomboy, growing up. Accessing that athletic movement and male physicality was always very easy for me, because I'm so tall, and I'm certainly no stranger to adolescent cockiness; that was me as a kid too. That part of it has always been lots of fun.

As I look back, one of the most fun and challenging male portrayals that I ever did was a Ruggiero in *Alcina* in Paris. You can see loads and loads of that in YouTube.

I looked back at some of those, and I almost forget that I am me, because the way that they costumed me, the very contemporary style of Robert Carsen in directing that production, sometimes I look at those videos and I think "I look just like a guy!" And it surprises even me, because I sort of don't remember it. There is a lot of not remembering about the development of that character, because it was a long time ago. But when I look at it, I see this suit – it was a sort of neo-cut black suit with a white shirt and a skinny black tie, and I had one of the best boy wigs I've even worn in my life. The way that Robert encouraged me to find the contemporary truth in my movement was something that changed it all for me. I tried later to incorporate that into Octavian, even though Octavian is an 18th century teenager. Also, into Sesto – even though Sesto was a Roman, certainly in a much more classical age. Check out that Alcina, because that was one of my favorite male portrayals.

OL – OK, I will. So, let's switch to contemporary opera. How was for you the experience of having characters created for you, in Jake Heggie's opera *Dead Man Walking*, in John Harbison's *The Great Gatsby*, and Tobias Picker's *An American Tragedy*? Is there something interesting to contrast and compare these three experiences?

SG – Well, it's great, first of all because you are breathing life into something that has only ever existed on paper before. That can be said of any role that you are doing, but in world premiere, when it's a new opera, the roles are yours and the composer's, the director's, and the conductor's to construct. There is no precedent. You can discover things, and no one can say that it's right or wrong in your performance. They can't say "Oh, that's not how Régine Crespin did it!" or "It's not how Tatiana Troyanos did it" because it's never been done. So, you have the freedom from comparison. You have the freedom to create – and to collaborate – something that nobody has seen before, and maybe something that nobody has thought about, in that way.

Certainly, with something like *The Great Gatsby*, it's an iconic American novel. It was an iconic movie. I went back to the novel, mainly, for my source, because it's dangerous to recreate something from a movie, although the woman who played my character, Jordan Baker, in the 1974 film with Robert Redford, is Lois Chiles, and I met her recently; in the past year I got to know her a little bit, and we had a good talk about Jordan Baker in terms of playing her, the character. Music adds a whole different level to a characterization. It brings a personality that a book can't access, because music has a whole other level of expression of a character and of storytelling.

OL – You did interact a bit with Susan Sarandon, the actress who did Sister Helen Prejean in the *Dead Man Walking* movie, right? I saw a picture of the two of you together.

SG – Oh, it was just a photo op, I never talked to her about it. She wasn't really interested in talking about it! [laughs hard] I think she owned her own

Sister Helen and she didn't want to share her with me! [laughs]!

OL – Interesting! [laughs]

SG – But Sister Helen herself was a huge influence, obviously. Getting to know the actual person… That's what I was about to say: that the world premiere of *Dead Man Walking* is in a category of its own, in terms of my experience with world premieres. *An American Tragedy* was wonderful, but I played a character similar to the one I played in *The Great Gatsby*. I played a privileged, rich girl in the earlier part of the 20th century, and that was sort of like Jordan Baker. So those two characters were not completely different. Sister Helen, however, is a real person, obviously, and her mission is a very, very… oof!... emotionally loaded calling. What she does is extremely important work, and it shook me to my very core, in just about every level that there is. Playing Sister Helen changed my life. Playing Sondra Finchley did not change my life. [laughs]

OL – Did you have any input in terms of the living composer there, to adapt the vocal lines?

SG – Sure, yes, in all three of those. John Harbison who is a very brilliant man, with the part of Jordan, we didn't have a lot to change. Everything was, to my recollection, pretty fine just the way it was. Tobias Picker, we did work a little bit on Sondra; I think we changed a few phrases that I wanted to sit better in my voice. Now, with Jake, this was Jake Heggie's first opera! He is brilliant, it's a brilliant piece, I love that piece, but he was very eager for feedback. There were certain things where the tessitura stayed a little too high for a little too long for a mezzo, so we encouraged him to be a little more tessitura-friendly with this part. Also, because it fits the character Sister Helen better. I mean, Sister Helen is not a high-flying hysterical-sounding person, and if write in the upper register for too long, it can start to sound that way. Jake Heggie is one of my best friends.

OL – Do you have any projects for new world premieres?

SG – Not any official ones, no.

OL – So, let's talk about your latest CD. Your "Virgins, Vixens, and Viragos" has no fewer than 14 composers from Purcell to Sondheim and explores iconic female characters. Please tell us how you selected this theme, and the songs.

SG – Well, Malcolm Martineau and I had been talking about it for a long time. We wanted to do a sort of female-centric collection of songs. Malcolm, having a brain like a song encyclopedia, was just throwing these stories out at me, the stories of these characters. For instance, we always wanted to do the *Fiançailles Pour Rire* [Poulenc's song cycle], which is not necessarily about a single person, but it's about different kinds of love a woman goes through. There is maternal love, there is heartbreak, there is jealousy, there is sassiness, those are just different facets of a woman and her love.

But if you go back to the first half of that program, we've got *The Blessed Virgin's Expostulation* [Purcell] – Virgin Mary is the most iconic female that there ever was, so we figured that was a pretty good place to start. [laughs] And it's perfect, it's a great piece.

Then we moved quickly through *Mignon* [from Goethe's novel "Wilhelm Meisters Lehrjahre"], who is a great literary character, and certain a female who had her challenges from being an abandoned gipsy child, adopted and possibly abused along the way, and kept in secrecy – she had quite an epic journey, so we wanted to do a collection of Mignon songs of all the different composers, as you know, which was a different take on it rather than doing just a Schubert Mignon, just the Wolf, we mixed them all up [also Schumann, Liszt, Tchaikovsky, and Henri Duparc, which I think it's an interesting study of the way the different composers treated that character.

And of course, then there is Lady Macbeth, who lets out the really evil side of these ladies, and she has her little crazy bit at the end. It's a more restrained telling than Verdi's, perhaps, by contemporary English composer Joseph Horovitz.

Anyway, Malcolm knew a lot of these songs, and between his suggestions and the ones that I knew, we just thought it was a good overview. We were calling it Good Girls and Bad Girls, because the whole first half is good girls and the second half is basically bad girls. And we wanted to include something a little more light-hearted at the end and we put in some more comic music theater takes on the woman and her love. We got the Cole Porter piece *The Physician*, and then there is of course Steven Sondheim's "*The Boy From...*" which is a story about unrequited love. She couldn't understand why the boy from "Tacarembo La Tumbe Del Fuego Santa Malipas Zacatecas La Junta del Sol y Cruz" was not giving her the attention that she wanted, and then she found out that basically he was gay! [laughs hard] So, that's a classic unrequited love story!

We just had fun with these explorations of female characters and their take on love.

OL – Great! So, You are a French knight! You got the Chevalier dans l'Ordre des Arts et des Lettres title! This is neat!

SG – Yes, I have also the Legion d'Honneur!

OL – Opera Lively Press has published a book by your colleague Jay Hunter Morris.

SG – Oh! [enthusiastically]

OL – Yes, "Diary of a Redneck Opera Zinger."

SG – Can you believe it? Isn't he funny?

OL – He is! The book is hilarious! And he explores a lot the fact that he comes from Texas, and ended up singing opera. There is a part about the French car he bought, un Citroën, that is very funny – how a big Texan ends up in a tiny French car.

SG – Yep!

OL – And you are also from Texas, and became an expert in French music, an unusual combination!

SG – [laughs] How did that happen?

OL – Right! So, that *is* the question: how did that happen?

SG – [laughs] Well, I always had a very, very active imagination. When I was a young girl, I dreamt of things that were French – French culture, and the French language, because growing up in New Mexico and in Texas, I dreamed about European elegance and culture and élan and food, all the wonderful exotic things that I didn't have in my surroundings. I was a pianist all along, and I've always played a lot of Débussy piano songs, Ravel, and all that kind of thing. Already I loved French music, then when I started studying voice when I was about sixteen, my teacher started giving me Fauré songs, right out of the bat! And Débussy songs, because I could already play them, so I knew the musical language. So, it was just natural that I would gravitate toward that, and when I got into college I was studying Massenet, a lit bit of Berlioz, some Reynaldo Hahn in college, then when I got to the Manhattan School of Music, that blew the door wide open, because I got to do *Chérubin* of Massenet.

In a conservatory setting you can spend six months studying an opera, and studying the words. We had a wonderful French diction coach who had us read the play over and over, like it was a libretto. And so, French started coming very easily to my tongue and to my brain and I was just loving it, it was harkening back to my dreams as a little girl, of going to France some day and seeing the Eiffel Tower up close. So music took me there.

OL – When you got the Légion d'Honneur, how was it for you?

SG – Oh, it was amazing. In fact, I got it I believe on opening night of *Iphigénie en Tauride*, at the Met. The French Consul came to the opening night party and gave me this award. The Commander of the Order of Arts and Letters I got actually at the Ministry of Culture in Paris, and that was very special, because all my French friends came, and the Minister of Culture gave it to me in his offices, in a ceremony. That was really thrilling.

OL – Your impressive discography has thirty items, and you've won so many prestigious accolades in your career, that you must feel very fulfilled. So, what else is challenging, after you've accomplished so much? Where do you want to go from that, to remain fresh and interested? You've done everything.

SG – [laughs] Surprisingly, I have not done everything! [laughs] There is still a lot… That's not to say that I will do everything, because that would be an impossible goal to set. I'm probably looking at maybe ten more years of singing if I'm smart and if I'm healthy, knock on wood. So the clue is just to keep reinventing yourself, and keep doing new things, and try not to recreate, but keep creating.

OL – Any projects coming up?

SG – There are some new roles I'm looking at; there are roles that maybe I was offered fifteen years ago and wasn't ready to look at yet, like Clairon for instance in *Capriccio*, maybe Countess Geschwitz [*Lulu*], those kinds of things that are challenging and interesting, but I don't have to carry the whole show. It's not Octavian. It's not to say I just want to do smaller roles, because I'm still doing lots of *Les Troyens*, and lots of the roles that I've been exploring in the past five years or so, but it's in terms of keeping repertoire fresh and keeping my mind engaged, and keep wanting to learn new things.

OL – So, after those ten more years of singing, let's say when you retire from singing, what would you like to do; teach voice?

SG – No! [emphatically] I don't want to teach voice! When I work with young students, my passion is to share the passion that has always excited me, which is finding the truth in the musical communication, the expression. I'd like to coach. I like to help a young singer unlock how they feel about a piece and what they want to express within a piece; what it makes them feel; what emotions it brings out and what they'd like to communicate, and to find the best and most effective way to communicate that. That's always been what really excited me in my own career, in my own portrayals, whether it's a Ned Rorem art song, or whether it's a Didon.

OL – Would you like to stage direct?

SG – You know, I thought about that. I'm daunted by that, because I think that there is so much to learn, and so much to manage when you are a stage director! Sometimes I marvel at the amazing directors that I've had and how their overarching vision seems so clear to them, and how they manage these big groups of people and get them all to do what they want! [laughs] I have great ideas, and maybe in the past five years most directors that I've worked with will tell you that I fancy myself as an assistant stage director anyway [laughs hard]! Because I do have very strong ideas about how I want to tell the story, and sometimes about how other people should tell the story too! [laughs]

OL – Did you have any input in this *Grande-Duchesse* staging?

SG – Oh yes! I mean, it was a great collaboration. Lee Blakeley is fabulous. He has great ideas. He knows that I've been doing this for a while, and that for the most part I know what I'm doin. I know how to tell a story, so with his vision and his concept, we work together to find the best, most effective way to do a scene or to express an idea.

OL – You are a US ambassador for UNESCO.

SG – Well, I'm not anymore; that was a three-year thing.

OL – OK. So, what are causes you care about and plan to be active in, to make an impact?

SG – Right now I'm working with an organization to rebuild a music school in Haiti. They had an amazing music program going in Port-au-Prince, then it was wiped out when Haiti underwent the terrible disasters that they did. The children and the people who are running the program are so dedicated to reviving it, that they've been laboring under terrible, terrible circumstances, like trying to train children to play a violin in a tent. So we are working hard at it, because they have an enormous desire to rebuild their music training program. Their kids have great talent.

OL – Admirable. And what did you do when you were with UNESCO?

SG – I travelled to different meetings and historical sites, and worked on preserving certain folk art, and folk music initiatives for different cultures around the world, mostly in South America.

OL – Nice. Now, let's end by getting to know the woman underneath the artist, if you don't mind. Would you tell us about your extra-musical interests?

SG – Well, I have just taken up a new hobby, just this summer – jewelry making. I became fascinated. Here in Santa Fe there is a lot of crafty people, and by crafty I mean people who do crafts. [laughs]. I've always had an eye for wanting to create things with textiles. I've never been much of a seamstress, though. Out of a desire to create something for myself, I just tried it one day. I was going to make some bracelets; it was just so much fun, and offered me a creative outlet to make something beautiful, and now I'm making them for my friends, for my family, and myself, and my mother… So, it's a lot of fun, and I'm doing a lot of experimenting with different kinds of beads and techniques.

OL – What else do you like? Gourmet food?

SG – Oh yes, I love to eat gourmet food, and I have a lot of friends who are winemakers, so I've been learning a lot about wine over the years. Good wine is something that I'm very interested in – drinking and learning about it! [laughs]

OL – That's my second biggest interest, after opera!

SG – Really?

OL – Yep. So, do you cook?

SG – No. My boyfriend is a great cook. I think I chose very wisely [laughs], finding someone who is a great cook. Also, another thing that I've been learning about recently is children, because my boyfriend has seven-year-old twins. I wouldn't call step-parenting a hobby, but it is certainly something that has taken an awful lot of my brain, these days. I find if fascinating. I never had children of my own, so being around these children and being a step-mother figure to them has been such an eye-opener, and really has brought such joy to my life! It's fascinating, because I became interested in things that I thought would never apply to me, like techniques for educating young children, and how certain things are better than other things; just getting really involved in it, in a way that I never thought I would have a need to.

OL – How are you as a person? What's your personality like, and your take on life in general?

SG – I don't know, what do you think? [laughs hard]

OL – [laughs] Really lively and friendly, I would say!

SG – [laughs] That's pretty much it! That pretty much sums it up. I'm not very equipped to answer that; you may ask some of my colleagues. I'm a person for whom, I guess, friendships and connections are very important. I have friends in this business with whom I've been for twenty-five years, people I grew up in the business with; we started up together: Renée Fleming, Barbara Bonney, Thomas Hampson, I consider them my family.

OL – [Having misunderstood her] Barbara Hannigan?

SG – Barbara Bonney.

OL – Ah, OK. I think I have Barbara Hannigan in my mind, because I've just seen this spectacular new opera with her, *Written on Skin* by George Benjamin, and I can't stop thinking about it. Have you seen it?

SG – Oh, no, I didn't.

OL – It's spectacular, I think it's one of three best contemporary operas I've ever seen.

SG – Wow! I'm sure you are going to see *Oscar* when you are here.

OL – I will, of course!

SG – David Daniels is another one of those people I consider my family.

This *Oscar* is a very important piece.

OL – Yes, contemporary opera is one of the main focuses of Opera Lively. Oh, I did forget to ask you one question I was curious about: how did your love for opera came to be? You started as a pianist, then you were singing art songs… I assume you didn't plan in advance to be an opera singer.

SG – I was in music theater in High School. I played Maria in *The Sound of Music*. That was a big eye-opener for me, because I had never done anything theatrical before. I was always a bit of a ham… [laughs] I was a kid who was jumping around on the tables at family reunions, trying to get everyone's attention, because I was the youngest of my family, and the youngest of our whole complete extended family. And the youngests, they are always vying for attention. Once I was in that musical, I loved the opportunity to be on stage and to become someone else, and the challenge of creating another persona and saying someone else's words, and just becoming another character – I loved that! Now, everyone thought – because where I come from no one knows much about opera – that I was going into music theater. "Oh, you will big a big star on Broadway," they said, when I was eighteen.

I was in college at Texas Tech, and I had been a competitive classical pianist for ten years, and for me classical music was really where I was at, and I thought, "Well, classical music and theater, that combination spells opera." So, it seemed so incredibly difficult and impossible to imagine, to learn all those languages, and all the music history, and sing operas written by Mozart after I played all the Mozart sonatas and concertos, and to sing these things would just be the most incredible experience imaginable; so that's what I wanted to do!

OL – What was the first opera you saw?

SG – The first opera I ever saw was *Così fan tutte*, live. Texas Opera Theater was touring through my hometown of Midland, Texas, and they played in my high school's auditorium. I watched Despina with fascination, because she was funny; she sang Mozart, and she got to drink chocolate. And I thought, those are three things that I like very much. [laughs] Comedy, Mozart, and chocolate! So I thought, "I want to sing the character Despina one day." But I didn't; of course I sang Dorabella.

Then when I went to Texas Tech, the first opera I was ever in was *Faust*. And I did not sing Siébel, because I was just a kid, tiny kid, I was in the chorus. I think I was the chorus woman who discovers Valentin stabbed and dying. Then when I went through schools, we did scenes. We didn't mount the whole *Der Rosenkavalier*, but I did Octavian scenes, *Falstaff* scenes, and I did *Così*. *Hänsel und Gretel*, we did the whole opera. *Die Fledermaus*, we did the whole opera. We did a lot of Gilbert and Sullivan, so I sang a lot of those parts. So it certainly got under my skin. I had a great teacher at Texas Tech, and when I finished graduate school with her I moved to New York and went to the Manhattan School of Music, and got a lot of exposure to a lot of different things, and here I am!

OL – Yes, world-famous! One of the best in the business!

SG – [laughs] How in the world did that happen? I don't know, but I feel very, very lucky.

OL – That's all I had, and wow, we got one hour, that's great!

SG – Well, you are lucky that it's a Sunday afternoon, and I'm just watching it rain! [laughs]

OL – I loved it; it's one of our best interviews to date, I think.

SG – Oh, how sweet! Thank you, Luiz; thank you so much!!

Frederica von Stade

Flicka is a living legend. I felt privileged when I met her in person. Ms. von Stade is a beloved artist in our opera community. Her phenomenal discography on video and audio media (with the amazing number of 119 items!) contains some of the most exquisite operatic performances on record. We are also thrilled to know that the veteran singer is coming out of opera stage retirement (she remains active in the recital circuit) for the East Coast premiere of the new American opera *A Coffin in Egypt* by Ricky Ian Gordon. Flicka is not only a great singer, but also an extraordinary human being, involved in advocacy, leadership, and charitable pursuits. It is a great honor for Opera Lively to have been granted an in-person interview with one of the *Grande Dames* of opera. We met Ms. von Stade in the context of her recital sponsored by the The University of North Carolina at Chapel Hill, College of Arts and Sciences, Department of Music, and the William S. Newman Scholarship Series, on March 5, 2013. Later in this book we have an account of her Master Class for the UNC opera students (chapter nine).

Opera Lively - Your program, "An Evening With Frederica von Stade," is a compelling arc with your reminiscences about your life and career. Some parts are extremely funny, light, and entertaining, while others are pungent and even a bit bitter at the very end, with "Send in the Clowns." How did you develop the concept for this program?

Frederica von Stade – I started actually maybe two years ago trying out little bits and pieces of it and incorporating speaking and telling stories, and as I was doing it, I went further, and I thought, "oh yes, this corresponds with that time of my life. It's not too egotistical and it's not in such detail that I think would be off-putting, so I thought it would be fun, and it's been fun for myself as well because a lot of the music of different periods has been important to me in forty years of career. Plus a lot of the concerts that I've been doing for the last couple of years have been sort of retirement concerts, so there it seems appropriate.

Recitals and concerts have changed in my forty years in the business. They used to be a little bit stricter. You usually sang in two or three languages and very often didn't include English if you were American. And now it's changed, as the generations of foreign-speaking audiences exist. I think we've had to change it. Having *Winterreise* is very challenging for an American public that don't speak any German, even if you see the translations, because the point of *Winterreise* is a musical and a real journey. So, I don't know that we have built the public to really understand and enjoy that, and I'm a firm believer that we are entertainers. We are artists, we study great music, but Adele is an artist too; she is a great singer and she writes her own things; there's not a big difference. We are there to give joy, pleasure, whatever to people, and if they enjoy a lighter program, so be it.

OL – That's exactly what I said in my review of your program, that you are such an entertainer. That program was so entertaining!

FVS – Oh, good! [laughs] Good! Well, it's fun, at this point in my life I don't do that many things, so when I get a chance to, I really, really enjoy it. I enjoy every minute of it. I began my career with the great joy of singing and I'm ending with this joy of expressing myself through song, and it's fun.

OL – The last song in your program – "Send in the clouds" from Stephen Sondheim's musical *A Little Night Music* - when you say this line here – "losing my time this late in my career" – do you feel some psychological impact of going away?

FVS – I feel the impact. In this song, the way Sondheim wrote it, the character Desirée actually split up; she's been rejected by her true love, because she didn't realize that he was her true love for years, so he's married someone much younger, so that's what it's about; it's about someone who has lost; her timing is completely off. She should have stayed in love with him when it was appropriate. And they do get back together in the end.

But I do not feel a gram of bitterness. I don't feel a gram of envy for the young voices coming along. I feel nothing but a celebration. I'm not sad about leaving, at all. I think I had better than I deserve. I loved every minute of it. I'm a little bit at a point where I can't remember. People say "when you sang this" and I think "I don't think I ever sang that song" but I take their word for it. I remember seeing a marvelous older singer at a party. They put on her records. She listened to them not as a great diva who was applauding herself. She listened to them as though she was watching her grandchildren play. And that's how I feel. I have grandchildren, and it's the most exciting thing that has ever happened to me. My grandchildren are tops. I feel like I'm watching or thinking about something that was very joyful. I know that there was a lot of sorrow and pain and anguish there as well but I'm sort of left with the joyful part. [laughs]

OL – You say that these are pre-retirement concerts, but you are engaged in two new operas.

FVS – Yes!

OL – So, you're not about to quit!

FVS – I know! When Patrick Summers asked me to do it, I felt that also in a way that at this time of life you just say yes to what you want to do and see what happens. I'm working hard on it already, and I love the subject and the music. It's like a challenge, like taking courses at a later stage. So, it's fun. I just say "yes to the dress." There is one of those terrible programs in television, a reality show about choosing your wedding dress: "Just say yes to the dress!"

OL – So, you do look back at your illustrious career with a great dose of joy.

FVS – Yes, I do! One of the most joyful parts of it has been the people I've worked with, the colleagues. Jim Meredith who is here, Marilyn Horne, Luciano Pavarotti, Plácido Domingo, Michael Tilson Thomas, Seiji Ozawa, when I actually do enumerate any part of that I think "oh well, have I been blessed, to be in the presence of these people, participating with them!" Because opera singers are really fun. They really are fun. Rehearsing in opera is very serious and we work very hard, but there comes a funny moment,; it bursts like a bomb, and it's fun for all of us to be together. There is really not the back-stabbing jealousy that people would like to think there is. It's fun to think about it but that's not been my experience at all.

OL – I hear that you are very beloved by your colleagues.

FVS – I have had so much fun with them, you know? We've shared so much of our lives; we've been away from our families at times; we've been in different countries together; we've gone on adventures between performances… You get very close when you are rehearsing eight hours a day, especially in the operas I did, like *Le Nozze di Figaro* where it is sort of a family situation anyway.

OL - While interviewing a Grande Dame of opera like you, a singer of legendary stature, we'd be highly interested in compelling memories. I know it's too vague a question, but since you've prepared a program that is autobiographic, I bet that you've been giving some thought to it. So, here we go: do you have a couple of really essential crossroads or defining moments in your long career that might be of interest for your fans to hear about? Something very dear to you or important to you?

FVS – Oh, so much is extremely important and dear to me. In the beginning I was such a novice and such an ingénue, not in role but in my thinking; I knew so little about it! I didn't know to be frightened, almost like a child. They learn an instrument before they learn it's hard. I've had extremely funny times with colleagues. The dear ones have been unusual. There's a famous maestro, Carlos Kleiber…

OL – Wow, one of the greatest.

FVS – Yes, Carlos Kleiber… actually I was invited to do a Rosenkavalier with him, but I knew that he was probably one of the greatest artists of all time and I was frightened to do it with him, so I didn't do it. But about two years later I was in London recording, and there was a gal that I knew very well from DECCA who was a friend of his. She brought him to my house and at that point I was having my second baby. My first baby was two and a half and she had spilled tea on her face, so she was in terrible pain; it was just awful, we went for treatment every day; it was one of those horrible accidents. So this friend brought Carlos, and I thought "oh my gosh, what am I going to do?" And he sat with my daughter. He entertained her by singing nursery rhymes to her from a book; she sat on my lap, and he just sang the entire book to her. And she was fascinated by him, because she didn't know him, and he just sang for her. I'll never forget that moment. It was so kind.

Another one that I remember – unbelievable – we did the opening night of *The Merry Widow* and I was with Plácido at the Met, and we were upstairs at the opening night party, and I had invited my husband, and my father-in-law with his wife – his first wife had died, and this was his second wife. He had Parkinson's. He was thrilled to be in New York and to go to this party and meet Plácido. He had terrible shakes. By mistake he knocked a glass of wine over. I could see him, his face drained, he was so embarrassed. Plácido and Marta, his wife, stood up and they put their hand in the wine and they blessed themselves. They said, "we were hoping someone would do that; you have no idea what good fortune this brings; it brings blessings on everybody at the table." Plácido probably doesn't remember that he did it, but I'll never forget it.

OL – Wow, very interesting! Back to Carlos Kleiber, he had a reputation for being reclusive and sort of odd; but then, in person, he wasn't?

FVS – Oh, no. At least my experience with him was that he had a depth and a kindness… I will never forget my encounter with him; I wish I had done the opera.

OL – Was that the one Anne Sofie von Otter did with him?

FVS – Yes, exactly. And at the time he was recruiting. I think he had just conducted *Otello* at La Scala. I went to one of the rehearsals. It was unbelievable.

OL – I rank him as the number one conductor of all time.

FVS – Yes, he was absolutely brilliant. Brilliant, brilliant.

OL - In a couple of hours you'll be engaged in a master class. You've conducted master classes at a number of universities and conservatories in recent years. Let's talk about some of the trends you've been observing as you instruct these young talents. First of all, has the training vocal performance students receive now, changed in any significant ways since you were a student at the Mannes College of Music?

FVS – I'll tell you how it's changed. On the one hand singers are better prepared; more ready mentally and musically to walk on stage. They are very beautifully prepared. Probably in this music school [UNC Chapel Hill Department of Music] and all the young artist programs that exist all over New York, San Francisco, Houston Grand, Dallas, the Lindemann, Chicago, they all have these extraordinary programs, so in that regard they are way ahead of certainly where I was. On the other hand I think they tend to over-emphasize the vocal things they are doing, and not really express what the works are about. I think the biggest worry I have in the trend is that they all seem too big, too loud. In the preparation I did for this class, there is a Saint-Saëns song [she sings a bit of it] and there is also a Fauré version of it, so I listened to quite a few people sing it, and the most enjoyable was Louise Homer; it was breathtaking, and what was wonderful about it was the youthfulness of it. Everybody seems to be darkening their voice and thickening it, and in my experience the singers who have remained true to themselves like Kiri Te Kanawa, Kathleen Battle, Teresa Berganza in my day, have had the greatest longevity and terrific success in their singing. Joyce DiDonato never drives her voice. Susan Graham never drives her voice. They treasure that lightness and fluttery sound. The danger of darkening and thickening and making voices heavy is that you don't hear words as well, and sometimes you don't get the nature of the song. It gets bogged down. So that's the biggest thing. I don't think it's the singers' fault.

OL – Why are they doing it?

FVS – I think they are doing it because most orchestras play too loud, because we don't have someone like Carlos Kleiber keeping the orchestra way down. Way down! I blame electronics. I think people walk into an opera house and expect to hear what they heard in their ear buds or on their Hi-Fi, and that's not the point. The point of opera and singing is that you hear the singers. If you are eighty to one, there is no way you can. I think orchestras take on a more exciting and interesting sound when they go from loud to soft, from forte to mezzo-forte, from mezzo-piano to piano, from soft to loud again. Another person who is a genius at that is Claudio Abbado. He could go from pianissimo to forte and it was a sixty-miles highway. There was every degree of it, and I don't think that is often explored. People are more thrilled with the big sound and the big boom, and voices cannot always take that, especially not young voices. They just need to be reminded that what carries is the slimness of sound, not the volume of sound. And if you don't have a big voice, don't be hard on yourself; don't try to make it into a big voice. Have the voice you have.

OL – I just attended a master class with Lawrence Brownlee; he stopped the singers all the time, saying, "can't you sing this, piano?" "If you keep the dynamics down, people in the opera house will try to listen to you."

FVS – Yes, exactly. For vocal technique and for longevity, when you master the hard parts of your voice… one of the reasons you sing loud is because you can't sing soft. If you work and work and work and that's what it takes to control that part of your voice, the rest of your voice falls in line. If you blast it out – and I've done it; I'm not speaking as one who has mastered it, I'm almost seventy and I'm still at it… [laughs]

OL – Yes, when you sang that song, "why did they shut me out of Heaven? Was it because I sang too LOUD?" you sang very loudly and the public startled and laughed.

FVS – Yes, especially for mezzos, if you manage that – it's around E-F-G, it's the hardest part of the voice, the passagio – you will go higher and you will be able to manage the lower part of your voice. If you blast it hard eventually the sound spreads and then you can't do it. Then you can't sing soft; you really can't do it without closing your throat. I've done it, and I know the pain of that. It takes a long time to recuperate.

I think sometimes it's the agents, the managers, who need to be very careful about what a young singer sings, and when they sing it and at what house they sing it.

OL – We were having a discussion at the website exactly about this. People are driving to the Met and listening to Met Opera Radio on their car sound system with eight speakers, and they crank it up, then they park and enter the Met and think they will find the same sound. If these people can't realize that what comes from their eight speakers is not the same direct relationship they can have with the unamplified beautiful voice of a singer from the stage, they don't even belong in the opera house in the first place – what are they doing there? They should have stayed in their cars.

FVS – Yes, yes! And it is the only thing left that is not intercepted electronically. That's throat to ear. That's why opera still exists: people need that. Look at pop singers – very often the public would like to hear them without a microphone. Everything changes when there is a microphone.

OL - Some leading international singers who are now teaching or serving on voice competition juries have expressed concern over what they view as a trend at opera houses to cast young singers in inappropriate roles. They believe these new talents are not being given the chance to properly develop

– like singers can do in houses like those in German-speaking countries where they hire a cast for the entire year. What are your views on this?

FVS – Oh, I agree with that. We are very lucky in San Francisco because we have a wonderful general manager who sang; he began his career as a singer. He really knows voices. He can pick them out. One of the gals who runs the Merola Young Artist Program there is one of the finest. She also was a singer for years, Sheri Greenawald; she knows voices. They are very careful about what singer should sing, what they are ready for. It's not always just the voice. It's the emotion. You never want to do anything to step on the self confidence of a singer, because as much as they use their voice and their talent, they are using their self confidence. What enables you to get out there and be free, is that you feel you can do something and you have something to contribute, and if you are out there in the wrong piece, chances are that it's not going to work, and you have to be careful.

Like the Charlotte aria. People will sing it. I heard young singers singing the Letter Aria and when you're singing this of Charlotte, you have to look at the first two acts, you have to look at the size of the orchestra. There is almost no excuse in today's world, because you can't get on your computer without finding ten versions of an aria. It behooves you to either have the best advice, which is what I had, or get on there and say, "oh my gosh, the first two acts, Charlotte sings in the lower middle voice everything, and then the second two acts, boom, high." The orchestra is a big orchestra at times, in that piece. So you got to know that; you have to have your coach or your voice teacher tell you "beware." Sometimes I hear kids singing Verdi, and in my opinion until you are thirty you shouldn't even touch it. Even the great big voices, they worry me the most, because once they are big, everybody wants to hear the big sound. So they push them to be bigger, and I think they should be singing Mozart, and learning to refine all their abilities. Bel canto is the best place to start, with anything.

OL - There is also frequent discussion today about the impact visual and online media are having on singing careers. Some believe it has led to an over-hyping of talent that hasn't matured yet; others contend that it has contributed to an overemphasis on singers' physical appearance. What are your thoughts about this?

FVS – Oh, I have to say, I'm all for TV, I really am. A great voice comes along, and you don't care about anything; you want to hear that voice. There is no danger that a voice will be eliminated because of the size of the singer or the look of the singer. Now I must say, singers are more and more beautiful. Really, the young singers, the Adler Fellows, they could be models. But a voice like Montserrat Caballé comes along, and you could have her playing Cherubino and I'd listen to it.

OL – Yes, we see some bigger ladies like Leah Crocetto and Deborah Meade, and they are doing fine.

FVS – Yes, yes, they are doing fine. I'm all for that. I don't think it's really affecting anything. Look at Luciano; Luciano was enormous, and had that big television career as he did. He was Luciano! I don't think it's a danger, and I applaud it. I think it brings opera to many more people than they would ever be able to go. I think Peter Gelb is doing an amazing job. I love the incorporation of all the new modern day projection techniques and everything. It's fascinating, I'm all for it.

OL – I see. Please walk us through the ins and outs of a master class. What can be accomplished in such occasions, and what are the limitations?

FVS – For me a master class is a misnomer. I'm not a master; I'm still working at my voice. Maybe Isaac Stern is a master. Many of my singer colleagues are masters. I've always struggled with my technique. I'm always working, always have been. I think what happened to me is that I was almost rock-solid in my technique and my career took off, and then my teacher died. I was learning and singing, and I got into bad habits. So I had to go back and re-work. But it is hard to re-work when you are out there. So some things always eluded me.

So with me, my master classes are not me impacting my brilliant information. I think they are opportunities for people to perform. They are a little unnatural. I think they should be done in here with all the singers participating, and not an audience. But they are also fascinating to an audience to hear different things. A, I think it's an opportunity for the kids to perform. B, I can share my experience with them. I can say – "You do that for two more years, you lose your voice!" Which I've never said to anybody; I never had to, but I'll say – "Look out for this part of your voice, slim it down there." Or, on interpretation, "Make up your mind what this song is about. There's no right or wrong answer, but be sure that you know what you are trying to say, because if you don't and you are just thinking vocally, it gets very boring for the public." And, "Then, explore all the variations of loud and soft, all the variations of fast and slow, of rhythm, and have them related to something concrete, not something vague; something very specific. If you can, paraphrase poetry and operatic words. In other words, put it in your own words. First of all translate all words. Don't have, you know - 'it means I went out the door and jumped up the window.' With poetry sometimes it's hard, but find a place where you are almost singing in your own language to an English speaking public, because that's what you will remember; you won't remember to take a deeper breath when you are out there. You're hyped up, and what you hang on to are the ideas and the intentions. Intention, intention! What do you want to get, over there? Sometimes what you want to get across is – 'This is hard but I am fantastic because I can do this.' I mean, that's what Rossini is about! And you can add to that – the basic bravado, you can add to the intention."

OL – Very nice answer!

FVS – Yep!

OL - What would be your most decisive advice to a young singer facing the realities and hardships of an operatic career these days, in this time of economic crisis?

FVS – First of all, "Don't get bogged down in it, in the realities and hardships, because you really don't know." I don't know what is going to happen next week with the Sequester [Editor's note – The agreement in the U.S. Congress to cut federal funding across the board for all federal programs], and chances are that music singers who are wrapped up in their careers, their voices aren't going to know. One marvelous example was that I was introduced yesterday to this wonderful young conductor Tim Myers from this new company here [Editor's note: Timothy Myers, artistic director and principal conductor of the North Carolina Opera], in that with such a limited budget you can put on these great productions, especially if you are going to do something like *Aida* which they are planning to do. So, you have to innovate, you have maybe to find a way of doing it semi-staged, of building platforms, using projections, but always having the essence: voice and orchestra and story. It's a time when we have to innovate; we cannot fall back on "Yes, the Philadelphia Orchestra will last forever." It didn't. It won't. The wonderful rich people who have made these things go on can't do it anymore, so we have to find a reason to make it work. We have to bring it into our time. But more than ever, we need the intimacy of song and the intimacy of music and the connection that it gives to people.

There is a wonderful quote from this incredible teacher who started the "El Sistema" in Venezuela, his name is José Antonio Abreu, and he gave a conference in Berkeley. He taught Gustavo Dudamel. He said, "For many, many people, the only source of human dignity for them is through music." My uncle who came see me for this last couple of days just got back from Cuba, and he said "On every street corner people are making music." What happened in the awful time of the Holocaust? There were these choirs started. Music is what takes you out of the incredible grief and worry that we have today. It gives you those moments of relief.

There is nothing that the young singes can do to plan about it. What can they do? They can't raise the money, so why worry? Be joyful about your singing; you have this gift, take care of it, don't be hard on yourself, and keep at it. The greatest singers are not always the ones that are rewarded.

OL – Joyce DiDonato, I interviewed her too, she said – I'm paraphrasing, I don't remember the exact quote, but something to the effect of "What we need to do is produce, sing, perform great opera; do it well, and that should take care of it."

FVS – Yes, that's it!

OL – And she said, "We should stop apologizing for our art form, and stop saying that we need to do this and that to attract the young audiences. They will come, if we present good opera to them, because opera is important and essential."

FVS – Yes, exactly.

OL - What do you like most about working with young singers?

FVS – I love hearing their voices, I really do! It's not like I think back to how I was at that time. I can't remember so well. But I just love hearing them, you know? I'm always amazed by the human voice. I love knowing what they have ahead of them, knowing the joy of singing.

OL - Very early in your career, you attended master classes yourself with Maria Callas. Do you have memories of that event to share with us?

OL – Oh, it was fantastic! Maria Callas gave these classes at Juilliard, and I was only able to get into one of them. The first thing she did, was that she turned her back to the public. She put her full attention on the singers and unlike the wonderful play by Terrence McNelly *Master Class*, she was nothing but supportive. A lot of what she said was about volume. I remember, someone did an aria from *Madama Butterfly*, and the pianist was just playing as loud as can be, and she asked "Why are you playing so loud?" He said, "I'm trying to give the idea of an orchestra with just one instrument" and she said "But look at what's written. It's pianissimo! You can't make the sound of the orchestra. Make the sound of the piano, but it's got to be soft!" I kind of remember just studying her, noticing how beautiful she was, and her wonderful hair; she was dressed beautifully. I think I was more taken with that [laughs] than with what she actually said!

OL - At one time, you wanted to be on Broadway. Would portraying the diva in *Master Class* be something that would appeal to you?

FVS – No, I could never do it. I'm not a large enough personality to do that. But I loved the play, and I consider Terrance McNelly our great American playwright. And he's passionate about opera, and that's clear. I always wanted to be on Broadway, but now I see how nice my life was without having to do a show every night and how I've been able to have a family and nights off, and I treasure them as much as all my singing experiences, so… I'm glad I didn't do it, if I could have.

OL - You not only conduct master classes for new operatic talent. You also work with the students at Saint Martin de Porres Elementary School in Oakland. You've taken some of the older children to opera rehearsals. Please elaborate on this – your goals and objectives, the children's responses, etc.

FVS – Oh, I was an educator at the Convent of the Sacred Heart, it's sort of an order that is devoted to teaching. Not long ago I was at Catholic charity events and I met this marvelous nun named Sister Barbara Dawson, who was also a Sacred Heart nun. She was talking to me about music. She is the head of the school. She is an immigration lawyer but was asked to save the school. There are only sixty students; they didn't want to have to close the school. So, she had been there for about five years then, and we got talking, and I said "I'd love to come and see if I can help you." So I started some music program at school. It's K through 8th. One campus is K through 5th, and the other is 6th through 8th. We started with singing, of course, and had a wonderful young girl who taught it, and the kids all loved it. At one point we took five of them to Washington, DC; they sang at Kennedy Center in honor of Senator Kennedy. We started a violin program, and so I just went and helped the teachers. I didn't teach myself, but I got the violins out. When the kids had to leave to go places, I took them. I'm on the Board and still very much involved with the school. I've seen what it has done to some of these kids. We started four years ago with violins, so now we have 4th Grade Violin, and they are progressing. The people who are dumbfounded are the parents. Our children come from very low income families. They would never be able to afford private lessons. They can't believe their kids can do this. For the children it gives them a great chance to perform and see everybody applaud them and have great affirmation. It gives them one-on-one training. So I just keep at it. We just hired a new violin teacher.

OL – Are they kids who were already spotted as having inclinations and talent for classical music in a magnet school, or are they having their first encounter with it?

FVS – It's definitely their first encounter with it. It's a regular school. They have never heard of anything having to do with classical music. And as for taking the kids to operas, I have taken them to four operas, one of them being *Don Giovanni* which is four and a half hours long. I took the older kids, the 8th graders. Not a single one of them has ever wanted to leave. They've been fascinated by it, as much by the mechanics of it, as the singing, as the opera house. Many of these kids have never been to an opera house; it just opens their eyes. We've had this conservatory come and do an opera in-house at the school for them, *Hänsel und Gretel*. This year the San Francisco Girls Chorus is coming to perform. We just take them to as much music as we can.

OL – I've shown your *Hänsel und Gretel* DVD to kids…

FVS – Oh! [laughs].

OL – And I also had a nine-year-old at home and showed her *Le Nozze di Figaro*. She was fascinated. Her mother, a friend of ours, was taking the girl back home from school but lost her house key and got locked out, so she phoned her husband to rescue them; well, he is a doctor and was busy at the hospital so he said it would be a while. As it was a very hot day, she came to our house to wait for him. The kid looked bored and the mother asked if I had some cartoon on DVD to play on TV to distract her. Being that my own kids are grown, I said, "No, I have no cartoons, but I do have opera!" "Opera?" – the mother said, "that's not going to work!" I said, "well, we'll see." So I fired up *Le Nozze di Figaro* and the kid was amazed, and glued to the screen. When her father arrived and wanted to take the family back home, the girl said "No way, I got to watch this 'til the end!" They tried to drag her out and she resisted, pulled back, and they ended up having to let her watch the whole opera.

FVS – Oh, that's so exciting!! [laughs]

OL – When you took the school kids to the opera, were these traditional productions, or were some of them updated or otherwise unusual stagings? Do you think they would be more interested in contemporary operas, or standard repertory works updated to the present time? Does it make a difference?

FVS – I've done very traditional productions, and very, very modern ones. Unless they interfere with the actual process of singing, I'm all for innovation. I don't mind it updated; I think if it works, it's interesting.

OL – Oh, I'm glad to learn that you feel this way, but I rather meant to ask about the Saint Martin de Porres kids when you took them to the opera, in terms of their reaction to different production styles. Do you think it is needed to update opera when we present them to the younger generation?

FVS – No, I don't think so. I mean, it would be like updating a painting. Are you going to update a Vermeer or a Michelangelo? No. If it's part of it, great. There was a production – *The Rake's Progress* – it's a hard opera to understand, you are never totally sure of what is going on. There was a very modern production of it, done by the man who does the Cirque du Soleil, and it was fascinating, full of gimmicks; it was such fun, and the kids adored it. But that's not what got them there. And it's not what kept their interest, the whole time.

OL - Later this month, you'll be appearing in Saint Martin's Gala. What's on the program there?

FVS – Oh, our Gala is a short little presentation. We are honoring a priest who is Irish, this year, so we are singing Irish songs.

OL - There is concern, not only here in the States but also in Europe, that children no longer have the connection to music and singing that those in previous generations did. A few years ago, a group of well-known German opera singers made a recording of folksongs and lullabies just to preserve this material. Is there a need to preserve a similar repertory in America?

FVS – It breaks my heart. It's not just what you sing to them, it's just that they sing. When I first became aware that children are not singing anymore was with my step-grandchildren who were in Kindergarten, and come Christmas time, none of them knew any Christmas carols! Well, to me that's obscene! So I started going into their classes and teaching them Christmas carols, and doing programs in the public schools to try and get them to put music in there. Not every child is born with a scientific brain. There are those who are inventive. Everybody should sing. Singing is in our human nature. So is dancing. It doesn't mean you have to be a dancer or a singer by profession, but we've taken this away from children. I bet that if there was an experiment and they put this back in the schools – it won't happen, at least not in my lifetime – I bet it would be life altering for the nature of the schools. The school system is not working, clearly. Music helps; there's been all sorts of studies. Music helps with Math, it helps with concentration.

What children today do not have – both privileged and underprivileged children – is quiet, is silence. They do not know what silence is. The world is so loud! What do you learn from music? You learn music, but you learn silence. You learn the value of silence. You learn the value of control and discipline. And you see that what you can do on Monday you can do on Friday, as you work on it. Think of the lessons of that. Now we are getting more and more computers in school… I don't know… why wasn't this number one on the ballot? I do not understand. Because if you changed the education system in the United States, probably the prison system population would drop. Every problem we have, practically, is related to education: not being educated to be good citizens, not being just plain educated to get good jobs; it's a real challenge. Our families at this little school are heroes and heroines, given what they've accomplished with what they have.

OL – Absolutely. I loved your answer. Now, let's move onto something else. The Baby Boom generation grew up hearing the great Broadway musicals of the '50s and '60s, and knew many of their songs. You've also included some musicals in your career. You've recorded Magnolia in *Showboat*, Maria in *The Sound of Music*, and Claire in *On the Town*, to name some of your roles.

FVS – Oh yes, I just love doing these, oh! [excitedly]. I grew up with this. The world was safe when I grew up, and I used to take the train from New Jersey to New York with my dear friend, when I was fourteen, and we'd buy standing passes to everything on Broadway. We'd go to a matinee and an evening show, and it was safe enough to take the train back home late at night. I saw everything. I saw *Annie Get Your Gun* with Ethel Merman. I never saw Julie Andrews. Ah, everybody. Elaine Stritch, so, that's a musical I've been in love with most of my life. My idea of dying and going to Heaven is walking in a Broadway theater and hearing the overture. Just the sound of it, there's something about it. I think it is the proximity to the smaller, intimate space. For me to get to do these things that I did, *The Sound of Music* which I've loved all my life, I grew up with [sings a song from it], it was just Heaven.

My wonderful friend Kiri [Te Kanawa] is the one who really started it. She is the one who, with *West Side Story*, started the tradition of opera singers being able to sing this, because it is not easy. You don't change your voice, but you sort of change the style a little bit.

OL - You've also sung Hanna Glawari in *The Merry Widow*. The conductor Christian Thielemann recently observed that people don't realize how difficult operetta is. How would you compare singing operetta roles to singing those in opera?

FVS – I'm in love with *The Merry Widow*. I think it's the most wonderful piece in the world. It has more genuine charm than almost anything. The orchestration, oh! [sighs]. The idea of it, the melodies… [sings a part of it]. *The Merry Widow* may be easier than some of the other ones. They are very hard. Just like in our own tradition, Gilbert and Sullivan operettas are very hard, very difficult to sing.

OL – Why?

FVS – It takes a certain style. These works have five thousand words; you have to keep great rhythm. Sometimes things are very wordy, you don't really get to sing. You have to get that right balance between voice and song. It's a challenge.

OL - Contemporary operas have been an important part of your career. Jake Heggie composed the roles of Mrs. De Rocher in *Dead Man Walking* and Madeline in *Three Decembers* for you. You're scheduled to perform in the world premiere of his latest opera, *Great Scott*, in Dallas in 2015. Can you please tell us about that?

FVS – Oh, I'm so lucky in my association with Jake Heggie! He's been one of the treasuries of my life. He is as great a talent as a great human being. To do this part in *Dead Man Walking* was fantastic; also in *Three Decembers*. He is writing this new piece for Joyce, *Great Scott*, and he very sweetly asked me to play the Benefactor in it. I said, "of course" and I'm really excited about that.

OL - Before then, you'll be starring in the world premiere of Ricky Ian Gordon's new opera, *A Coffin in Egypt*, next year in Houston, and I'm even more excited about it. I understand this opera has only one character, Myrtle. Tell us more about it.

FVS – It's very interesting. It's based on a Horton Foote play. I'm still learning my way through it, not just learning the piece but learning what's going on, really. I've read a lot of Horton Foote in preparation, trying to understand. My impression is that he is a very precise person, in trying to be very precise about an event and what one's memory is of an event, and how one's memory of it can form one's character and one's own life. Fundamentally, it's about a woman who is reflecting on her life. She had a very unhappy marriage to a man who from the beginning had a mistress, a mulato mistress, and flaunted it. She was terribly embarrassed by it, and at one point couldn't stand it, so she took her daughters to Europe, to live all over Europe. She was very beautiful as a young woman, and people fell in love with her in every continent. She took her daughters with her, and they took ballet lessons and lived the European life, then for some reason she comes back, and by then his mistress has gotten sort of fattened, and then he was going after some young girl, and everything had changed when she went back. She had loved going riding on the prairie and there was no more of that. Her husband was home a lot of the time. Eventually the father of the girl he was having an affair with wanted to kill him and they had a fight, and the father was killed. In the opera, everybody is dead when she is sitting on her porch reflecting upon all of this. She says – "I'm still poisoned by it." It's a study in her character and her reflection. This is what she saw, and it is filtered all through these beautiful negro spirituals that have soothed her.

I don't even know whether I like her, of whether she is just a woman who let bitterness overtake her life. It's a real exploration for me. There is no other singing, so I'm a little nervous about that. There will be actors, and there is a lot of dialogue.

OL - Does this type of work place a greater burden on the singer, who has to carry the whole show?

FVS – Yes. I'm nervous about it, to tell you the truth. But I just said "Yes." Oh, yes, it will be different. But I also have a lot of time to prepare. It's with one of the finest directors of all time, who also wrote the libretto, Leonard Foglia, so that makes a big difference.

OL – I'll be sure to attend it. It will show at the Academy of Music in Philadelphia, right?

FVS – Yes!

OL – I'll be there!

FVS – Great!

OL - We are thrilled that you are performing in new American opera. We believe that our country, in spite of the economic crisis, has been relatively more active in terms of advancing the art form, than our European friends who created the art form but seem relatively – with exceptions – stagnant in terms of new opera. Do you see an American style of opera developing, these days?

FVS – Oh, I definitely see an American style, and I think it's because we have some great American composers right now, really great. Ricky [Ian Gordon], Jake [Heggie]… to have the success he's had is unheard of. Dead *Man Walking* is always being given in some part of the world. Continuously, it's had ten new productions, it's incredible. *Moby Dick* is harder to produce, but it's had a triumph. Three Decembers has been done all over. He has commissions. Ricky Ian Gordon has done amazing things. He's just debuted another piece. I just think it's a very, very exciting time. And I think our public wants it. They love the traditional operas – who cannot love *Bohème*? But they also… it's the pleasure of hearing your own language, in the American idiom, too. It's very exciting, and they address very interesting subjects. In *Dead Man Walking*, it was approaching an extremely important part of American culture or lack thereof, to examine the prison system. So to do it through music was incredible. When we first opened, there were people who walked out. And then we had to give an extra performance because it was so popular.

As many people were pro the death penalty as were against it – there are two sides to everything. If you know nothing but brutality your whole life, it becomes your life. And that is where the mistake is. You can't just remove people. You have to remove what is making them that way, and that's what we are not doing.

OL – I just saw Kevin Puts' new opera *Silent Night*. It was very beautiful.

FVS – Yes, that's fantastic. It's having a big success.

OL – And it's his first one. I'm excited that he is doing next *The Manchurian Candidate*.

FVS – Yes, me too! Back to why this piece *A Coffin in Egypt* will be so challenging, is because there is a retroactive story, but it is as much about character – the character of this woman – as it is about what happened to her. Sometimes that's a cerebral idea, an intellectual idea. Not always the opera tells a linear story.

OL – And she doesn't seem someone you can identify with, because you are quite the opposite person!

FVS – [Laughs] Yes, yes! But it's always fun to explore.

OL - On a different subject, you've made more than 70 recordings and won numerous awards for them. Do you ever listen to your own recordings? Among all of your recordings, which were your personal favorites, or which do you consider to have been the best?

FVS – No, I never listen to my recordings. The only one I listen to is one I made of Brubeck songs with Dave and his son Chris, and it's mainly because my daughter is in it. She was seventeen. I love that recording, I love Dave Brubeck and I love his son Chris, so it brings back a lot of happy memories, but no, I never listen to them.

OL – But anyway, even if you don't listen to them, which ones are your favorites?

FVS – I have listened to them over the years, but only when I had to. The only one I feel [hesitates, searches for the word] proud of, was a recording I did of Mahler's Fourth, with Abbado. I had the opportunity to sing it many times with him in concert, and I loved it so much! I love this concept of Heaven that Mahler gives – having asparagus, and Sicilia, and baking the bread, it meant so much to me, being a Catholic. The words have great meaning to me. I love the symphony. It was very carefully done. Anything you do with Claudio has a very special quality about it. He is very true to what he believes, and he works very hard to get it out of an orchestra, and that was the Vienna Philharmonic, so that, I am proud of!

OL - I particularly love your *La Cenerentola* film directed by Ponelle. Do you have memories of that production to share with us?

FVS – Oh, I loved making that. I loved Jean-Pierre Ponelle, he was one of the greatest directors of all time. A task master with more taste than any man I've ever known. Chic! Costumes, sets, everything… he is a genius. To work with him, you work hard, and you are very satisfied at the end of the day; you really feel you've accomplished something. We filmed it in an old factory in Vienna, and created the sets. I had my girls with me. It took forever. It took a long time to do everything. But I loved the production so much, and I loved all our cast. It was fun; I had never done anything like that. Someone like Jean-Pierre, you put your total faith in him. You just know that you don't have to make any of the artistic decisions because you're being looked after.

OL – That's another DVD I've used to introduce opera to "non-believers" sometimes.

FVS – Yes! [laughs] It's such a sweet opera too; it's such a sweet take on the Cinderella story!

OL - In late April, you're traveling to Austria for a "Salute to Vienna" recording. That sounds like a wonderful event. Can you please tell us about the activities there in which you will be participating?

FVS – They are preparing a New Year's Eve concert and filming it; I'm just the hostess. I'm in to sing the Vilja Song, and I'm already nervous about it. It will be fun to be in Vienna. It's going to be with the Vienna Choir Boys.

OL - I must say that we were terribly saddened to learn of the recent death of mezzo soprano Zheng Cao. We know you were tremendously supportive to her in both her singing career and her battle against cancer.

FVS – Oh, my Goodness, I know… She was… A person like this girl comes along once in a century. First of all, one of the most exquisite voices I've ever heard. The very reason it was so exquisite was – beyond her vocal chords – that everything she ever did, even in rehearsals, was connected to her heart and her soul. And she as a person was one of the most expressive people I've ever known, and hysterically funny. Very direct, very outgoing, very appreciative. I mean, it was amazing. And all through her illness, we went over to see her a lot, and she always had a big smile. She was in a constant struggle to stay alive, and she married this wonderful man who was her doctor, David Larson. The reason she saved her voice was because she didn't have full brain radiation, she had what is called gamma knife radiation, and that's why she could still sing. I saw her the week before she died, and then I was away. Her voice was still there. And she was starting to be in a lot of pain. I thank her with all my heart for working so hard to stay alive for all of us, because we loved her so much.

A group of her friends and family are giving a memorial service for her in June, and we went through all the venues in San Francisco, and the only one big enough is the opera house. And David Gockley [SFO general director] is giving us the opera house on an afternoon when it's closed, and I can bet you it's going to be filled. An extraordinary girl!

OL – Is there something being done, like a recording, to celebrate her memory?

FVS – There are a couple of things. There is going to be a new song cycle written by Amy Tan and Stewart Wallace who did the piece that she was singing when she found out she was sick, called *The Bonesetter's Daughter.* When she was still feeling well, a group of us got together and established an endowment in her name for either a Pacific Rim singer or a mezzo-soprano, so when one of the kids becomes an Adler Fellow or a student in the Merola Program, their trainee program will be underwritten in her name.

OL – Nice. Changing topic: did opera make you grow as a person, psychologically speaking?

FVS – [Laughs] I guess. Everything makes you grow, that happens to you in life. I'd say, it certainly gave me a running-over cup of satisfaction and joy; very hard times as well. I didn't have to leave my children as often as one would imagine because I took them with me a lot, but every time I went away, I couldn't even look at the date coming up because it upset me so much.

I'm sure opera does make you grow. You learn to do a lot, because opera is not only singing; it's a lot more than that. First of all, learning a new piece, doing photo sections, speaking, it's a lot of things, dinners… it's busy. Then if you are managing a family as well, it's double busy.

OL - What roles had the most psychological impact in your person, and why?

FVS – I would say *Dead Man Walking*, because I played a woman who suffered probably the greatest thing that any mother can suffer – have their child die. And, in addition, to feel responsible, because of having failed him. Her reason for failing him was the abject power of poverty. So, I was able to look at some of the decisions I made for my life, for my kids, that weren't the best for them, and explore that through this character, and it was really hard, really hard and very powerful. The other one to a certain extent is Mélisande, in *Pelléas et Mélisande.*

OL – I was about to suggest that.

FVS – Yes, because with Mélisande, it is very hard to find the key. She is not this, and she is not that. She is not all one thing. The best way I can describe her, really, is that she is young, and she's been abused – that's what we learn about her. And that's a very special circumstance – the youth, and then the abuse – because that makes kids operate a certain way. That's what I think she is. And I believe everything she says, because any of her lies which are proven to be lies in the opera are lies of necessity. That's how kids deal with trauma in their lives, they lie about it. They have an alcoholic mother at home, they don't tell anybody, they say "My Mom couldn't make it because she is sick." They learn to lie, so you have to believe them for that, because of their purpose and their intent.

I don't think she has any bad intentions. She is young enough to not see some of the consequences of what she might do. It's actually very beautifully written, because she really doesn't say much. [sings] "Non… oui… je ne sais pas… peut-être…" And all these people are going on and on and on about it. Pelléas, it's also youth, it's that rushed blahblahblah of youth, and it's almost like all these people want to impose themselves on her and form her to be what they want her to be, and she is just who she is, which is a young, damaged girl.

OL – And such a death scene! I think it's one of the two best in all of the opera, the other one being in *War and Peace*.

FVS – I know. I agree with you. Very beautiful.

OL – And probably very impactful to do on stage.

FVS – It is! The fun part of it is, when you are rehearsing it for hours and hours and it's after lunch, you are going to have a little snooze when you are lying there [laughs].

OL - Do you plan on publishing your memoirs? Or writing a libretto? Or doing something else to preserve your legacy (which is of course already preserved in your recordings – but I mean, beyond that or in addition to that)?

FVS – No, I do not plan on publishing my memoirs. To preserve it, I'm doing something for the Cal library [University of California Berkeley], ongoing interviews, just memories. I don't really have many mementos from my career. I just haven't preserved letters. Now I wish I had, but I didn't. Anything I do have I will give to the library at BU [Boston University]. I'm not going to do my memoirs. The closer I'd come, is that I'd love to write a children's book. Some kind of a silly children's book, maybe about opera, maybe involving my dog who I love.

OL – I interviewed Sylvia Sass in Budapest, and she is writing the libretto for an opera called *Callas*, about Maria Callas, of course.

FVS – Fabulous!

OL – And she wrote three books, and they are beautiful books.

FVS – Fantastic!

OL – And I think your career is just as great, I think you should!

FVS – Maybe I'll change my mind in the years to come.

OL - How are you as a person? I suspect, from your recital, that you are energetic, funny, passionate… But tell me more.

FVS – Yes. [laughs] But I also… there is a deep part of my soul that is very sad. I felt I was born into sadness, because my poor mother, my father was killed in April before I was born in June, it was just a very sad world I came into, because she was so devastated, losing her husband, and her father died shortly thereafter. To give birth to a child without your spouse, it was very, very hard. So, there is a deep core of sadness inside me. I got to explore it through opera. Because I was brought up so strictly in the Catholic faith, I truly believe in the opposite of joy which is sorrow, and I believe in them both. You can't always control the biggest element in your life. They are both there so you might as well get used to it. You are not going to live a life that is free of sorrow and pain.

OL – But you are also very funny. I laughed so much during your recital yesterday!

FVS – [laughs] Well, I have a heritage of humor from this favorite uncle, Freddie, and I suspect my father was a lot like him. He is the funniest man in the world. All my family, they are eight children, and I've been pretty close to them my whole life; I love my aunts and uncles. There are only three left now, but I loved every one of them in a different way. To raise eight children who were pretty balanced and copacetic, is kind of a victory for my grandparents. I loved my grandmother, I worshipped my grandfather. I used to follow him around like a dog. He wouldn't speak much. If he got up, I'd get up, if he went out the door, I'd go out the door, I just adored him.

OL - Besides your daughters, granddaughters, and your students at St.

Martin de Porres, what do you care about or like to do outside of classical singing?

FVS – Oh, what do I care about? [laughs] I love doing things with my husband. I love actually fixing things. He can do anything; he is very gifted. I love working on a project, painting or building. We are doing a little bit of that now. He is a great sailor, and I love just being with him when he is sailing, because he is just so happy; he just feels like he is true to himself when the wind is blowing and he is on the sea! I have five step-grandchildren and I love being with them as well. This grandparenting thing is the best thing that has ever happened to me, because I feel that I'm getting back some of the time that I missed with my kids. And to see your child being a parent is amazing. I thank the Lord that I am getting to see this, and see how she is doing it, what choices she makes, what she insists upon, how she structures their lives.

OL – I envy you. My daughter and her husband don't want children. They have a cat, so now I have a grandcat.

FVS – A grandcat! [laughs hard].

OL – I do have a son; he is still young to be a father, but maybe, in a few years.

FVS – Yes…

OL - If you arrive at a point when you can't sing anymore due to the natural aging process, will it be a big psychological blow?

FVS – No, I don't think so. I feel age in my voice right now, but I'm determined to find my way through it. My teacher, Mr. Sebastian Engelbert, he used to sing every day until he was eighty-four. I mean, he wouldn't go on the Met stage. I won't do anything that isn't age appropriate anymore. The woman I'm playing in *A Coffin in Egypt* is ninety; I think I can pull that off… [laughs]. You can't expect more than that of a singer my age; I don't think anybody would expect that of you. But I don't see a reason to stop. We've used our throats more than anybody else, so like if you exercise, those muscles will stay in shape. I haven't sang a lot for the last six months, I have a lot of work to do to get that sound [sings a bit] out of it. Because if you don't use it, you lose it. Just like when you haven't exercised in a lot and you go do a sit-up and you think your body is going to break in two. And then, five days later, it's not that bad. And that's what it takes. It just takes different exercises, maybe some adjustments and different repertoire. Mister

E sang until he was eighty.

OL – I was pleasantly surprised yesterday in your recital. You still got it!

FVS – Yes! [laughs] My friend Kiri is singing all over the place. We both know we are old, and we don't try to do the things that we can't, but there is a lot of music out there that is possible. Tony Bennett is an inspiration too. You just have to keep working. You can't expect that you don't have to work.

OL - Who are some of the current singers that you admire, today?

FVS – Oh, there are so many I admire, there are so many wonderful tenors now… Joyce [DiDonato] and Susan Graham are top of my list because I love them both and admire so much what they do and how they sing. I'll always love Plácido until the day I die. I love Anna Netrebko, love her! She is the most passionate, generous singer with this personality that just butts you on the head, I just adore her, I adore everything I've ever heard her do.

OL – I interviewed her, and I think it was one of my weakest interviews because I was as star-struck as you were with Maria Callas… So I wasn't very articulate in my interview with her because I was so fascinated!

FVS – She is very funny, and very articulate, and very kind. She is just larger than life, and totally natural. She throws herself into everything. Joyce does the same, as you know.

OL – Yes, absolutely. I love those two. And what about the tenors?

FVS – The tenors, I love Piotr Beczala, I just love his voice, and I love him as a person. I love Stephen Costello, young tenor. I love Matthew Polenzani.

OL – I love him two. I interviewed him twice and met him three times, and we've exchanged some email; he is such a nice person!

FVS – Oh, I love his singing. He has such a heart! Some of the others, I'm not all up on it; you'd be amazed at how often I do not go to the opera. When you start the grandparenting thing, if you are on duty, you are really on duty and it's hard work when you are taking care of little kids. That's why I'm not an expert in opera. If I didn't sing in it, I was going home and was not going to go to the opera, which is a shame, to a certain extent.

OL - What about historical singers, who are your favorites?

FVS – Oh, I just love them all. Teresa Berganza, I adore. Janet Baker, almost top of the list. Luciano, that's who I listen to all the time, Luciano and Plácido. Kiri, I adore. She's my generation, though. De Los Angeles broke my heart every time I heard her sing – talk about true, really true singing! I sang at the Met with some amazing, amazing voices! I loved Corelli. I loved Nicolai Gedda, very funny man. I sang one thing with Birgit, who cannot love her and be amazed by her? Pilar Lorengar was one of my absolute favorites. Just so many…

OL – Do you feel that singing was better before, than it is now?

FVS – I don't think so. I think we have some great voices, now. I think the aura around singers was different, then. The world of singing was a bit more amenable to a life. Singers stayed in one place longer, they didn't get into a jet plane the next day, so that they could have a life more easily. But that already started in my generation; it was hard to be in one place. The world was different. I think a Maria Callas comes once in a lifetime, really. People are still talking about her today. I think Anna [Netrebko] comes very close to that type of a personality, that commitment to singing, that commitment to her work, that bravado, that exquisite voice. I never like to say Maria Callas around another voice because I don't think anybody should be put in that position, but I think she comes very close to it. Renée Fleming is one of my most favorite singers in the world.

OL - What was the most difficult role you've ever performed in your career, and why?

FVS – I did one run of der Komponist [*Ariadne auf Naxos*] in Hamburg and decided on the spot that my voice wasn't right for it. I didn't have that thrust that it takes at the end to do it, that part [sings a bit of it]. I could do Octavian in the right circumstances, but just knew that it wasn't right.

OL – About longevity of career, we've talked about how admirable it is that you are still creating new roles and you continue to perform opera on stage. Any advice for singers willing to also have long careers?

FVS – A couple of things, which I have violated, but I can talk about them. Never drive it, never push on it. Thank it every day for what it does for you. I always tell a story – I'll probably mention it today in the master class – there was a wonderful guy at Glyndebourne named Yanni [?], he's Hungarian [Editor's note – we were unable to obtain clarification; Yanni is a Greek pianist; we aren't sure of the spelling of the name Ms. von Stade referred to], he had a drawing of some poodles by his piano, and I asked, "Yanni, why do you have this picture here?" and he said [she reproduces a heavy accent], "My darling, that is your voice. If you are good to your poodles they will do tricks for you; if you are bad to them, they will bite you!"

OL – [laughs]

FVS – Really, it takes something like, "don't get mad, if you can't do something, keep at it; you don't get instant reward with the voice. You can work on coloratura for three months, and still not get what you want, but six months later it will be there. Never underestimate the value of work. Don't wear yourself out, though."

I really love doing songs with different pianists, because you get a new take on it. Someone might go faster, someone might rush here, and it is fun to get those new ideas. You can disagree with them if you want, but try them; see if they fit.

OL - Of the honors you've been granted – the Ordre des Arts et des Lettres in France, Honorary Doctorate from Cleveland Institute of Music, the American Academy of Arts and Sciences, etc. – which one is most dear to your heart?

FVS – Oh, I'm always thrilled with the doctorates. I just basically go there thinking – "Are they nuts?" [laughs] So, that's how I feel about them. What I'm always thrilled by is that they're presented at a graduation, almost always, and I feel the energy of the young people, of what they have done to get there. The most moving for me, was when I got an Honorary Doctorate from Georgetown University Medical School; it was one of the first ones I got. The graduation was at the Kennedy Center, and of course since it was a medical school and they study for so long, there were a lot of children there, and wives and husbands, and every girl that walked across the stage I thought "that could be my daughter" who gave her life's blood to graduate and become a doctor, so I was very emotional about it. That's the part of it that just thrills me.

OL - Looking back at your career, any regrets? What would you have done differently?

FVS – No, I don't have any regrets. I don't regret the bad times. Well, maybe one thing. I still don't work as hard. I wish I had worked harder. The best part of my life, without a doubt, has been my family, and I have often chosen that over spending three hours working on my voice. I do regret that. I should have worked harder.

OL – I think you are too humble. You are great!

FVS – No, but it's very hard for singers to confront their voices. Because you are sort of confronting something that is imperfect about yourself, and they will do anything to avoid it, sometimes. And the only way you are going to improve it, is to confront it, and say, "I need to do this," and what's so bad about that? Pianists lose their fingering, so…

OL – Thank you for a lovely interview!

FVS – Oh, my pleasure, thank you!

.

Magdalena Kožená

Czech singer Magdalena Kožená is a beloved artist with 29 CDs in her discography. While better known for Baroque and Mozart, she has a diverse repertoire that includes mezzo roles performed in all the great opera houses, and has made incursions into modern and contemporary music as well, with a very impressive concert and recital resumé. This interview is from February 2013.

Opera Lively - Let's start by asking about this recital at the UNC Memorial Hall, which you also just did in Baltimore and will do at Carnegie Hall. Part of it was commissioned to commemorate the 100th anniversary of Stravinky's The Rite of Spring, as part of a series of concerts with this common theme that have been happening throughout this season at UNC Memorial Hall. Can you please tell us about the program, and how you made your selections of the music you are bringing to us? [Editor's note – the program included Mussorgsky - *The Nursery*; Marc-André Dalbavie - *Three Melodies on a Poem* of Ezra Pound (2013); Ravel - *Histoires Naturelles*, Op. 50; Rachmaninov - *Six Songs*, Op. 38; Bartók – *Dorfszenen*].

MK – I chose this repertoire, among other factors, in respect to the pianist I'm having. Of course, I'm having probably the best pianist I would ever be able to have, in the person of Mr. Yefim Bronfman. I wanted to do some Russian repertoire since Stravinsky comes from that part of the world. Especially Rachmaninov, because the piano part in the Rachmaninov songs is as difficult as any piano concerto by him, and there aren't many pianists in the world that can play it this way.

The Mussorgsky that opens the first half is a fantastic piece of music. It is very much like a recitativo type of mini-song cycle. It's about a little child talking to his nanny – actually in some parts it's a girl, in some parts it's a boy. It is very charming, with a very special musical form. The third piece also in the first part is the Ravel, *Histoires Naturelles*, which again has this recitativo style of songs, talking about animals and the resemblance of certain animals to people. It's very important for the audience to have the booklet with the text to read, because some of the lyrics are very funny and witty.

In the middle of the first half, it's where we put this new piece by Marc-André Dalbavie which is very atmospheric. I think it's a nice counterpoint to these two sparkling, brilliant song cycles.

I've mentioned the Rachmaninov that comes after the intermission, and then the Bartók is very much close to where I come from, because he actually arranged Slovak folk songs. I come from the Czech Republic, but the Slovak language is extremely close to the Czech language, and also, I studied in Bratislava which is the capital of Slovakia. So, these songs are extremely familiar to me. I'm singing them in the Slovak language. There are two possibilities; it is also possible to sing them in Hungarian, but they were originally Slovak songs, so singing them in Slovak is even more authentic.

OL – I understand that Mr. Dalbavie has written this second piece specifically for you and Mr. Yefim Bronfman. Can you please tell us about it? It's new music. You are a Baroque specialist. Is there a place in your heart for contemporary music?

MK – Yes. First of all, I think it is important to do modern and contemporary music, to somehow carry the future of classical music. Another aspect also is that it is very special if somebody writes a piece for you. I have already done a cycle of songs by Brett Dean, a brilliant Australian composer who wrote them for me. See, we sing today a piece by Mozart, for example, but often he wrote it with his thoughts in some specific singer of the time. Many of the opera composers had in mind special singers or voices that they liked. So, when we sing this music, we have a bit of disadvantage because it wasn't done for us. We are at a disadvantage regarding pop singers as well, who get songs made for their skills and their voices. I find it very refreshing when something is written for me and I can say to the composer, "look, this doesn't sit very well for my voice, can you just change it?" We can work together with the composer and get the best fit for our personality and our type of voice. It's very thrilling work to do.

OL – You did sing the role of Mélisande, which is not contemporary but is modern and innovative. Do you find it more vocally challenging than your other roles?

MK – No, I have some trouble thinking of Débussy as modern… [laughs]. In a way, it was written a very long time ago, and now we can look back and call it a very classical piece [laughs]. Of course it takes longer to learn than a Handel role. Memorizing the harmonies is more complicated. But at the end, I love very much this type of music that tells a story like a narration. It's speaking to people rather than just singing simple melodies. Take Italian opera, for example. I love it, but I'm not the hugest fan of bel canto. I mean, it's beautiful, but for me, for my character, it doesn't go that deep. It's more about the beauty of the voice and the line, but what I'm more after, is to say something interesting in terms of drama and text, so I do love modern and contemporary music.

OL – How do you relate to such an enigmatic character as Mélisande?

MK – I like not only singing Mélisande, but also playing Mélisande, because she can be a lot of different things, depending on the director. We don't know where she is coming from. We can't guess much about her past. But there are little clues and it is all very symbolic, in a way. So, everybody sees her differently. I like very much to interpret her a little bit differently, each time, and to find some hidden meanings there. It's a very interesting character, for me.

OL – Let's talk about your homeland, a little bit. I was there last summer in your beautiful capital city, Prague, and I interviewed mezzo-soprano Ms. Jana Sykorová who was in the title role of the contemporary opera *The Elephant Man*, and contemporary composers Mr. Martin Smolka (of the opera *Nagano*) and Mr. Marko Ivanovic (of the opera *Enchantia*) who is also a conductor and has conducted an orchestra in your hometown, the Brno State Philharmony Orchestra. Do you happen to know any of them or their music?

MK – I know their names, all three of them, but I've never met them in person and wasn't able to get familiar with their music, since now I live in Berlin and I'm unable to spend as much time in the Czech Republic as I would like.

OL – How is opera doing in the Czech Republic?

MK – Like in a lot of places, not only opera but culture in general is suffering with the economic crisis. A lot of programs are being cut in the Czech Republic and the theaters don't have that much money to hire guest artists. The situation is not the best. But at least, I think we still have a very deep tradition of interpreting Slavic music. There is still quite a lot going on, in terms of concerts. We also have a number of fantastic Czech musicians who have had great careers abroad. But I'd say that the situation in the opera houses themselves, in the Czech Republic, is not the happiest, at the moment.

OL - There is a very rich musical tradition in the Czech Republic, back to the centuries when the Austro-Hungarian Empire still existed. Mozart's *Don Giovanni* had its world premiere in Prague. You frequently appear at two major international festivals, the Prague Spring Festival and the Concentus Moraviae Festival. I know the Concentus Moraviae Festival is devoted to music from the 17th and 18th centuries. Can you tell us a little more about these events and the roles they play in the cultural life of the Czech Republic?

MK – Yes, I'll rather speak of the Festival Concentus Moravie rather than the one in Prague, because I like very much the idea of bringing music to smaller places. In capital cities there are always great artists in attendance, so I find it important to take the music deeper into our country, which is very historical; we have an amazing number of churches and castles and places that are fantastically suitable for chamber music and Baroque music. This festival every year has very strong dramaturgy, and they concentrate in one theme and find perfect venues to fit with the music together. It's a very nice summer thing, relaxed in a way, but also you can see how much the people in smaller cities appreciate music and the artists that are coming to their places.

OL – One of your solo recordings featured the music of Dvořák, Janáček and Martinů – the three major composers of your homeland - with Graham Johnson for DG, and it won the Gramophone Solo Vocal Award of 2001. You are said to be the most successful Czech classical music artist in the world, today. Do you see for yourself a mission of diffusing the music of your homeland?

MK – Yes, I feel very privileged for being able to do that. Of course, Czech music is something I grew up with; it's my own language, and this is always the music I feel most comfortable with, in a way. I think there is quite a bit of a treasury there in our repertoire, especially in songs. Of course, for singers who are not Czech, they won't be as familiar with the language, and it is quite a difficult language to learn! [laughs]. But I must say; now everybody knows the operas by Janáček, they play them everywhere, and I'm always stunned to see how fantastically my non-Czech colleagues can sing in the Czech language. There are lots of people who do it brilliantly. But still, you know, to learn a Martinů cycle is still quite a challenge for people who don't speak Czech, so I feel privileged and feel a sense of duty to present this music to people abroad.

OL – Yes, it's unfortunate that so many opera lovers know little about Czech opera beyond Smetana's *The Bartered Bride*, Dvořák's *Rusalka*, and Janácek's operas. Last year, there was a revival of Josef Mysliveček's opera, *Il Medonte*. Few people have heard of Mysliveček, yet he was a major influence on Mozart and an incredibly prolific composer. He wrote 26 opere serie, which is not a small output. Who are some of the other Czech composers that you feel have been underestimated or neglected?

MK – I really would like for the world to know a bit more about Martinů. Everybody knows Dvořák and Janácek as our two greatest composers, and they are, obviously, but I think Bohuslav Martinů should be just as well considered. I recently did one of his operas, *Juliette*. There is a recording with Sir Charles Mackerras of fragments from it. This opera was written in Czech and in French, so it can also be given in French. I think it's a raving masterpiece, and it deserves more attention than it has had.

OL – Sir Charles Mackerras was such a specialist in Czech music… now that he is gone, has it been more difficult to carry on?

MK – We have Jiří Bělohlávek who is an extremely famous Czech conductor and performs these pieces a lot, abroad. I think I could also name my husband [laughs] as someone who does a lot of Czech music, not only because of me, but he was probably the second person who conducted *Osud*, Janáček's opera that is not very famous. He has conducted a lot of Janáček. This music is especially appreciated in England, I sometimes think, even more than in the Czech Republic, it's paradoxical. My husband is probably one of the most prolific conductors of Czech music.

OL – OK, so, let's talk conductors. You've worked with some of the greatest; for example, Sir John Eliot Gardiner, Mariss Jansons, Sir Charles Mackerras, Bernard Haitink, Claudio Abbado, Marc Minkowski, Nikolaus

Harnoncourt, and of course you're married to one of the most brilliant conductors in the world, Sir Simon Rattle, with whom you have recorded extensively as well.

MK – These are a lot of people. [laughs]

OL – Yes, but let's focus on a specific question that we're always curious to hear about, since we are a website that specializes in opera, even though we also love non-operatic classical music. But regarding opera and conductors, what makes of a conductor, a good opera conductor? What guidance does a singer need; what are the characteristics in a conductor that make opera singers most comfortable to work with them?

MK – Everybody is different, but what I like about the relationship between singers and conductors, what makes me feel comfortable, is first of all, to have trust. You know, some conductors like to control everything, and maybe sometimes they do it too much. Of course, they have to control the various elements of the orchestra and the singing in order to put everything together, but everybody does their best – both the musicians and the singers – when they feel that they are appreciated and that they can bring their own ideas and the conductor trusts them. A good opera conductor should understand the general singing technique, so that they won't destroy the singer by making us repeat everything many times! [laughs] Also, they need to guide and to breathe together with the singer. Conductors who don't do a lot of opera often forget to breathe with you. An opera conductor is a really good one if he doesn't forget that thing – that we need to breathe!

OL – Who are some of the conductors who do this particularly well?

MK – There are some conductors I absolutely adore to work with. I love to work with Mariss Jansons, for example. I did a lot of great Baroque things with Marc Minkowski, he is someone I find very exciting. He is a real stage animal as well. He himself would like to be an actor. He understands the drama of it. He made Baroque music for me very lively, a bit out of this authentic interpretation. Sometimes some of the groups can be very strict. People have very particular ideas about how it was, in Baroque. For me, Marc brought very much life and spontaneity to it.

OL – So, I take it, from this answer, that you prefer Baroque music in modern instruments rather than in period instruments, given that the period orchestras can indeed be very particular about how the music needs to be played and how it was played at the time?

MK – No. I think that Baroque music in Baroque instruments, for me, is the best combination. First of all, there are different pitches. Some music was written in a specific pitch, and even if it is a half tone, you can feel the difference in the voice. And also, the period instruments have softer colors. Modern instruments are always very bright, very brilliant. But I love a lot more the sound of a flute that is soft and round. Especially the wind instruments, I find very exciting to match them to the voice. But you know, I'm not the type of person who will say that Baroque music can only be played on period instruments. I for instance work with a Canadian orchestra called Les Violons du Roy, which plays modern instruments, but they concentrate in Baroque music, and they play fantastically, in style! So this is what matters; if you feel the music right; the kind of instrument is less important.

OL – What is your comfort zone, in terms of singing alongside instruments and orchestras that are tuned to different values of A?

MK – Well, it depends. Vivaldi was written in A440, Handel in 415, and there was even a motet that was written in 390 something. Rameau, for example, is almost impossible to sing, it's almost one tone higher on a modern instrument. Some instruments, like wind instruments, can only play in a particular pitch, so it really varies with the composer, with the time period, the place where the music was written. I think you can always feel what is right, what fits with the original intention, when there is a match between the music and the original instrument.

OL - Some opera singers are taken aback by the pitch of period orchestras. Sir John Eliot Gardiner was talking to us about how opera singers tend to sing too high and when they get to perform with the Orchestre Révolutionnaire et Romantique which practices a lower pitch, it throws them off. I would assume that this is not a problem for you, since you've done so much work in Baroque music.

MK – Not at all, I wouldn't see that as a problem, no.

OL – Let's talk about your discography. You have a very extensive discography – we've counted 29 CDs. If one of our readers wanted to buy a collection of Magdalena Kožená essentials – let's say, your favorite three or five – which ones would you recommend as particularly dear to your heart?

MK – I think it very much depends on people's taste because there is quite a bit of different music. Still, I like my first CD in the international market, the one with Bach's arias. When you listen to old recordings you always think "oh, I would do this one differently," but I think there is something very pure and innocent when you record a CD at the age of 22. I was doing mainly Baroque music at that time, and it was a pure joy to make my first CD. Somehow I think it comes across very natural and in the spirit of Bach's music. So this is one I know people like very much and I kind of understand why. I personally of course tend to go for later CDs, like my last one with the Berliner Philharmoniker, where I sing Dvořák's *Biblische* songs which I like very much; it's quite rare to hear them with this orchestra instrumentation – it's normally done with the piano. But Dvořák did orchestrate the first five songs and they're not often performed this way, so yes, I like it. But it is very hard to choose.

OL – So, you do listen to yourself. I once talked to a singer who told me that once his CDs are out, he never listens to them again.

MK – I normally don't. Sometimes when I do the pieces again I want to actually hear how I did it. Recently I've listened to a lot of my CDs because DG is preparing a special double-CD compilation with highlights of all CDs, for my coming birthday. I wanted to be a part of the choice. But I have to say, I don't like doing that, very much, because I always hear something that I would like to do differently. It's really not much fun to listen to my own CDs. [laughs]

OL - Let's talk about your beginnings. Your father was a mathematician and your mother was a biologist, so neither one was a professional musician. Yet music obviously was an important part of your life very early on. You wanted to be a pianist, but you broke your wrist when you were six years old and so you focused on singing instead. Six! How early did you begin taking piano lessons?

MK – No, actually I started piano later, when I was eight. I was in the children's choir from the age of six. About this broken wrist, it wasn't exactly like this. This is a kind of journalist version because they find it colorful… [laughs hard] But if you want to know the truth, I was always singing since I was one; apparently I was singing before I could speak. I fell in love with the piano in Kindergarten. That was the main thing I wanted to do, but since my parents were not musicians and we didn't have much money we didn't have a piano; it was complicated. The teachers said, "you have to do something for this girl because she really wants to do it." Then, I was tapping on some gas heater because it reminded me of a keyboard. I really gave real signals that I wanted to do it. So I started in a very professional children's choir with the Brno Philharmonic Orchestra, and we got a really strict socialistic training, and I loved it very much, but I never thought that I had a particularly good voice, I was very much tuned into becoming a pianist. When I was fourteen at the time when I entered secondary school, I wanted to play the piano and I broke my hand, so I tried singing with this thought that "next year I'll do the piano exam and then I'll switch to piano." I did the exam and passed it, so I decided to study both, which was quite unusual but I got an exception. So the first four years I studied piano and singing. But then, when I was sixteen I met a lute player, and we started to do Renaissance music, like Dowland, and pre-Baroque. Suddenly I was also a member of a madrigal octet and I started to earn a little money with singing, and I was only sixteen years old. Somehow I discovered that singing was in a way more natural to me. Also, I had less stage fright as a singer. As a pianist I always felt a little bit alone at the keyboard. With singing, I could see the people and kind of communicate with the audience; it made me feel more relaxed about it. When I was eighteen, I had to really decide what I was going to study next, and then I made, I think, the right choice to become a singer.

OL – So, this initial encounter with the piano at a young age happened at school, not at home.

MK – Yes. My kindergarten teacher played quite well children songs on the piano for us. Then this children choir Kantilená that I got into at age six specialized in Renaissance music and modern, contemporary music. So we did a lot of things like Orlande de Lassus, and a lot of Czech contemporary composers; it was very particular and unusual to have these two opposite styles.

OL - After your studies at the Brno Conservatory and while you were still at the College of Performing Arts in Bratislava, you were a prize winner at the Mozart International Competition in Salzburg, and you and were chosen as "The Most Talented Performer of the Czech Republic". Then, your career took off pretty fast. Was it difficult in any way, or confusing, for a young lady to suddenly become famous?

MK – Well, you are that young and things are going well, you kind of take everything for granted. I appreciated it. What was amazing is that I lived in this closed, socialist country, and couldn't travel. When I was sixteen, it was when the Velvet Revolution happened, and then with everything I had learned, I could suddenly go abroad. This wouldn't have happened to me if I were ten years older; I wouldn't have been able to suddenly become an international singer if I had started at a later age. When I look back at it from a distance, of course not everything is great about becoming famous so young, and there is some kind of truth in going through it in a slower process. This is the sort of thing you only realize later in your career, that maybe it would have been nice to have had more time to study this and that. But at the time, I was rather happy with what was happening, and was just taking it day by day.

OL – I'd like to talk a bit about your recording career. An artist of your magnitude is in a stronger position regarding the recording industry than most colleagues. So, we understand that by this point in your career you probably can get DG to agree with any project of yours. What kind of interesting surprises can we look forward to, in the future?

MK – Yes, I am of course planning for some recordings. I am still one of the few lucky people who have contracts with a recording company. We all know that it's not the greatest time. Who knows? I can't imagine people buying CDs in ten years. It's a very old-fashioned medium, already. But still, things are happening, and I'm preparing my next CD. Very recently, the idea came up of doing the repertory for voice and organ, because there is quite a large such repertory that is hardly recorded and is sort of fringe. There's André Caplet, there is Lili Boulanger, there is Bizet, and there are Hugo Wolf songs orchestrated by Max Reger; it's a large repertory that is hardly ever done so I thought it was an interesting project for recording. I have more projects; one is a pure Monteverdi CD with La Cetra which is a pretty specialized group playing old instruments.

OL – How do you discover all this music? Do you do a lot of research?

MK – I do some research. Also, in the field of specialized Baroque music, I ask people who know more about it than me; people who really spend time in archives, and then they advise me.

OL - Your very impressive discography includes a number of opera recordings. Studio recordings of operas are much less common now than they were 30 years ago, and some singers even feel at a bit of a disadvantage in the studio. They need to have the theater, the audience, to really get inside their characters and the drama. What are your feelings about this?

MK – Nowadays we hardly record any operas in studio. There are advantages and disadvantages. I always think that if you can do a live performance, there is this atmosphere, there is this adrenaline, but of course it's never that perfect. So it depends on what you are after. I think we are now a little bit forced to be perfect; everybody is cutting every note and people are used to having the CD as clean as possible, but often the live recordings are still for me, somehow, more human, and even if there are some intonation problems and some notes are less beautiful than they could be, it's still more exciting than to do this surgery stuff.

OL - You came to perform *Carmen* relatively late in your career, for a mezzo. We'd be curious to know why it took you so long to portray that phenomenal character. Was the reason for the delay; a vocal one, or something to do with the psychology of the character? Or just, the opportunity took long to materialize?

MK – I was offered to do it several times over the last fifteen years, but I never felt quite ready. I was waiting for a proper occasion, because *Carmen* can be done in very different ways. What we are used to in general is making *Carmen* this big, almost Italianate opera where everybody expects Carmen to have this huge chest sound. This is not who I am; this is not what my voice is. I don't think it's the only way, and don't think it's the way the role was written, because the Opéra-Comique where it was performed for the first time is a small theater and the singer had a light soprano voice, and she was more an actress than a singer. So it was for me a little bit like – I don't want to say it – cabaret style songs. If you go through the score, you'll see that Micaëla and Don José have very melodic lines like in Italian arias, but Carmen actually sings songs. She is out of the regular society, I see her a little bit as a cabaret singer. In a classical production with a traditional conductor, it doesn't come across this way, so, I was waiting for a production with someone who has the same opinion; it took some time [laughs].

OL – I did watch some YouTube fragments of your performance, and it was indeed interesting. So, you've sung in concert arias from roles that are generally regarded as soprano parts, such as Despina – though it's not that unusual for mezzos to also be cast in that role – and Vitellia. Are there other traditionally soprano roles that you feel would be suitable for your voice?

MK – I recorded arias from Despina and Vitellia but wouldn't do the roles complete on stage. Maybe Despina yes, but later; it's often done by older, experienced singers [laughs]. But Vitellia, no, I wouldn't sing the whole role; the last aria is done in arioso and is possible for mezzos, but the first aria and the trio are really for the soprano voice. But I for example sang Cleopatra from *Giulio Cesare* which is a soprano role, but in Baroque music it's a little bit different; it's often not so high. It depends on how high you are going to decorate the *da capo* arias, and it's up to you what you do with it; there is more choice, but normally I stay within my mezzo possibilities. [laughs]

OL - Your voice, like that of all singers, must be evolving. Where is it taking you next?

MK – In a way I don't think my voice has changed somewhat dramatically but, yes, with maturity and the older you get, the voice gets a big richer and heavier. Now I feel more comfortable in Mahler than ten years ago. On the other hand, I'm also losing some things. Coloraturas that were extremely easy ten years ago – I'm still doing them and it's good to practice them because they keep your voice in technical good shape – but it's not as easy as it used to be. You gain something, you lose something but in general my voice is getting a bit richer especially in the lower register, so I can more easily do something like Brahms or Mahler.

OL - In 2003 you earned the title of Chevalier de l'Ordre des Arts et des Lettres by the French government, so now you are a knight, just like your husband. Do you have memories to share with us, about the moments when you learned that you had been granted these prestigious awards?

MK – Yes, I remember. At that time I was married to a French baritone, my first husband, who got quite irritated that I was becoming a French knight, not him. [laughs hard]. I thought it was a bit early. I was very young and of course I was very honored to be a French knight. I felt that I'd have to do for French music something special. It made me feel very happy.

OL – And you do celebrate French culture, right?

MK – I have to say, I do a lot of French music. In my recitals, I actually do mainly French and Czech pieces. I do some Russian and German, but everybody is doing Schumann, Schubert, and there are lots of fantastic German singers who sing their music and I love it, but I think that French music deserves a lot of attention. It's harder for the public, because the emphasis is not on melodious tunes, but rather on the impressions, on the text. I was doing this recital in Baltimore two days ago and people found it hard. People would say, "this repertoire is not my kind of thing but I love your voice." I'd say to that, "you need some time to get into this repertoire; you need to listen to it maybe longer." It's more demanding for the public, but I don't give up; it's worth it, trying to make people love this kind of music as well.

OL - Is it very difficult to raise a family when both parents are international music stars of the first magnitude, with busy schedules?

MK – Yes, when it gets complicated is when your children start to go to school. I used to travel with my children. I have my younger son here with me; he is only four, I still can do it with him, but with the other one who is eight, you can't take him from school, so we try to organize our schedules in a way that there is always one of us in Berlin. But it's not so easy, not always entirely possible. But I think it's not the hardest task. Of course it's not easy to have a career and to have children. I would recommend it to every singer, even though sometimes maybe you don't give such fantastic performances because you haven't slept all night. But you get something that in a way is more important, which is the real life. You see the priorities more clearly, and what is most important for everyone and for me. If you have a family, even if things don't go the way you want, you always have someone to go back to. I think there is nothing sadder than singers – or artists, not only singers – who suddenly finish their careers, they are in their fifties, and although they still have thirty years to live, there is nothing much happening. That must be very difficult, because when you are a famous artist attention is always on you, and you are also living from this energy, and I think the cut is very dramatic. It must be very hard to live through this situation. I love my job and I'm happy for this opportunity to do it, but it's nothing to compare with having family and children.

OL – So, how do your children relate to your music and your husband's music? With genes like these, are your children Jonáš and Miloš very musical?

MK – They are very musical, but they are not especially interested at the moment. Of course the little one is still very little, and we are not the kind of parents who would try to put violins in the hands of our children at age three and force them. I really believe that if you want to be a musician, you know it from early childhood. It's not because you just like it; it's rather a must; it's a passion. I was just crazy for it, I didn't want to do anything else since I was three. My husband was the same.

What my goal would be to actually bring my children to accomplish is that they'd love music. They wouldn't need to be musicians. Music is a wonderful thing to have in your life even if you are not a musician but rather a passionate listener. That's very important. But I'm against forcing children to do something that I would want them to do. The older one has started in a choir and he really likes it; actually he has a very good singing voice. He does a bit of piano but for the moment he can only play music from *Star Wars*, it's not progressing very well. [laughs] But the choir might be nice and he is very sociable, so he likes to make music with other people; it's easier for him than just sit and practice alone. We'll see, but I don't think we are bringing up two professional musicians to the world of tomorrow.

[laughs[

OL - Do they attend already their parents' performances?

MK – Yes, they like it, especially when it's opera, because they have the visual side. They loved *Carmen*, and thought that it was a perfect piece for children. [laughs] It's harder to bring them to *Pelléas et Mélisande*. [laughs] But *Carmen*, my son was really thrilled to see me killed at the end. [laughs] I was really afraid that he'd be scared or would experience some sort of trauma from it, but he said, "Oh mom, if you were so terrible to me as you were to Don José I would have killed you too!" [laughs hard].

OL – Fantastic! [laughs] We know Magdalena Kožená, the spectacular singer. How is Magdalena Kožená, the person, wife, mother? Would you please – given due respect to your privacy of course – give us a hint or a flavor of what your personality is like?

MK – [laughs] That is a very difficult question.

OL – Yes, I get that a lot. [laughs] But often, this question brings about some interesting answers.

MK – [laughs] OK, I'll try to give you an interesting answer. Well, I like to laugh. It's a very Czech thing. We deal with every problem with black humor. I think I'm quite sarcastic; I'd say, and funny, in a way. Sometimes I have too big a sense of responsibility. I'm always on time; I prepare a lot for everything. Some singers can come to a pre-production and they don't know it. They learned it by the end, but they have this sense of learning it during the process. I always have to be prepared 200% otherwise I would be too nervous about everything.

OL – What else do you like to do, other than your music, and being with your family?

MK – I love nature very much. If I could choose, I would live somewhere in the countryside, in a farm. I love mountain-hiking. I practice Yoga a bit. I like to cook. I don't have much time but I like to read books and I like theater and paintings.

OL – Coming back to what you said about the Czech thing, maybe what I'll say is a gross generalization, but like I said at the beginning, I was recently in Prague and interviewed three Czech artists, and talked with other people. Some of them told me that the Czech people are suspicious of everything and very pragmatic. It's the country in the world with the largest proportion of atheists which constitute the vast majority of the population. They supposedly are weary of any sort of organized institution that would control their lives. Maybe it is in function of the oppressive political situation a few decades ago. Is this how you see your people?

MK – Yes, very much like you said. It's very interesting, I thought about it many times, because we are not the only country that had a history of oppression by others, and the other countries that were in the same situation are very different, like Poland, and even Slovakia, with whom we were together for a long time – they are much more into religion. There is something about the Czechs – they like to be smart and do everything on their own. When Czechs emigrate abroad they don't tend to make communities with other Czech immigrants. People prefer to be on their own and deal with everything intellectually. There's just something purely Czech about that, and I think you get a hint of it when you read books by Hrabal or Kundera. You get very much this Czech spirit, and sometimes I find it even annoying, you know? Sometimes if you are abroad and you are a Polish person and somebody speaks Polish around you, you come and say "Oh, you're Polish, what are you doing here?" and people start a conversation. But Czech people, they hear someone else speaking Czech – and I found myself doing it too – they are going the other way! [laughs]. And this is how we are all like, and it's hard to explain, but it is true.

OL – Thank you so much for your time. I'll be there tomorrow for the recital. We're glad that you're bringing this music to our town.

MK – Oh, you're welcome. You did a fantastic job with these questions. Thank you very much!

DIVISION ONE – INTERNATIONALLY ESTABLISHED SINGERS

CHAPTER TWO - THE TENORS

Juan Diego Flórez

The most famous light lyric tenor of the last several years doesn't need much introduction to our readers, of course. Opera Lively was honored to present a short interview with the outstanding tenor the day we launched our website in late 2011. A couple of years later and after Opera Lively's growth including more than 125 exclusive interviews with prominent artists, it was our pleasure to address Mr. Flórez again, this time for a long in-person interview at the Met in early May 2014 on the occasion of his performance of Prince Ramiro in *La Cenerentola.*

Opera Lively - Before we talk more specifically about you, let's address the character Prince Ramiro. What is the recipe to do this role well? Do you have something to say about the psychological characteristics of this character, if any, that might make of him more than a stock character?

Juan Diego Flórez – Prince Ramiro is a prince of course, but he is different than all the characters in the opera. He and Cenerentola are the normal ones. The other ones are always playing a role or being greedy or not true to themselves. Instead, Ramiro and Cenerentola, they just search for love, although it may sound as a cliché; not convenient love, but pure love. That's why in this production in the Met we are different than the others.

We are not made up; we practically don't have make-up on. We look natural. The other ones look white in their faces. They wanted to make us different in a way.

OL - Are there any vocal challenges in this role?

JDF – Vocally it's a high tenor Rossini role, so what it means is that it is very virtuosic with big high notes, and a lot of runs and coloratura singing; all that bel canto can have is in there.

OL - This production has an extraordinary cast. Can you tell us a little bit how good it is to work with your illustrious colleagues?

JDF – Well, of course. We can start by talking about Joyce DiDonato. She is a magnificent mezzo-soprano and she is like my sister. We have worked so much together, and we know each other so well… The rest of the cast, also, I have worked with each one of them, especially Alessandro Corbelli and Pietro Spagnoli. They are friends. With Pietro, for example, I made my debut with him. So, it's very easy to work with them, and so pleasurable!

OL - You were born in Lima in 1973. I'm very much interested in your South American background. I'd say that arguably together with the late Bidu Saião you're the most accomplished South American opera singer in history. So, let's start with your childhood. Your father was a singer and your mother a music-lover. How early did music enter your life?

JDF – Music, always, but the classical music, really when I was seventeen. In my house we didn't have classical music. My parents never listened to it, or to opera, but towards the end of high school there was a teacher who wanted to do Zarzuela at school, and I took part in it, and asked him if he could give me some lessons. He started to teach me voice, by imitation. I tried to sing like him, and then I wanted to enter Peru's National Conservatory, but not because of classical music but rather pop music. I used to compose and sing my own songs and I wanted to know how to read and write music. So, I went to the conservatory and auditioned with singing because I had already had lessons with this teacher. He taught me "Questa o quella" and Schubert's "Ave Maria" and I got in. But in the conservatory I discovered really what classical singing meant, and I decided I wanted to do that; but before, I wanted to be a pop singer, a melodic ballad singer.

OL - So, you started by writing your own songs and singing pop, rock, and Peruvian music. Do these first steps still influence you today, as a classical musician? Do you think they inform you in any way, or did you leave it all behind you?

JDF – I think everything that you listen to, that you like, what you grow up with, is part of you, and you bring that to your music and to your singing. I cannot say no. That's part of what I am and of my background, and I sing with that.

OL - As a teenager in Peru, how did your peers and friends see your classical music vocation? I was talking with maestro Marco Armiliato and he told me how all his friends – and himself – were into soccer, while he was also into classical music, and his peers found it really weird. Any similar experiences?

JDF – Yes, of course, because they were going out to parties and drinking, and I was going out with my friends from the Conservatory, with classical students. We would go to concerts, and of course we would go out and drink and go to parties as well, but it was another crowd. My other friends would say, "where are you going; aren't you going out with us?" and I'd say "no, I'm going to a concert." "What do you mean, a concert?" they'd say. [laughs] But I always played football; I kept that, and I still do it, and enjoy it so much!

OL - So, you came to Philladelphia to the Curtis Institute at age 20. Was it difficult for a young man your age to make this leap?

JDF – No, because I wanted to discover the world; I wanted to go away from Peru not because I didn't like it, but because I wanted to explore, as a young person. For me, it was great. I found that scholarship with a lot of dedication and effort. I found it myself; I came to audition, I got in, I found the money, and I studied in Philadelphia for three years. It was great because I entered the voice program. It meant I should just sing art songs, but they didn't have a tenor for the opera program, and they took me practically into the opera program, being only twenty. They gave me operas. I arrived there in September 93, and in November 93 I was singing *I Capuleti e I Montecchi*. I didn't know anything about Bellini, nothing, and I sang it, and then I sang *Barbiere*, then I sang *Il Viaggio a Reims*, and another one… That gave me so much experience, but I was really lucky that I didn't get ruined in my voice, because I wasn't really prepared, but I just did them. It all gave me experience and made my debut very fast, because I had my debut very early also, at 23.

OL - Then, you met Mr. Ernesto Palacio who had a huge influence in your career. Can you tell us more about it?

JDF – Yes, in 94 I met him. He was a singer at the time. I was in Peru on vacation. He represented something big to me: a Peruvian tenor who sang at La Scala, at the Met, and who belonged to a tradition of singers with Luigi Alva, and before, Alejandro Granda, who sang with Toscanini many times. I auditioned for him in Lima, and he said to me "I want you to have a career." He helped in every way he could. He made me do a CD right away, then another one while I was still a student. He got me international auditions; the first one in Bologna, for the Rossini Festival. They accepted me to sing a small role. You know, the story goes that the tenor cancelled and I went on to sing the big role, and this is how it all started.

OL - Yes, Corradino in *Matilde di Shabran*, on short notice, and you stepped in. You learned the role in just a few days.

JDF – Yes, a lucky break, unexpected of course, and then they called me to sing at La Scala.

OL - Yes, four months later you were singing at La Scala. Was this incredibly fast rise to fame psychologically difficult for a young man, 23 years old?

JDF – I was kind of unconscious. I was doing everything and not really realizing what I was doing. After Pesaro, immediately I went to Ireland to sing *Don Pasquale*, and *L'Etoile du Nord* by Meyerbeer, and then I went to La Scala. It was one after the other, and I made my debut at La Scala and then I did a concert there. I started to sing in several houses in Italy, one after the other. The Royal Opera House Covent Garden came also the following year. I was studying a lot because everything was a new role, but I had the facility; I played the piano, I could read the music… I think it is something that every singer should learn. Many singers don't know that, how to read music. They know it but not well enough so they always depend on somebody who is going to teach them the music.

OL - The Peruvian public and cultural institutions seem to be, and justifiably so, deeply in love with you, given the large number of accolades, awards, and honors you have received from institutions in your country. You are even on a postal stamp there. How emotional is it for you to go back to Peru to sing?

JDF – It is very emotional, especially because of the children. I have a foundation, and when I go there I feel the love and the thanks from all those children of the Sinfonia por el Peru, my foundation, similar to the Sistema in Venezuela. I have a recital in Peru on May 13, with a pianist, but in the middle of the recital we are presenting the National Children's Orchestra, and that is a great achievement because the foundation is only three years old, so I'm happy about that. I'll be doing a lot of work during those four or five days I'm going to be there. In Peru, I'm recognized and I am kind of a hero. Many people haven't heard me sing, in Peru, but they are still proud. It's something else. Many people have heard me but many haven't, but they all love me in a way, because I'm making them proud and feeling important in the eyes of the world, and for Peru that's very important; that's the reason why.

OL - Your popularity in your home country is impressive – crowds flocked to Plaza Mayor to see your wedding ceremony. How about the rest of South America – do you have any intention of trying to enhance the popularity of classical music and opera in neighboring countries? Any collaboration with Venezuela? Any plans for say, Argentina and/or Brazil?

JDF – No, I don't have any plans, but I know I'll be doing it anyway, and that's good. My only intention is to help these children through music – not only classical. The program is not only classical music. I know that with my singing I'm making the opera world a bit more popular, but popularity is not one of my objectives.

OL - How did you get the idea for the foundation?

JDF – I went to Caracas for a concert and I saw the Sistema and decided that I wanted to do this in Peru also, and got to work on it right away.

OL - You are also UNESCO's Goodwill Ambassador. What responsibilities come with that?

JDF - I got this prize and this title because of my foundation. There is no responsibility per se, except to continue what I am doing, but now under the patronage of the UNESCO, and that's a good and important thing because it makes it easier to achieve my objectives.

OL - You are really the king of bel canto. In the future, other singers will look back at you for inspiration. So, when you look back, who were the past singers who inspired you?

JDF – When I started, I was seventeen in the conservatory; I got hold of cassettes. Pavarotti was the first tenor I heard, and Alfredo Kraus. Both really impressed me, and I thought "how do they do that, how do they sing like that?" And then, of course, throughout my career I have admired many tenors and I always listen to performances from other singers, not only tenors, and I learn from everybody.

OL - Other journalists must have asked you so many questions about bel canto, that I'd like to focus a bit on your latest CD, "L'Amour." I listened to it last week and was thoroughly impressed. I'm a lover of French opera and knew all those pieces. I thought that your voice was a bit darker in this repertory with meatier and rounder colors as compared to the bel canto light tenor roles. Is this an evolution in your instrument, and are you planning to go deeper into these roles?

JDF – Yes, my voice changed a bit when I hit 39, 40. I felt more comfortable in these roles, so I did *Guillaume Tell*, *La Favorite*, and I felt really, really well. In this CD I sing with this slightly different voice, not because I want it, but because it's how I sing now. This year I'm doing *Roméo et Juliette* in Peru, and *Werther* in 2016. I'll be doing *Les Huguenots*, and operas like that – *Lucrezia Borgia*, *Lucia di Lammermoor*, but I'll still be singing Rossini. [laughs]

OL - How did you select the tracts for "L'Amour"?

JDF – By investigating. The Internet is great these days; you can even go into libraries. I did it by myself. I got a nice group of pieces; some known, some others a little bit less known. I made a nice mix.

OL - In your extensive discography and videography, what are a couple of your favorites? If someone wanted to get to know your artistry and asked for your advice on what to buy – your best recordings - what would you say?

JDF – I don't like my CDs [laughs]. I listen a lot to all those tracks before the CD comes out, because you have to help with the edition of the CD. You have many takes on a track and they ask for your advice when they are putting it together. But then when the CDs are out, I don't listen to them; I'm kind of tired of them. But I would recommend this last one, "L'Amour"; I really liked this one. About the DVDs, I really liked the last one I recorded, *Guillaume Tell*, I don't know if it is out already; and also the ones before last, *Matilde di Shabran* and *Zelmira*.

OL - I love that one. So, *La Fille du Régiment* with Natalie Dessay – it was an iconic production. Mme. Dessay has retired from the operatic stage. Do you miss her? What was it like, working with her?

JDF – She hasn't entirely retired. She still does some things. My experience with her is amazing because she is a great actress and a wonderful person, and we had a lot of fun together. That's the word: fun; a lot of laughs and a lot of discoveries about each other. I learned a lot from her and her passion. She is one of my best partners.

OL - Comic operas are one of your greatest strengths. However you are equally good at tragic roles. Do you have a preference? Which genre is harder to pull off?

JDF – Serious operas are more difficult because they are very static. You have to be credible while moving little. With comedy you can really explore the space. Especially in serious bel canto operas, they are very static and are made of just singing; that's why these operas work well in concert form, because there isn't a lot happening on stage. It would look very silly to just move around. I enjoy both, but comedy in the bel canto is more fun, because there is less of a convention. If I do something more dramatic like *Werther* or even *Orphée* that I'll do in 2015 at the Royal Opera House, there is more to act there, because it's less conventional theater; it's more like real theater.

OL - Do you have favorite stage directors you love to work with? I think most of your productions are traditional rather than Regie – but not always – there was for example that *Rigoletto* with the animal heads and a lot of nudity. Any opinions there?

JDF – I've worked with lots of directors but I like more modern productions. I don't like it when I arrive at a new production and everything is so conventional and old-fashioned. I think the public doesn't want to see that anymore, either. But I like the modern productions when at least they make sense. When they don't make sense, it's just craziness; then I don't like it because I don't know what I am doing on stage, and they don't know it either. You ask questions of the director on why he is doing certain things, and the answer comes as "I don't know." [laughs] It's for you to interpret.

OL - Tell us about your work as a composer, please. What are your projects?

JDF – No, no, I'm not a composer, I just have some fun [laughs]. I do arrangements for Peruvian songs because they are not arranged and I need to sing them in my concerts. There is a song, "Santo", that I composed for a CD. I think it's my best work with a classical orchestra, but that's not what I usually do. I don't have any projects as a composer [laughs].

OL - At this point in your career you have practically accomplished everything that there is to be accomplished. How do you keep yourself challenged and interested? What goals do you still have?

JDF – I'm always interested because I like to explore the voice, the technique, the ways of breathing in a better way, and to see how others do it. For me the part of the mechanics of doing it is fun. I'm always curious and interested in singing. I enjoy singing. I enjoy rehearsing and performing; I'm not tired of doing that. I'm tired of traveling, of being on planes and away from home, but never of performing.

OL - I think technically speaking, your most impressive feature is the extraordinary control you have over your voice and your pace. I think you are one of the most precise and elegant singers I've ever heard. How do you do it?

JDF – Well, I study. Not so much, I'd have to say, but when I study I like to study well. I found that with the slight change that my voice had in the latest years, I have to study again, because with the technique I used to sing with, I could continue to sing but it wouldn't be perfect because my voice has changed a bit, so I have to adjust for this bigger center. So I had to study deep and nice again and I had lots of fun doing so, even going into the science of it and the muscles involved in breathing. I have a friend who made echographies of the muscles to show what happens in your muscles and lungs while you sing. I read books about other singers and what they do. For me, it is a nice journey.

OL - What advice do you have for younger singers?

JDF – I would say that they should think that the teacher is only 20% of their preparation. The rest is them. They have to work by themselves. They have to record themselves in rehearsals and listen to the recording. They have to do their own experiments. Otherwise if you think a teacher will make of you a great singer, you are really wrong. I'd advise them to be prepared, musically.

OL - I heard from other singers that you are a very nice man. One of my interviewees, Jessica Pratt, was once in Peru and said you were the perfect host, taking all the singers to visit Lima, and she was just incredibly impressed with how personable you were – such a stratospheric star, but so accessible and friendly. So, let's talk about the man JDF a bit. How do you define your personality?

JDF – I think I like people; I like to be with people, but I can seem sometimes distant, because at the same time I'm a bit reserved and I like my privacy. I'm a really private man. My family is the most important thing, but if I have to be the host when somebody comes to my country or to my house, I like to enjoy people. Sometimes they have to ask me to keep it down a bit [laughs] because sometimes I'm too jokey. I joke all the time. I wasn't like that; I think I was more serious in the past, but I became like that, now. I don't take myself seriously, and I don't take anybody seriously.

That, in a way, has made me go into this career without a lot of problems. Sometimes singers come to me and say "I don't know what the stage director meant when he told me that I wasn't doing this like that, and I told him that I am doing it, and he said to me that I should look the other way, and I told him – no, why?" I tell them, "why are you making your life difficult? Just say yes to anything they tell you. Just smile; you know, the rehearsals are long; he maybe will forget about it and then you'll do what you want." There is always an easy way to respond. I never understood some of my colleagues who respond in a sort of violent way when they are told that they are doing something wrong; and then there is a confrontation, there is tension, and sometimes the whole production is ruined because of these things; it's best to just smile and try to arrange it in the course of things. I've always been friendly; and then I end up doing what I want.

Directors and conductors need to show that they are the leaders – because they are! – and they need to show their authority. You just have to smile to that, because if you fight, then it causes a lot of problems. So, that's how I've been going about this career, by never having conflicts with colleagues, directors, and conductors.

OL – So you are an easygoing person.

JDF – [laughs] Not always, but in general, yes.

OL - Your daughter was just born in January – Lucia Stella – congratulations! Your son Leandro is about 3. How do you juggle your career, and your life as a father and a husband?

JDF – That's a nice question. I do everything, my calendar, thinking of them and how we can be together. Everything in my future is done that way. I'm always asking my wife "what do you think if I accept this opera?" Then we think about it, and we decide accordingly.

OL - What are your other interests in life, besides classical music?

JDF – I like sports – tennis and football. I have a group of friends in Europe, and I like to enjoy time with my friends. It is very important, I think. There is not much more than this. Oh, and I like wine and food. [laughs]

OL – I heard that you cook as well.

JDF – I cook, but not so much, anymore. I used to cook. When I'm alone I cook more, but not complicated things. I know a lot of Peruvian dishes. If I have to cook, then I cook.

OL – Thank you very much for this lovely interview and for your time.

JDF – You're welcome.

Jay Hunter Morris

This interview from January 2013 captured Jay in the rising moment of his career, after his nice "rag to riches" break that catapulted him into international fame by singing Siegfried for the Met in HD broadcast of their "Machine" *Ring*. Ever since, much has happened in Jay's career with other *Rings* and additional roles. The personable tenor also published with Opera Lively Press his funny and compelling memoirs, our best seller with enthusiastic reviews, "Diary of a Redneck Opera Zinger." This phone interview (which we will reproduce in its casual conversational style that demonstrates the singer's friendly demeanor) marked the start of Jay's enduring relationship with Opera Lively.

Opera Lively – Hello, Mr. Morris!

Jay Hunter Morris – Hello. Call me Jay!

OL – OK, great, call me Luiz. So, I'm Luiz from Opera Lively. Is this a good time to talk?

JHM – Yes, it's a very good time, Luiz. Glad to meet you, sir! Thanks for calling!

OL – I'm the one who should be thanking you. I'm reading online your "Diary of a Redneck Opera Zinger" and I'm laughing so hard that you'll probably find my serious questions very boring.

JHM – [Laughs] Good, that's the idea, I hope so!

OL – So, thank you for talking to us. We have half an hour, right?

JHM – Yes, sir. I have a three-year-old son, hopefully he won't be coming in here pulling on my ear too often.[laughs]

OL – [laughs] OK. So, I saw in your website, you had to cancel your appearances as Siegmund this month in Florence because of shoulder surgery. We were very sorry to learn about that. Are you OK? How are you feeling now?

JHM – I'm doing really well, now. Yes, I had shoulder replacement surgery here in my right arm, November 12, but I feel really good. I'm ready to get back to singing, I've been off for a couple of months. You know, you have to refill the well every now and then. I tend to work hard for a while, and then I manage to get a couple of months to lie down and rest. I wish I didn't have to have my body cut open to do that [laughs] but it needed to get done.

OL – I'm glad to hear that you're well. Was that performance in Florence at the Teatro Communale going to be your debut as Siegmund?

JHM – Sort of. I have sung the first act in concert before, and I covered Plácido Domingo in Los Angeles, so I got to do all the rehearsals. And then, of course he came in for the performances. I feel like I've been through a couple of productions of Siegmund.

OL – I see. Will this one with NC Opera be a concert performance, or staged?

JHM – Concert.

OL – OK. In general, some singers have found concert performances of operas to be less strenuous than a staged opera; however some others, such as Siegfried Jerusalem, felt that concert performances were more difficult in that they restricted his ability to move. What has been your experience?

JHM – I love concerts. I prefer them, just because they are all about the music. It's the same thing for rehearsals of staged opera productions. Everybody is different, but my favorite part is the Sitzprobe, which is the day we just stand and sing with the orchestra, and we are not distracted by sets and acting and colleagues, all this other stuff; it's just about the music, and we don't get to do that very often. I've probably only sung a dozen concerts in my life. I *love* it, I'm so excited to just come and rehearse this music! I think your audience is really in for a big treat. As I look at the program, that's a fantastic night of music.

OL - The role of Siegmund actually lies quite low. Does this pose any particular problem for a tenor? Do you find it difficult?

JHM – Oh my gosh, no! I love this music. Listen, compared to Siegfried?!? It's such a pleasure, there are such great tunes. For us tenors, I like singing high. I enjoy singing high notes and I feel that I've worked it out for these last twenty years that I can handle the tessitura pretty well. I've been at this for a while, and I just now am comfortable singing low. I enjoy it. It sorts of takes the pressure of the role off, the possibility of the voice cracking. There is nothing worse than standing in front of a paying audience and splattering and cracking your voice all over the place. It is not fun! I feel like with Siegmund I have a really good chance at having a good evening, so it makes it the whole evening and even the whole rehearsal period such a pleasure!

OL - In a sense, Siegmund is similar to Captain Ahab or Peter Grimes in that he's an outsider, perhaps even a social outcast. You're obviously not in that category – you seem to be such a happy fellow, so how do you "get inside" of these sorts of characters mentally or emotionally?

JHM – You know what, I do the same thing that I've been doing my whole life, and that is, I use my imagination. To me, it's easy, because it's outlined for me. You know who this guy is, he is running for his life, he is an outcast, everywhere he goes people disagree with him, he is put down, he is pushed away, he has always been fought against. We have not only the guidelines of who he is as a personality, but also the text and the music. I feel like – especially with Wagner – that he is so clear! He defines who the guy is, and it is up to me to just use my imagination and step into his shoes. Like Ahab. You put on that peg leg, you put on that hat, you get the scar, and you just step into the guy. People who are in opera are in showbiz. We put on a performance. I've been doing this in one form or another for my whole life, and it's what gives me the most pleasure and the most joy, it's to step into somebody that is completely different from me.

And Luiz, listen. Can you imagine the year that I got to have last year! I mean, I got to sing Siegfried, who is this 17-year-old demigod, and to me the polar opposite of him as a character, which is Captain Ahab, the single-minded, driven antithesis of Siegfried. This is what I love to do. It's fun, it's such a joy for a few hours to get lost completely in the music and in the story! I think that's why people go! We go to movies and plays and music; we want to escape the noise of our lives for a few hours and step into something completely different.

OL – Let me ask you a question about Siegfried. We often debate on the website about some traits of his personality. He has this heroic, driven side, but also sometimes he is depicted by Wagner as a sort of naïve fool that can be easily manipulated. How do you relate to these two sides of his personality?

JHM – Oh, gosh. That's easy. You know what? He is young! He is naïve. We all… I was there for a minute. I was seventeen and I thought I knew everything, and yet at the same time I was encapsulated into this protected innocence. I have a lot of things going to draw from in my own life. I've got a nephew that I hang out a lot with when he was sixteen, seventeen. I know how he acted and how he thought, and how he carried his body. It's playacting; it's just using our imagination and stepping in somebody else's skin. I very much can relate to Siegfried. I wish I were seventeen and fearless and naïve and not quite limited by Father Time.

OL – Yep. Let me ask you a kind of risky question. Feel free to say "Well, let's not go there" if you prefer. Jon Vickers was a noted Siegmund, and also a very devout Christian. He once turned down an offer to sing *Tannhäuser* because he found the role morally repugnant. Like Mr. Vickers, you had a very religious upbringing – your father was a Baptist music minister and your mother played the organ at church services. After you graduated from Baylor University, you were involved in ministry yourself. Does your background have any impact on how you view certain roles? Many people would probably find an incestuous relationship between twins to be pretty objectionable. Does what Siegmund does get in your head in some way?

JHM – [Pauses] No, not at all. In fact I think that's the first time I've given it much thought. It's showbiz. It's not who I am. I'm not stepping out and saying that I approve of this. I'm just playing the character. I enjoy playing the crazy guy. I enjoy playing Canio who is vengeful and kills his wife and her lover. I enjoy playing that but I don't approve of that type of behavior. There are some things that I don't want to do. I don't really want to curse a whole lot. I don't want to do anything that is going to make my mother uncomfortable if she is sitting out there in the audience. I don't really want to be one of those fellows who go out there without their shirts or pants on. It's not good for the audience, or for me.

I've been asked to sing *Tannhäuser* recently, and I passed on it too, but not for the same reason. That's a big, long, hard sing. There are a handful of really big, long sings that I'm going to step in for, but there are some that I will say "no" to, and that was one that I did say "no" to.

Wife Meg, son Cooper Jack, and Jay (photo credit Jay Hunter Morris)

I have a moral compass that is very strong. It came from my youth and all of my adult life. I feel very compelled to be a man that my mother and my father would be proud of. More importantly, I want to be a man that my wife can look up to and my child can think that I'm the best guy in the world, but rarely what I do in the operatic world influences that. It's more how I behave at home.

OL – Yes, nice! So, I was about to ask you about Tannhäuser and you won't do that. What about Rienzi? Any plans to sing it? You've sung most of Wagner's heroic tenor roles already except those two and Parsifal.

JHM – Yes. But you know what I want to sing? I want to sing *Meistersinger* again. It's probably been eight years or so since I sang it in San Francisco and in Frankfurt, and I love it. I want to sing Lohengrin some more. I'd love to sing Parsifal. But I've learned over the years that we can't do everything. We all change as we grow. We can't sing the same repertoire all the time. I went through a period when I was younger when I sang all the romantic Italian roles, and then I went through a period when I sang a lot of Czech and Russian, the Slavic things. You find different things that you are drawn to, and more importantly, that are offered to you. I said for years that my repertoire was whatever anybody would pay me to sing. Anything anybody asked me to sing, I said, "Yes, please." And just over the last couple of years that has changed, and I'm able to say, "You know what, I want to sing Siegfried, I want to sing Tristan."

If I take six months of my life to learn Rienzi, I'm probably not going to sing it more than three or four times. All over the world, it's not done very often. There are four or five roles that I'd rather sing than Tannhäuser or Rienzi. Especially now, I'm reminded as I step into this new year, after the amazing year that I had last year… I mean, I got to sing my first Tristan in concert with Zubin Mehta! Can you imagine such a thing? I sang Siegfried at the Met! This new role that I love so much, Captain Ahab in this amazing new opera! I got to have an absolute career year. And as I stand on the cusp of 2013, I want more! [laughs] It's so fun, it's so good!

OL – Good for you!

JHM – It's such a joy to get to sing this incredible music with an orchestra like the Met orchestra, with such colleagues. One phone call, and all of a sudden I'm standing there singing with Bryn Terfel and Deborah Voigt! I want to do this more! As I stand here looking at my schedule of the next couple of years, it rings true that I can't do everything. I have to pick a few solid things that I wish for. That's the specific things me and my manager, my wife, and my support team, my inner circle of five people are hoping for and wishing for and welcoming. I've got a big banner that runs constantly across my mind, that says "I can't force great things, I can't force the world to give me opportunities, but I can make great opportunities welcome." I'm hoping to get opportunities to do this handful of roles that I really covet. Somebody, someday, will give me my first Peter Grimes. I can't wait!

OL – Right, because one risk would be to be kind of typecast as a Wagnerian stylist, because you also want other things, right? Otello, for instance.

JHM – Absolutely! I really want the acting roles. I want to be the guy that gets to go crazy and kill people. I want to be the guy with the myopic view of the world that is consumed with hate for this white whale. I want to be that guy who wins the girl. I spent many years either being the supporting character or being the understudy, being out in the audience, waiting, watching, preparing, I think that's why I felt so prepared when the call came for me to step in as Siegfried, both in San Francisco and at the Met. It's because I spent a lot of years thinking, "What do I want to do when it's my turn? Who do I want this guy to be?" I understudied three men doing great jobs as Siegfried. That gives you time to envision and prepare yourself, and think, "How do I want these characters to sound when I get my turn?"

OL – Yes. I read your point about thinking "Oh, I will never get the big break." And then you did, of course. We are all thrilled for you. But I want to ask a more psychological question. The big break, the sudden fame, does that mess with your head in some way? Do you feel that there is any downside to this incredible exposure and fame that you've achieved last year?

JHM – Absolutely not. [laughs] I haven't found yet if there is a downside. I've had a great run. Twenty years ago I decided, "I want to try and sing opera." I'm from the South, so my vision was, "I'm going to put my bait in the water and I'm going to see if anything bites. I'll get a job and if I don't, then I'll go do something else." I haven't always been on top. I've spent a lot of time in the valley. The best thing about these big breaks is that I get to sing this music. All of a sudden I'm singing with the Met Orchestra, have you heard them? The San Francisco Opera. All of a sudden I'm standing there, looking down on Zubin Mehta throwing me cues to sing Tristan – there is no downside to that. I can't think of anything negative.

I'll be honest with you. The most challenging part about this is the pressure. You cannot deny that the night before, and then the days before singing Siegfried on an HD broadcast, knowing that the camera are going to be down my throat, up-close and personal, and I'm going to be on 100-feet high IMAX screens all over the world, opera lovers from all over the world will be sitting up there and watching and judging and hopefully being entertained. There is a very real and very tangible pressure there. I did a lot of pacing, and I did a lot of staring into the abyss. But as soon as that orchestra started tuning, I was fine, I was at home on the stage, I was relaxed. I didn't know how it would end, if I'd still have a voice at the end of the night, if the audience would love me, or if the critics would love me, and I still don't.

OL – Well, you did great. I think that by now you must have realized that you really did great, no?

JHM – Yeah, but I mean, that doesn't mean that the next time I go out there it won't be different. That's the most exciting and challenging thing about Siegfried, is that with something that long and that challenging, you just don't know if at the end of the night you are still going to have a voice left. So, I take this love that I'm getting from the audience and I'm savoring it. It may be old hat to some singers, they may have been getting it their whole career, but I haven't. And right now I get emails from people that are not my family or friends, that take the time to write me and give me support and love, and I read every one of them, and I appreciate it and enjoy it. It's nice! Truly, it's such a luxury to be loved and respected, right now. I know very well it's short-lived, and it's not unanimous, not everybody likes me. I've heard the CDs of these recordings from the *Ring* and I've watched the videos, and you know, I like what I do most of the time. I'm not entirely pleased, and I'm not finished, I've got a long list of things that I'm working on and I want to do better. I think I'm going to do better this year than I did last year. But all of this good stuff that is happening really since Francesca Zambello told me she wanted me to be the Siegfried in San Francisco, that started everything – since that day, to Peter Gelb giving me my opportunities there at the Met - it's all be such a pleasure, such a joy! I *swim* in gratitude every day, I am so thankful! Because it could have been somebody else. All of these rides were supposed to have been taken by another man. So, look, I'm grateful, and I'm thankful every day and I look forward to getting over there and giving it another shot and do my best.

OL – But what about all the pressures that can come from this? From now on, you are in high demand, there will be traveling all over, less family time, staying in hotels all the time, and so forth. Is this something that makes you think "Oops, maybe I got too famous, too suddenly" or is it the case that drawing from your inner structure and your inner strength, you feel that all of that will be fine?

JHM – All of that will be fine. Listen, it's not like you think. I am guilty of thinking that you sit there and you stand in front of the Met audience and they are giving you some love and you hear from people out that saw it in the movie theaters, and I get all the support from friends and colleagues, but that doesn't necessarily translate into jobs. There was a time last year that we though, "OK, my calendar is going to fill up quickly, and I'm going to get to sing all over the world" and people said "Oh gosh, you are going to be in great demand" – it's not really like that. I have gotten a good handful, as you can see on my schedule, of very good jobs, thank goodness. Peter Gelb is giving me some more shots, and I get to come back and sing two of the *Ring* cycles this year. But it's not like all of a sudden I can't leave my house because there are paparazzi out the door. I mean, let's keep it real; this is opera, not the movies. As passionate as I think that our fans are, they are not knocking the doors down, and neither are all of the opera companies of the world all of a sudden flooding my inbox with offers. The best thing is that I'm going to get some chances to sing some more great music, and to sing with some of the best singers in the world.

For somebody who has been trying to do this for so long, twenty-three years now… You know, I've been friends with these guys for a long time. I've been friends with Bryn Terfel for twenty years, we've played golf together in Santa Fe in 1990 when I was an apprentice there. I love his singing and I've bought his records. I never thought I would get a chance to share the stage with him. Most of the people who are up there singing in the *Ring* at the Met have been stars at the Metropolitan Opera for a lot of years – Bryn Terfel, Stephanie Blythe, Debbie Voigt, they've been there for years. So, it's just… to be me and to get to watch for twenty years, and then all of a sudden to be out there sharing the stage with them, woooo, it's good, boy!

OL – Let me ask you about modern and contemporary works. You did do some 21st century operas and some from the second half of the 20th century. Do you find this repertoire to be more difficult as compared to the 19th century and early 20th?

JHM – Certainly, a lot of it is. Most of the time it comes down to tunes, to having something that is easy on the ears, something that takes root in your mind and is easy to remember and easy to perform. You take that against a piece like, say, *Wozzeck* that is such a challenge. It's a different game, completely. I've been very lucky. I was in the world-premiere production of *A Streetcar Named Desire*, I was in *Dead Man Walking*, *Grendel*, *Doctor Atomic*, *The Fly*, I got to be a part of several world premiere productions of new operas, and I've enjoyed them, it's great. I'll tell you something, I've never loved a show the way I loved *Moby Dick*, and not just because I got to play Ahab. Everybody from the orchestra players to the backstage personnel, we all felt this unifying passion for this piece; it's such a great production!

Listen, it's just like you. You go to work in the morning, and you sit down and you take a look at your case files, and you take each individual on their own, and you look them in the face, and that's what we do with opera too. I take each individual opera and role and I sit down and I say, "OK, this is a chapter of my life, I'm going to do the best I can", whether it be Puccini, or a Czech piece. I'm going to have to work for six months on the language. I have never, ever felt anything but privilege, to get to sit down and say, "OK, you know what, I'm going to learn this new role." Even if it is these new modern pieces that are often so difficult. I'm getting paid to sing, so I count my blessings, and I sit down and do my studies, and I know that I'm lucky that I get paid to sing.

OL – Right. There are some composers right now who are really pushing the boundaries of music theater today – people like Salvatore Sciarrino or Heiner Goebbels. Goebbels even thinks opera houses as performance spaces are becoming obsolete. Where do you see contemporary opera headed? What do you feel will be the future of the art form?

JHM – Hm… I don't know where this technology is taking us. What do me and my colleagues, as artists, as singers, talk about? – We want a compelling story, we want music that is engaging and enthralling and captivating not only for the audience, but for us, and we want a production in a staging that is new, that is fresh, that uses this technology that we've got… because you know what? We are in showbiz just as much as the movie theaters are, and musical theater is. New operas have got to meet those criteria. It's got to be a good story, it's got to be well set, the music has to be all those things we've just talked about. That's the reason I'm so excited about *Moby Dick*. Because of their use of 3D projections, and the stage, and the way Jake [Heggie] wrote the score, everything came together. For the composers, it's an enormous challenge and an enormous burden to write something that hasn't been done before, but is still so captivating to the audience. We've got to be entertainers. I don't know where all this technology is taking us, and thank goodness it's not my job to figure that out. My job is to go out there and tell the story and I'll do my part as best as I can.

OL – Great. Let me go back to something I skipped in my list of questions here. When you have to sing such a long role as Siegfried, how do you prepare yourself in terms of general health, physical condition, warming of the voice? Do you have a routine, do you get all superstitious, saying "I can't do this or that because I'm singing Siegfried" – what is your routine to prepare for such demanding long roles?

JHM – My wife calls it the cocoon. [laughs] She and Cooper generally stay away during those periods. I go to work and to rehearsal, and I go home. That's about it, I don't waste much energy on social life. I exercise a lot to keep my stamina. But here is the thing: you've got to sing well. If I sing well for two hours, then I've got a good chance for singing well for another two hours. If I go out there and scream, and sing poorly and use poor technique, come off the breath, and don't use my support, I don't have a chance. This is what is so exciting about it and frightening, this is why I go into the cocoon for *Siegfried*. This is why when I'm not on stage I'm so nervous, and I'm so terrified. There's some very, very challenging music at the end of the opera. Now, we might rehearse Act III of *Siegfried* for three hours in the morning. And if I do it isolated like that, I have a really good chance of doing it well, I think; I feel like I've worked it out to a place that I'm going to get through it OK, my voice is going to be strong and fresh. But you put that at the four and five hour mark, after I've already been singing act I and act II, it's a whole different game! So, knowing that, people ask, "Do you save your voice in act I and act II" No, I don't do that. My best game plan is to save up all of my energy, so that when that curtain goes up I can sing well, I can act well, I can feel strong, for the five or six hours. If I sing well the whole time, then I have a chance at finishing it.

OL – I see. Now let's go to the last part of the interview, with a little more about the person Jay. First of all, your family. Cooper, how old is he now?

JHM – Cooper is three and a half.

OL – Wow! Is he already aware that Daddy is an opera singer? Does he go to the performances, stay on the side wings, or go interact with the musicians, anything like that, do you take him?

JHM – A little bit. He comes to rehearsals, more. He certainly knows that Daddy fights the dragon, and he knows all about Moby Dick and the white whale, and he knows all about the orchestra. I talked to him, we've been studying all the orchestra sections. Meg my wife comes and brings him, he will sit out there and see the orchestra, sit on the edge of the orchestra pit sometimes. Not a whole lot, because whenever he sees me he screams Daddy!!! [laughs] So we haven't quite worked on our theater etiquette and on our good behavior, he hasn't been old enough for that yet. But he's been watching conductors on the Internet since he was a little boy. I've got a baton for him, and he likes to walk around and swing it, and believes that he is going to be a conductor one day.

OL – Wow! That's fabulous! [laughs]

JHM – Yeah, I like that idea too!

OL – So, what about your wife, she is in music as well, right?

Cooper, Jay, and Meg (photo credit Jay Hunter Morris)

JHM – Oh yes, is she ever! She is the real star of the family. I met Meg [Gillentine] when we were both living in New York City and she was singing and dancing on Broadway. She sang and danced for ten years on Broadway, she was in *Fosse* and *Cats* and *The Producers*, in fact she is about to do *The Producers* here in Atlanta at Fox Theater. She won awards; she won the Helen Hayes Award for Best Actress as Lola in *Damn Yankees* a few years ago, and she is very talented. We've got such a great life right now; we travel, we see the world, I take the time and sing for a while, next week Meg is going to rehearsal and I am going to be doing the babysitting and full time Daddy day care. She gets her chances to do the things that she loves, and I get a turn every now and then.

OL – Wow, super nice!

JHM – I also have some family down there in Raleigh. I've never been to Raleigh but I have a stepbrother there. My father passed away when I was thirteen and my mother married again when I was older, a very good man, and I have a stepbrother named Jeff Beckett who is pastor at Salem Baptist Church there in Raleigh [It's actually in Apex, a suburb of Raleigh]. And so I'm going to have the chance of visiting with some family again. He's got a big family, four kids. Also, Eric Mitchko, I don't know if you know this guy or not.

OL – Of course I do! [He is the general director of NC Opera]

JHM – You know, he and I go back. He was my manager. He worked for Columbia Artists Management, for several years and he was my agent, and took care of me, so I'm very happy to get to come back and spend a little time with Eric.

OL – Were you musically inclined since a young age? How did you get into this in the first place?

JHM – No, I was your average teenage American. I wasn't special. No one, not my mother, not my high school choir teacher, would have predicted that I would get to sing at the Metropolitan Opera. I sang in choirs, I played guitar and piano, I was very active in church music that was the foundation for me, singing in the church and being involved in the ministry.

To be honest, I was sort of bored with church music. Contemporary music, and country, and the little rock-and-roll and stuff, there wasn't a lot of challenge in it for me, I wasn't very good at it. I wanted to find something to be really good at. So, when I realized the breadth and the scope of what opera singers do with their voices, I just thought, "I want to try that, I want to see if I have a voice for this." I sort of stayed alive in the business, sometimes by the skin of my teeth… It wasn't a calling. I didn't grow up listening to opera, or singing Italian art songs around the house; it came to me later, and sort of came to me slowly.

OL – Do you recall the first time you attended a live opera?

JHM – I certainly recall a performance that changed everything for me. That was at the Dallas Opera, I saw *La Traviata*, I don't remember how old

I was, but it was after college; it was the moment when I said "I really want to try and do that. I'm bored musically, with the other parts of my life, I'll just give that a shot." So I went back to grad school. That was when I sought out that teacher in Dallas [Editor's note: his teacher was recommended by Alfredo Kraus] and said "I want to give this a go!"

OL – Maybe the last question: how do you describe yourself as a person? What's your personality like?

JHM – I don't really know the answer to that! I mean, I'm very comfortable in front of very big crowds, I'm not very comfortable in front of small crowds. My mom asks me to sing a hymn sitting around the table with my family, I'm a nervous wreck. If I have to sing at church in front of three hundred people, I'm a nervous wreck. I need the costume, the make-up, the lights, the orchestra. Whenever I get to step out and be somebody else I'm very comfortable. Whenever I have to be me, that makes me a little bit more nervous.

OL – Wow, one wouldn't have expected that, reading your book. You were so natural and frank… You did expose yourself in a very candid, interesting, and funny way.

JHM – Well, let me tell you about that. Those were just emails to my family. I never sat down to write a book. It's just whenever I have to write to my mom and say, "Oh my gosh, you are not going to believe what happened to me today." And I just saved them over the years. I got a lot of love over the years for it, it took a little life of its own. The emails got sent around and I heard from a lot of people that enjoyed them, but it was *hard!!* It was *really* very difficult for me to put that out there for public consumption, because that means that I think it's OK, that I am to some degree a writer, and that was a big challenge for me. [Later Opera Lively Press published this book in paperback and e-book formats]

OL – Thank you for a very interesting interview. I'll be working on it today, while I watch the NFL playoffs. High brow and low brow entertainment… A friend of mine said that opera is more violent than football.

JHM – [Laughs hard] I like it! Thank you very much, Luiz, it's been a pleasure talking to you

Lawrence Brownlee

In this interview from March 2013 we get to meet this charming and down-to-Earth man and exquisite light lyric tenor who is a favorite of the Metropolitan Opera and other prestigious houses around the world. The occasion was his recital and master class at Asheville Lyric Opera (in chapter nine later in this book there is an account of the master class).

Opera Lively - We hear that in your childhood you came from a disadvantaged background in your hometown of Youngstown, Ohio, and then became an international opera star. This is a very compelling and admirable journey. We'd like to start by asking you about your childhood. What were some of the experiences you had to go through, and likely, strengthened your character?

Lawrence Brownlee - I came from a lower middle-class family. My father was a person who believed in hard work. When I think about my career and all the things I've done and been fortunate to accomplish, it's because I had that great background through my parents, of working hard. We weren't exactly poor; we always had things provided for us. However, we never felt like things were given to us; we had to work for them. So, seeing my father and seeing the area that was around me where there were a lot of people who did suffer from poverty, did strengthen my character. My father was such a good role model for me! He made us realize that work, work, work is important to be successful in anything. I have sisters and brothers who are all successful in what they do, and it comes from that background.

OL - In your biography, classical music wasn't a staple of your family background, but music was. Would you please tell us about your first encounter with music in general, with musical instruments, and musical genres?

LB - Yes, I played the drums, the piano, the trumpet, the electric bass, and organ a little bit; I played around. Music was always around me, and that time was the opportunity for me to experiment, also with singing, with dancing, and other things like that. Classical music wasn't a part of it, but the fact that I got a chance to be involved in so many different types of music opened up my mind to think that all music is important, and I could find some enjoyment out of any genre that is out there.

OL – We know that your high school – the Youngstown East HS – offered you some opportunities for musical training, and then at the end of it you were discovered by Dr. David Starkey - Voice Professor Emeritus of the Dana School of Music of Youngstown State University – who played a significant role in your education (like he did for Gary Lehman as well). Then, you earned a Bachelor of Arts degree and made it into arguably the finest school of music of all American universities at Indiana University, where you earned your Master of Music. Your career got some exciting boosting with your participation in Young Artist Programs of two fine opera companies, Seattle Opera, and Wolf Trap Opera. Then, a big break came to you: you won the Metropolitan Opera National Council Auditions in 2001.

LB - Yes, things happened very fast. When I graduated from my Masters Degree I was fortunate to win the Metropolitan Opera Auditions. I think that that was the critical moment that started a lot of things. Yes, I was successful before then, but it was that competition that really opened up a lot of doors. It got me my agent. Because of winning that competition, it got me the recording of it, which was used to send to Milan, La Scala, at the age of twenty-eight to get an audition. And then, when I got the audition they offered me the role. Many things after that started happening. The fast track did start because of the Metropolitan Opera.

Again, my father was not a philosopher but I always quote him. He said "when the challenges are there, it's what makes you step up to the plate." You don't get ready. You are ready when the challenges are there. Opportunities are there. You don't say, "OK, here's an opportunity, let me go back and get ready." I'm always already ready. I'm prepared for when the opportunity comes, and I seize it.

OL – So, suddenly you were singing at La Scala. You had your debut there in 2002 in *L'Italiana in Algeri*. Were you scared to death, with all those loggionisti who boo singers at the smallest mistake?

LB – Yes, they are crazy and they will crucify anyone. But I'll always say that the reason why I was there at La Scala wasn't just by accident. I came and sang the audition, and they offered me the role; it was because I felt that I really could count on what I had prepared. So, I wasn't thinking "oh, am I going to say my words right; am I going to sing the right rhythms; am I going to sing in tune?" I knew the piece well enough that I felt like I was there because I was prepared. Many of the greatest singers in the world sang there before me, but they are not different than me, if I pinch them, they will probably say "ouch." [laughs] So, I feel like we are all flesh and blood.

OL – You sang - with no less than the New York Philharmonic - a concert version of *Porgy and Bess*. Let's talk about that opera. What is your opinion of *Porgy and Bess*? It drew some controversy in the African American community. What is your position regarding this controversy?

LB - My opinion of *Porgy and Bess* is that it's a great piece of American music. It focuses on Catfish Row, an underprivileged black community. It has helped careers in many ways. A lot of people think that it has hurt careers; I don't necessarily agree. It is true that sometimes you can get kind of just singing *Porgy and Bess* because that's what happens. The reason why I never performed it on stage – I did it only in concert a couple of times – is because my role, Sportin' Life, is not a legitimate classical voice role; it's a jazz role. For Bess, it is a tour de force, it's really a vehicle to show you off; for Porgy, for Jake, for Serena, for Clara, all those people have roles that they really can sink their teeth in. Sportin' Life on the other hand can be sung by someone who doesn't need a voice. Not that a voice would be wasted in it; that's not what I'm saying, but it's not appropriate for a classically-trained, real bel canto singer.

OL - Let's address African-American classical music. There is a large number of operas by African-American composers, which I personally feel deserve more exposition. I'll mention, among others, an opera I saw live, *Highway One*, by the great William Grant Still, whom I rank among the best American composers of all time – he was, like you, a Kappa Alpha Psi brother.

LB – Yes, I knew that!

OL - I've also seen *Dream Lovers* by Samuel Coleridge-Taylor. Of course Scott Joplin's *Treemonisha* is a masterpiece, of which I've seen fragments on stage, and listened to the existing recording with the Paragon Ragtime Orchestra. And these are just some of the ones I got to know, and I'm sure I'm missing many others. I did hear isolated pieces such as art songs and psalms, from other noted African-American composers including Nkeiru Okoye, William Banfield, Leo Edwards, H. Leslie Adams, and T.J. Anderson. There's also contemporary composer Donal Fox (I've heard him playing one of his pieces in world premiere), and also Florence Price, Moses Hogan, Margaret Bonds, and Roland Carter. So, there is a very rich tradition of African-American classical music that I feel most of our fellow Americans don't know very well. Do you feel the need to diffuse this music? Any plans to record, for instance, a CD with African-American art songs?

LB - It's funny that you say this, because tomorrow I'll be offering some spirituals in my recital. The pianist who is playing with me has arranged some newer spirituals. I feel a responsibility to try to bring out and highlight some of the African-American composers that are out there today. I'll say that the reason I haven't done it thus far is because I've been really focusing on singing bel canto, because I've been told that it's what my voice is, and I got a chance of performing it in various places. But I think that there are people out there writing wonderful music, and I hope it is recorded and brought to the light. I hope people can have a better appreciation for the African-American experience. There are some wonderfully gifted composers and musicians who could really make a name for themselves and put these wonderful pieces of music and literature in front of people. I hope it can come out, and the only reason I haven't done it, is because I've been doing Rossini, Rossini, Rossini! [laughs] But the songs I'll be performing tomorrow will get to a CD, and it will be one of the first steps when I'll get a chance to do some of that music as well.

OL - Not only there are outstanding African-American composers, but also great performers. While many African-American female opera singers achieved great success, such as Leona Mitchell who sang at the Met for 18 seasons and won a Grammy, Gloria Davy, Hilda Harris, Martha Flowers, and the great internationally famous and sublime artists Kathleen Battle, Leontyne Price, and Jessye Norman, among others. It's been more difficult for male African-American singers. You are certainly a path opener for your community, and I don't think that any other African-American male operatic singer has achieved your prominence this day and age, except maybe arguably on your same level, your colleague Eric Owens. But there were predecessors, notably George Shirley, whom I had the pleasure of listening to, in recital, and was able to shake hands with. He was the first African-American tenor to sing leading roles for the Metropolitan Opera, where he sang for 11 seasons. He is today the Distinguished Emeritus Professor of Music at the University of Michigan - Ann Arbor, has performed more than 80 operatic roles in a 53-year career, and is a Grammy winner. His repertoire reaches as far as singing songs in Wolof language that survived from the time of slavery, for example, "Do Bana Coda." He established an annual competition for high school students featuring arias composed by African-Americans. Mr. Shirley was preceded at the Met by Robert McFerrin, baritone, who was the first African-American male to sing at the Metropolitan Opera, although not in leading roles. There were also Greg Baker, and Mervin Wallace, and of course the great Vinson Cole who, like you, won the Metropolitan Opera National Council Auditions and went on to a great career in Europe; and then back to the US, he sang with the Met and San Francisco Opera. Do you look up to these predecessors,

Mr. Brownlee?

LB - Yes, of course. I was fortunate to meet George Shirley and Vinson Cole; I actually have a picture of the three of us together. And I have another picture with Martina Arroyo, Harolyn Blackwell, Roberta Alexander, and many of them I had the good chance to meet. I have so much respect for them, and I feel like even some of the things that they've endured are the reason why I can perform in some of those stages where I am today. So, I think it is important for us to have a real History lesson of the people who came before us. There were some fine voices there. When we think of African-American opera singers, it's mostly women – Leontyne Price, Shirley Verrett, Grace Bumbry, Reri Grist, I mean, I could go on and on, Martina Arroyo, Jessye Norman, there are a lot, and fewer man. Many of the men were just as talented, but maybe they didn't get the opportunities for whatever reason, but thankfully people like George Shirley and Vinson Cole and Roland Hayes really worked on who they are as singers, and that made room and opportunity. Things became more and more relaxed. One thing that George Shirley told me early on, he said "every man opens the door for himself." He said, "yes, you may say that what I have done opened the door for you, but a man has to do it for himself." That right there taught me a great deal of humility. He didn't want to take any credit for it. I'm not taking any credit for making the road easier for someone coming after me, because I feel like the reason why the door is open is because of the work that someone does.

OL - Now let's talk about the emotions of creating a role in a new opera – the role of Syme for Lorin Maazel's new opera *1984*. You were at the world premiere, in no less prestigious a place than the Royal Opera House in 2005. Can you tell us about that production?

LB - Oh, the role of Syme! [laughs] I got this role when Lorin Maazel asked me to do an audition for him. He said to me, "do you have a high D?" I said, "I think I do." He said, "just sing it." I said, "like that, just sing it?" He said, "yeah, just sing it." I said, [laughs] "can I do it in a scale, up a scale?" So I did it in a scale, and I had sung *Carmina Burana* which has high Ds in it. And he said "you are OK." So I got the piece, and it has, I think, nine high Ds in a row, which is stratospheric. But it was a wonderful experience for me to work with someone like that. I have a great deal of respect for him. To see that piece created, and in the context where it was, with many gifted artists involved in that production, was a very important time for me. And it was the first and only time I've been at the Covent Garden in London, but hopefully I'll get a chance to go back, and they are working on that now. But it was great to create that, and it was the first role I've ever created.

OL – Was it very different for you?

LB – Yes, it was very different, because the precedent hadn't been set. You know, if you do *The Barber of Seville*, how many people have done it? How many tenors, and versions, and cuts, and theaters, and countries in the world? But in this case, there is no precedent set, and you have the chance – and the responsibility – to create. You say, "OK, I want to make this so." The person that comes after me has to really work to exceed my level, so I felt that responsibility, and I know he wanted me to do it several times after that, too.

OL - 2007 was a great year for your career: a debut at the Metropolitan Opera House, and another one at the Vienna State Opera – arguably two of the top five opera companies in the world. By then, you must have felt – "that's it! I made it!" By now, there aren't too many hallmarks left for you, if any – you've sung with the Berliner Philharmoniker, you've sung at Wigmore Hall and Carnegie Hall already, and on March 28 you'll have your first solo recital there. Your performance in Rossini's *Armida* was broadcast live to the entire world on Met Live in HD; you've even sung for the US Supreme Court. Your performances have been released on solo and ensemble CDs, and on DVDs, with a growing discography containing already several items in prestigious labels such as DG, DECCA, EMI, Sony, Naxos, and Opera Rara. You've been around the world, as far as South Africa and Tokyo. What else is left to accomplish? At age 40 now, you're in a very strong phase of your career as a recognized and experienced performer, but there are many years left in it, hopefully, so what are some of your future goals, to stay fresh and motivated?

LB – Oh, you know, I just came from Vienna, and I had a chance of sitting down and having lunch with Plácido Domingo. And this is a person who is, what, seventy-two, seventy-five – I don't know his age exactly – but this is a person who is constantly evolving, so I never feel like I've arrived, that I'm done. What is there to do? Many things. Now I'll be doing more Mozart, there are a couple of new works that are being considered for me, some recordings that are coming up, so I feel like the maturity and the growth that I've had in these years will come out now. The recital disc that I made years ago, and hopefully the one that I'll make now, will be different, because people will see more maturity, more growth. And the voice changes, so… what is there left for me? Constantly be on the stage, and be amongst artists that inspire me, that motivate me to work to continue to try and improve who I am as a singer. There is a lot for me to do, and I fell like hopefully, they say, a tenor gets his best years in his early forties, and I just hit forty.

OL – You are right at the peak – not to mean you'll come down from it; we hope you stay at it for a long time. Do you see yourself walking away from bel canto?

LB – I feel that I have only scratched the surface of bel canto. I will be exploring some other things in bel canto. Then maybe I'll get into some of the lighter French things and into some Mozart. With performing now, a lot of times we are contracting jobs that will cap in three, four, five years down the road. Where I will be at forty-five is different from what I am today. What I've established in the thirteen years of my career, gives me the opportunity to say, "OK, you know what, I'm going to take a risk, a calculated risk, of saying this is not right for me." There are other times when I'll say, "I may try it, maybe this will work."

OL – Such as?

LB – For example, *La Favorite* is one of the things. There's been a couple of other things people have mentioned. I'm not interested in singing the Duke in *Rigoletto* at this point. I could probably get away with it in some places, I know people who have similar voices to mine who have done it and have been successful. But I feel that there are still lots of things for me to sing in the bel canto repertory. Who knows, in one year from now, what the voice may take on in color or shape that will allow me to do some of these things? Somebody told me that it's the voice that tells you when to move on and to do some of these more daring things, if you will. Hopefully I will sing in a way that I will not rush up the process, but the natural process of maturing for the voice will happen, and I will get a chance to do these things that are out there and right for me.

OL - Your next Met performance is in *I Puritani*, in 2014. Is it too early to ask about that?

LB - No, because I've already done *I Puritani* twice, and I feel like, again, this will be better, hopefully, if I'm healthy as possible and I am singing strongly. This will be an opportunity for me to do it better than I did last time, and hopefully I'll show some growth. Of course, in such an important stage like the Metropolitan Opera, I'm excited about that. I haven't done Bellini at the Met. It will be the way I do it. Pavarotti sang *Puritani* at the Met, and other people; it will be different than that, but that's OK. And I hope I can say something about *Puritani* that people will respect and enjoy.

OL - Let's finish by getting a taste of the man Lawrence Brownlee rather than the opera singer, as artificial as this separation may be. How are you as a person? What do you like to do besides opera?

LB - I always say to people that opera does not define me. I want to work hard at it and do it as best as I can, but I have many hobbies outside of opera. I am a passionate photographer. I like to work with my cameras. I was looking at the photographers a while ago [Editor's note – Mr. Brownlee before the interview was delivering master classes and there were photographers documenting the occasion] and admiring their cameras. I have Nikon, they have Canon. I've invested in some really good photography and that's one of the passions that I can enjoy. I always try to make my life on the road as comfortable as possible, because I have to be away from home.

My family is very important. I have a lovely wife and two kids. I always try to stay connected with them. Also, I have a passion in salsa dancing and salsa music. Sometimes I "dee-jay" salsa. Also I'm very passionate about table tennis. I like the idea of doing something. A lot of times when I go salsa dancing, people don't know that I am an opera singer. I don't wear it as a badge of honor, I don't go out saying "I'm an opera singer!" Sometimes I walk on the streets and no one has a clue about what I do, and that's great for me. Sometimes I'm on the streets and I hope that no one has a clue, but someone comes and says, "are you this person?" and I say "yes" and I enjoy it. But I do a lot of things outside of opera. I'm a passionate, passionate fan of the Pittsburgh Steelers football.

OL – By the way, the coach was a member of your fraternity as well.

LB – Yes, yes, Mike Tomlin, yes, I did know this as well, he is from the William and Mary chapter, a college in Virginia. William Grant Still, and many other decorated people were from my fraternity, and I'm very involved in that. That's a very important part of my life. And of course, my faith, who I am as a person, all those things matter. Opera is what I do but is not who I am. I like to do many, many things, and I always say, if I walk away from this, I will be happy, because it's not the only thing I can do. I know I will enjoy it, because if I give my all to opera, I can say, "OK, I did it, I'm happy with that" and I can put my focus and energy in other directions.

OL – Thank you so much for your time.

LB – Absolutely, my pleasure!

OL – And you know, witnessing your master classes, you are a brilliant teacher, you should consider going into that if you ever stop singing!

LB – [Laughs hard] Thank you, thank you!

Giuseppe Filianoti

Italian lyric tenor Giuseppe Filianoti performs frequently in both sides of the Atlantic and has recorded six CDs and six DVDs of various operas. We talked with him in March of 2013.

Opera Lively - Today, you are one of the world's leading lyric tenors, but the first university degree you received was in literature. Was singing then not your first career choice?

Giuseppe Filianoti – Yes, I earned a degree in literature, but it was simultaneous with my degree in singing at the Conservatory. I earned both at the same time, in 1997. My passion was singing music, I was born with it. But my other passion was and still is literature. Maybe my first dream was to write books or to be a journalist, or get involved in research in English literature, Italian literature, everything. But when I started my musical training in the Conservatory in my hometown, I discovered that I had a gift. My teacher entered me in some competitions, and every time I'd win the first prize. So that kind of life took first place in my interest. Today I read a lot of books; they are my best friends when I'm alone and not working as a singer.

OL – So, you graduated from the Universita degli Studi in Messina, and you went through voice studies at the Francesco Cilea Conservatory.

GF – Yes, the literature degree was in Messina, Sicily, but the Conservatorio Francesco Cilea is in my hometown of Reggio Calabria in the mainland, separated from the island of Sicily by the Strait of Messina. So I was attending the Conservatory in my hometown in Calabria, but took the boat daily, to go to Messina in Sicily, to study at the university.

OL - What previous experience in singing did you have before you entered the conservatory? Were you a member of the choir at your school or church?

GF – Yes, I have to be very grateful to the sisters. My first school was run by Catholic nuns. Every morning we had to pray to God, and there was a choir to go together with these religious rituals, and I was a member from the time I was very young, six years old. So, the sisters would ask me, "Giuseppe, sing less loudly" because my voice would predominate over the choir. So, they decided to put me as a soloist. For five years, every morning the choir would sing with me in this position of soloist. Singing was a natural gift and a pleasure for me, and the sisters immediately discovered it. I have to thank them for putting me through this experience. For them, the praying and the singing was just as important as studying the school subjects.

OL – Were your parents and siblings also interested in classical music?

GF – No, in my family I was the first one. And I'm still the only one. [laughs]

OL - When did you attend your first opera performance? Which opera was it? What impressed you the most about the experience?

GF – My first opera was in Messina. In my town of Reggio Calabria we had a beautiful, beautiful theater but it was never put to work. The closest real opera house was in Messina. I went there to attend live opera for the first time, and if I'm not mistaken, it was *Il Barbiere di Siviglia* with Rockwell Blake. The second one was *La Traviata*, with Salvatore Fisichella. At the time I already loved opera and knew very well about the stories, and knew the arias and duets of the most famous operas. So, when I saw live opera on stage for the first time, it was a nice experience, I was fascinated by that. I immediately wished that one day I would do the same, on the operatic stage.

OL – I interviewed Luca Pisaroni. He grew up in Busseto in Giuseppe Verdi's home region.

GF – Oh, wow!

OL – Yes. He said that as a young boy who loved opera in Italy, he was considered by his classmates to be weird, because all the other boys were into soccer, and he was into opera [laughs]. Was it something that happened to you as well?

GF – [laughs] No. When I started to really learn how to sing opera, I was in high school, around the age of fifteen to seventeen. When my classmates discovered that I could sing opera, they actually appreciated it, and they always asked me to sing at school, before the lessons started. They would tell me, "Oh, you're like Pavarotti, please sing for us!" But they did find it a bit strange, that style of singing, and some of them would ask, "what is that??" Because in our culture, the opera lirica is not as popular now as it was in the past. I am thirty-nine years old now, so when I was a teenager, we were in the late 1980's and early 1990's, and it was a very different situation from the 1950's and 1960's when everybody was in love with opera. So, at the time, I was trying to imitate Pavarotti, but I did it because I listened to him on my own and loved it, not because of a family tradition or a shared interest with my classmates.

OL - You also won a two-year scholarship to the Accademia at La Scala. Can you tell us what your two years there were like? What sort of training do the young singers there receive?

GF – This was one of the best experiences of my life. I grew up in a small city in the South, so, being in Milan at La Scala which is the premier place for opera in Italy was really exciting. I went there and auditioned for Maestro Riccardo Muti, and he immediately said, "OK, stop the audition, I want this tenor!" And after that, he followed my career very closely, and I have to thank him, because he always wanted me around and I learned a lot from him. He taught me how to sing opera, how to respect a composer, how to do the phrasing. Over there at the Accademia, another very important person in my learning was Leyla Gencer [editor's note – the famous Turk soprano who became the teacher of operatic interpretation and the artistic director of the Accademia for young opera singers at La Scala, once she retired from the stage]. She had this big quality of the old style of *fraseggio*, and was an expert in interpretation. I learned how important words are in opera, not just the sounds. It is important to interpret the feelings and show the results through the words. One also needs to know how to not exaggerate in the interpretation – you can't do too much, but you can't do too little, you need to reach equilibrium. The Accademia taught us the best Italian traditions that unfortunately we are now losing, even in Italy. It was a very good experience, yes.

OL - While you were there, you met the great tenor Alfredo Kraus, and he became your mentor. Of all the things you learned from him about style, artistry, and technique, what do you consider some of the most important?

GF – Alfredo Kraus was unique in opera. He was the living tenor that was closest to my taste. He was always a clear singer. He had perfect control of his breath and of his singing technique. He was also a gentleman, as a man. I think having him as a mentor was the most important experience I ever had, not only in Milan, but later. He was always open to giving me his impressions and advice. Of course, along the years, there were many great singers, but if I have to chose an interpretation to look up to, I always choose Kraus's version, for his elegance and nobility.

OL – Yes, and he had a lot of longevity in his career.

GF – Yes, he took a lot of care regarding his voice. That's important. Every singer is different, and the repertory never works the same for each person. But Alfredo Kraus was able to feel his body. If he understood that he was going against his body, he would always stop, and say, "no, this doesn't work for me or for my voice." You should never push beyond what your voice can do. This is what all singers need to do; we need to listen to our bodies and respect them. We are like sportsmen. We work with our minds but also with our bodies. If you use up your body too much or the wrong way, you'll lose your body and you won't be able to sing any longer.

OL - You made your professional debut when you were 24 years old, singing the title role in *Dom Sebastien* in Bergamo. By your mid-20s, you had made debuts in leading roles at some of the world's major international opera houses. So you rose to the top of your profession very quickly. For some people, early fame can spell trouble; they don't handle it well. How did you keep your emotional balance?

GF – That's true. I started singing at La Scala at a young age, but I was lucky in the fact that I didn't get prematurely involved with a recording label. Sometimes these labels throw their artists too quickly into worldwide exposure, and people make mistakes. I made my small mistakes as well at the beginning of my career but then I learned with my mistakes and learned how to manage my career. Today, the problem resides in the fact that sometimes these recording labels decide to make a star out of someone, but there is nothing there to sustain it. Maybe these artificially made stars can sustain it for one or two years, but then, if you don't have a very strong mind and good ability to know yourself, your career can destroy you.

But I was very lucky in my beginnings. I was able to sing with the best stars and the best directors, and learned a lot from them. I sang with Renato Bruson, Mariella Devia, Daniela Dessì, who were the best ones in my generation. I was able to develop some good experience out of the Italian theaters, and when I went on to other major houses in the world, yes, it was fast, but never under too much pressure.

In the past, this was how it went for everybody, including Pavarotti, Kraus… today it is different. Today instead of this gradual learning and exposure, there is this publicity machine that takes people in their first or second year and convinces them that they're the best, and put them out there on TV and so forth. I was lucky to have been spared this business-oriented model when I was learning the ropes.

OL - You won several important awards, and the second prize at the 1999 Operalia. How was that experience for you?

GF – It was very important for me. Before that, I had won another one that was very instrumental for me as well, the Francisco Viñas Competition in Barcelona. I won the first prize in the Viñas, and immediately after that I won the second prize at the 1999 Operalia in Puerto Rico, the Domingo competition. I shared second prize with Rolando Villazón. The first prize was won by the Bulgarian bass, Olin Anastassov. Joseph Calleja also won a prize at that Operalia; he was the youngest prize-winner. We were all there in the same competition; it is a nice memory to have.

OL – And did Domingo open doors for you? Did he help you in any way after the competition?

GF – Domingo is a wonderful person and singer. He always called me back. He called me to Los Angeles to sing *L'Elisir d'Amore* a few years ago. Just recently he called me for a concert at the Arena di Verona to celebrate the Operalia there. If I need something and I have to call him, he will get me what I need, for sure. I only have good things to say about him, and I have a big respect for him. I know that he is there, and if I need something he will help me.

OL - Word spreads very quickly around the opera world when a wonderful new talent has been discovered. Houses begin offering the new star all sorts of roles, and some of them may really not be appropriate for the individual's voice at that point. Did you also have this experience? Perhaps some houses wanted to engage you for some of Verdi's or Puccini's heavier roles?

GF – Sometimes, yes, but not too often. I've had to deal with some strange demands, especially from some important directors, for example, for *Pagliacci*, or for *Il Trovatore*, or many times for *Norma*, but I knew they weren't roles for me. They may think, "all right, we need a lyric voice and not a spinto for this role." It may even be an interesting experience to have, but you cannot cancel the tradition that is behind these roles, and the audience is savvy enough to balk at these vocal compromises. It's better not to risk this sort of thing, so, I have always turned down offers that I thought were not well suited for my voice. Why should someone take on those risks? So, yes, I had this kind of experience, but was wise enough to say, "better not!" [laughs]

OL - Most of the roles you've sung are clearly in the lyric tenor repertoire. But you've also expressed elsewhere the desire to sing Peter Grimes, and you are under contract to sing Pelléas in the near future. Grimes is often sung by a heldentenor, though Britten actually wrote the role for a lyric tenor. But Pelléas really is a baritone role. A tenor can sing it, but aren't there technical challenges involved in that?

GF – True, I have accepted this *Pelléas et Mélisande*, and yes, I'm a lyric tenor, so this appears to be in contradiction with what I was just saying, but there is a particularity. If you listen to my lower notes, I'm OK with that; I can sing in the lower register. My voice is not that of a *leggiero* that would have a lot of difficulty with the lower notes. I can easily lower my voice without forcing it. I consider this opera as one of the best in the 20th century, I love this opera and I love Debussy. It is so difficult, but musically it is something special. So, I said "yes, I want to have this experience," like I did with *The Rake's Progress* and with *Capriccio*, because I think we should give ourselves the pleasure of singing some beautiful music that we love. These are less popular works than, for instance, a *Rigoletto* or a *Lucia,* but sometimes you need to enjoy your work by doing something that is on a higher personal level for you.

OL – Right, if you like literature so much, you must enjoy the libretto for *Pelléas et Mélisande*, which possesses high literary quality.

GF – Yes, exactly! And not only that, but the music has such a great atmosphere! It's like a symphony! It's nice to go a little bit outside of lyric opera and explore another style. I like it when a role comes around that is not among the biggest workhorses. such as *La Clemenza di Tito* – it's Mozart but not among his most famous four operas - and I love Mozart. And I know that Mozart is not really for my voice, because my voice is better suited for *Werther*, *Manon*, and *Hoffmann*; that's where I feel at home. But I am a musician, you understand? So I like to do music that I love, sometimes, as long as it doesn't destroy my voice.

OL – Do you play any instruments?

GF – I play the piano.

OL - You've also sung Stravinsky's Tom Rakewell and you've expressed the wish to sing the title role in his *Oedipus Rex*. But you once described a lot of modern music as possibly overrated. What is it about Stravinsky's music that appeals to you? Or perhaps should we no longer consider his works to be "modern" music?

GF – Yes, if someone asks me to sing *Oedipus Rex*, I'll say yes. Stravinsky's *The Rake's Progress* is a masterpiece. I enjoyed playing the role of Tom, and I enjoyed learning it. It is a very difficult role to learn and remember, and it is hard to keep up with what is going on in the orchestra. The story is wonderful. So, I definitely don't consider Stravinsky to be overrated. There is quality there, unlike in some other modern pieces.

OL - What about operas from the late 20th century or the 21st century? Are there any contemporary roles that you would like to sing?

GF – No, I think this is not something for me. There is too much dissonance in this music. I think we are going too far with that. I believe that the singing voice still needs at least a little bit of melody. I don't feel comfortable when it is extremely dissonant. The modern works I've mentioned before are still sufficiently melodic, but the contemporary ones are not for me.

OL - You've sung Ruggero in *La Rondine*. What alternative ending do you prefer? The one where he confronts and abandons Magda who then kills herself, or the one where she abandons him and he begs her to stay?

GF – I think the ending where she kills herself doesn't work. I've listened to it but I've never seen it live. I prefer the version that I just did at the Met, where she says, "this is not for us, bye, bye." I think it is the easiest and simplest way to end that opera. I don't think we need to make of Magda something very tragic. This is an especially light opera, in terms of Puccini's output. I don't think the big drama suits it well, like it does in the similar story that is in Verdi's *Traviata*. *La Rondine* is what it is, a lighter story. Puccini tried to change the ending to give more power to the drama, but then this kind of tragedy is not compatible with the rest of the opera.

OL – Yes, *La Rondine* was commissioned as an operetta, originally.

GF – Yes, but then, Puccini was not able to do it as an operetta [laughs]. It wasn't in him! So, he said, "let's put some drama into it, now!" But the opera wasn't born this way, and you can listen to the lightness in the score, so if you change the ending, you destroy the structure of the work, the way it was born.

OL – Yes, interesting. But let's go back a little to Maestro Riccardo Muti who had, as you told us, a significant role in your early career. Can you give us a taste of what the great Maestro is like?

GF – Yes, Maestro Muti, I love him. He discovered me at La Scala, I worked a lot with him. He is very demanding. He wants professionalism from his singers and musicians. He studies a lot, and requires everything to be very clear and precisely worked. Every time I do something with him, I discover new aspects written in the music that I hadn't noticed before, that nobody else was able to dig out. He masters the old tradition of Italian opera. I feel very lucky to be able to work with him. I must say, I believe him to be the best conductor, nowadays.

OL – Very nice. And is he very supportive of his singers?

GF – Yes, you know, he is very supportive of the opera! For him, what is very important is the music, and the opera. So if you demonstrate to him that you feel the same way, he will like you and support you to the end. He is very nice.

OL - Your background in literature must be instrumental to inform your stage work, right?

GF – Every time I prepare for a role and the libretto was taken from a work of literature, I make a point of reading and studying the source. The librettist needs to cut a lot of things from the source when writing the libretto in order to fit the story into the available time, given the added time for the music. So, if you want to have a wider and deeper understanding of the character, you need to go back and read the book. That's very important, because then you discover little details that you can incorporate into your interpretation of the role, by yourself on the stage. For example, it was very important for me to explore the source for *Werther.* Sometimes you have to also explore history, to better understand historical characters like Titus in Mozart's opera *La Clemenza di Tito*, and not only read the libretto by Caterino Mazzolà, but also go back to Metastasio's piece, and study sources that give you some vision of the actual Titus. I always try to impart some meaning into my acting on stage, to do my work from the standpoint of an idea.

OL - Are there any books or plays that you think would be good source material for a new opera libretto that nobody has thought about, yet?

GF – It's difficult to answer this. Books are something very individual.

Everybody has his or her own relationship with a book. We like books because in them we find something to develop in our mind and feelings. I believe that books have literary value when they help in the understanding of human behavior and human feelings. So basically any book that fulfills this role can be turned into a good opera, because we go to the opera in search of the same thing – you want to get yourself immersed into the position of those characters, and to get involved with the dilemmas that they are going through. So, in our real lives today, people rarely stop to think about emotions, but if they go and watch *La Traviata* or *La Bohème* and they cry, it's because these works put them back in touch with the deep human emotions that they may be skipping in today's hectic world. Literary works achieve the status of classics exactly because they are able to evoke these emotions. So, there are many books that can qualify for a good opera – but then, if the music is not up to standards, even the best libretto won't sustain an opera. You can have fantastic music with a bad libretto and still have a decent opera or even a masterpiece, but the opposite is not possible. So, if one selects a great book on which to base a libretto, it is still no guarantee that you'll have a good opera, because you need to add exquisite music to it, so it's hard to say what books would be successfully turned into great operas.

OL - You found a lost song from Cilea's *L' Arlesiana*, and made sure that it was incorporated into the score. This is unusual for a singer. Do you worry about critical editions, and what score is being used in your performances?

GF – This is a nice story; I found this song because I was born in the same city where Cilea was born. So I went to the Cilea museum there and found many manuscripts, and was reading through them, and found something that sounded very familiar to me, and I kept thinking, "where did I see this before?" Then I went to the first autograph copy of L'Arlesiana and it was there, but wasn't in the subsequent editions that were being produced. It was the second aria for Federico, and it is very beautiful, so I asked the Maestro to put it in, and he did. But I don't usually do that. For Cilea, it is a must for me, given our common origin. I want to do the best for his music. For other composers like Verdi, Wagner, Donizetti, Rossini, there are so many scholars that have looked into it; I don't think it is up to the singer to do this kind of research. But in verismo, not everything has been discovered, so I was glad that I was able to do my small part to contribute to having a more complete and accurate version of *L'Arlesiana.*

OL – Back to our preparation for an opera role, you said you do extensive research on the literary source, when available. Regarding the musical side, how do you study the role?

GF – First, I listen to all the past recordings of the role, if possible. Then I play the piano score by myself, note by note. Next, I go to the voice coach and sing the role with piano accompaniment, to commit everything to memory.

OL – I'm always amazed at how you singers can memorize three hours of text and not miss a single word.

GF – It's actually not so difficult, because there is the melody to guide you. The melody gets so closely associated with the words in a singer's mind that when you are singing the melodies the words seem to just pop up and be the right ones. If you use the wrong word it suddenly doesn't feel right. Think of a well known pop song – if you had to memorize the lyrics and recite them like a poem without the music, you would likely make more mistakes than if you had to just sing the song, then the words would come to you. Well, I can say this, but maybe it is not true for everybody. For me, it's this way.

OL – Yes, it must have to do with how a musician's brain is wired; what seems very easy to a singer may not be so easy for a regular person. Beyond the singing, there's also the acting. Many reviewers have praised your acting skills as well as your singing. You also have some theatrical background, don't you?

GF – I've been lucky to have worked with some of the very, very best stage directors. But I think to be frank that I do have a natural gift for acting. So, I take my acting very seriously. Every time a stage director wants me to do something, I need to be convinced. I want the audience to understand my character, and that is very important to me. So I have my own strong ideas about the acting, and I need to work with the director on them until we're both comfortable with what I'll be doing on stage. Because many times, what you do in your acting is closely related to the music, so the two need to really fit together, and the directors need to have an understanding of this. Voice, and acting - one doesn't need to destroy the other one. They have to be integrated into one whole.

OL - You've sung the Lensky aria from *Eugene Onegin* in concerts, although I believe you haven't done the complete role on stage. The Slavic languages can sometimes be difficult to learn for people who are native speakers of the Western European languages. Did you have to work with a coach or teacher on the Russian pronunciation?

GF – It's not difficult to sing in another language, for me. I sing a lot in

French but I don't speak French. I think that the pronunciation for a singer comes with the territory, because if you are an operatic singer, you have a special skill for the musicality of sound; in the music, but also in speech. So, the sounds of speech even if they come in an unfamiliar language, are easy to discern and reproduce, for a trained singer.

OL - You frequently sing at La Scala, which has long been one of the world's most important opera houses, and one with many traditions. One of those traditions is a very passionate, vocal audience that doesn't hesitate to let those on stage know what it thinks. The *loggionisti* are legendary. Many famous singers have discovered what it's like to displease a La Scala audience. But all of your experiences there have been positive, haven't they?

GF – Yes, I had beautiful experiences there. But I don't like the way they treat the singers. We need to respect the singers. There is a long tradition there at La Scala that the ticket-paying audience is entitled to expressing exuberantly their dislike, but one needs to understand that a singer who goes on the stage is always trying to do his or her best. The singer is not trying to live a lie and fool the audience; the singer is trying to do his or her job to the best of his or her ability, so, if the audience doesn't like it, it is best not to applaud. Silence is very eloquent to a singer. There is no need to boo.

I was mostly lucky there at La Scala which was my home, the place where I was trained, so I have good memories from there and was given some love from the audience, as this local product – but I don't like the way they treat some of the other singers. We are human beings, we give our lives to the art form and to be able to stand there on the stage and sing, while the audience gave only a couple of hours of their lives to that moment. Some of these behaviors can be very destructive to the mind of a singer; the audience should take that into consideration.

For the same reason, I don't really read what the critics say. It's easy to go and listen to someone, and write about it, and contest what the singer did. It is easy to judge. But it is not as easy to sing, and there is a lot that goes behind that in terms of effort and preparation, so, sure, singers can be criticized, but some measure of respect and some civility should still prevail.

This phenomenon is causing La Scala to self-destroy in a sense, because many big singers don't want to go there to sing. The *loggionisti* at La Scala yell at the singers, tell them to go home, and that's not so polite.

OL - When you made your debut at La Scala, were you at all concerned about the audience's reaction?

GF – I was in a sense born there. Singing at La Scala for me is like singing at home. But still, every time I put my feet there, I'm scared, as is everybody! I'd be a liar if I said otherwise. Anybody who says "oh I don't fear singing at La Scala at all, I'm just as relaxed there as in any other house" is a liar. Because they will find any little mistake, they will not let go of any little sound that you produce and is not what they expect. Never! [laughs] They did this to Callas, to everybody, so… [laughs]

OL - Opera is such an essential part of Italy's culture. But with the current global economic problems, some opera houses in Europe and North America have been facing significant funding losses – whether from public or private sources. What is the current situation in Italy?

GF – It is the worst situation in Italy, among all the other countries. It's a pity, I know, but it is true. Many opera houses are closing. They can no longer afford the important names in opera, and they've been asking the younger people to perform there; it's not a good situation. In Italy we don't have support from donors and philanthropists. It's only from the state, and the state is giving close to nothing, now.

OL – Do you think the opera houses in Italy will be able to change their funding structure and survive?

GF – The problem is with the political situation. It seems like the current politicians in Italy are strongly against culture. I don't know if the habit of sponsorship and donation can thrive in the Italian culture. We don't have this type of behavior ingrained in our culture, so it is quite hard to start now. This is my opinion, I don't know if it's true or not, but I'm not optimistic about it.

OL - Will opera houses become more cautious and conservative in their productions?

GF – Yes. Some audiences may want to see something new and spectacular in the staging, but that costs more. You spend less money in paying singers and orchestras than you spend in the physical production, so, that part will also suffer. It may be a good thing, because some balance is needed. Maybe people will pay singers better if the productions are less ambitious. Big stagings, costumes, are very expensive, so, they'll have to moderate that part, also.

OL - Avant-garde opera productions are very popular in the German-speaking countries. But what about Italy? Do houses and audiences there prefer more traditional stagings?

GF – In general, yes, but it depends. If you propose to the Italian public a very extreme production like we see in certain German houses, they will kill you, that's true. If you do something modern but respectful to the text and the music and the opera, the Italian public will like it; a production doesn't necessarily need to be traditionalist to be successful in Italy. But when a stage director puts blood where there is none so to speak, and profoundly changes the opera, the Italian public will not accept it.

OL - *Rigoletto* in Chicago – how is it coming about?

GF – It's a production from 2005 and it is a very, very traditional staging. It's like going back to the past. Sometimes, it's OK. It's a pleasure. [laughs]

OL – Yes, we do tend to have more traditionalistic productions in the United States as compared to Europe. What do you prefer, the American or the European style?

GF – I wouldn't properly talk about an American or European style. I'd rather say that I prefer what I call an intelligent staging. It can be modern, it can be traditionalistic, but if I work with someone like Graham Vick or Robert Carsen who do very intelligent work, I will accept just about anything, be it modern or not. They work very strongly in getting the best of the characterization for every singer. They do not try to say "this is not *Rigoletto*, now this is my opera, so I will change it." No, for Vick or Carsen, first comes Verdi, then it's the music, then it's the libretto, and last is the staging. We put all these elements together, but they don't try to impose anything that goes against the will of the composer.

OL – Have you ever refused to participate in a production when you profoundly disagreed with the director?

GF – No, because I always try to find a solution. There is always a solution, if you talk to them and explain why it is not possible to do certain things. I have never been forced to do something very strange that I didn't agree with, in my career.

OL - Mozart, Donizetti, Verdi, Puccini, and the French (Massenet, Gounod, Offenbach) – please tell us about your thoughts in terms of singing the music of these different composers.

GF – People say that Mozart is honey for the voice. Sincerely, this is quite a silly thing to say. It all depends on the way a singer is built. A big person with big vocal folds will be able to sing Wagner but then that same singer won't be able to sing Mozart. Nature gives to each of us a different instrument, so you can't say that Mozart is good for everybody. We lyric tenors are a bit lucky in this territory, because we often can do a little bit more or a little bit less and have a slightly wider range in our repertory, because we are not too *leggiero*, and not too dramatic. So, Gounod and Massenet are best for me, but I can still explore a little bit of Puccini, but not too much. Similarly, I can explore a little bit of Verdi, but not too much. I can however go back safely to Donizetti and Mozart, as I did.

But you can't sing Mozart the same way you sing Puccini. If you are a lyric, you understand that singing Mozart teaches you a way to be more classical. It's like a painting. If you see a classical painting, there is a particular beauty in it, and when you see a modern one, you can see another kind of realistic beauty. When you sing Mozart you have to sustain a beautiful tone, and stay there. When you sing Puccini, you need to go out and let go and give more passion. All these composers have different ways to work the musical line, a different style, and you need not only to have the appropriate voice for them in terms of weight, but also you need to understand the style and what kind of phrasing is expected of you.

Puccini has a warm color, but if you try to put too much color in Mozart's music you'll end up singing too loudly; you need to find a clearer voice for Mozart. Callas understood this very well. If you listen to her in a heavier role, then you go and listen to her *Sonnambula*, her color there is very different. She was able to adapt her voice to the style of the composer. But this notion that Mozart is honey is dangerous. Most people understand that singing a role that is heavier than what your voice can offer is damaging, but the reverse is also true. A heavier singer can also damage his voice by singing light Mozart. I've never sang *Così fan tutte* because I think it is too light for me.

OL - I particularly like your DVD of *Medea* with Ms. Anna Caterina Antonacci, whom we've interviewed as well, a lovely and intelligent lady. Any memories of that production to share with us?

GF – Yes, she is something, Anna Caterina. That production had another great stage director, Hugo de Ana; I did some beautiful things with him. He did that staging with very low budget. All the costumes were second hand and recycled. There was only one set for the entire opera; the theater couldn't afford any set changes. But he got the best of what could be done with that limited budget, by focusing on the feelings of the different characters. I remember him saying: "We need to put together this opera with the kind of atmosphere that we saw in the film *Zorba, the Greek*." He wanted to recover that age full of superstition in the original story, in a sort of verismo acting coupled with the more ancient music. It was very nice; he was able to pull off this big contrast, but without disrespecting the music. That production was very beautiful.

OL – Yes, it was. Can you tell us about some of your plans for the future? Any new roles you are currently working on?

GF – I'm scheduled for several *Rigolettos*, but in terms of new roles for me, I'm studying *Simon Boccanegra* and *I Due Foscari*. I'm sort of retiring Mozart for now and going deeper into Verdi. Donizetti gave me so much… so another role I'm preparing is Roberto Devereux.

GF – What do you think of the future of the operatic art form in this hectic world we live in?

OL – I don't know, it's so strange now, they are trying to do a new kind of opera that is closer to the way the cinema industry approaches the audiences, with all the business side and the marketing and the polished images. But I try to do my best to help the kind of opera that I value continue to survive. However, an isolated singer can't do much. The only thing we can do is to sing as best we can. I hope that money comes back to the arts. You cannot do good opera and enjoy opera without money. But I hope that the future will be less of this business-oriented model, and more of good musical quality.

OL -To finish, if you don't mind, some more questions about your life outside opera. Are you married, do you have children? If yes, how do they relate to having an opera-singing daddy?

GF – I am married and have a son who is eight years old and lives in Italy. His name is Riccardo and he attends school. For him, my being a singer is normal; I'm just his Daddy, I don't think he thinks of it in any special way. He went to see me in a few rehearsals. But now with him in school and with the fact that I sing so often outside of Italy, there isn't much opportunity for him to see my work; it's not so easy. But he saw all the videos that I have recorded. He tries to imitate my *Rigoletto* every time [laughs].

OL – Nice! What do you like to do besides opera? What kind of person are you, in terms of personality (outgoing, more reserved, etc.)?

GF – I like to read books, and to explore the city where I am, and see the local museums. As a person, I'm very reserved. So, those who know me well often ask me how I transform myself so much on stage. It's probably because I have some things inside myself that I need to tell, and don't normally do it with my reserved self. The best actors are those who have a lot to tell, and try to show it on the stage. In real life I'm just this normal guy, so the possibility of being another person on stage appeals to me. In real life, I think I'm very boring [laughs hard]. No, I'm kidding. I can actually be very funny with my closest friends. Most of my friends think that I'm very funny. I always find a way to make them laugh. But then, I also like to have my own time and to read my books. I don't really enjoy going out and going somewhere with a lot of people to drink and so forth; it's not my way.

OL – Thank you so much, this was a lovely interview.

GF – Oh, thank you. I loved it too. I'm happy that you liked it. Ciao!

DIVISION ONE – INTERNATIONALLY ESTABLISHED SINGERS

CHAPTER THREE – THE SOPRANOS

Diana Damrau

Opera Lively met Ms. Damrau in person in New York City in late March 2013 during her Traviata run at the Met. She is one of the leading coloratura sopranos in the world with an extensive discography of more than 12 CDs and an equal number of DVDs.

Opera Lively - You're making your role debut as Violetta here at the Met. This is a part you've been looking forward to, but it's also very demanding. It's sometimes said that Violetta needs to be sung by three different voice types. How have you prepared for this role in terms of vocal technique?

Diana Damrau – I prepared for Violetta my whole career. I started as a coloratura soprano and was able to sing all the light repertoire for my voice, and then with time, and now with two babies and changes of hormones and with age, my voice, thank God, has not lost the high notes and its agility but it has gained in warmth and also in lyrical and dramatic potential. So, my voice is really ready, and I'm also ready as a person. Violetta is a very, very complex role. It's a role of a woman that contains the most opposite and the most extreme feelings. Violetta knows that she is going to die; she is a courtesan; she finds love and she gives up her love for the sake of Alfredo and his family. These are big decisions and big problems that are thrown at her from the moment she meets Alfredo. To live through all this, I think you can't do it as a young singer. You really have to know life, and know what it means to lose something, and what it means to be loved. Yes, *Traviata* was always my dream since I fell in love with opera by watching the Zeffirelli movie when I was twelve. For me, this is the most beautiful thing humankind has created – what people can do with their bodies and their voices in this beautiful, dramatic story. Thank God I now have the possibility to play this role and my voice can do this; I worked for this the whole time and now I can; it's the harvest!

OL – You are singing in this Willy Decker production, following the footsteps of Anna Netrebko and Natalie Dessay. How do you plan to make of this version something unique, the Diana Damrau version?

DD – I think everybody is different. We are not copies of each other. We all have different voices and we can show different aspects of Violetta. Anna's connection and chemistry with Rollando Villazón and their ability to play together was instrumental to show this great love of these two lovers in Willy Decker's production in which Violetta and Alfredo get much more time on stage together than in other productions. Natalie Dessay also had a different approach. All of us worked with Willy Decker. He sees and feels what each of us is capable to do, and he goes in that direction. It's never a remake, it's always new, when the cast changes.

OL – Saimir Pirgu who is singing with you is a very young and exciting tenor; we interviewed him too, and I love him. [Read Saimir's interview in volume 1 of our series)]

DD – Yes, absolutely, Saimir is the perfect Alfredo. He has the youth, he has the fire for it, and he is handsome as well. We work well together, on stage.

OL - In a couple of months, you will also sing Violetta at the Zürich Opera in a production by Jürgen Flimm. His approach seems to be somewhat more traditional than Herr Decker's. Have you had any opportunities yet to discuss the Zürich performances with Herr Flimm?

DD – Oh, I have not seen the production, yet. I don't know what is going to happen there, in Zürich. It will be a big revival, in this big opera house that has a lot of repertoire productions, so we get one week of rehearsals. We do our best. All of us put our thoughts and our experience into it. There is no possibility of working with Jürgen Flimm every second of the staging, but surely it's going to be thrilling.

OL - A few years ago, you said that Violetta was probably the farthest you would go with Verdi roles, or perhaps Amelia in *Simon Boccanegra*. Do you still feel that way, or has your voice developed to a point where you may consider some of his heavier lyric roles?

DD – As you said, Amelia for sure would be a good role for me. But the bigger ones are not so possible for me.

OL - Since you've been adding more bel canto roles to your repertoire, are any – or all – of Donizetti's Tudor Queens parts that you want to sing? Or *Lucrezia Borgia*?

DD - I want to do the Donizetti queens, with time. *Roberto Devereux*, I love that opera, and I think I can sing it, but not now. Later, later. For now, I'll stay with Violetta for a nice while. I'll enjoy this. And then I'll probably go further in the Mozart and Richard Strauss repertoires.

OL – Since you've mentioned Richard Strauss, two other noted bel canto sopranos, Montserrat Caballé and Teresa Stratas, not only recorded the role of Salome but also sang it in staged productions. Do you think that might ever be a possibility for you?

DD - I wouldn't do Salome, it is too dramatic and I don't want to hurt my voice.

OL - Your repertoire includes several comic roles, from Adina, Rosina, and Marie in *La Fille de Regiment* to Zerbinetta and Aminta (*The Silent Woman*). Some have said that it's actually more difficult to do comic roles well than any others. What have your experiences been?

DD – Well, sure, regarding comic roles, playing a great comedy is by far more difficult than a tragedy. Comedies are faster; there's more timing; there are moments when your acting needs to be on the point. It's much, much faster so you must be always ahead. I love both comedic and tragic roles. You can't imagine how much I enjoy singing Violetta, finally. It's such a deep role with dramatic moments, and lyric moments, and soft moments, and moments of anger and power, moments of fragility, there is everything in this opera. It's a real drama, a real story, very very deep, so I love that. But sure, to play a Zerbinetta or Aminta, or like we did *Le Comte Ory*, where we really had to invent a lot to make it funny, is always very enjoyable. You can't just make it for the sake of being funny; you can't sit on a joke. You don't have to laugh when you play comedy. It's the public that has to laugh, and that's difficult. Sometimes you think you are funny but you are not, because you are doing too much. You need the right dose.

OL - Another 20th century role that some lyric and coloratura sopranos have sung very successfully is Lulu. Is that a part that would interest you or suit your voice?

DD – Oh, Lulu. I know, Lulu is a child-woman. Lulu is a wonderful role to act. I would do the play immediately, without the music. For myself, I have a problem with Berg's *Lulu*. For me, it's too long, it's very dramatic, and my ears and my soul don't really get friends with the music.

OL – I see. Now, 21st century opera: you sang the role of Charrington the Gym Instructess in Maazel's *1984*. This opera had poor reviews in England but better reviews worldwide. What is your opinion of it, and is singing contemporary opera something that appeals to you?

DD – Well, yes! Before that I did in Vienna *Der Riese vom Steinfeld* which is also contemporary music with extremes for the voice – I had to hum until the key of E, on stage, at the end of the opera, so I had to have voice left for that moment. The Maazel opera was fantastic in another way. I had two small roles, the Gym Instructess and the Drunken Woman. The Gym Instructess, the music for her is like the one for the Queen of the Night. You have to be there and be pinpoint accurate. It's a very dramatic role with really strong coloratura, and *staccati*. I had to do speaking and shouting on top of the music, and do a whole body work-out. So that was a great challenge, and I loved it. The Drunken Woman was a character role with belching in the lower voice. She had to throw up on stage. I can't do that! This was extreme acting! Fun acting, because he made me do really terrible things on stage, we had fun rehearsing it. Everybody was afraid of me! It was pretty nice. Also, it was high and low, I had a combination there between opera and musical technique.

OL - Later this year, you will sing the role of Moll Hackabout in Iain Bell's new opera, *A Harlot's Progress*, at the Theater an der Wien. The libretto by Peter Ackroyd is based on William Hogarth's etchings with this same title, which actually preceded Hogarth's "A Rake's Progress."

DD – Iain Bell is writing this opera for me. Now, the opera is finished, and this year it's the world premiere. Because it's written for me, we have discussed everything. His music is lyrical but acid, if you want to describe it. He creates wonderful atmosphere. There is a lot of power and a lot of responsibility for the singer. The lines and the language, with the melody… oh, Iain is brilliant. And he writes for the voice, for a singer with classical technique. Moll Hackabout is the harlot of the title. It's like a Manon story. She has a syphilitic mad scene at the end of the opera so it's much darker, and interesting.

OL – Indeed, both Moll and Manon involve the downfall of a girl from the country. You are also a noted Mozartean stylist. Some noted opera stars, such as Birgit Nilsson and Siegfried Jerusalem, said they found singing Mozart to be healthy for their voices. Yet others contend that the notion of Mozart as a "tonic" for the voice is a myth, that singing Mozart well is actually quite difficult. What are your thoughts on this?

DD – Yes, Mozart is quite difficult, but that's why it is healthy for the voice. You have to be aware of every note and how you sing it, and you have to have good and clean technique. Singing Mozart is good for the brain, first. And then it's good for the voice. But when you don't have good technique, Mozart can kill you.

OL – Oh wow, this clarifies the issue very well; thank you for your answer. When one looks at your repertoire, one sees as many roles in Italian or French as in German. As recently as a decade ago, there was a much more rigid stereotyping of singers. Italian singers were supposed to sing the music of Italian composers, and German singers were supposed to sing operas by German or Austrian composers. For the Met to cast Hildegard Behrens as Tosca or Plácido Domingo as Lohengrin was really quite unusual. But that no longer seems to be the case. Did you ever experience problems with opera houses outside the German-speaking countries casting you in Italian or French roles?

DD – No, I've never had problems with that. I have to say, now comes the real utopia, because my teacher, she told me "Diana, you must have dreams, you must have the impossible dream; having dreams is good for you; have some for your private life and for your profession." So, I had the impossible dream of me as a German coloratura soprano. I was very young then, when we had this conversation. I said "one day I will sing *La Traviata* at La Scala di Milano" – and you know, everybody is afraid of La Scala. They will throw boos and tomatoes at you. So, we thought that a German singing that role over there, would never happen. But I'm opening the season on the 7th of December, in a new production of *La Traviata* at La Scala di Milano in the year of Verdi!

OL – That's right, it can't get any better than that!

DD – Yes, it can't! But I'm terrified! But I've had roles at La Scala already.

OL – And how did they treat you?

DD – Very nicely, thank God! Sure, it's wonderful to have singers with original language there, singing in their mother language – Germans singing in German, or Italians singing in Italian, because you have the real feeling for the sounds of the language, because you know what feelings and thinking really lie behind those words. Germany, specially, is such a complex language. In English you have one adjective expressing a feeling, but in German for the same feeling you have five different ones, and each treat a different aspect of it, and you have to really understand it to be able to render these nuances. But nowadays, all singers are very much in touch with the importance of language. When they sing, they transport a lot of information through the language, so everybody is very keen on having proper pronunciation and knowing what is going on behind each word. You need to know every single word. It is not necessary to speak the language but you must know every word, not only in direct translation, but also in what lies behind the word with its layers of meaning. When I prepare Russian songs -- I have Rachmaninoff in my Lieder recitals at the moment -- I take Russian coaches and I want to know everything that is behind each word. I need to actually feel the country and its people, in the writing. It's what we have to do, and it's possible. I mean, you have to have some talent for that, and the time to learn.

OL – It seems that convenient air travel and continuing development of rapid communication technology have all helped to make opera truly international now. But some people have complained that this internationalization has come at the expense of stylistic authenticity. Do you think that there is a risk that this will maybe homogenize too much the way people sing opera, so that singers will lose a bit of the Italianate style, or of the German style?

DD – Well, I hope not. No, I don't think so. It depends on which level you are thinking. If you are thinking The Metropolitan Opera, and Wiener Staatsoper, and Paris, and London, and Munich, really in these top houses, the top should happen and will happen. It all depends on us singers, how seriously we take everything, to keep that style well characterized and pure, and we should honor our coaches and our conductors who give us this knowledge. The teachers should keep and transmit this knowledge to the new generations of singers, so that it is not lost.

OL – Good answer! Opera has long held a very important place in

Germany's cultural life. Almost any city or town of any size has a theater where operas and operettas are performed, and the smaller houses have been valuable training grounds for new singers. You began your career at the theaters in Würzburg and Mannheim. But the global economic troubles of the past several years have really hurt some houses. They've had to cut back on the size of their ensembles and orchestras. One thinks of the current situation at the Cologne Opera. What impact do you think the reduction in public funding to opera houses will have on the future of opera in Germany? At the Salzburg Festival, Alexander Pereira is actively pursuing public-private partnerships. Do you think more theaters in the German-speaking countries will move in this direction?

DD – In Germany and Austria we are still lucky to have the support of the State. But it is undeniable that with the crisis, everybody should consider contacting private sponsors to keep this going. Art is food for the soul. It's our history. It's more important than a lot of business people think.

OL - You've often sung the part of Gilda. With all of the changes to social and sexual mores in Western society over the last 50 years, it may be difficult for people today to understand or sympathize with Gilda's situation, since she doesn't fit the mores of the modern woman when she supports her rapist. How do you create empathy for such a character with the younger audience?

DD – I think Gilda is just a young, very young girl, for the first time in love. I'm not sure if the Duke really raped her. But even if he did, her love is just so big that she sticks with this idea and wants to prove to her father that he will change. Probably he has told her, when she was alone with him in his palace and she finally realized that he was the Duke, some sort of idea that made her give in. In his earlier aria he says she is the girl that could have touched his heart. He has some feelings for her. I'm not sure if he raped her, I actually don't think he did. But yes, she has to turn and explain it to her father, and she is all tormented in that moment. It's the biggest thing that has ever happened to that young girl. I think even modern young women can relate to this moment that Gilda is going through.

OL - You and French harpist Mr. Xavier de Maistre recorded a selection of Debussy songs for Sony, and your joint recital at the 2009 Baden Baden Festival was televised. How has your concert program developed since then in terms of the selection of material you perform?

DD – I'm a maniac with songs, and especially the French songs and melodies. You don't hear that repertoire too often, but already doing studies, I delved deep into all the Debussy, Chausson, all those composers and their music. I try to do them as often as possible in recitals. There aren't so many opera performances of music like that. Maybe one day I'll do Mélisande. We'll see. But especially the melodies, and the French music with its elegance and purity, appeal to me. I'm very interested in Impressionism.

OL - You are a member of Bavaria's Maximilian Order for Science and Art, which includes some of the greatest singers and composers of the current century and the past two. This is really a very select group, isn't it? How does it feel to be part of an Order that includes Brahms, Meyerbeer, and Richard Strauss?

DD – This was like the German Nobel Price. It is like being a knight. It's a great, great honor to be selected to be a part of this group.

OL – You got a long list of awards from your country. You've even received the title of Kammersängerin from the State of Bavaria. You must be very popular there.

DD – Yes, in Bavaria, yes!

OL – Are you recognized on the streets, there?

DD – No… no… well, sometimes. You know, the opera world is small. I don't do the yellow press circuit… I'm calm.

OL - I'd like to ask you about some of the charitable work you do. You have appeared in benefit concerts for the Fascination Regenwald Foundation, which supports protection of the world's rainforests, and for Frankfurt's "Städel" Museum. How did you become involved with these organizations?

DD – The doctor who found the Fascination Regenwald Foundation comes from my hometown, so it was just a question of time for we to get together. If I weren't an opera singer, then I'd probably be in the rainforest, do some storm research, something with nature; this is very dear and important to me. And the "Städel," well, art helps art. I'm always there to help art, to help poetry and songs. I'm now on the Board with Thomas Hampson's song project.

OL – Oh, nice, we've talked to him about his project; he was one of the first interviewees in Opera Lively's beginnings [Editor's note: read his interview in Volume 1). Now, to end this interview on a more personal note, you are a mother of two boys (and I'm having the privilege of meeting your baby right now!) [Ms. Damrau had her baby with her during the interview], and you're married to a singer. Would you please tell us a little about the person Diana Damrau, how your personality is, and what you love to do besides opera and your family?

DD – I think I'm a positive person. I am very curious, I want to learn things. I want to get deeper into things. I love movement. I am very energetic. I'm giving. I love my children and my family. I need nature. Being always in big cities, I need to escape somewhere, into nature. I need some space to think and regroup, recharge the batteries. I love animals. I hate violence against anybody – animals, children, everything.

OL – Thank you very much for a lovely interview!

DD – You're welcome!

Eva-Maria Westbroek

Eva-Maria is understaded and humble, while being very intelligent and a hugely sophisticated artist with exquisite technique. She is very appreciated by her colleagues who talk about how approachable she is and how professional, with an uncanny facility to learn new and difficult roles. We interviewed her at the Met in March 2013 at the end of her Francesca da Rimini run. Very active in Europe, she got phenomenal reviews in America when she debuted at the Met in *Die Walküre*, and her Didon in *Les Troyens* at the Royal Opera House was equally successful.

Opera Lively - You are Dutch, but anyone who listened to your interviews during the Metropolitan Opera broadcasts would have been impressed by your very idiomatic English. You sound like a native speaker. How come?

EMW – I don't know… I guess, I learned from watching television in English. In Holland everybody has to speak another language, because nobody wants to speak our language. (laughs)

OL - You are a spinto, right?

EMW – I think I've been a spinto, forever.

OL - Your instrument has wide range, is beautiful, polished, strong and powerful, with nice projection. A musician friend of mine is of the opinion that you are best in non-Italian roles. However, as a spinto soprano, your voice must be ideally suited for many Verdi heroines. So far, you've sung Desdemona, Amelia in *Un Ballo in Maschera*, and Leonora in *La Forza del Destino.* Any comments?

EMW – I really love both Italian and non-Italian roles. I think Verdi and Puccini are extremely healthy for my voice. They just line me up in a very good way. Shostakovich is all right. Richard Strauss is also very vocal. And Wagner, you have to be a little careful, not to be too declamatory and lose your musical line.

OL - You are one of the world's leading Sieglindes today and have sung the role at many different opera houses. When you sing a role frequently, how do you keep the character fresh and interesting for yourself and for the audiences?

EMW – It's really nice if you have a new conductor. You do a role with James Levine, it's very different from doing it with Antonio Pappano or Simon Rattle, so I'm very lucky to have these great people who are inspiring, and they make you think about it differently, again.

OL - Three of your roles are those of unhappily married women who become romantically involved with other men: Sieglinde, Katerina Ismailova, and Francesca da Rimini. Any comments?

EMW – It's interesting, because they have so much suppressed emotion! When you suppress something, it becomes bigger, so these passions that they have become bigger than those of someone whose life is easy and normal. When you have to suppress your love, it becomes unbearable.

OL – What do you think of the score of *Francesca da Rimini*?

EMW – Oh, I think it's amazing. I really love it; I think it is so special and interesting! I'm not a scholar or a musicologist; I just go only on how it makes me feel, and I think it's fantastic. The more you know it, the more you like it.

OL – Yes, I love the wordless duet.

EMW – Isn't it amazing?

OL – It reminds me of *Der Rosenkavalier*.

EMW – Yes, yes. It is beautiful.

OL – One of the best moments in all of opera.

EMW – Yes, it's divine. It's so poetic! I also love the words in this opera, they are so amazing! It's nice how through the book they get together; it's a highlight for my career, to be doing this.

OL – I thought you did very well.

EMW – Oh, thank you, so you did enjoy it! It was a good show, yesterday!

OL – Yes, it was! Moving on from Zandonai, Wagner and Richard Strauss are important parts of your repertoire, but a few years ago, you said that you didn't think Brünnhilde was in your future. Do you still feel that way?

EMW - I still don't think she is in my future. I may do little things from the role in a concert but I really don't think I have that type of voice. I'm not a Hochdramatischer soprano.

OL - A few sopranos have sung the roles of both Elisabeth and Venus in the same performance of *Tannhäuser*. Would that appeal to you, or is Venus also more of a role for a Hochdramatischer soprano?

EMW – I don't want to do Venus. It's hard, harder than ever.

OL - You will sing your first Isolde this coming November at the Semper Oper in Dresden, and then in Bayreuth in 2015. This is one of the great Wagnerian roles, and I'm sure you must be looking forward to it very much. What are some of your thoughts about this part, in terms of its technical challenges?

EMW – Yes, I'm looking forward to it very much. I'm really working on it. The thing I find to be the most difficult about it is its length, because it is so long! You want to pace yourself, and you want to scream in the first act because it is so exciting, and then you have the second act which is so lyrical, so you have to be technically prepared, and think technically, a little bit, so, that might be difficult. I hope I can do it… but I don't know, you know?

OL – Psychologically, there is such a shift as well between the acts!

EMW – Yes, yes! I love her transformation, it is amazing. From being so angry, she is so in love; it's phenomenal, wonderful.

OL - I know that you do extensive research whenever you prepare a new role. Can you please tell us more about that process?

EMW – I do what I can; I read about it, I go online… Now it's so easy, that we can go online; it's wonderful. I read what people say about it, and I read the text. Sometimes I go back to the literary source, but not always, because I don't always have the time.

OL - When you are working on a new role, do you listen to records as part of your research? Or do you prefer to come to a role "fresh" without being influenced by the way in which others have interpreted it?

EMW - Yes, I really do listen to older records. I know that some people don't want to be influenced by their predecessors, but I really do, I like it.

OL – Your husband is a singer as well, and you have sung the roles of Sieglinde and Siegmund together. There are some singer couples – Peter Seiffert and Petra Maria Schnitzer, for example – who make a point of frequently performing together. How often are you and Mr. Frank van Aken able to sing together? Do you make specific plans in your schedules for joint appearances?

EMW – Yes, he is doing the Tristan in Dresden, so this is going to be very exciting. And there is another *Walküre* planned for the future. I'm not sure if I'm allowed to say where, but yes.

OL – You're both avid record collectors, right?

EMW – Well, more, him. Actually, only him. I couldn't compete with that! He came to New York and he was hysterical; he just bought so many records here again, and it's such a heavy material to carry around! He is one of those who say "I got this series now complete!" Also, he is so interested in older voices!

OL – So, that's where you get some of the old records you use in your preparation for new roles?

EMW – Yes, I do use them!

OL - You've described Minnie as your favorite role. What about this character and the music appeal to you?

EMW – I love Minnie very much for a lot of reasons. I love the music, I find it really divine, and I love how she is really a real person. I feel very close to her insecurity. She is so feminine and so cute, but I love it that she is also a lioness. She has everything. She is a true person and could be one of my friends.

OL – So you identify with her? Are you a strong woman?

EMW – Yes, but then she says "io non son che una povera fanciula oscura e buona a nulla"[I'm just a poor and obscure girl, and good for nothing] – I find it so sweet! You feel that way sometimes. I find Tosca much harder to identify with, because she is this sort of diva; she doesn't show this vulnerability; this makes her not as interesting.

OL - You are also well known for singing the title role in the world premiere of Mark Anthony Turnage's opera, *Anna Nicole.* What was your reaction when you were asked to sing Anna Nicole Smith? How much did you know about the real woman at that point?

EMW – I always thought that Anna Nicole was a fascinating figure, one of the most beautiful people ever, so I have to say, I was very surprised they asked me, and also flattered, but also very scared, because I thought, "my God, what it's going to be?" I got the score and I read the text and everything. I thought, "oh my God, what am I going to do??" Knowing that it was this wonderful team, it was so much fun... I really loved it.

OL – Contemporary music is a bit more challenging for the singer, right?

EMW – Yes, I'm not a really great musician, so it took me a really long time to learn it.

OL - Did your impression of this woman change as a result of portraying her onstage? What are your views of her now?

EMW – It did, actually. I really fell in love with her. I saw lots of footage of her in the Internet. You see this girl that is one of the most beautiful people ever, and how she has to sparkle in this amazing charisma, and how that makes people around her go crazy. In the end it turned against her. Also, in the rehearsal room, everybody in the beginning was saying, "God, did you see that episode of the Anna Nicole Smith show?" Of course, those were very depressing. But in the end, we were all saying "it's a tribute to Anna," because we all fell in love with her. Isn't it great? I was so happy! The best compliment for me was that two of her close friends came to see the show, and they liked it. I asked, "would Anna have liked it?" And they said, "Oh my God, she would have loved it!"

OL – Nice! Some of the other characters depicted in Mr. Turnage's opera are still very much alive. Do you know if the Royal Opera House was ever contacted by any of them or if they opposed the performance?

EMW – Yes, there were lawyers checking out everything, and they had to change some scenes. There was a scene in which we were supposed to act like we were sniffing coke on stage, and we were not allowed to do it.

OL - Last year, a group of us from Opera Lively had the pleasure of hearing you sing Didon in the Royal Opera House's production of *Les Troyens*. In 2010, you sang the role of Cassandre with the Netherlands Opera in Amsterdam. How would you compare the two roles?

EMW – Cassandre is of course a very dark and interesting character, but Didon's story appeals more to me, because I'm a romantic. And Didon's music is just so divine! I can't get over it! The quintet! And the ending scene is so amazing! I hope I get to do it again. I wish I have another try. It's quite low for me.

OL – Could you do both in the same production, like some of your colleagues did?

EMW – No, I couldn't. I was exhausted! Cassandre is very declamatory in the middle voice, and that is always quite tiring. I personally find it very tiring.

OL – Yes, she often says her line in prophetic tones and speech-like tones.

EMW – Yes, especially in that last scene with the Trojan ladies.

OL – Régine Crespin and Shirley Verrett performed both roles.

EMW – Yes, and Jessye Norman, and Debbie Polaski. I learned it the first time when I covered it in Salzburg for the Festspiele. It was actually a big break for my career because Gerard Mortier heard me do an orchestra rehearsal, and then he invited me to Paris, to sing there.

OL - I'd like to ask you about the early years of your career. How did classical music and singing come into your life?

EMW – I had some luck. My father played the piano so we always had classical music around the house. It wasn't like it was new for me; but there was never opera or singing, really. We had one Kathleen Ferrier record, and that was it. But I was always singing. I wanted to be like Mahalia Jackson; I was always singing huge spirituals and screaming my head off. So, my dad said, "why don't you take singing lessons?" instead of violin, which I was really not good at; I had no talent for it whatsoever. So I went to see a woman who lived in the area, and she said "you have to do opera, your voice is for opera." Then she gave me a record, and I was struck by lightning.

OL – How old were you?

EMW – Sixteen.

OL – As a teenager, you were a fan of Mahalia Jackson, Nina Simone, and Billie Holiday, right?

OL – Yes, still.

OL - But have you sung any popular music since then? How do you feel about so-called crossover music? Would you have any interest in performing or recording music outside the classical genre?

EMW – No, I'm not good at singing their music; I prefer that other people do it. I sing it under the shower. Diana Krall, and K. D. Lang, I love them all. And Nina Simone, of course, is amazing. But you know, I don't think I'm good at it.

OL - Your career began to move forward again when you joined the ensemble of the State Opera in Stuttgart. You were soon singing leading roles with them, and you've described your time in Stuttgart as a very happy one.

OL – Yes, it was.

OL - What in particular did you like about the environment at that house?

EMW – I was starting out, so I was quite inexperienced. It was a wonderful theater, with a fantastic leader. We had really good people. What they did was not like we see now in some of these opera houses where they get stars to do the first night and then the ensemble gets to do the rest with two weeks of off and on rehearsals. No, we were the stars. So, if you were in the ensemble, you were doing the lead role. It wasn't like they hired other people. And that was amazing. I got to do so many wonderful roles, with great rehearsal periods and wonderful conductors. And of course, the greatest thing was to be settled somewhere so that you could have a social life.

OL – So, now, with all the traveling, is it a lot more difficult?

EMW – Yes, although the fun thing is that now that I've been doing it for so many years, I keep meeting the same people in other places. I keep bumping into them. Especially when you do Wagner, you see the same people all the time. [laughs] So, it's like a family!

OL - You also received the title of Kammersängerin there in Stuttgart; do you feel very special about it?

EMW – Yes, I do, it was wonderful. I don't know if I actually deserve it so much.

OL - You've said you might have remained with that company longer if there hadn't been a change in management.

EMW – Yes, I was in Stuttgart for six years, and then the intendant left, and it was extremely emotional, because we were really a family, and so the family was being broken up. And then they did this sort of gesture for a couple of us, and it was special and emotional; we had a couple of good-bye concerts, and in my last performance we were all weeping, because we were all leaving.

OL – So, with the change in leadership, did they stop having that sort of special consideration for the ensemble singers?

EMW – No, they didn't; it's just that it was different people and they wanted their own gang. People wanted to bring in their own, and I understand that. That's how it is, that's change; everything changes all the time in life.

OL - You are involved with the international charity Musicians Without Borders, right? Can you please tell us about some of the projects on which this organization is currently working?

EMW – Actually, not yet. Someone put it somewhere, but I never really got to meet them. I tried to be part of it, but it never worked out. But I do want to be part of it. I think they are an amazing organization. They go to places like Bosnia to make choirs for women from all sorts of background, so they try to, with music, help people communicate. They try to put musical schools in places where everything is destroyed. I think music can bring so much life and love and understanding to people!

OL - At the end of April, Queen Beatrix will step down and The Netherlands will welcome a new King. Will you be able to attend any of the celebrations connected with the enthronement?

EMW – No, they didn't ask me. But I love the Queen, I love her very much.

OL - Looking toward the years ahead, may we ask you about some of the new roles you'll be performing in two or three years from now, or any recording plans you have?

EMW – I have no recordings planned. Isolde of course is a huge, big challenge. *Kat'a Kabanova*, I'm very happy to be doing that, too. I'm really excited that I did *Manon Lescaut* for the first time, and I'm going to do that again; I totally loved singing Manon Lescaut. It's so wonderful!

OL – The first time I saw one of your DVDs, was *Lady Macbeth of the Mtsensk District*. I thought it was spectacular, and I kept thinking, who is this great young singer?

EMW – Oh, cool, I'm so glad, thank you!

29. How are you as a person? Reserved, or outgoing? How do you describe your personality?

EMW – Ouch! I don't know! It's always hard to say it, about yourself. Ah… I'm not reserved, I think. I like people, I like to have fun, I like harmony. I don't like to fight. I like to have a nice time, all the time.

OL - What are some to the things you like to do outside of opera?

EMW – Actually I have to admit that my life revolves a lot around opera. I have a dog, I love my dog. I really love going in nature and walking the dog, and going in bicycle trips. I cook for friends. I go see my friends and my family; that's what I do.

OL – Thank you so much for this lovely interview!

EMW – You're welcome!

Barbara Hannigan

Canadian soprano Barbara Hannigan is just amazing. She conducts, dances, plays the piano, and sings, and champions modern and contemporary music like nobody. She is also a phenomenal actress, and talking to this multi-talented woman in July 2013 was a pleasure. We called her on the phone from Santa Fe; she was relaxing at home in Canada.

Luiz Gazzola for Opera Lively - Thank you Ms. Hannigan, for doing this. I'm very impressed with your Agnès in *Written on Skin*. You are a wonderful artist, so it will be my honor and my pleasure to interview you, having talked at length with the composer George Benjamin about this piece [read his interview in chapter 10] – he is obviously another great admirer of your talent. Let's start by talking about your character. It's a very emotionally intense character, one that must resonate with a performer's inner core. Please talk to us about the psychology of the character.

Barbara Hannigan – The psychology of Agnès? Obviously the role is about liberation. As far as she is concerned, she is dealing with a situation in which she didn't know how oppressed she was. The way that I play her is that from the beginning it is clear that she is frustrated, but she doesn't really understand why; she doesn't know what she is missing. As the opera goes on, this boy comes into the house, and he evokes feelings in her that are confusing and very strong. He encourages her to think and feel. Then the trajectory of events is quite intense.

OL - What exactly triggers Agnès sudden defiance of her abusive husband?

BH – Nothing is a sudden choice for her. Every step that she makes is one small step, and that is made very clear in the libretto at the beginning. She is remembering how she took her shoes off and that she wouldn't make a lot of sound, and she quietly walks up the steps to the boy's room for the first time, to see what he was painting. She walks over to him in very tiny little steps. I don't think she talks to herself "I am going to have an affair with him and change my life." It's really more "I'm curious, I have these feelings inside and I don't know what they are, so for the first time in my life I'm really going to follow my heart and my instinct."

OL – Yes, very interesting! You are right, now that I think of it – it is indeed gradual, not sudden. Why do you think Agnès kills herself? Would it be a matter of control, to rob her husband of the opportunity to murder her?

BH – You are right, that's part of it. It's her final act of power, certainly. It's a very powerful and defiant act for her to do that. At that time suicide was the ultimate sin. It's also a liberating choice, because if she stays, either he will kill her, or will make of her life a living hell, so her only escape, really, is to jump off the window. She has liberated herself intellectually, sexually, emotionally, and has begun to be her own person. She is no longer owned by her husband, and so this is her final act of ownership: "I decide how I die, and when I die."

OL - *Written on Skin* has scenes that are of a devastating eroticism, but done in a classy way by stage director Ms. Katie Mitchell without showing any… skin.

BH – Right!

OL - I personally see it as a lesson to be learned by certain Regie directors. What are your views on the issue of Regieoper?

BH – It's an interesting question. I see that term used and I often have the feeling that it is used in a negative way, against directors who don't respect the real story of an opera. They will take an opera and turn the story upside down, and make of it something very different than what the singers are singing about, and everyone needs to twist themselves upside down and backwards to try and make it work. But my feeling is that I do think opera needs very good directors. It's no longer a performance of standing and singing, and pretty costumes and pretty sets. The public also wants to have good actors and good direction even when they are seeing traditional opera like bel canto or Mozart or Handel, as well as with contemporary works like *Written on Skin*.

I just want to work with a team that clicks, when you have a director who respects the story and the characters, and who has an understanding of the music to the best of their ability. Then, we have a conductor and a music staff who are also supporting this Gesamtkunstwerk. Then, we have a very special situation. If I look at two operas I did this year, *Written on Skin* and *Lulu*, that's what we got. In *Written on Skin*, there was Katie's beautiful and intense direction. She kept talking to us about how she didn't want our gestures to be "operatic." She didn't want to go to Opera Land. She wanted it to be real and feel more like theater, or even more filmic. She was constantly telling us to do less.

With *Lulu* directed by Krysztof Warlikowski, there was hesitation in the opera world about his work, which I cannot understand, because he is absolutely an extraordinary colleague and director. He worked very much from the center of the story of Lulu. When I walked into the very first rehearsal and we began to speak, I thought "We have exactly the same ideas about this woman." All the crazy things I did in *Lulu*, going on pointe [ballet shoes], falling down, time and time again being pushed around the stage, any of the extreme physical things I did in that piece, certainly fit what was happening both in the libretto and the music. It all made perfect sense.

We really need this compatible marriage between the director, the conductor, and of course, singers who are interested and willing to do more than just stand and sing, to really incorporate – in the true sense of the word – the characters.

OL - How do you feel about the smashing success of *Written on Skin*? Did you expect this much ever since you laid eyes on the piece?

BH – I didn't. First of all, I often don't think about whether something is a hit or not. But certainly, when I get a new score, I think "Is this a good score?" I make my decisions very quickly. Sometimes my perspective changes over the period of rehearsal, but quite early on in the process I have an opinion, shall we say. [laughs] But I didn't have any idea that this would be such a success. As we were working with Katie during the rehearsal process, it became clear that this was something very special. We started to really love the piece and the process of working on it. As we got to the dress rehearsal in Aix-en-Provence, people had been coming to the rehearsals and there was a lot of buzz about the piece.

We were in the biggest theater in Aix-en-Provence, and it was a risk to put modern opera in this theater where the Berlin Philharmonic had done the *Ring*. The response was extraordinary for opening night, but then there were no tickets to be had – it was just completely sold out. This was a wonderful feeling and a wonderful surprise. Except perhaps for Amsterdam – I wasn't there, I was singing *Lulu* at the time so I couldn't be part of that – every other location we've gone to, the opera has been sold out. Even in Munich, I've never seen an audience respond like that. The curtain calls just went on, and on, and on.

The opera appeals to the heart of the public. They become wrapped up in the story as if it were a kind of thriller. I don't think they sit there saying "Oh, I'm enjoying modern opera." They don't seem to think of it as modern opera. They are so engrossed in the story, because it is transfixing. Then they go home and tell their friends, and they read about it, and everyone comes. I haven't heard any negative words. No one has come up to me and said "Oh, what a waste of time." It's been the opposite.

OL - I know you're no stranger to creating new operatic roles and I'll ask about it a little later, but right now, to remain on the *Written on Skin* topic, let me ask you this: The experiencing of creating a role for a piece that is being heralded as the best masterpiece of the 21st century so far, and one that is in all likelihood destined to withstand the test of time, must be thrilling. Any comments on this particular effect of – let's call it this way, immortality - that this is likely to have in your legacy as a singer?

BH – First and foremost, it's a great honor and it is very good fortune to be part of this. It's a combination of a long commitment that I had to music – to singing it and performing it, and particularly, modern music. I've premiered over 80 works, and I know every one of them won't be a hit or a masterpiece. I didn't know what I was getting into with George's opera because I hadn't seen a single note of the score when I said "Yes, I will do it." I didn't even know the story.

When we look at the history books and look at the singers for whom particular roles were written – like Mary Garden who premiered Mélisande, or we remember Maria Malibran or Adelina Patti – all these singers were modern music singers. I'm really excited that my name gets in some way to be beside those names. It's a great, great honor.

OL - How did George Benjamin pick you?

BH – I don't know! I've known George for quite some time, and he certainly knows my work. We have many, many colleagues in common. He's seen me perform. All I know is that he came up to me in Luzern quite some years ago and just flat out asked me if I would be in his opera, and once we sorted out the times and so on, that was really it. He had an idea when he asked me. He knew the character of the piece that I would sing – I didn't. He very much wrote the part for me, so he had the upper hand. He knew what he wanted and what he was doing – I was a bit in the dark. I had to discover the part scene by scene.

I think every composer that I work with projects something of themselves on to me, or on to any of the people for whom they are writing. In George's case, as you know, Agnès is a very heart-breaking character. She garners a lot of sympathy from the audience. I was thinking yesterday – if he changed the story a bit, it didn't have to be a woman, it's not particularly that; it's just one of these persons who need to free themselves. Everyone has the opportunity to go through that at some point in their lives, in a small way or a large way.

OL - Can you please share with us memories of the composition process, and how George got input from the singers? I know that George invited you all over to talk about the tessitura.

BH – He already knew my voice and my repertoire. He looked at the pieces I've sung and knew what my voice can do. That said, I went to his house and we very carefully played a kind of compositional game together, where he would write a few notes and then ask me to write on the music paper what kinds of notes I wanted to come next, then he'd write a few more notes and I'd write a few more notes. By this game, he started to see how my voice likes to move. One of the things he saw is that I love to make very large leaps from low to high or from high to low. If you look at the role of Agnès, that's what happens. She starts with very small intervals in the opening scenes, and then as she becomes liberated the intervals become larger and larger until the final aria which has a range of an octave and a fifth. She is constantly leaping more than an octave in her most fantastic final aria just before she kills herself. George really listened to me, which I loved.

OL – Isn't it incredible, how he manipulates the music to fit the situation? This opera is so brilliant! I think it is one of the top three contemporary operas I've ever seen, and I go as far as ranking it in the top twenty of all time. People gave me flack about it, but I stand by it. I think it is one of the top twenty operas ever composed.

BH – Yes, I think you are right.

OL - How hard is the Agnès role as a sing, as a vocal challenge, even though it was written for your voice?

BH – It's hard to sing, yes. It is difficult. But it has a natural progression of the role, so as the energy builds up, it gives me the energy to sing. As the character becomes more and more energetic I'm also energetic, and as she starts to break out then I need to break out at the same time. As long as I do a good warm up… and when I start to sing the piece in performance, it also warms me up, vocally. It doesn't start with spectacular high notes, or spectacular pianissimo. It's very controlled in a middle voice way, then it spirals and becomes bigger and bigger and bigger. So actually this makes it easier to sing, at least for me.

OL - Those who have seen the world premiere and the Covent Garden run have by now associated the three main roles with the role creators, you, and your wonderful colleges Mr. Mehta and Mr. Purves. How is for you, the work with other casts now that the opera is being revived everywhere? I asked George and he said he did not have to adapt the vocal score to other singers, so far.

BH – It was quite early on that Bejun Mehta had to be replaced. We had a wonderful guy in Toulouse named Tim Mead. He brought something very different to the role, he brought a kind of tenderness and compassion which was really sweet to experience, and he sang beautifully. I really enjoyed it. And then we had another countertenor in Vienna and Munich, Iestyn Davies, who had worked with Katie Mitchell before, so he particularly understood her appreciation for a certain kind of acting. I also enjoyed working with him. Vocally, everyone is different, and Bejun has some incredible strengths, especially in the lower register which is very difficult for countertenors, so sometimes I miss that particular beauty of tone, but everyone has their strengths, and all three countertenors that have sung the part have bought something to it.

Only once we had a different person to replace Christopher Purves, only in Vienna, and it was a Norwegian singer named Audun Iversen, and I thought he did a very good job, but there wasn't as much…[she hesitates] Because Bejun had to be replaced several times, I'm used to working with different countertenors, but with the new Protector we only had a few performances, and it is more difficult to connect if you know you are only going to do it once. I think he did a beautiful job. He was younger and he was a really big guy – I mean, a lot younger than Chris. The thing about playing it with Chris is that I was the young wife, whereas with Audun we were more or less the same age and it leveled out the playing field a little bit. When I'm the oppressed wife with the much older husband – Chris Purves is not that much older than me, but on stage he looks older and I look younger – it's a different dynamic.

OL - You've just finished another sold out run of this spectacular opera in Munich, and I know about the Paris run later this year. Do you have plans to revive the role, and if yes, where and when, if you are at a liberty to say it?

BH – Yes, there are plans to do it in New York in 2015. It will be fully staged; not in an opera company, but part of a festival. I'm not authorized to be more specific. There are plans for us to return to Covent Garden for it, and we will also do it in concert form in Toronto, and there are other offers coming in as well. There is a ton of interest. It's a pity that I won't be able to do them all.

OL - Not only you have incorporated into your repertoire this gorgeous role of Agnès, but you risk to become a quite iconic Lulu as well. Can you tell us about the impact of playing and singing Lulu?

BH – Ah, it was amazing. It was really one of those "the role of your lifetime." It's such a huge part; to prepare it is more than one year of work, not just vocally but also emotionally, in the attempts to incorporate such an extraordinary character. I felt really fortunate that we had Krysztof Warlikowski as our director, because he and I worked very much of one mind. I'm happy that he and I have other projects together in the future. We have two more operas that we will do together. It was very hard for me to let go of *Lulu* when I finished the nine performances in Brussels. It had been sold out and incredibly well received by almost all the press. It was very hard to say goodbye to this vision. I have the feeling that I didn't really say goodbye. I think Lulu became part of everything else I do. What she taught me as a character has infused other roles and even other concerts I did ever since, including Agnès.

OL – Interesting. Now, let's shift to other aspects of your illustrious career. First of all, I'd like to ask you why a Canadian-born artist has been so prolific in Europe but hasn't been back to perform in your native North America as often – maybe just a question of opportunity, but if there are specifics about this choice I'd like to hear about them, if you don't mind. We miss you here, Ms. Hannigan. Any plans to sing and conduct more often this side of the Atlantic?

BH – I am asked for lots of things in North America. I'm really particular about what I do, and often times it's just a matter of the calendar, with something not fitting. I do come to Canada every couple of years to sing with the Toronto Symphony Orchestra and I have a wonderful relationship with them. I do have plans in the major cities in the United States over the next couple of years to do various programs. I'm really happy with those relationships. I think you'll see once the seasons are announced for 2015 and 2016 that I'm over in the States a fair bit doing some really wonderful repertoire and also bringing some special pieces that I created in Europe to the United States. So, I'm really looking forward to that.

OL - Then, we can't help but being amazed at your artistry combining singing, conducting, dancing, and playing the piano. Would you tell us how this multi-talented career came to be like this? How do these passions have intertwined with each other in your training? What fulfills you more as an artist – singing recitals and concerts, singing opera, accompanying yourself on the piano, dancing, or conducting? Of course, most probably, all of the above, but still, there must be some difference in your enjoyment of these different aspects of your art.

BH – Well, the singing is of course the central guiding force, and I think everything else is an extension of that. I always played piano, and occasionally I will play accompanying myself in public, but only for special projects. I am not going to go play a concerto somewhere or anything like that. It's more having a kind of theatrical aspect to it when I sit down and accompany myself.

The conducting is also an extension of the leadership I have when I sing. Certainly I try to be the best musician that I can be, so I've always had a strong awareness of what my colleagues are doing in the orchestra. When it was suggested to me that I tried to conduct as well – actually it wasn't even my idea – I became quite addicted to that way of studying a score and that kind of preparation. It is really very addictive to prepare a score with that depth. I don't have as much time as I would like when I'm "just the singer" but when I have to prepare a score for conducting it does take a lot of time and a lot of attention, but it's the kind of work that I absolutely thrive on.

As far as the dancing goes, I have had dance training as a younger person and I have done a lot of modern dance pieces in which I also had to sing, over the years, but it became a much more prevalent part of my work since 2010 when I started working with Sasha Waltz, the choreographer in Berlin.

I had always been quite a physical performer and I've always been in a strong physical condition, but when it started with Sasha, it was eight hours a day of dancing and training, and I was singing as well, and was expected to be one of the dancers. I was intimidated by it at first, but I also felt in a way quite liberated and very excited, because I was doing something that I have always dreamed of. I always wanted to dance, but I had to choose music because where I came from in Nova Scotia you couldn't do everything, otherwise you would spend your entire life in the car, driving from lesson to lesson. It would have been impossible; then I chose to focus on music, and it is fantastic that later on in my life I actually get to live another dream.

OL – Did you take conducting lessons, or was it self-taught?

BH – When I began conducting, when I made my debut, to be honest I actually hadn't had more than a few hours of coaching. It came quite naturally, but I didn't have a disciplined technique. I just did it. Maybe it was just like the dancing. I had some lessons as a young person but I actually just went out there and did it. Now I am taking lessons. When I prepare a score, I work with Jorma Panula in Finland who is the conducting guru, a fantastic teacher. So now when I prepare a score I go to Helsinki and I work with him. It gives me more confidence and confirms a lot of the instincts I have. He is not showing me how to conduct. He is helping the conducting emerge out of me as a musician. He doesn't say "move your arms like this or like that." He is really drawing out the most efficient and most musical way of showing the orchestra what I want. That's what I really needed; I think it's what every conductor needs.

OL - You have sung with some of the best conductors of today. Does your work as a conductor yourself, informs your interaction with them? Do you have a better say than other singers when you work with conductors?

BH – Yes, I think that's true. It works the other way around too. I always respect all my colleagues, but now I do see the score in a different way. I know how difficult it is to conduct, and when I'm working with conductors, it probably makes the working together a little bit easier because I know what they are trying to show me or what they need from me, and I realize more clearly what I need from them. There are just so many things going on that they need to control or be aware of in the orchestra! So I guess I have more empathy for what they are doing. I get to work with such amazing colleagues; players and conductors. Sometimes I'm pinching myself and thinking "How did this all happen?"

OL - You are very devoted to Baroque and to modern and contemporary music, a somewhat unusual combination. Would you tell us what attracts you in these very different approaches to music; one so tonal and melodious, one so fragmented? (By the way, I must say, I also love both).

BH – It's something about the purity of the sound creation that I really like about the Baroque and classical music. There is something really clean about it, about the tuning and the architecture of the score, and I could see that comparison as well in the modern repertoire. It is why often in the singing it works very well side by side, having those two styles of music as my focuses.

OL - What do you think we need to do to expose more the traditional operatic audiences to all the extraordinarily good work being done today by some of our contemporary operatic composers? The audiences sometimes are spoiled with the romantic pieces and don't accept as well the dissonance and atonality of the modern pieces.

BH – One of the most important things is the way programs are made. If we put an entirely contemporary music program on a season, it's very hard for the audience. It's like looking at four very difficult pieces of modern art side by side – it's exhausting. I like to have programs that are mixed but have a true line, of course, of some connection between the pieces, but they are also like a journey where you have moments that are very intense and drain a lot from the emotional side, from the intellect, and other moments which are slightly more restful and allow us to have some piece for a while. It's like a landscape. Those people who are making programs – sometimes now that is me, because I'm doing a lot of programming as well – need to consider the stamina of the audience. We want to challenge them, and we want to appeal to them especially in an emotional way as opposed to an intellectual way. How can we draw them in to the dramatic component of the evening? It's the most important thing.

I don't like all kinds of contemporary music. I'm very, very picky about who I promote and what music I sing. I'm very careful, because I know that when I sing a particular contemporary piece, I am telling everyone "This is what I want you to listen to." So, I need to be very, very strict; and I am, about what I will agree to sing.

OL - We on Opera Lively make a point of covering new works as much as we can – I'm here in Santa Fe for the world premiere of *Oscar.* So, like I said you are a very frequent role creator. Besides Agnès, you have taken part in the world premières of Pascal Dusapin's *Passion* (Lei) at the Aix Festival, Louis Andriessen's *Writing to Vermeer* (Saskia) for the Netherlands Opera, Jan van de Putte's *Wet Snow* (Liza) for the Nationale Reisopera of the Netherlands, Michel van der Aa's solo opera *One* with film and electronics, Luca Mosca's *Signor Goldoni* (Despina) at La Fenice and Gerald Barry's *The Bitter Tears of Petra von Kant* (Gabrielle) for the English National Opera. I don't mean to ask you about all of them because it would be too lengthy, but would you please pick some that you care about the most, describe them briefly to us, and share with us some of the experience of singing these characters?

BH – *Passion* by Dusapin is a major work in my repertoire, I would say. I performed it in three different stagings. We had three different directors for this piece. It was written for me. Well, all of those pieces were written for me. I loved that I was able to explore the character in three different ways, and continue to do so, because we still have performances of that opera in the future. It's a very special piece for me.

Gerald Barry is really a composer I admire greatly. He is a friend, and he is an artist whom I honor very much. *The Bitter Tears of Petra von Kant* was the first opera of his that I did, then he wrote a Strindberg play called *La Plus Forte* – The Stronger – into an opera, for me, for one soprano and orchestra, and I've been performing that for several years, although we've never done it staged; we've only done it in concert. He also wrote *The Importance of Being Ernest*, and the role of Cecily was written for me. And now he is writing an opera on *Alice in Wonderland* and I will be Alice. So, he is a very important colleague in my life, and he is an incredible creative force. One of the things about him that is so special is that he's got a fantastic sense of humor in his music, because music doesn't generally tend to be very funny. Ligeti can make things funny, but there are not very many other composers who can do that, and Gerald Barry is one of them.

OL - Please tell us about the "Let me tell you, for soprano and orchestra" you'll be singing soon and in 2014.

BH – It's a half an hour piece, by Hans Abrahamsen who is a Danish composer, and Paul Griffiths who is a Welsh writer. It's a very special piece. I've just gotten the score for it, actually, and I'm so excited, because the premiere is in December with the Berlin Philharmonic, and it came out of a book that Paul Griffiths wrote about *Ophelia*, from Shakespeare. To make a long story short, I basically asked the Berlin Philharmonic to commission Hans Abrahamsen to write a piece for me and the orchestra using text from this book. What I find amazing about it is that before the score was even written, we already had many orchestras that were interested to have me come and sing it, including the Göteborgs Symfoniker, the Rotterdam Philharmonic with Yannick Nézet-Séguin, and we will sing it at the Concertgebouw; we will sing it in Birmingham; so it's an amazing project, and it is a very special piece. You will be able to watch it in December in the Digital Concert Hall in Berlin; they will broadcast it online. What I love is that it came from the artists; it didn't come from a manager trying to put famous people together. It came from me, Paul, and Hans, just from the artistic idea we brought, and tried to bring it as we have done, to the highest level. To have the Berlin Philharmonic premiere it is just extraordinary; we still can't really believe it.

OL - Your impressive discography boasts 13 items already that I could count (maybe more that I haven't noticed), between DVDs and CDs. Do you have favorites? Would you describe to us a couple of very special CD items for you, and how you got to select the music for them?

BH – I don't know, because I never listen to them. First of all, it's a Dutilleux recording, *Correspondance*, that's probably the most important to me. It's a piece that I sung for almost ten years and I worked very, very much with that composer, and with Esa-Pekka Salonen and the Orchestra of Radio France. We made this beautiful recording which has been very, very well received. I would say that people should listen to that piece, definitely.

The other CD of course that just came out was *Written on Skin.* [This recording is of the world premiere in Aix. The opera was also recorded on DVD at Covent Garden with the same prodution and almost the same cast including Ms. Hannigan].

Again, I can't say that I actually listen to them. I make the recording, but I don't listen to it once it is out, although I have it. [laughs] I remember those days when we recorded *Written on Skin*; they were live performances in Aix-en-Provence, and I know the feeling, and I know that the recording is a very good representation of those incredibly exciting moments around those first performances of what you have said is a masterpiece.

And the third recording that I like a lot is *Les Illuminations*, by Benjamin Britten, which I recorded with the Amsterdam Sinfonietta. I'm very happy with it; I think it's a very good piece, and I'm happy that I was able to record it with that group.

OL - Let's end if you don't mind by a couple of questions about the person underneath the artist. Please tell us how was for you, growing up with this passion for classical music.

BH – I come from a very small village in Nova Scotia. When I was growing up there wasn't any Internet. We didn't have a public transportation system, so we couldn't go out to attend a concert or something like that in an easy way. We could get in a car and drive one hour or two hours, but we did a lot of music in the home. The school music program was very important, because we had very, very good music teachers. The kids, my friends at school, everybody was excited about music and music-making. It certainly wasn't anything sophisticated that we did, but I really loved making music for as long as I can remember. It really was love. It wasn't that I liked it, it was that I loved it. When I moved to the big city, to Toronto, all of a sudden I could go to the Symphony five nights a week. I could hear chamber music programs, and I could spend several hours in the library listening to recordings and scores, and that was like a festival for me, because I was so hungry and so curious!

OL – How old were you when you moved to Toronto?

BH – I was seventeen.

OL – Was your family involved in music as well? Were your parents musicians?

BH – My parents were involved in music in an amateur way, nothing professional. But my sister studied cello, and she is a professional cellist. She lives in Montreal. She had really seriously good training with Yehudi Menuhin who took her when she was fifteen to a summer program in Spain and in Switzerland. She was a very high level musician. My twin brother did his degree in music. He focused on jazz, but he didn't stay in the business; he decided to go into something else. Three out of the four kids really studied very intensely. We all played the piano, plus another instrument, plus singing lessons, choir camp; a lot of music all the time.

OL - Please tell us about your extra-musical interests. What else do you enjoy and love, in your life outside of the performing universe?

BH – The thing I like to do most other than making music is to cook. I love it. I tend to make really elaborate meals and to create recipes. I can't follow a recipe. It's not in my nature. I will read books and cooking magazines, whatever, but I always have to make up my own path, which is probably like my music career as well, [laughs] I certainly don't follow a recipe in my music career. That's one of my main hobbies. The other thing is that I can't say I'm very good at relaxing, because I like to work, and I like to work hard, but when I'm home like I am now, I can sit and read a book, and I can visit with my family, and I can enjoy the beautiful nature that we have in Canada, and that's very important to me, to reconnect in a very basic way with my surroundings.

OL – Do you have any causes that you plan to be active in, like education of children, or something like that?

BH – As far as teaching goes, I do like to give workshops for composers and master classes for singers. I like working with kids, but I find it exhausting. I think every teacher knows what I am talking about. [laughs] It's really exhausting. It gives you a lot of energy but it also takes a lot of energy from you, and right now what I'm expanding into, in the conducting, is taking pretty much all of my time. So, I don't see myself doing a major educational program and spending a few weeks of every year teaching.

OL - I know that this question is always a bit of a challenge but it is very nice for our readers to get a flavor of the person: how do you define your personality? How are you, as a person?

BH – I'm pretty high energy. [laughs] I have a lot of energy. I'm very positive. I have literally trained my mind to be very positive in the way I approach everything that I do, kind of like sports psychology, so that I can be as healthy as I can. I suppose I'm quite driven. I like to work hard; I like to keep a very fast pace. It's hard for me to sit still. It's hard for me to relax. For me, relaxing is studying, or making programs for a festival, so this is a little bit funny. I think I'm a pretty happy and positive person. I have down times when I feel frustrated and less positive, especially when I'm tired or things are going wrong. I like to have schedules of what I'm doing. For some reason if something goes wrong I don't have a lot of room to adjust. Certainly my colleagues usually say that I'm pretty positive and fun to work with and pretty intense. [laughs].

OL – One can tell, looking at your schedule. [laughs] I'm grateful for this interview, you answered our questions so well and for so long! I'll be thrilled to see you in New York in 2015, or maybe sooner. I was about to travel to Paris to go see *Written on Skin* there, but it coincides with my son's college graduation.

BH – Oh, I see, you can't miss that. Well, I'm glad that we talked, and that we had the time to answer all the questions. Thank you so much!

DIVISION ONE – INTERNATIONALLY ESTABLISHED SINGERS

CHAPTER FOUR – THE BARITONES AND BASS-BARITONES

Greer Grimsley

Dear readers, brace yourselves for one of our most interesting interviews to date (done in July 2013), especially if you are a fan of Wagner's operas. We have interviewed the very intelligent, insightful, experienced, and knowledgeable American bass-baritone Greer Grimsley, who specializes in the Wagnerian repertoire and was a phenomenal Wotan in the latest Metropolitan Opera complete *The Ring of the Nibelung* cycle. We talked to the singer in person at the Met Press Lounge, about his long career with appearances in practically all great opera houses in America, Europe, and even Asia.

Opera Lively – You are quite the Wotan specialist. You've sung it twice with Seattle Opera, once with the Deutsche Oper Berlin, once with Oper Köln, once at La Fenice, and once in Shanghai. You are doing the Met *Ring* next [at the time this interview was done], and returning for a third Wotan in Seattle. So, let's focus a lot on this role. First of all, how do you see Wotan's psychological traits? One might say that he is a rather emasculated boss god, given how he must obey his wife, and how the delicate equilibrium of power limits his ability to do as he pleases.

Greer Grimsley – I see Wotan as having many, many human features. He is called the King of the Gods, but for Wotan, this is a god that was created in the image of the men who were living at the time and who needed this god, so he has a lot of these human traits. The whole idea of bargaining and getting the best deal and sometimes doing a little shady dealing was what life was like when people were living in this feral time. People had to make truces with those they didn't like just to survive. So why shouldn't their gods have to do the same thing? In that sense Wotan doesn't see the repercussion when he does get the gold and it is cursed. In *Rheingold* Wotan doesn't look ahead to see the ramifications of his actions. It's all about "let's get this done. We have to pay the giants, and then everything will be OK." Throughout the rest of the Cycle he – in a very human way – spends his time trying to correct his mistakes.

The thing about [laughs] being henpecked by his wife, you could look at it this way. I choose not to. I believe in *Rheingold* there is still a very caring relationship between Fricka and Wotan. This makes the break between them in *Walküre* so tragic. In their final scene together in act 2 of *Walküre* she tells him - reminds him - of the rules that he himself has set up. So he is trapped by his own rules. She says, "You cannot do this. You cannot allow this. This goes against everything that you have set up in the first place." Erda warns Wotan in *Rheingold* that if he doesn't return the ring the gods will not live forever. He wants to fix this for everyone, not just for himself, because he feels that he made this mistake.

OL – In listening to Wotan trying to justify his philandering to Fricka, we almost have the sense that we are hearing Wagner attempting to justify his own behavior in this regard. How much of Wagner's own personality you think is reflected on the character Wotan?

GG – I think there is a lot of it reflected, as with many composers. I think they impose a certain amount of themselves into their work. I have to say that there are times when I agree wholeheartedly, and then there are other times when I'm convinced that he did write things that were greater than himself. For what we read about Wagner as a man and the music he created, we find that they are often at odds. Perhaps he wrote some passages for some of his friends, as an inside joke. Who knows? That bears some more research, I think [laughs].

OL - The theme of redemption is one that frequently occurs in Wagner's operas. We see it in the *Ring* with Brünnhilde's sacrifice. Two of your other Wagner roles, the Dutchman and Amfortas in *Parsifal*, are central to this idea of redemption. What are your own views of these characters? Maybe

Wagner was trying to reach redemption regarding his own personal life.

GG – I've thought often about this: redemption through a woman. I find that interesting because of Wagner's relationship with his mother. Wagner's operas are full of things Freud would have a field day with. There is redemption. There is also acceptance. Women throughout his operas represent transformation for his male characters.

OL - In the first part of *Siegfried*, in the encounter between Mime and the Wanderer, Wotan refers to Mime's brother as "Schwarz Alberich" – dark Alberich – and later to himself as "Licht Alberich" – light Alberich. This has led some people to suggest that Alberich and Wotan represent two sides of the same personality. Do you agree with this view?

GG – Yes, although I don't think Wagner intended it to be that way. It's long before Freud, and it's long before any other major psychological breakthroughs. I can't imagine Wagner actually intended that. He was very interested in Eastern philosophy. There is a balance to things – the Yin and the Yang. I think that intrigued him, as well. I found that very interesting when I was first studying the *Ring*, and it is an interesting way for him to distinguish the two of them. Perhaps it's two different directions, two paths for life. We as humans naturally seek balance and symmetry, which includes the bad and the good – the dark and the light.

OL - Wagner's anti-Semitism has made him a more controversial figure than many other composers. Can we separate the artist from his or her views? Or does one necessarily influence the other?

GG – Yes, that's a much talked about subject. This is not to excuse anti-Semitism. It is awful in any age, but it was a time when in public it was a lot more acceptable, which as I said is never right or justified. He did have a grudge with the major Jewish composers in Paris whom he felt did not help him as much as he thought they should. Whether or not that was true or whether it was just his ego speaking, he felt very betrayed by Halévy and Meyerbeer. I think that colored his outlook. He spoke specifically about the "Jewish music-makers". I'm not trying to excuse it, but I also mentioned earlier that I do think he managed to create things greater than that bigotry he carried. And then you have *Parsifal*, all through it he has this phrase repeated over and over – "through compassion you will know." Through compassion! And this is from a man who has written those awful things and has behaved awfully, but at this point in his life perhaps he saw things differently. I hope so.

OL – Do you give any credence to the idea that the Nibelungs are metaphors for the Jews?

GG – You can read it that way. I tend to not to. They are mythical creatures and there were creatures like that in the folklore at the time. Also, the Flying Dutchman is supposedly the "Wandering Jew". I haven't found anything to corroborate this. I do find it interesting he had Jewish conductors, he insisted on Jewish conductors to conduct some of his pieces [Editor's note: e.g., Hermann Levi], and a gentleman by the name of [Karl] Tausig who was also Jewish was the person who did a lot of his piano reductions for him. Wagner wanted his works associated with only the best. It's interesting that he was able to do this despite the bigotry. I believe it was more important to him that his operas be the best they could be.

OL – Let's switch to the singing and acting. Arguably the best Wotan moment is the long scene with Brünnhilde when he strips her of her condition of being a goddess. Tell me about your emotions during that half hour of gorgeous music and great theatricality.

GG – Of course I'm very emotionally involved. I have a daughter, and to really connect and sing that music – first of all, it's such a gift to get to sing it! Secondly, it's such a wonderful scene! Some of the things that he says to her at first are so horrible! I could never imagine myself saying them to my daughter. But the emotion of having to say good bye forever to your daughter… I don't think I've ever sung it without having tears in my eyes.

OL – Now, tell me about the vocal challenges of the role. What makes Wotan difficult? What are the different challenges you encounter in the three different operas where Wotan appears?

GG – That's a great question. I believe the challenge of Wotan is that you have to show his exuberance and the youthful blindness in the first scenes of *Das Rheingold*, but towards the end of *Das Rheingold*, the lesson is starting to be learned. Then as you go into *Die Walküre*, there is a more worldly quality that you need to have in your singing; a more settled and focused quality. For *Siegfried*, you need to convey the sense that Wotan has learned so much more than he knew in the previous operas, and that he finally sees the way that this is going to be resolved. He is on a spiritual journey. The way I see *Siegfried* for Wotan is that he's resolved a lot of his issues. Instead of being a conqueror of things, now he conquers knowledge. He is completely focused on that, and he's learned so many things, which he tells Erda. Showing these different qualities of Wotan's character is a big challenge, and you have to think about it without jeopardizing your technique and your basic sound, but you also have to act with your voice as well. This is true of any opera, but in the *Ring* you have to show all of these delineations between the three operas.

But yes, it is a huge challenge, and the stamina that is involved, you have to know that you can do it, and then do it. The biggest vocal challenges are stamina, the vast range changes in the three different operas, and the massive orchestral density. Combine all this with complicated text and the need to stay focused over long periods of time and I believe this is why Wotan is so daunting and yet so deeply rewarding.

OL – Of the three, which one is the most difficult?

GG – I would say *Die Walküre* is the trickiest for me because I can lose myself in the emotion.

OL – Right. So, what is your opinion of Robert Lepage's staging and his famous Machine? I confess that I am very ambivalent about it, feeling that it makes the huge Met stage seem cluttered. For the singers, is it an asset? An obstacle? Both?

GG – I'm the sort of person who looks at things as a challenge and tries to make them work. There are many things about this Lepage design that show promise and a new direction for opera, but it can be challenging. There are physical challenges, but those aren't things that I ever shied away from. When I was a young singer I worked with a few great acting teachers. Their one common idea was "Don't say, 'I can't do that.' Always say 'let me try that.'" It would have been fun to be there at the beginning of this Lepage *Ring* and play with it as well. As long as you have time – and this is always the enemy of non-profit theater – when you have a concept piece like this, you need the luxury of time for singers to feel comfortable, but that takes money. Unfortunately we don't have a lot of that, even at the Met. It's wonderfully funded and rightly so, but time is always an issue. Having only seen the Lepage production on television before starting rehearsals here, I found it much more impressive sitting in the theater. I would have gone even further with some of the projections. It's an interesting concept, to me.

OL - In any case, is singing Wotan at the Met more challenging or more exciting, as opposed to the various other times when you did it in other houses?

GG – Singing at the Met takes on a very different aura, because it's the Met, and it's a great honor always to be here. I think about the singers I used to listen to who stood and sang on this stage. To be able to perform on the same stage makes it hard not to have a smile on one's face the entire time. It's amazing, it really is.

OL – When you sing a particular role so frequently, what do you do to keep the character fresh and interesting for you?

GG – It happens by itself because I'm always looking for something new. In Tito Gobbi's book about *Tosca*, he said he always found something new in his Scarpia. He must have done a thousand Scarpias. I remember reading that book as a young singer, and thinking "of course, you have to find something fresh, some different way." But with the *Ring*, it is so dense that you could sing it for twenty years and still find new things in it.

OL – So, let's talk about the other *Rings* you've participated in. I'd like to compare and contrast these different productions, and ask you to share with us some memories of them, or at least, three of them: Seattle, Berlin, and Venice.

GG – OK. Seattle has the distinction right now in the world to be the only natural looking *Ring* left. It's not a concept *Ring*. We take a great deal of time to find the relationships between the characters, even when we remount it. There is quite a long rehearsal period for this. The scenery is beautiful. It's a wonderful treat for the eyes, if someone is tired of seeing concept pieces. It's a beautiful, beautiful *Ring*. People respond to seeing the characters actually speaking and relating to each other.

That said, the Berlin *Ring*, I love very much as well. It's a piece of history, it's a concept but it is done in such a way that you still tell the story, and for me that's always been the deciding factor. Whatever way you dress it up, if we are still telling the story, if we are still dealing with the interactions between the characters, that's what is important to me. It's great fun; I have a great time when I'm there to do it. I hope they keep it; I hear rumors that there is a new *Ring* happening in Berlin at the Deutsche Oper, but I hope that older *Ring* doesn't go away completely.

Also, being in La Fenice to do this was amazing! Because this is where Wagner died. I would go on walks, just off the Piazza San Marco, and I got to this park and there was a bust of Wagner. It's amazing to be in this theater. I was there many years ago before the first house burned down. I got to see the old house. The rebuilt house is an exact replica. The acoustic is fabulous in this theater! One of the biggest thrills was running into the audience and listening to the Ride of the Valkiries. That was the same production that the Cologne Opera did. Once again, it was updated, but it was updated with care, with the idea that we were telling the story. I have no eye patch in that *Ring* cycle but I think it worked well. It's when you start messing with the relationships that you get in trouble.

OL - You've sung Wagner roles with a number of American opera companies, but also with houses in Berlin, Venice, Cologne, Prague, Copenhagen, Barcelona, and Nancy. European houses, especially those in Germany, are known for their more adventurous stagings. What has your experience been with these Regietheater productions?

GG – There have been some crazy things. You just have to say, "OK, people are going to come see this opera." That's what I start thinking. If something is completely, completely crazy I try in a very diplomatic way to talk to the director, because sometimes they have a very fixed idea about the interpretation, but as long as we are telling the story, the craziness that is around us really doesn't matter. Regardless of what production I'm in, I try to keep the relationships between the characters as true as possible.

OL - I am very curious about the experience of staging the *Ring* in Shanghai. How did the Chinese public react? Any differences in awareness, enthusiasm, or understanding?

GG – I was greatly surprised, because I didn't expect what I saw. I was excited to go to Shanghai, because I had never been to China. The thought came to me: 'I wonder… this is so foreign to Chinese culture, this kind of Nordic myth, and the music as well is very challenging for even Westerners.' I think you have to embrace Wagner first. The performances were sold out every night and people went crazy. I didn't expect the audience to respond that way, but it was exuberant. It was amazing. It was very rewarding.

OL - - Earlier in your career, you sang Escamillo in *La tragédie de Carmen*, Peter Brook's condensed version of Bizet's opera. In late 2012, the Teatro Colón in Buenos Aires performed a condensed version of Wagner's *Ring* cycle arranged by the German composer Cord Garben – not without controversy, one might add. If an opera company offered you the role of Wotan in Herr Garben's arrangement, would you consider it? What do you think of this trend of performing abridged operas?

GG – I would look at it as interesting; I would have to take a look at it, yes, but I would have to see what was cut, what wasn't, because everyone has a different idea of what's important to the story. But I think that's a great way to get people interested in the *Ring* without having to invest five hours in four different nights the first time. You can give them a taste of what this music is, which is an amazing experience. To be clear, I still believe the best way to truly appreciate opera, especially Wagner, is to see it without abridging it.

OL – Do you see any risk that due to budget constraints, this fad of abridged productions would lead people to start cutting these pieces all over the place?

GG – There is always a risk, yes. One of the big expenses is scenery. The idea of using these projections and animation might help with having the scenery not being one of the major cost factors. The cast can be large, but some bel canto pieces also have large casts. It's then a question of going overtime. Some places that do the *Ring* regularly have a separate budget for the *Ring* aside from the usual season. So the *Ring* is very expensive and an abridged production might respond to that, but I hope other houses will continue to put on the full cycle, and people will continue to fall in love with this art form like I did.

OL – Good. Your other signature role is The Flying Dutchman, whom you've portrayed all over the world even more often than Wotan. Again, tell me about some of its vocal challenges.

GG – OK. I think the biggest challenge is that in the first act you are asked to sing this huge declamatory aria full of angst and pain and regret, and then in the second act for the first part of the duet, you have to sing as if you are a Lieder singer, and really finesse these words. Then in the third act you are back to this huge declamatory rejection of Senta when you think she's cheated on you. It's managing to do those things while still keeping the beauty in the sound throughout all of it that is challenging.

OL - Your other Wagnerian roles are Telramund in *Lohengrin*, Kurwenal in *Tristan und Isolde*, and Amfortas in *Parsifal* – any favorites?

GG – Any time I get to do them, I love doing them. I love them all. I really do. My first Wagner role was Telramund and I really enjoyed singing that character. I've heard it screamed a lot, but I think the role has a bigger impact if you sing it like bel canto but in Wagner style.

OL – Your repertoire does weigh heavily in Wagner, but you have had a long list of non-Wagnerian roles as well, about in equal parts between

Italian, German, French operas and a bit of Hungarian opera: Scarpia in *Tosca*, Macbeth, Amonasro in *Aida*, Jokannan in Salome, Don Pizarro in *Fidelio*, the villains in *Hoffmann*, Mephistopheles in *Faust*, the High Priest in *Samson et Dalila*, Escamillo in *Carmen*, and the fascinating Bluebeard, among others. First of all, I'd like to ask you as an opera lover that I'm sure you are beyond being a performer – do you feel a strong superiority of Wagner over the other operatic traditions? Or do you think that the Italians, French, and Eastern European composers are enough of a match?

GG – They are all inspired and inspiring. There are operas that are just as satisfying as Wagner's operas, and I'm grateful to sing them. I was just talking about this. *Bluebeard's Castle* is an amazing work. It is fascinating, and this was the only opera Bartók wrote. It was for a contest. I remember when I was learning it, I kept thinking, 'why didn't he write more? This is an amazing work, and he understood how to write for the voice so well and instinctively!' The psychological part of the piece is also amazing.

OL - Given the language barrier, was it more difficult to learn?

GG – It did take more time, that way. The Hungarian, there is a way to sing it. Although I've never sung in Czech, hearing it, it sounds more difficult than Hungarian.

OL – Well, Hungarian is such a particular language, in a class of its own…

GG – Yes, it is.

OL - You have quite a rogue's gallery of characters across a wide stylistic range. You are a true bass-baritone in that you sing roles such as Macbeth, which are clearly in baritone territory, as well as Mephistopheles in *Faust*, who is normally sung by a bass. How do you keep your voice healthy across these registers?

GG – I just sing as I was taught, with the bel canto technique. I try to keep it as even and easy as possible. I never try to force a particular sound in either direction; I just sing. So far that's kept me really healthy, along the way.

OL - About modern and contemporary opera, you have participated in *Peter Grimes* in the role of Captain Balstrode, and you have created the role of Cankya in the world premiere of *Ashoka's Dream* in Santa Fe. Please tell us about your views on contemporary opera, and on the experience of creating a new role, and the challenge of singing modern and contemporary music.

GG – Actually I enjoy it. It doesn't come my way as much as it used to. Once you start into the Wagner repertoire, for some reason people think you are not interested in other things. But I'm always interested in different things. With *Ashoka's Dream*, this was Peter Lieberson's first opera, I believe, and it was the story of the Bhudda. The challenge of contemporary opera, when you learn it and perform it, is that you have to learn something that is not part of the standard repertoire. By that I mean that when you sing it, your audience shouldn't be aware that it is so new. You need to sing it like you mean it, just like you sing *La Traviata* or any other standard opera. And I think it's a challenge because sometimes we get caught up in the newness of it. Working on the character is no different than working on the characters of the standard repertoire when you work on them for the first time. There are sometimes musical challenges. The composers can be quite complicated. But once again, I look at it as a challenge and I try to conquer it.

OL - You're going to add Claggart in *Billy Budd* to your roster of bad guys next year. While some of the characters you sing are more complex individuals, it's hard to find many redeeming qualities in someone like Claggart – or Scarpia or Pizarro. How do you approach such characters? From a theatrical standpoint, how do you find a way to "get inside" these unpleasant individuals?

GG – That's a good question. I remember when I was going to do my first Mephistopheles in *Faust*, I was thinking 'How do you do this? How do you play this?' I ended up reading *The Screwtape Letters* by C. S. Lewis. It's interesting because those are basically conversations with the Devil. The Devil perceives himself as not evil, but being fully justified in doing what he is doing. That's the approach I take with these kinds of crazy characters. They are convinced that they are justified, in their minds, that their behavior is the right behavior. They think "of course it's not wrong" and they find all these reasons to do what they do. We see it in many countries where politicians behave that way. They justify their actions by saying, "Ah, it's for the country, it's for the people."

OL – Interesting. You have a rarity in your repertoire, Heinrich Marschner's obscure *Der Templer und Die Juden*. Please tell us about that one. Why was it important to revive it?

GG – Yes! [laughs] It was at the Wexford Festival, and that was many years ago. Wow! Thanks for finding that! [laughs] They like to do interesting works that aren't done very much. Many people know Marschner's *Der Vampyr*, but *Der Templer und Die Juden* is a very obscure work. It's basically the story of Ivanhoe. You know what, I think it deserves revival. Having done it, I enjoyed it very much. He was a precursor to Wagner, and you can hear those musical influences that are about to happen in Wagner.

OL - Performing in opera not only makes a lot of physical demands on you, but also requires a great deal of emotional intensity to bring a character to life. How do you "wind down" after a performance? What do you do to relax and recharge your batteries, so to speak?

GG – If my family is with me and we have an apartment, we go back to the apartment, or we go out. I may have a beer, and just being with friends and family is relaxing.

OL - You're from New Orleans. How are things in New Orleans today?

GG – They are going well. Actually I was just there. I just performed with New Orleans Opera before coming here. The recovery is going really well. At one point New Orleans led the nation in startup businesses. They've created a lot of incentives for people to come back, or to come to New Orleans and create businesses. A lot of the important centers like the French Quarter and the uptown area didn't get as damaged as a lot of the outlying areas like Lakeview. There are pockets of houses that are boarded up, and look like the hurricane happened yesterday, but my second name for New Orleans now is, "La Fenice". It is rising out of the ashes.

OL – Good! The tenor Bryan Hymel, who is also from New Orleans, is making quite a name for himself as well. Have you and Mr. Hymel ever had an opportunity to meet?

GG – No, I haven't met Bryan. My daughter is studying singing in New Orleans and she's done a master class with him. She knows Bryan because she was with my wife who is a singer, when they sang *Das Rheingold* down in New Orleans together. She can't say enough good things about Bryan.

OL - In the world tour of *La tragédie de Carmen*, the title role was sung by a mezzo named Luretta Bybee. Was this how you and your wife met?

GG – Actually I met her just before that. We were young singers doing our first *Carmens*, for a now defunct touring group from Houston, called Texas Opera Theater. I was Escamillo and she was Carmen. We met on tour and fell in love during that time. We heard about auditions for Peter Brook for *La Tragédie de Carmen*, and we flew to New York during a break of the tour to audition for him, not telling him that we knew each other, and we were both hired. Sometimes things happen the way are supposed to.

OL - As opera singers, you and your wife have careers that take you all over the country and even to other parts of the world. So you're faced with even more challenges than most dual career couples. How do you balance the demands of your careers with the needs of family life?

GG – The challenge was committing to spend the money to see each other. We always find a way to see each other within a certain time frame. It was challenging, especially when our daughter came along. I wouldn't change any of it.

OL – You've enjoyed a long and well-established career. What advice would you give those who are still studying? What are some of the things to which they should pay particular attention?

GG – I would say to young singers, to make sure that your technique is second nature, and that you spend time exploring and finding the artist in yourself. Spend time finding out what you want to say, what is important to you to share with people. As young singers, you get a lot of people saying "oh, you should do this, you should do that" and you need some quiet time to sit and really discover who you are, and why you want to do this. It's very important.

OL - In general, what do you see as some of the risks or weaknesses aspiring singers face today?

GG – It's not so much that I see weaknesses. It's a reaction to how things have changed in the business. Before, when I was a beginning singer, there were many touring companies. As a young singer you could learn on your feet – get really valuable experience – on these tours. Houston, San Francisco, City Opera, the Met all had tours. It was a huge learning process. Nowadays – and I don't fault the singers on this – there are no places like this to go, other than a few very selective young artist programs. So I see a lot of young singers stay in college and rack up a huge debt. There are smaller companies that are looking for young singers, but still, there aren't enough opportunities for all of them, so a lot of young singers are working on their doctorates when they should be out there singing. But it's scary out there. I would be thrilled to see touring companies be revived.

OL - Speight Jenkins once compared your voice to that of George London. And when one listens to YouTube clips of you and Mr. London singing the same aria – Scarpia's Te Deum, for example – one can definitely detect a certain similarity in timbre.

GG – Yes. I have been told so, and I'm always flattered and honored.

OL - When you study a new role, do you listen to other singers' interpretations? Who are your idols? Who inspires you?

GG – Yes, I listen. Actually I came to George London very late. I like to listen to older recordings because there is not so much studio mixing. You can find old live recordings and you can actually hear what I call the air in the sound. More often than not you can hear certain musical traditions that I listen for. I like to listen to different conductors conducting the same piece. I like to find out, for a role I'm doing the first time, how my predecessors interpreted it, musically. It feeds what I do. As a young singer, I listened to a lot of tenors: Jussi Björling, Richard Tucker, Del Monaco, Gigli, Pavarotti, Domingo but also I listened to baritones and basses like Bastianini, and Capecchi, Tito Ruffo, di Lucca, Milnes, Pinza, Tozzi, Panerai , Siepi. Then someone told me, "You should listen to George London because you have some similar qualities." OK, I did, and once I listened to him, it was very strange because I understood how he was making his sound. It's hard for me to explain but I understood what was happening in his throat when he sang. I certainly adore the legacy that he left. It's amazing! He was one of the people that I studied what he did in the *Ring*; also Hans Hotter, and the great Thomas Stewart. These are my three Wotans I referenced, to see how they handled it. And it's not to imitate. I don't imitate, but it's to hear how they negotiate certain things in the music that are difficult.

OL – Now let's talk about your beginnings. How did vocal classical music come to your life? Was music in your family background?

GG – No, I say I'm an anachronism in my family. My father liked to play guitar and sing Country songs. I did not grow up in a family of musicians; not at all. I remember in sixth grade, we had the option to pick an instrument and we learned the basics with little simple songs, and I picked the trumpet. And then this program ended, and I kept the trumpet and kept teaching myself how to play until High School. I got into the High School Marching Band and I was also in the choir. I liked to sing as well but didn't think that this would be my career. All through High School I was thinking that I wanted to be an archeologist. And then when I was a junior in High School, I got to see my first opera. The first opera I saw, I was in, because they called the school and asked for some volunteers to be extras. Oddly enough, this opera in New Orleans was *La Juive* with Richard Tucker singing the only performance he sang of it in the United States, because he died before the Met got to do it for him. I remember being so impressed and so inspired by Mr. Tucker! This new art form that I found, combined two things that I absolutely loved, singing and acting.

After that I started to explore a little bit more. Then in my senior year a friend of mine, Anthony Laciura who is a very fine character tenor but is now an actor in Boardwalk Empire on HBO, told me, "You know, you have a good voice, you should go study with my teacher at Loyola." So I auditioned for the Music School at Loyola University and got a scholarship. It started me on my way.

OL – Nice! How did you get interested in the music of Wagner?

GG – I had dear friends who kept saying, "You are going to sing Wagner one of these days." And I would say, "No, no, no, I don't think I ever will." And they would take me to operas to convince me, and it actually did work. My interested was sparked by going with my friends who insisted I should be singing some of this, and yes, I ended up doing it. [laughs]

OL – What are your interests outside of opera?

GG – Archeology is now a hobby, so if there is anything of interest where I am, I usually try to get out and go to it. It's easier to do that in places like Rome, and Tel Aviv, and Greece, and in many other European cities there are museums to do that. I love fishing when I can have time to do that. And also I love to just get out in nature and hike.

OL – How are you as a person? Can you describe your personality?

GG – [laughs] That's a very good question. I would say, I am curious, accepting, pretty much most of the time trying to look on the brighter side of things.

OL – So your daughter is interested in singing. Do you take her with you to your performances?

GG – She has been going to them all her life. She is 21 years old and is a junior now at the college where I went, down in New Orleans, Loyola University. She just sang the role of Cunégonde [*Candide*] in January. She is an English major and a music minor and has a real gift for singing.

OL – Genes from both sides.

GG – I think so, but how we got a coloratura, I'll never know, from a mezzo and a bass-baritone. [laughs]

OL – Thank you for a lovely interview.

GG – Wow, wonderful, wonderful questions. It was a pleasure.

OL – The pleasure was mine, and our readers'.

Ildar Abdrazakov

When Opera Lively talked by Skype with Ildar back in October 2012, even though the Russian singer had already had many Met appearances and an impressive discography and was very well received in Europe, he hadn't exploded into the American public's eyes and ears like he has now, with iconic roles in important Met productions such as *Prince Igor*. It is with fondness that we've been witnessing his rise to fame also this side of the Atlantic.

Opera Lively - Let's start by talking a little about your background. You were born in Ufa, in the Republic of Bashkiria, which was also the birthplace of the great dancer, Rudolf Nureyev. Your father was a stage and film director, and your mother was a painter. So it sounds as though there were many creative influences in your life when you were growing up, both at home and in the community.

Ildar Abdrazakov – Yes, growing up in that environment was fun. My father's place of work was just a few yards from home, so I was always there. My mother's on the other hand was one hour away; she had to take the bus to go there, and as a matter of fact I saw her work only once. I went there once, and there she was, in that big pavilion, painting. I can't say it impressed me very much. My father's work, however, was fascinating to me. I mean, it was the TV, and the theater, and there were stage directors and singers and actors, I loved to watch and be in touch with all of that. When I was four years old my father gave me a part in a Christmas musical that he was directing.

OL – Four years old? Wow! How big was the part; were you a character in the show?

IA – Oh, it was a small part. It wasn't even a real speaking part. I just had to come in, say Hello, and move around. I was in for just a few minutes.

OL – Music was important in your family, right? I know that your family enjoyed singing traditional Bashkir songs, and your father played the violin.

IA – Yes, he played the violin, accordion, mandolin, and piano. But he never formally studied music. He was never in a conservatory. He learned it all by himself.

OL – Did he love opera?

IA – He loved music, but opera, I don't think so. But he learned to love it once my brother Askar, who is also an opera singer, started to sing in the small opera house we had in Ufa. I used to go watch the operas with my dad, when my brother performed.

OL – I see. So, you developed an interest in the art of singing because of your brother?

IA – Yes, it was thanks to my brother. He is seven and a half years older than me, so when I was in grade school my brother was already in a conservatory. He would come home and sing all day long, from the morning until the night. I enjoyed listening to him, and then one day I thought, "hm, maybe I could sing, also!"

OL – How old were you when this happened?

IA – I was thirteen years old when I got interested. One year later, at age fourteen, I started to take singing lessons with my brother's teacher, but just once a week, because I was still too young. Later I got into the same conservatory and studied formally with the same teacher.

OL – Were you already sure at the time that you wanted to be an opera singer?

IA – Actually my first idea was to either sing choral music with the philharmonic orchestra there, or to sing pop music. But then I started to sing in the chorus at the opera house, and things evolved from there. At the time, I never thought that one day I'd be singing at La Scala, at Covent Garden, and other countries. I started to sing small roles at our local opera house. As a matter of fact I wasn't even expecting that I'd go to Moscow or Saint Petersburg! But then I started to win competitions, and while competing, I met all these people who had sung for the major opera houses, and they told me that I had a good voice and should audition for the opera houses. And then I auditioned for Maestro Valery Gergiev at the Mariinsky Theater, and he accepted me.

OL – Maestro Gergiev is coming to my town this Monday. He is here to play Stravinsky's *The Rite of Spring* with the Mariinsky Orchestra.

IA – Yes, I know. I spoke with him today and he told me about his tour in America.

OL – So, your first name, Ildar, means Gift to the Country in your language. Did it become a reality? Are you a celebrity in your homeland?

IA – Yes, yes, they know me, especially in Ufa. When I go back there and go out with my friends to restaurants and other places, they do recognize me.

OL – Nice! Does it get to be intrusive?

IA – No, the people from my home town love me and they wish me well; they follow my career and say beautiful things to me.

OL – How important was your time at the Bashkirian Opera House in your development as a singer?

IA – It was essential for me to develop in a low-pressure environment and to become more secure as a singer. I started by singing small parts, like Zuniga in *Carmen*, or Don Basilio in *Il Barbiere di Siviglia*, and several small parts in Russian opera. It was like being in an opera studio for me. I worked a lot with great stage directors there, and great conductors, while at the same time I had my teacher there very close, and she could tell me what was good and what was not, for my voice. She supported me a lot.

OL - At the age of 22, you made your debut at the Mariinsky Theater in St. Petersburg. You were singing Figaro in a production of *Le Nozze di Figaro*, and your Susanna was a young soprano named Anna Netrebko. Tell me about it.

IA – Working with her was very special. Of course, at that time, no one knew who Anna Netrebko was [laughs]. It was in 1998. She was a regular person; not the big star that she is now. At the time we were good friends. We worked a lot together, and partied together, went to restaurants; we spent a lot of time together.

OL – And then after she became famous you continued to work with her, and just recently, last year, did *Anna Bolena* at the Met with her. I was there, by the way; I saw you on stage, and liked what you did.

IA – Oh, thank you.

OL – So how is it, to work with her now that she is so famous?

IA – Oh, she is the same! She is so interesting, and so funny, I love her. I'm very happy to work with her, and very happy for her and her big career. It is a lot of fun for me, to think that I've worked with her from the beginning when she was starting her career in Russia, all the way until now at the Met when she is such a star!

OL – I think it is a pity that out of 381 opera productions this season in the United States, there is only one Russian opera – a single production of *Eugene Onegin*. In recent years there were more, like *Boris Godunov* or *Khovanshchina*, but currently there is only one scheduled. Is there a way for you as a Russian singer to try and change this situation, to promote Russian opera in some way?

IA – No, it's not really something that a singer has control of. It's really up to the opera house managers, conductors, and stage directors. For me, it would be even more difficult to have an influence on this, because ever since I left Russia, I stopped singing the Russian repertory, for a long time. Only this past March, a few months ago, I had my first opportunity to sing Russian opera outside of Russia – I did a *Khovanshchina*. So, there is only one *Eugene Onegin* this season, huh? I don't know why. Maybe it is because of the Verdi and Wagner bicentennials; they may be paying less attention to Russian opera. Well, at least we had a recent a production of *Boris Godunov* that was given in different opera houses in the world, the same production. That was good.

OL – Do you see many differences in the professional environment between Russian houses and Western opera houses?

IA – I think the main difference has to do with how the administration of the opera house operates and deals with the singers. The Mariinsky is my home, I love the Mariinsky and feel comfortable there, but in some other opera houses which I won't name, it wasn't the same thing. They'd hire you, and would tell you, "OK, you're here to sing this role, and the rest of your time, you're on your own." Over here at the Met they make you feel really comfortable; they call you and ask you if you need something, they inquire whether there is any way they can somehow help you… Covent Garden is like this as well; they make you feel at home.

OL – What about the audiences; do you see differences as well?

IA – Yes, of course. The mentality of the audiences is very different, in different countries. The Russians want a big voice. If you have a big voice, that's good, it doesn't matter how you sing. In Italy, the preference of the Italians is more linked to how you sing, to your musical phrasing, and whether or not you fit the style of the composer – there is a style for Verdi, a style for Mozart, and they'll require that. Also, if you have any small vocal failure – say, you have some congestion and your throat scratches a little – the Italians will immediately boo you. American audiences are generous. They come to watch and have fun; they want to enjoy the opera; that's amazing and is beautiful. They don't boo if you make a mistake – maybe they'll applaud less. I never heard boos in America; singing here is more comfortable.

OL - During the late '90s, you won several important voice competitions. Probably the one which had the greatest impact on your career was the 2000 Maria Callas International Television Competition in Parma, since it led to your recital debut at La Scala a few months later. That must have been quite an experience. You were 25 years old, and you were singing in one of the world's most famous opera houses. How did you feel? Were you nervous at all?

IA – Yes, that was a very special moment. First, I did not want to participate in that competition. But my friends and the people who supported my career insisted that I had to go. They said, "you must go, this competition is good for your voice, you will win, you will take the grand prix." I said OK, auditioned for it, and they invited me. There were three elimination rounds. These three rounds took four months, because they had 673 competitors - lots, lots of singers and just one prize. And I did it all, and survived all the rounds, and when the jury said that I had won, I thought I was dreaming; it was unreal! (laughs)

OL – And then you went to La Scala, and your career took off.

IA – Yes, three months later I was at La Scala, and my European career went very well. And then in 2004 I had my Met debut.

OL – Yes, as Masetto in *Don Giovanni*, right?

IA – Yes, exactly.

OL – So, let's talk about Mozart a little bit. Now you are one of the world's leading interpreters of the role of Don Giovanni. What comments can you make about singing Mozart?

IA – You know, people say that Mozart is honey for the voice, but I don't really agree. I think that singing Mozart is more difficult than it seems, especially because now we have to sing it in huge houses with a complete orchestra. In Mozart's time, the orchestras had half the number of instruments of a modern orchestra, or less. So, one could sing with half voice as well… not anymore. For me, it's difficult. I need to warm up my voice for twenty to twenty five minutes to sing Mozart. Another difficulty is that Mozart's operas are very active. In many Verdi operas you can stand there on stage and breath and sing. In Mozart, you have to be moving all the time. You need to warm up not only your voice, but your body too!

OL - Please tell us about the *Nozze di Figaro* production by Jonathan Miller at the Met, in which you'll be singing the title role.

IA – The first performance is tomorrow [10-26-2012]. It's a beautiful production, very stylish. The sets and costumes are beautiful, I like it. It's not a modern production. I did Figaro many times, and as a matter of fact, traditionalist stagings of it don't change very much; they are similar.

OL – The production of *Anna Bolena* at the Met was a very traditional staging, with costumes that were influenced by Hans Holbein's portraits of Henry VIII and his wives. With your family background in theater and film, you are very knowledgeable on the subject of theatrical productions. Do you prefer more traditional stagings? Or, do you like the more avant-garde productions?

IA – I prefer traditional, beautiful productions. I do like modern productions but they need to be intelligent. Last time I did *I Vespri Siciliani* in Turin, it was an updated production to our time, but it was beautiful as well, respecting the story. I believe you can see it on YouTube; look it up, I think if you see it you'll agree with me.

OL – OK, I will. And then, right after this one, you have Don Giovanni in the Michael Grandage production at the Met. Is it difficult to be in two title roles at the Met in a row?

IA – No, these operas are not difficult for me even when they come one after the other like this, because I've done them many times. Just a few days ago I sang Don Giovanni in Washington, now I'm doing Figaro, and then Don Giovanni again. So it's just a question of getting to know my new colleagues and putting everything together, but it is not difficult.

OL - With a few exceptions, opera's handsome young heroes are tenors – or countertenors, in Baroque opera. Basses typically sing the roles of villains or the Devil, fathers or old men, or buffo characters like Mustafa or Don Pasquale. Do you ever wish that, just once, you could be the handsome guy who gets the girl?

IA – [laughs] No, I actually prefer the dramatic complexity of the bass roles. See *Moïse et Pharaon* for example, it is interesting to play a man such as Moïse, this patriotic strong character. I prefer the deep characters. But sometimes I also feel very good in the buffo roles. For example, *L'Italiana in Algeri* is one of my favorite operas. I love to play Mustafa, he's a great character and very funny. I love acting on stage.

OL – *L'Italian in Algeri* is indeed a gem, and very funny. So, you like the multi-dimensional characters.

IA – Yes, yes, and it is not only that. It's also because their music is beautiful.

OL - As you look forward to the progression of your career in the years ahead, do you have any interest in singing roles in the German repertoire – Sarastro, Rocco, Kaspar, some of Wagner's bass roles?

IA – [laughs] No, I don't see my voice going that way. I'm more into bel canto with its legato. Besides, I don't speak German and I find that language very difficult. I like the French repertory as well. I like the roles that have lots of color. It is important to me to understand all words in the libretto, and I can do this with Italian and French, but not with German.

OL – By the way, congratulations on the two Grammy Awards that you won for Verdi's Requiem in the categories of Best Classical Recording and Best Choral Performance, with the Chicago Symphony Orchestra under Riccardo Muti released by CSO-Resound. Are there any more recordings planned that we can look forward to?

IA – Thank you. I would love to record more in the future. I have several ideas I am considering, but currently there is nothing concrete planned.

OL – Let's talk about some of your other recordings. They include *Rossini Discoveries* with unpublished arias by Rossini (conducted by Riccardo Chailly, Decca), *Messa Solenne* by Cherubini (Bayerische Rundfunk Orchestra under Riccardo Muti, EMI Classics), Shostakovich's *Words of Michelangelo* (BBC Philharmonic under Noseda, Chandos) as well as Rossini's opera *Moïse et Pharaon* (orchestra of the Teatro alla Scala under Riccardo Muti) which came out on both CD and DVD. Which one did you like most, to perform and record?

IA – You know, I don't really have any favorites. I've listened to them just once. As a matter of fact I don't like to listen to myself on recording. [laughs]

OL – Really? [laughs] You don't like to listen to yourself?

IA – No, I don't. [laughs]

OL – That's interesting. And how do you select what you record?

IA – Again, it's a question of conductors. They invite me. I don't get much say in whether we'll do this or that. They invite me and say "let's do this program" and I say yes and feel very happy about it.

OL – Would you tell us a bit about yourself as a person? What do you like to do in your spare time?

IA – I like to play golf. I enjoy going outdoors for barbecue with my friends. I like the beach and swimming at sea. I go jogging on Central Park and go to the gym. And of course I love to spend time with my children, but I don't have enough time for it; I end up only spending a few days with them. My youngest is nine; will be ten years old in January.

OL – Do they like music, and do they come to see you on stage?

IA – Yes, they do, they come to see me, and they love music. My son plays the piano.

OL – Are you a more reserved person, or are you easygoing?

IA – I'm very easygoing.

OL - You are still very young at 36. How do you deal with fame? Is it disturbing in any way?

IA – No, not really. I love what I do. I prepare my parts, rehearse, and go sing them on stage. I don't allow myself to get all impressed and say "wow!" I try to think of it as my work, and I just go and do it. I'm very happy with it all.

OL – OK, thank you so much! Like I said I've seen you on stage in *Anna Bolena*, and you're a great singer; I look forward to seeing you again in a future opportunity.

IA – Thank you. All the best!

DIVISION TWO – EMERGING, REGIONAL, OR YOUNG SINGERS

CHAPTER FIVE – FEMALE SINGERS

Lisette Oropesa, soprano

This interview from May 2013 at the Metropolitan Opera features a delightful young lady who is so amiable and warm that we'd easily be personal friends with her and her charming husband (we met the young couple three times) if life had placed us together. We are rooting for Lisette from now on, although she doesn't really need it, given her blossoming career. She was singing Gilda at the time, and simultaneously doing the small part of the Wood Bird in *Siegfried.*

Opera Lively - Let's first talk about this production of *Rigoletto.* Please tell us a bit about the director's idea of staging it in Las Vegas.

Lisette Oropesa - I think the idea of updating *Rigoletto* is something that can be easily done because *Rigoletto* is just about people, relationships, and vengeance. The only thing that is a little bit weird is the idea of the powerful curse, because back then a curse held much greater weight than it does today. But I think what we can do by taking it into a modern setting is that Rigoletto kind of self-fulfills the prophecy of the curse. It becomes much more of a psychological type of opera. But really, it's set in the Rat Pack time; I've heard many people say that using the Mafia, using the very idea of the power struggle between a boss and a guy who works for him is absolutely relevant today. The father-daughter relationship can be put in any time period, really, so any setting would have been great. I really like doing it in this modern period because it's a little more freedom to act in a contemporary way. People can relate to it. They've seen movies that take place in this time period; some people grew up in this time period, so they can see a picture of something that relates to them a little more closely.

OL - Now let's talk about Gilda. What are some of the vocal challenges you see in this role?

LO – All over the place. The entire role is extremely difficult. The aria "Caro nome" I've sung many times, ever since I was a young singer. Well, I'm still a young singer, but when I was a student. It never gets easier, because of where it comes in the opera. Gilda comes in and sings two very big duets and then sings "Caro nome." It is extremely exposed, and sits quite high. You have to be able to lift your voice again and make it sound exquisite because it is the aria people have been waiting to hear. And then in the second act when she has been raped and comes in to tell Rigoletto about what has happened, she sings "Tutte le feste," which sits much lower and musically is more dramatic. She is confessing something she is quite ashamed of, for the first time to her dad, so vocally it is much more difficult to place. And then the quartet and the storm trio are very loud, very full, energetically charged sections with heavy orchestration; and then the death scene is all high and very light and has a lot of dynamic contrast. So it is never easy; there is no moment in the role at all where I feel – "ah, I can relax now for a little bit!" Never. In fact the contrary is true because I need to be always warmed up, but not too warmed up because I don't want to get tired. It's an extremely difficult role.

OL - What about her psychology? Much has been said about whether the Duke raped her or not. In this production, he did. Still, she remains loyal to him. How does a modern woman like you relate to the psychological traits Gilda exhibits?

LO – Whether or not she was raped does change it a little bit, because if she was more willing, the ending makes more sense; it's easier for her to sacrifice herself for him. We understand it more as an audience. The fact that we do play this as a rape means that she is dealing with a different, perhaps abused, mindset. A lot of times you see women in an abusive relationship coming to the defense of their abuser. They don't go to the police, they don't tell other people, they make up excuses, they stay with him for a long, long time, they stay with him to their dying day. Why? Because psychologically they are insecure. They don't want to lose him. So I have to come at it from a point where this is a person who has been abused and perhaps has an insecurity there, a very deep insecurity. Also, the way that Rigoletto treats her...Rigoletto, the way we are doing it in our production, he is not the warm kind of sweet, loving daddy that will give everything for his child. His character is not like that anyway. No, he is very strict, he is very direct, he is very cold sometimes, he doesn't want to share, he doesn't want to have an open conversation – in a way it's another type of abuse that she is having to put up with.

Her decision in the end to throw herself into the sacrifice I think comes from an idea of feeling like there is nothing left to live for, and also coming from an idea of "this is what I want and I'll do anything to get it, I absolutely don't want him to be unhappy." She becomes so strong in the sense that she will sacrifice herself in the way a parent would sacrifice herself for a child. She becomes a parent for Rigoletto too; she sacrifices herself for him, because they will kill him too, maybe. It's a coming of strength.

OL - You're simultaneously singing Wagner while you are doing a full Gilda. Is it challenging to be at the Met involved in two different roles even though one part is smaller?

LO – Yes, despite the fact that the part of the Wood Bird is small, it doesn't matter. I have to come, I have to get dressed, I have a costume that they give me, I have to warm up, I have to prepare. And it's a tough little part, because it is sung with very challenging, spoken-type rhythms; it's all about the speech, all about the text. You can't just fly through it (no pun intended), you have to concentrate for the whole second act. So yes, and also going back and forth between *Rigoletto* and *Siegfried*, you're here, it's still a time commitment. I had two performances in one day, at one point.

OL - How do you feel about the current *Ring* production at the Met? Any thoughts on Lepage's Machine, which has been a bit controversial with opinions all for or all against it? I particularly find that it clutters such a huge stage like the Met's – is it half an asset, half an obstacle, or both?

LO - I do feel it's both. The assets are that you can project beautiful things on it, the planks can do different things, and be manipulated in really beautiful ways. For example, in *Das Rheingold*, when the giants come in they look like two giant hands, which I think is fascinating; it's a really cool thing that they can do. It can turn upside down and people can walk across it. It turns the entire world where the *Ring* is set on its head. At the same time in operas like *Die Walküre* where the characters are having a one-on-one relationship, then sometimes the set can seem overwhelming like it's in the way, because the drama between the characters is overshadowed by this giant thing looming there. I feel that there is a balance. That's why you have to have great singers and great actors. But really, you have to have space in order to express these great emotions, especially in *Die Walküre.*

OL - Now let's focus on you and your career. Your parents emigrated to the U.S. from Cuba, and your mother is an opera singer – also a soprano. She put her career on hold to raise a family, but music must have been an important part of your childhood. Do you sing with her? The tenors Daniel Behle and Björn Casapietra have both made recordings with their mothers, the sopranos Renate Behle and Celestina Casapietra. Now that you're established in your career, have you and your mother ever given a concert together or performed in a program together? Is this something you may want to do in the future?

LO – I would like to plan to sing a concert with her. She doesn't know that yet but I'm going to try to get her to do that. There are some plans in the works.

OL - How early did you begin to take voice lessons? Did you study with your mother?

LO – I studied with her my whole life. I never took formal voice lessons from anyone except her, until I went to college and I studied as a voice student. My mother all my life gave me a very good foundation of singing, because she was always singing, always practicing. I was in Church all the time singing with her, and listening to her and imitating her. Sometimes to be funny but even as a small child I was singing in an operatic way. For years, while I grew up she developed my voice very well and gave me an appreciation and an understanding of what it is supposed to sound like, from a very young age.

OL – What age?

LO – Oh, very small, I was singing when I was three. I have recordings of myself when I was three years old.

OL - When you were 21 you won the Metropolitan Opera's National Council Auditions. How did you prepare yourself for this competition? Any memories of the event to share with us? How was it psychologically for you, to come and win it?

LO - Well, I didn't think I would win it. I didn't even think that I would make the finals, or the semifinals for that matter because it was the first time I had ever done a major competition. I thought I would maybe make the regional and that would be it. But I just kept progressing and progressing, and I was just in shock the whole time, because things were going so well, and eventually I realized that I had a shot at winning it. I learned a lot because you get coachings from people here for that whole week between the semifinals and the finals. You coach and work every day. And I realized "this is really serious stuff." So, I was very nervous.

OL – So, did you go directly from that to the Lindemann? Did the competition open that door?

LO – Yes, exactly. When I was here during the competition they asked me if I was interested in the Young Artists Program and I said yes. So the week after I won the finals, I came back and sang an audition for Maestro Levine and the rest of the faculty for the Young Artists Program. They invited me to join the program that very day. I moved up here that summer and started my work here.

OL – What does a program like this do for a young singer? You have coaching, and languages…?

LO – Coaching, languages, and more. There is a set of people who run the program, a set of singers, and pianists. We all work together and we also work separately. We have coachings with the young artist pianists, and when I was in the program, John Fisher who would coach us several times a week, Ken Noda also worked with us a lot; on top of the musical part, we also had language coachings several times a week. We had many, many master classes with different opera singers – Renata Scotto, Mirella Freni, Sir Thomas Allen, it was a lot of people. I was always getting something from someone all the time. It's like school. And we got to see all the final dress rehearsals of the operas.

OL – How long does it last?

LO – It's three years. For international students it's two.

OL – It's probably better than any college.

LO – Yes, it's school of music times ten.

OL - You were still in the Lindemann Program when you sang your first major role at the Met, Susanna in *Le Nozze di Figaro*, with Erwin Schrott. It sounds a little like a Hollywood script, but I think you were replacing another soprano and made a great success of it. Were you nervous at all when you found out you would be singing one of the leading roles? What was going through your mind then?

LO – Yes, I was covering, and the leading soprano was pregnant, and quite far along. I remember getting a phone call and being asked to sing the final dress and first performance. I was nervous because I had had very little rehearsal. It felt very last minute, but that's how it happens sometimes...as a cover you have to be prepared for the most sudden changes. Looking back, I think probably it wasn't the easiest way to make a big role debut. I had only sung very small roles at the Met before. I had been on the stage, I had been with the orchestra, I had been in the process but I had never done a big, big role like that. So I was very nervous. But as soon as the curtain went up I just said, "you know, it's Mozart, I love Mozart, I am just going to sing it like I love it and do my best, I know that I have the energy, the enthusiasm for the role." It ended up being a huge success.

OL - Since then, you've sung a variety of roles at the Met and worked with other major international stars. In 2008, you sang Lisette in a production of *La Rondine* with Angela Gheorghiu and Roberto Alagna. What was it like working with them?

LO – Wonderful! I loved being in *La Rondine*. That was the first time I had done a pretty large role in a new production in HD. So, I was very excited to see how that was going to work. Everybody was coming to see us in the theater and we were wearing all these cool costumes, 1920's stuff. I loved Gheorghiu and Alagna, I'm a huge fan of both of them. They were so gracious! Wonderful colleagues! I have a funny story. One time in a performance I had forgotten a prop. I was supposed to have a notepad that I was supposed to give to Roberto Alagna and tell him to write something down and I didn't have it in my pocket. And I reached in my pocket for it and it wasn't there. I didn't know what to do; I was in the middle of the performance. I looked at him like "I don't have it." And I tried to telepathically tell him, "memorize what I am going to tell you instead of writing it." And he communicated back "OK" and he played along, "yes, I'll remember that." Then he went in his pocket and pulled out a pencil – I don't know how or why he had that – and he wrote down on his hand what I was telling him. And I thought, "he is a genius." It was the nicest thing he could have done because he totally fixed the whole situation. He is the perfect professional.

OL – Super interesting, thanks for sharing that.

LO – Oh, sure!

OL - At the Met, you also created the role of Miranda in the Baroque pasticcio, *The Enchanted Island.* There is controversy about it. Many European commentators didn't like it, and kept complaining about singing in English these baroque arias. I found it spectacular, I loved the idea of a modern pastiche in English, going back to Baroque music. What were your memories of that? Is there a difference in the way you prepare a role in a pastiche and the way you prepare a role in one of the standard repertoire operas?

LO – Yes, the preparation was a little different because it wasn't an established piece. Everything was kind of tailored to the artist. I didn't have any say in what I was singing, but the people with the bigger roles had more collaboration, being able to say "I want to sing this aria," or "I don't want to sing this one," "this key is good for me," things like that. As we were going, sometimes they would rewrite things. People would say, "you know, this recitative is not so comfortable for me, maybe we should rewrite it like that." It was very much like working on a brand new piece. But at the same time, we were doing different, obviously established, composers so we had to remain respectful to the style. I loved the production, I thought it was fantastic and beautiful as well, I think it was gorgeous to watch and very fun to be a part of. The story was interesting and neat in the way it all came together. The cast was phenomenal. I really feel like it was one of the greatest successes we've ever had at the Met.

OL - You have a wide-ranging repertoire, from Baroque roles to Wagner. How would you characterize your voice in terms of Fach – in what kind of role you feel most comfortable in terms of tessitura and agility?

LO – I always say I'm a lyric coloratura. I'm not a straight coloratura because I don't live in the extreme top. My voice can move, but I don't think I'm a full lyric. Maybe not yet. I'm a lyric, but with coloratura. That's what I think.

OL - Two of the roles you've sung, Lucia di Lammermoor and Konstanze in *The Abduction From the Seraglio*, are both very demanding technically. Is Lucia the most difficult role you've sung so far? At times Mozart can also be quite difficult.

LO – You know, Konstanze is more difficult for me than Lucia, because Lucia is bel canto. Not that Konstanze is not. "Everything is bel canto," that's what I say, or should be sung like bel canto. Lucia though, the way it is written, has more of an arc for the character to develop. It's not as long a role as Konstanze. Konstanze's arias are extremely difficult, all three of them. And she has the duet with Belmonte which is huge. Then, the quartet, which is also huge; it's a big, big sing, and the orchestra is full blast. So I find *Abduction*'s Konstanze to be one of the most challenging roles in my repertoire.

OL - In addition to appearing with several U.S. companies, you've also sung with the Welsh National Opera, the Deutsche Oper am Rhein at Duisburg, and the Bavarian State Opera in Munich. Do you plan to remain based in the United States, or are you seeking more career opportunities overseas? Is performing at other major international houses one of your goals?

LO – I love living here. I want to stay based in New York when possible, but I definitely want to work in all of the great houses in Europe. My dream of course is to have a wonderful international career, and be able to sing in all the great houses; it would be a dream come true.

OL - Zarzuela has been an important part of the culture in Spanish-speaking countries, with Plácido Domingo and Montserrat Caballé, among others, both singing zarzuela roles. Cuba has its own particular zarzuela tradition – and you won the Zarzuela Award at the 2007 Operalia competition. Would you like to make of Zarzuela a part of your career as it progresses, and to advocate for its diffusion especially in the United States?

LO – It's very hard to get the opportunity to do a Zarzuela here. I'm not a big enough star yet that I can say "I want to sing this Zarzuela in Miami, put it on for me." If I were, then yes. Basically Plácido Domingo is the one who spearheads that repertoire here. Zarzuela is popular in Spain and in Cuba, and I would love to be able to do one, because I do feel like it's a beautiful art form. Especially in major cities in the US that have a giant Spanish-speaking population, like Miami, Houston, Los Angeles, places with a huge Hispanic community – it would mean a lot to them. I do want to try it, later on. I have an interest, and people have asked me about it, "please sing Zarzuelas!"

OL - In November, 2008, you participated in your first Lieder recital with the Met's Chamber Ensemble performing Brahms' *Liebeslieder Waltzes* with James Levine and Daniel Barenboim. Do you plan to include more Lieder concerts in your schedule in the future?

LO – Yes, I love German Lieder. I think that Lieder is very special. Right now I'm focusing a lot on opera but I do want to do more recitals because it's very intimate, and in a lot of ways more challenging than singing an operatic role, because you don't have the sets and the costumes and the acting to really distract people; it's just you and the piano! Yes, I have done a very nice recital with Ken Noda playing the piano. I shared the recital with another singer, his name is Brian Mulligan and he is a baritone; it was for the George London Foundation. And that was very special. It takes a lot of preparation; it's like preparing a role.

OL – Yes, singers I interview often tell me it's more difficult, because you don't have an arc, you don't have pauses to go off the stage for long stretches of an act, you have to mix different sub-genres and try to adapt your voice up and down, then it all gets to be more exhausting than singing a role in an opera.

LO – Absolutely! When I did that recital, I did Bizet, some songs by Mozart, arias from *La Sonnambula* and *Lucia*, a lot of stuff, so, yes, it can be very tiring.

OL - You've sung two leading roles, Gilda in *Rigoletto*, and Leïla in *The Pearl Fishers*, with the New Orleans Opera. It must have been a tremendous experience to go back and sing with your hometown company. What was it like when you came back there?

LO – Easy! Wonderful! Not easy as in "I don't care," but easy as in "Oh so nice!" Because when you are at home everybody knows you, everybody grew up with you; you always have wonderful support. The New Orleans Opera has treated me so, so well! Even after the hurricane, right when I went there to do *Rigoletto*. We had a very limited kind of rehearsal space, and a small theater that was mopped up for us to work, but it was very touching.

OL – How are things there, now? The main Performance Arts Center there, the Mahalia Jackson Theater, fortunately did not suffer a lot of damage, but economically there is a hit, as people dealing with the losses don't have as much disposable income, the population of the city has decreased, and so forth.

LO – They are better now, they are trying to keep their seasons going, but they don't do as many operas year round. But they've been revamping their seasons. Now that they are back at the Mahalia Jackson they are doing a lot better.

OL - The tenor Bryan Hymel, who is also from New Orleans, is making quite a name for himself as well. Have you and Mr. Hymel ever had an opportunity to meet?

LO – Yes, I have met Bryan Hymel. That's right! We've known of each other for many years, though I can't say that I'm close to him because we've never had the opportunity to work together, but we study with the same teacher here in New York, Bill Schuman. So we run into each other, and he is doing so well, I'm so happy for him! He is a marvelous, marvelous singer, and a very nice guy, so I'm glad that he's been so successful.

OL - When you've been back in Louisiana, have you ever been able to stop by Baton Rouge to visit Louisiana State University, perhaps speak with some of the voice students there?

LO – Yes, as a matter of fact I was there just a few months ago, giving a master class to some students and doing some small coachings. I have always taken voice lessons with my teacher there, Robert Grayson, and it's always great to see him again and catch up; I love to go home any chance I get to see my family.

Lisette's master class in Lousiana, personal picture

OL - Now that you're well established in your career, what advice would you give those who are still studying? What are some of the things to which the young singers should pay particular attention? Well, I'm saying that, but you are also very young, you are thirty, right?

LO – Twenty-nine, I'm not thirty yet! [laughs] Usually, it's just giving them ideas about how to interpret whatever piece they are doing. Sometimes, I teach them concepts about breath support because what I've noticed with young singers is that they need to learn how to manipulate their breath so that it works for your singing – I still have this challenge too; we all do. I try to give them a little advice on how to sing with your breath without a lot of pressure on your voice. I also pay attention to language issues when I hear them.

OL – What about career advice, and risks associated with it?

LO – Yes, I often get a lot of questions about the career. I try to be very honest with them about what it is really like, in our world. It is extremely competitive. There is not a lot of work to go around and there are a lot of singers, all trying to get the same roles. I tell them about the risks of putting in a lot of work and not always being successful, but they need to always stay positive, always work hard, and never feel defeated or feel that you aren't good enough. A singer will do a competition and not win and not ever know why. There are lots of factors. No one ever tells them, "you have a problem with your top" or "your voice is too small" or "you are too young" or "you are overweight" or "we don't like the way you dressed today." Rarely does a judge tell singers these things. So they go into it blind. They think they may have sounded great, but perhaps aren't aware of the little things that can derail them. So it's very important to be honest with them about what the issues are and how to fix them. Also what teh career is like financially...you don't learn about that in college, so yes, I'm very real with them.

OL – You were fortunate to have been to the Lindemann and all, but I was interviewing another young singer, Jessica Pratt from Australia who is having a nice career in Italy, and she was saying that these days there isn't enough mentoring. You escaped this fate, but for others, often people are thrown in the fire by greedy agents who want them to make a splash and make some quick bucks but then their voices get damaged and they get discarded for the benefit of the next wave.

LO – I think it's like that in any business. It's very cut-throat. And because we are singers, we are like athletes. You come in in your prime, you have a very good voice for a little while, you look great for a little while, and it is very much up to you, personally, to manage your voice. At the end of the day the only person who is responsible for it is you. You are the one who can say, "yes, I want to sing this role, but no, I don't want to sing that role." You have to be your best advocate all the time, and sometimes it means you must turn some things down, you have to put your tough shoes on and stand on your own, because a lot of people will try to manipulate you into doing things you know are not right, so you have to have good technique but also good understanding of your technique and who you are as an artist, and not let anybody mess with that.

OL - Many of today's stars mention great singers who were their role models when they were studying or beginning their careers. Did you or do you have a singer or singers whom you consider role models for your approach to singing, other than your mother?

LO – Yes, there are a lot of singers today whom I adore. I love Renée Fleming. I think she is one of the most incredible artists alive, one of the most fabulous singers, and incredibly intelligent. She knows so many languages, she is marvelous. I love Natalie Dessay, there are things she does, when I watch her, that move me so deeply, more than any other artist. I love everybody. You can learn something from everyone. Of course I listen to Callas and I adore Callas, I listen to her interviews, how she thought about things, how she approached things, and Scotto, I can go on and on. [laughs]

OL – Yes, and since you've been immersed in opera since age three, you were exposed to a lot of singers.

LO – Absolutely!

OL - You're active on both Facebook and Twitter. How important are social media for your career?

LO – Nowadays it is important because we are trying to build a younger fan base, get people exposed to opera from a younger age. The better you can do that, the better we will have people in the future coming to the opera and keeping it alive. And young people are so enthusiastic about opera, they really are! People send me messages every day about how much they loved the productions, or ask questions about something. Sometimes they are younger singers, sometimes they are audience members or fans. It is important to always remain open as an artist to younger singers because they look up to you, they want to pursue that, they get excited about it, they tell their friends, and that's how you build fans. If you keep opera only in the theater, it becomes very closed; a very closed world, and we want to branch out.

OL – What about outreach? With your background, you could be instrumental in addressing the Hispanic kids. In Venezuela, for example, there was a concerted movement to get disadvantaged kids who were involved in gangs, in touch with classical music, with wonderful results. Would you like to be involved in this kind of activism?

LO – I haven't had that opportunity yet, but when I was in Miami doing Pamina I participated in a lot of outreach, doing interviews and posting a lot of stuff in Twitter aimed at the young Hispanic community, although it wasn't a lot of outreach like going to a school and doing a performance there. It hasn't happened to me yet but I definitely believe in sharing with kids and with the younger community so that they see it is a safe and exciting place. In Miami they do invite students to the dress rehearsals, and the Met does that too, they invite kids to come to the final dress, which is huge, because sometimes it's their first experience with opera ever. You don't know who is in that audience – twenty years from now those kids could be running the Met. So yes, this kind of thing is extremely important.

OL – How is this coming season shaping up for you?

LO - This coming 2013-2014 season is one that I'm looking forward to greatly. I am making my debut with the Santa Fe Opera as Susanna in *Le Nozze di Figaro*, as well as participating in two new productions at the Met, both of which will be featured in HD. The first is *Falstaff*, where I'll be singing Nanetta; the second is *Werther*, where I'll be Sophie. In addition, I'll be performing in concert with the Pittsburgh Symphony in *Carmina Burana*, and will appear with the Washington Concert Opera in a single performance of Verdi's *I Masnadieri*. This is a season I'm really looking forward to!

OL – Besides opera and your family, what other interests do you have in life?

LO – First of all I have my husband whom I love so much! I'm very active in health and fitness. I used to be very overweight and I came to the Met and found out that losing weight would help me a lot, so I began to go into a fitness and health journey that has lasted for many years. A lot of people asked me how could I do it, and how should they do it, and I'm actually part of a couple of groups on Facebook that are health groups for singers. We all contribute and share information, and that's one thing I often get a lot of messages from young singers about – "I want to lose weight and I don't know how; can you give me some advice?" Health and fitness are a big part of my life. I run Marathons, I'm a vegan on a 100% plant based diet, I practice Yoga; I have a very strong connection with health and fitness. That's my other big thing.

OL – There's always a debate about looks in the current operatic environment but we do have some larger ladies who are able to have great careers, like Angela Meade and Leah Crocetto, who remain relevant in this

Live in HD and Blu-Ray disc era even though the emphasis on looks has been so intense. A few decades ago ladies like Montserrat Caballé were loved by everybody in spite of their body weight. But some of the younger singers today are experiencing a lot of pressure around this issue. Do you think this new emphasis on looks and fitness is a good thing, or is it limiting the talent pool for opera, since genes that codify for a great vocal instrument don't necessarily come together with genes that codify for great looks and a healthy body type?

LO – I do feel like it is important. Even Pavarotti said this. Singers are athletes. When you are on stage and you are singing, it's not just your voice, it's your abdomen, it's your entire body, you are moving around, you are getting up, you are sitting, you are going upstairs, you have to use your body. It's not just about your voice. You have to use your face, you have to use your expression. When you are up there and you are overweight, it's not just about how you look, it's about how you feel. Even Callas said this; she was getting too heavy. If you are overweight it's harder for you to climb upstairs, it's harder for you to keep your breath calm. When you get nervous and you are heavy, your heart is beating out of your chest and you sweat and you get uncomfortable. You sweat through your costume. It's not just about looking pretty. Looking pretty is fine, everyone loves to see someone beautiful on stage, we can't say as an audience we don't appreciate that, but also, it shouldn't be beautiful people who can't sing. Because we don't want that either; I absolutely don't agree with that at all. It's very important that your voice be in tip-top condition first; absolutely, it's the most important part. But you cannot neglect your health as a singer, because you are using your body. If you maintain a healthy lifestyle, you don't get sick as often, you recover more quickly, you don't sweat as much on stage, you are physically more agile and stronger, you are in a better mood, you are more confident, you sleep better, and all those are things that will boost your career. Fine, you look better too; yes, absolutely, you have better skin, you have healthier hair, whatever, all that is fine, yes, you look better. But absolutely, at the end of the day, your health is what makes of you the best singer that you can be, so don't neglect that.

OL – How are you as a person? How do you define your personality? Are you reserved, or outgoing? Would you share with our readers something on the person underneath the artist?

LO – [laughs] Yes, I took one of these personality tests, the Myers Briggs, you know what that is?

OL – Yes, I'm a psychiatrist and psychoanalyst.

LO – Oh my God, that's why you are asking this question! [laughs hard]. OK, here is what I am: I'm introverted, intuitive, feeling, and judging.

OL – Wow, I always ask this question in my interviews, and that's the most precise answer to this question I've ever heard from a singer! [laughs]

LO – [laughs hard] I think it's very important every day to wake up and find a reason for happiness. I believe that happiness is a choice. Keeping a positive attitude is very important. I'm not always a happy-go-lucky but I try and make every effort to be happy.

OL – Do you fear a bit that the meteoric success you've been having at such a young age might change too many aspects of your life, such as making family life more difficult and so forth?

LO – That is true. It's a big challenge. In fact I just had a conversation with my mother, who is here this weekend to see *Rigoletto.* Yes, it does take a toll on your routine – because you have no routine. You have no schedule. Every day you have a different set of things that you have to do. Sometimes you have to wake up in the morning and sing at 10 AM. Sometimes you have to sing at 11 PM. You have to maintain a certain look all the time, you have to maintain a certain persona. When you go to rehearsals you have to act professional, you can't dress like a slob and go to a rehearsal, you have to maintain a certain level of integrity as a professional. And you have to find a way to balance your time, because if you just live and eat and breathe opera, and you only think about opera 24/7 which is very easy to do, you go crazy, because you have nothing else to share in your heart, except opera singing, and it can be very stressful because then everything becomes about your voice, 24/7. I never wanted that to happen to me. I always wanted to be free to express myself, because I've been singing like I said since I was three years old, it came naturally to me.

OL – Some people will get into all sorts of rituals; they can't do this or that because they will sing tonight. For you, it does seem like it comes more naturally, you've been doing it your entire life. So, you are granting us an interview just minutes before you'll be singing on the Met stage. Most singers will say they won't grant an interview right before a performance.

LO – [laughs] Well, I have a very small part tonight [editor's note – Ms. Oropesa was about to sing the wood bird in Siegfried]. If I were singing Gilda tonight, I'd have said that we needed to pick another time. But I can't sit in bed and watch TV and wait for my performance. I do have a routine that I go through when I have something big and it is very stressful.

Running and exercising help me a lot with managing stress. I'm very lucky that I have a wonderful partner in my life who has always been so supportive and loving. I'm never alone, I never travel alone, he always travels with me. I actually feel very blessed.

OL – Good for you! Are you guys planning to have kids?

LO – No! [laughs] Not yet!

OL – Just like my daughter. I don't have grandchildren, but I do have a grand cat. She has cats.

LO – You have a grand cat! I love it!

OL – Thank you so much! This was really a lovely interview!

LO – Thank you! Thank you so much!

Isabel Leonard, both mezzo-soprano and soprano

Back to back, we get another great young American singer with a meteoric career, Isabel Leonard, and she is just as personable and friendly as Lisette. We met her over lunch in the Upper West Side in New York City, just recently in March 2014, around her *Così fan tutte* run.

Luiz Gazzola for Opera Lively - Mozart's music in this piece has a sensual beauty. He also does ensembles in this opera at his best – this is the quintessential ensemble piece. "Soave sia il vento" is arguably one of the most beautiful pieces of music ever composed. Please comment on the music of *Così fan tutte.*

Isabel Leonard – I do think that in *Così* Mozart did two things very well. Well, he does everything very well, but in this piece he did something so wonderful with the characters! The music he writes for each character is very specific to their temperament and their personality. With the rhythm and the way the line is written, he paints the picture of these characters in those musical lines. Then, of course, he manages to take all of these characters who are so different one from another, and put them together in ensembles where they become a unison voice. That's a wonderful and incredible thing, and very harmonic.

OL – What is your take on Dorabella's personality? Some people feels that she comes across as shallow or ditsy, but I'd say she is vivacious and spontaneous and unguarded, and she's also young and inexperienced. What is the key to singing and acting a good Dorabella? Are there vocal challenges, or is it an easy sing?

IL – Dorabella is a very tricky character to play because she is outwardly the first one to give in, so to speak. Everybody thinks that this means she is shallow or easy, but I always play her, personally, by remembering where the story comes from and what kind of history and cultural education these girls have. I feel that really helps understand their actions. For me, any great comedy comes from some sort of tragedy. In this tragedy, the girls, or Dorabella at least, truly believe that maybe they will be alone. If Ferrando dies, she will live alone, and at that time, that's not a good thing for a woman. So, I go with this. For me, this is a truth that I can understand. I don't necessarily relate to it, because as a 21st century woman it is very different, but I can allow myself to accept it.

Then, as I play Dorabella it is not hard for me. I don't judge myself playing her. I don't judge her choices, because one can't play a character and judge oneself at the same time. It is important to me to believe all the choices I make as Dorabella and to believe they are the right choices for her. You have to put yourself in a position where you believe in her truth. For me, her truth is that she flies by the seat of her pants. She does things, and thinks about them later. However, she does have that, in my mind: the fear of being alone. She is trying to make sure that she ensures her future, and her sister's future. She says it very clearly in the second act. She says "Fra un ben certo e un incerto c'è sempre gran divario." [Acto II, cena decima, recitativo – Between something certain and something uncertain there is always a big gap]. At that time, it is true. She is just saying, "this is what is going on right now. This is the truth of our situation at this moment. We don't know if they are coming back from the war." And it's true; I think we can relate to it today if we allow ourselves to get into *Così fan tutte* on the dramatic level, and not just see it as a kind of light comedy, because it is not.

In terms of singing, Dorabella is not an easy role to sing. It may sound easy because it is not necessarily very high nor very low; however, the arias for Fiordiligi are easier for me to sing, because Dorabella's arias actually sit higher in the vocal range. The ensembles are lower.

Everybody in that cast sings the whole show. Three hours of music nonstop is a lot of singing. For Dorabella, as a second soprano role, one of the biggest challenges is that you are not only singing harmonies – I love singing harmonies – but in the harmony position you are always following someone else's lead, generally speaking, which means that on a purely technical level as a singer spending three hours of always following someone else's instrument means that you never take a bow the way your muscles are meant to. You do it the way somebody else is doing it, so you are fitting in to somebody else's musculature all the time, and it took me years to find comfort in Dorabella.

OL – Wow, I wouldn't have imagined it! The issue of misogyny of course comes back every time we talk about *Così fan tutte*. However I don't really agree that this opera is misogynistic. What Alfonso demonstrates is that if we apply to people different standards than the ones we apply to ourselves, we run into trouble. He says "everyone accuses women, but I excuse them even if they have a thousand changes of affection in a day. Some might call it a vice, others a habit, but to me it seems a necessity of the heart." Alfonso's message in my opinion is that we are all human. I think it's rather an avant-garde view, for Lorenzo da Ponte's time. What is your take on this?

IL – Don Alfonso is a very interesting character. Most agree that Mozart was ahead of his time, and very provocative not only in this opera but others as well. Emotionally, in the time period, he liked to create a bit of a ruckus. *The Marriage of Figaro* was a big deal, pitting the classes against each other. *Così fan tutte* brings up a lot of issues that people didn't want to discuss at the time. I would have loved to see the first ever performance of *Così* and its response. Today, the issues which are raised in *Così fan tutte* depend on how the show is produced and who the director is. It can be very simplistic if you just go along with the text and you do the show the way it was written. It's a hard question to answer. Mozart likes to provoke uncomfortable feelings and delve into subjects which force a dialogue and in my opinion whether then or in the future, provoke social evolution.

As an actor in the opera, I have chosen not to try and fully understand Don Alfonso's intentions, because for me, the girls cannot fully understand his intentions. That's the whole thing: they don't understand what is happening. They don't understand why this was done to them, or why this is done to all four of them in the first place. For me, I don't agree, of course, with the way things are handled in the opera. I don't agree with the hurt. I find it sad, but depending on the director and everything, my job is to tell a story that is clear, and make the audience think about whatever is going on.

OL - Conductor Iván Fischer, talking about *Così fan tutte*, says "everybody is seducible, all of us, regardless of what we think about our own morals." What would you say to this?

IL – Well, I think it depends on what we are talking about. If we are talking about seducing a person romantically I don't know, because everyone has their own experiences. I suppose everyone has weaknesses. I know that I can be so-called seduced by a piece of chocolate, if I really want a piece of chocolate. I may say to myself "no, I shouldn't have it," but the truth is that I will have it. Everybody has their Achilles' heel; that's what I can say. I think some people are very good at protecting it, and others are sometimes in a position where they can't protect it, and it's not their fault. They can't. What about Zerlina! All the women in *Don Giovanni*, or Cherubino, the Countess, the Count! Roméo and Juliette… "Seduction" has a bad rap, but as everyone knows, it doesn't always have to be "bad".

OL - After all that they go through, people are not necessarily put together again at the end. How do you interpret the end of *Così fan tutte*? What do you think would happen next to these characters, if the opera continued in real life?

IL - If *Così* happened today, again, it depends on the people. I imagine for myself, I probably would move on with the new partner or neither at all. Ultimately, I don't think we know what we would do and that is why this opera always creates so much discussion.

OL – The opera seems to have a message of rationality. This piece involves the stripping away of romantic illusions. It pleads for rationality, for the age of enlightenment. Alfonso's tactics are brutal. But he is a man of reason. He says "happy is the man who looks at everything on the bright side and allows himself to be guided by reason." Do you agree?

IL – It's funny, because when you say rationality, I don't think of any of the things that happen to them throughout the opera as rational. I think of them as ludicrous. Despina coming in dressed up twice is ludicrous. The fact the girls can't recognize their men dressed up as Albanians is ludicrous! That wouldn't happen today, I don't think. Perhaps, decades later and other major physical changes could create that scenario… but, rational, nope.

OL – But this is an interesting thing, because Mozart didn't want them to wear a lot of disguise. In terms of stage directions, he wanted them to be recognizable.

IL – Is that in the libretto?

OL – No, but it is mentioned in historical accounts.

IL – Well, it does say in the score they come dressed as Albanians, not much detail as to how recognizable or not. Going with this thought though, I can argue it is a way of being provocative. It could mean several things. Either the couples don't really know each other that well in the first place, or it's about what happens to a person when they are under so much distress. Not only it is said that you are blinded by love, you can be blinded by distress, and the women are very distressed when the men leave, and they lose sight. They have to start functioning in their new reality, which is, the possibility of them not having the men there ever again.

OL – What do you think of this current production of *Così*, and particularly, the emotion of having maestro Levine back in the podium?

IL – Having Levine back is wonderful. There is just no doubt about it. It is wonderful to work with someone who enjoys making good music and has a deep connection with his singers. He supports us, as we support him. I don't romanticize about these situations, because the truth of them is that they are the best of all worlds. It is why we do what we do, to work with someone who is not only dedicated to his craft but is also dedicated to the people on stage. For me it's very simple. It means – we are going to work, and we are going to put on a good performance, a good show, because that's what our job is: to do this, and to do well, to our best ability, so that the audience can experience this fabulous thing. To have him there means that we are going to do that, and that's what's wonderful to me.

OL – You've done this role many times, in gorgeous productions. I particularly like the very modern one you did in Salzburg. Any comments on that one or interesting memories about it?

IL – The Salzburg production was the first time that I sang Dorabella. It was a challenge for me to do it for the first time in such a modern production, where the concept was turned upside down on its head. Like every production that I do, no matter how I feel about the production, or if it is difficult to understand conceptually, it's my job to make sense of it and to tell that story. That's what I do.

OL – Let's now talk about other products in your discography. I'd like you to comment on the experience of having been part of two extraordinary productions that got recorded on video – *The Tempest*, and *Giulio Cesare*.

Let's start with *The Tempest*, in which you sang Miranda. What do you think of the piece, and what are your memories from that production?

IL – *The Tempest* was a fabulous experience. We all knew we were part of something special from the first rehearsal with Thomas Adès. He is a fantastic man, so kind and patient! Adès has an incredible compositional voice. It's his voice. It comes through and it is wonderful. His music is complex and tricky to learn, but once you've got it, it's as natural as anything else that you've done. Of course, I loved working with Simon Keenlyside, Alek Shrader, and Audrey Luna. The experience brought us all together and we have remained friends.

OL – What about the *Giulio Cesare*?

IL – Another first. It was a very different experience. I was in France, and my son was only seven months old. I don't think I slept at all, maybe two hours at a time, every day. So, I don't remember a lot [laughs], at all! However, I remember enjoying my colleagues very much. I remember developing a friendship with Laurent Pelly. We've worked together since then, in different projects. I adore him!

OL – I interviewed him too, and found him brilliant.

IL – Yes, I like him so much! We were in Japan together doing *L'Enfant et les Sortilèges*, and *L'Heure Espagnole*. We had so much fun!

OL – Was it the same production he did in Glyndebourne, which was visually stunning?

IL – Yes, great evening.

OL – Another great production you were part of was *Dialogue des Carmélites* at the Met in 2013. What can you tell us about that one?

IL - *Dialogue des Carmélites* was absolutely fantastic! It was an acting and musical experience different than most of the other pieces I've done so far. I loved working with David Kneuss [stage director]. I love everything about the piece and the role of Blanche. Sometimes I sing soprano roles, sometimes mezzo, it depends on what fits. I speak French and love the French language, so it's very easy for me to get into it and I like to dig my fingers into the dirt of the situation. I had read books about that time period, about the Carmelite nuns and their history… It was very interesting for me to be a part of it.

It had also been my very first opera when I was in college! Frank Corsaro directed *Dialogue des Carmélites* when I was a freshman at Juilliard, and I was in the chorus. So for me to go from being in the chorus as a freshman, to last spring singing Blanche… was an incredible journey.

OL – Let's talk about your training a little bit. You are a native New Yorker and trained at Juilliard, steps from the Met. Any interesting memories of that phase?

IL – Juilliard was wonderful. I did my undergrad, my Masters and one year of an Artist Diploma. Thanks to my wonderful voice teacher and all the other incredible teachers and coaches I had, all of this has been made into a possibility.

OL – You studied with Marilyn Horne. How was it for you, to train with such a legend?

IL – I worked with Marilyn Horne in Santa Barbara, at the Music Academy of the West for a summer festival. She was the one that introduced me to Matthew Epstein, who became my manager, so she was very instrumental in launching my career. Working with her was really fun! I would bring in all this repertoire that she's done, like *Cenerentola,* and she would have me singing fun ornaments, just for fun, "try this, try that," and we'd play around.

She is an incredible woman, and someone whom I admire so much for what she has done, and especially for what she gives back. I am involved in education as much as possible and I will continue on this path alongside performing. Mrs. Horne has done and continues to do this. She is really an incredible model. It's admirable. It's an honorable thing to do, as an artist, to not just do your art, but to educate and inspire others, because that's how art is perpetuated. The only way is to inspire others to do it as well. She does that.

OL – You won numerous awards. Was it nerve-wrecking? Do you feel that this is an important path for a young singer? The Beverly Sills one must have been very special.

IL – I did only a few competitions. I was very lucky and very blessed to win some of these awards where they call you and they say, "Oh, you won an award!" and you kind of think "Why on Earth? I haven't done anything!" [laughs] In some ways there is more pressure because you think "Why me?" when at the same time it is great recognition. People think artists are the most self-assured people, but generally speaking they are not. Most can be pretty insecure, or unsure of themselves, so to receive any sort of recognition or to receive thanks, really it is a very good thing for an artist. I mean, everybody wants to know that they are doing a good job. I want to be doing a good job as a mother. If someone were to give me the New York City Best Mom Award, I would be thrilled! [laughs] Of course I would still think "No, I'm sure you are wrong" but everybody wants that kind of recognition.

OL – Great answer! Is the rapid rise to fame something that ever gets difficult to deal with, on a personal level?

IL – Well, I don't know if it's rapid or not. I don't really have anything to compare it to. I started working pretty young, because I didn't do any Young Artist Programs. I feel for me it actually has been pretty steady. I haven't sky-rocketed out of any one place. I have been working professionally very hard for eight years, and seven in school prior to that . All I can say is I've been working really hard for a long time and hopefully it won't stop. I have loads more I want to learn, experience and create.

OL – You have accomplished quite a lot already for a young singer. What are your remaining career goals? Where do you see your voice taking you?

IL - I hope for a slow and continuous development; to continue evolving appropriately in the different aspects of my life and career; not only to perpetuate work in the business of music, but in the world of music; to think about the question: what do people need? Audiences need different things as time goes on, and I believe it is my duty to present an experience to them that hopefully enhances their own lives in some way, however small. Music is an incredible binding force. I will be very fortunate if I can do this until I'm quite old and grey (well, I may go grey pretty soon).

OL – What would be your advice for a young singer starting today?

IL – For a young singer, I honestly don't know. I can't project too far into the future. It's hard enough to do this when we sign contracts three or four years in advance. I try not to project too much. For me, it's about staying healthy every day; singing as healthily as I can. I have other responsibilities in my life aside from my job, and so for me it's not about where my career is going to be in the next ten years; it is rather, where will my life be in the next ten years? What kind of life would make me happy? How do I find the incredibly difficult balance between life and this crazy career? I surely don't have any answers. For a young singer, the biggest thing I would say is make sure you get your technique sorted out. Technique is a very important thing.

OL – What about the business side, the exposure side, what would you say to a young singer?

IL - Everybody is different. If young singers like doing competitions, then by all means, do competitions. If you don't really like competitions and you find it to be a situation that makes you nervous, or freeze up, I wouldn't say it is necessary. Competitions don't really give you a career. Some of them put you in the forefront. The National Council Auditions give you more exposure. Auditions have you heard by certain people. But aside from the Met National Council, I don't know of a career that was launched solely by the winning of one competition. There is so much more than that! It's about working and learning all sorts of different things – how to sing, how to be in the theater, how to be a good colleague, learning all about yourself, being a performer; it's a lot.

OL – Going further back, how did opera come to be your career choice?

IL – Opera just sort of happened to me. I went to Juilliard because I wanted to learn how to sing properly. I wasn't sure at the end of High School if I wanted to do musical theater or opera. I went there because I thought "this is where I will get the best musical education" and it turned out to be the right place for me, and there I was entrenched in classical music, classical art songs, and I loved it. That's the direction I was trained in, but it doesn't mean I wouldnt want to go back and sing with a jazz band like I did in High School or sing musical theater. I would love to do *Camelot, Showboat*, and *Kiss me, Kate*, to name a few. It is all music I grew up listening to and that I can sing. It's just not what I went to school for.

OL – I noticed that your all time favorite musician is not a classical musician, but rather, the great Ella Fitzgerald. Please explain your choice.

IL – Ella Fitzgerald is absolutely one of my favorites. The singers we love, we love them because they have their own recognizable voices. We listen to the songs they sing, even if we don't know the songs, because it's them singing the song. That is why I love Ella Fitzgerald, Frank Sinatra, Sarah Vaughan, Doris Day…the list is very long. I happen to have an affinity for that era of music, and I love the music that they sang. I love Gershwin, Jerome Kern, Sondheim, and Bernstein, etc.

For me, it's about the music: these people with their voice, their interpretation of the lyrics, bringing something of themselves to the song, how to spin a phrase, and how to sing the line… I listen to several of them singing the same song and I would never say one were better than the other because they are all different interpretations of the same text, and each one of them are so honest that they are all true to me. It is music that I love.

OL – How do you juggle the career of opera singer and the fact that you are the mother of a young child?

IL – I will just say; with a lot of difficulty!

OL – Does your son come to the opera?

IL - I have never forced him to come to the opera. It's where I go to work, and if he wants to join me he can; if he doesn't, he doesn't have to. The invitation is open. He knows that it is open to him and a special place to visit.

OL – How do you define your personality and your take on life?

IL – My personality and take on life… I have no idea! [laughs] I can say what I try to do. I try to run my day with as much care and kindness as I can. It doesn't always work. I try very hard to feel and do everything that I possibly can for everyone that is close and dear to me in my life, and for my work. I am very detail-oriented. I can be incredibly organized. This is usually very good, but sometimes it is difficult when I can't get into a new score unless I organize something else that is going on in my life, and at that moment, I may really need to get into the music! So, sometimes I have to break certain habits in order to get along with my To Do list! [laughs] I have To Do lists all the time, all over the place. I take care of a lot. I do. I don't question it, I don't doubt it, I don't wonder why, I don't think it's unfair (well, we are human. Sometimes, we just think things are unfair!). I just have a lot to take care of. We all do. Everybody has different lives, different challenges in their lives, and I just try to get it done, as best as I can. [laughs]

OL – What do you like to do besides opera, and I suppose, your family?

IL – Of course my family is very important to me. my son, my mother, my friends… My son and I will do art together, sometimes. My father was a visual artist and he and I used to paint together, so when I have time we'll do some sort of art project, even if it's just drawing together. We like to do that, and we like to go outside.

I still love to dance, since I grew up dancing, so if I can go to a dance class (theater, tap, flamenco, etc.) I will. However, it is very challenging to find the time . But, I Just love, love, love it. I mean, the reality of the situation is that I have two full-time jobs, so time is scarce. I enjoy taking a long walk up Broadway, if I get the chance. If I have to make a phone call I'd rather walk and talk to someone than sit down.

Or, I love being quiet! [laughs] I like peace and quiet. I like simple enjoyable things, whether it's by myself or with my friends, my son… I don't like a lot of drama. I really don't. My friends will probably laugh, because there is so much drama in opera and there is so much drama in life, however I don't need it! [laughs] I'm happy to have drama in opera and nowhere else. [laughs] I don't know, it's hard to describe yourself. I don't think about it very much.

OL – Very nice!

Olga Peretyatko, soprano

Olga is another young Russian singer who is taking the operatic world by stomr, with some very important roles and DVDs under her belt already. She is very beautiful and expressive, with a divine voice. We talked to her in person at the Met, in March 2014 during her *I Puritani* run.
Opera Lively - Let's start by talking about Elvira. Some singers play her as a bit deranged from the beginning so that the mad scene doesn't appear like it is coming out of the blue. What is your take on the psychology of this troubled character?

Olga Peretyatko – I think she is really not quite sane from the beginning. Think about this time when Elvira lived. The role of the woman was nothing; just nothing! Of course you have your riches and your love and this conflict between what you should do and what you want to do, and this all got to her in a way that I don't think allowed her to be just normal. She was nervous from day one. I hope you have seen it in my performance. She was nervous but not quite mad yet; then she had her first mad scene in the finale primo which was just a psychological collapse. I believe she was thinking about what her life would be from that point on. She was left in the altar, and in Puritan society it was a catastrophe. Her life was over. If something happened to her wedding plans, it was supposed to be the woman's every fault. It was thought to be Elvira's fault that Arturo left her.

OL - I think there is some method to her madness. She starts by saying

"I'm not Elvira" – it sounded to me like a battle cry to escape the fact of her being the plaything of men and only existing to be ordered around by her father or by the men who wanted to marry her. As a modern woman, how do you relate to this kind of character?

OP - In our modern life now, in 2014, one can't imagine what it was like for her. That kind of collapse, I can't relate to it; I'm not Elvira.

OL - Do you always read the source for your roles, like in this case Sir Walter Scott's novel?

OP – Yes, I've read a lot about Elvira's time and her society which was quite weird. I have read Sir Walter Scott's novel and a lot of other books about the same topic, in Russian as well. A singer needs to be prepared, because everything you read and listen to, will be heard in your singing.

OL - Elvira is a role with such extraordinary past singers like Callas, Caballé, Sills, and Sutherland… Who are the singers who inspired you in your preparation?

OL – Mariella Devia. She was my teacher. Of course I have heard all of them that you've quoted, but when I'm preparing a role I try to refrain from listening to my predecessors upfront otherwise it will be a caricature of somebody else, which is exactly what I don't want. The first part of my preparation, I like to study alone with my pianist or just on my own because I can play the piano. Then in a second phase I do listen to other singers to get a sense of the traditions. For example, this finale primo has some ornamentation that is not written but was started by Callas, so now everybody who has the high D natural does it. It is beautiful; it shows your expression and it is a very effective line. Then I do study what everybody else did. For example, I observed Georgio Pertusi, a wonderful bel canto singer. I remember him in 2006 when I was at the Accademia Rossiniana for the first time in Pesaro, and part of our study was to see the rehearsals of others. We were young students with wide open eyes. I was speechless after his performance in *Torvaldo e Dorlisca.* He was the bad guy there, with a slow aria that was amazingly sung. Now I understand that you should learn from every colleague.

OL - What vocal challenges exist while singing this role? Is the Veil Song difficult?

OP – I can't say it's difficult. If you are prepared, if you have the right technique and the right voice, it's not a difficult role. It's similar to Rossini roles. It's long. It can't be sung by a pure coloratura soprano because in some parts it's written low and you need to have this power in the middle register and downstairs. You must have the extension and it can be a bit of a challenge, but if you have it, then you have it. I think the difficulty is more because it's long and there are changes in your mood, and you have to stay credible; otherwise someone will tell you "you are technically perfect but you are cold." But I laugh about it because I'm in good company: they said the same of Sutherland and Devia and Gruberova and so on. In this kind of staging you can't just jump into the orchestra pit. The previous production I was in was directed by Dmitri Tcherniakov and it was an absolutely different way of *recitare* and act. But here in this production we did what is right for this kind of staging. But regardless of the production, the connections between the protagonists are always the same. It's about passion, it's about love, it's about power. So, in summary, everything can be difficult, but it is easy if you have the voice for it.

OL - *I Puritani* is said to have a huge gap between the quality of the libretto and the quality of the music. Bellini famously said the plot didn't matter. What's your overall opinion of the piece?

OP – I can't say that the libretto is weird or stupid, because it is very theatrical. There are lots of different images from the beginning. The first scene we sing from behind the stage. It's church singing and is very special for 19th century opera. It is something new. Then you have the usual duets and scenes and so on, but it is a rare case of an opera for my voice type in which I don't die at the end. [laughs] It's a bit weird, but every bel canto opera is weird. You need to think that nowadays, Lady Gaga is the freak that entertains the public. At that time, Giulia Grisi was that kind of freak. The public wanted to see something strange on the stage. Madness was not something you'd see quite often in that time because the entire society was about etiquette. You couldn't show something like that in public. Then, the public came to the theater, to see it on stage.

OL – Fantastic! I had never thought of it this way. It's interesting!

OP – Yes! [laughs]

OL - What do you think of this veteran production of *I Puritani* by the Met? It is older than you are. [she laughs] What are its strengths? It's very traditional. Is it boring? Do you prefer the more modern productions, or one like this one?

OP – I did a lot of productions. Here, everything is about the singing. I enjoy this production. The painted background is beautiful and you have wonderful historical costumes. To put *I Puritani* in our time doesn't work. The problematic of this piece is about the Puritan society. That's why I think it is pretty correct, what they did. I like it. Being a veteran, old production, doesn't mean it is boring, no. We bring our own personality into it.

OL - I've interviewed Larry Brownlee and met him twice more; he is a wonderful man and a great singer. What can you tell me about the experience of working with him?

OP – I adore Larry! He is such an amazing colleague! Our generation of singers, we are all kind and we love each other. It's team work. It's not about "ah, who is the diva?" [laughs] It's not about who is more prominent or anything, we work as a team. He is nice. It's not our first meeting on stage. We did *Il Turco in Italia* together in Amsterdam, and his first Nemorino was with me in *L'Elisir d'Amore*. This is our third opera together, and next we do a fourth one in Aix-en-Provence which will be *Il Turco in Italia* as well. The bel canto world is so small, it's all the same people. [laughs]

OL - Being conducted by your husband maestro Michele Mariotti – is there any funny story to tell us about it?

OP – Funny? Not at all. [laughs] No, to sing with him is quite normal for me, because we met like this. He was conducting, and I was singing, in 2010 in Pesaro: *Sigismondo*. That was a strange opera, I'll tell you! To sing with him, is like to breathe; something normal. This production is the second one since we got married. All in all, we worked together three times. Now it's a happy time for us because we are together. It's not easy to be together with our lives and parallel careers. He is here, I'm there, and for months we don't see each other. That's why I'm so happy! [laughs]

OL - This is the first time you sing at the Met. What are your thoughts about the house and the audience?

OP – I love to sing here! The audience is great, the acoustics are great, everything is great! I enjoy it every day, being at the Met. The house is big but the acoustics are wonderful! You know, after I sang *Rigoletto* at the Arena di Verona for 16,000 people, open air… if you can sing there, you can sing everywhere. I enjoy working here, really!

OL - Now, let's turn to you, Olga, rather than Elvira. You started singing at age 15 in the choir of the Mariinsky Theater, but what happened before that? At what age did you get interested in classical music, and why?

OP – My father was an opera singer. He is in the choir of the Mariinsky Theater and has been there for almost 35 years. He started singing in the conservatory, and then I was born. So, he needed to earn money; that's why he came to the Mariinsky. So I came as well, and I was singing all the time, actually not just when I formally entered the choir at 15, but rather since I was 3. I enjoyed the public and the parties at home. I danced as well. I just needed the public; until now, I still do! [laughs] My first diploma was choirmaster. Actually it is very good because it gave me the musical base. I can read the music and play the piano, I'm good in solfeggio; everything I learned there is very important for my work now. All that happened to me was the right thing.

OL - So, you first wanted to be a mezzo, right?

OP – Actually I was a mezzo. My voice is quite low for a coloratura soprano. It's not a unique case. I extended my voice up and now I'm a soprano. I have a long range. It helps, and I try to work on it and keep this range. This is my exercise everyday: three octaves of arpeggio, to keep it. Now my voice is more mature, but in a natural way. That's what my teacher always said: don't push. Don't try to sing too dramatic roles too early. You'll have everything, but take your time.

OL - You are a Karate fighter, and you say it helps with opera. Tell us more about it.

OP – Well, I was. [laughs] Yes, what Karate is about is that you should have power. We singers are athletes. It's not hard power like that [grunts] but very elastic. The art of Karate is to be protected but not to initiate fights. You are very powerful but you will never fight somebody spontaneously. If somebody attacks me, I will win! So, it's quite peaceful. It's not about fighting, it's about art. So to be on stage with all these live broadcasts and the media and so on, you should have the nerves for that. Also, to be able to concentrate is very important, and I learned it with Karate.

OL - When I think of Saint Petersburg I have goosebumps, with all the great composers having their graves at the local cemetery. I imagine the city as this extraordinary epicenter of classical music. Maybe I'm romanticizing it a little. I've never been to it, but I plan to.

OP – You should!

OL - How was the experience of growing up in St. Petersburg?

OP – Oh, we should take two hours for that! In St. Petersburg there is this background: it's an amazing city! To be there is something very special, but in different ways. It can be very cruel, the city, like New York, but it is beautiful at the same time! The winter is very long… Of course we have almost two months of white nights, and everything is magical. You don't have nightfall, almost, and it does something to your head. You get crazy in that period!

OL - What can you tell us about the Mariinsky as a cultural institution?

OP – Gergiev did a great job. He created it. I mean, the Mariinsky Theater as a brand was there for hundreds of years before him, but he made of it what it is today. Now there are three theaters there; or two theaters and a concert hall, one of them brand new, and they are always full. Sometimes there are two full opera performances per day and the house is packed. Of course, there are many tourists but our people also goes there to listen to the music, and that's amazing. Yes, you should come to St. Petersburg, just to feel it! [laughs]

OL – So, from being a choirmaster, you went to Berlin to study singing?

OP – While being a choirmaster I was also singing all the time as the second alto. I did small solos too. Singing in a choir, it gives you the possibility of listening to your colleagues as well; that's important.

OL - Was it difficult to go to Berlin all by yourself at age 21?

OP – It was my very first trip to the West, in August 2001. I was totally in love with the city, because it is so special! You feel freedom in the air. A friend of mine was studying in the Berlin conservatory, the Hochschule für Musik Hanns Eisler, and I had just started to take private lessons in St. Peterburg with a soprano, and my friend told me "go to Berlin for an audition!" I did, and the professor told me to come again for an exam. Six months later I went back for the exam, and they took me. From 2002, my Berlin era started. It was a really difficult time because I didn't have any support and any money. I did everything to earn something. I mean, I wasn't washing the dishes at the restaurants, but I was taking every singing job everywhere I could. We created a quartet, and we sang a lot of small concerts, for example in hospitals and hospices. I'd earn 50 Euros to do this, and it was great money for me because I didn't have any. But it gave me experience, and now I can be thankful for that time, because it led me to everything that I have now.

OL – Then, when did you have your first lucky break?

OP – I count it from Pesaro, in 2007. I was there in 2006 for the Accademia Rossiniana, and I told you about Pertusi, and then the great maestro Alberto Zedda took this risk of giving me this big role of Desdemona in *Otello* in 2007. It was with Juan Diego Flórez and Gregory Kunde and it was a great success. Of course it was very dangerous for everybody – for me, and for the Festival, because I was young at 27 and I had a relative late start in operatic soprano singing which I started at 22. It was my fifth year, overall. After that, it was Aix-en-Provence with Stravinsky's Le Rossignol which was my first role in Russian. Robert Lepage did an amazing work there and we took the same show to New York at the BAM, Lyon, and Amsterdam. In Toronto, it was where Peter Gelb heard me for the first time, and he engaged me here for the Metropolitan, for another role, a small role, Fiakermilli in *Arabella*. There are three minutes of music. Then they changed their minds with my career growing, and asked me to do Elvira. Of course I was happy, happy!

OL - Was it difficult, psychologically speaking, to deal with your escalating success?

OP – What success? I mean, I am doing what I've always done. It's the same work. Maybe I sing better now, because I do try to be perfect. It's not possible, but I try. Where I'm now, it's because of a lot of hard work I did before. Therefore, somehow you expect something, yah? [laughs] If you work so hard, for me it's just normal. I work hard now, I worked hard before, and life is long.

OL – Oh, you said "what success?" I think the whole operatic environment in New York City is crazy about you. All the blogs and newspapers are saying great things about you.

OP – Thank you, thank you!

OL - In 2011 in the midst of a string of bel canto operas, you did Handel's *Alcina*. How do you compare the experience of singing Baroque versus bel canto?

OP – Eh… Baroque was a bit too much for me. *Alcina* was a great experience for me, but I did it just once. Maybe someday I'll do it again, who knows? They told me my voice was too big for the role. But you sing with your voice, you can't just change it. I don't believe that singers can sing it all. Therefore you should just choose your way and do your stuff, your fach. Maybe if I had to sing Handel again, I'd rather sing Cleopatra, maybe. That's interesting. I mean Alcina is a great role, really great, but I don't know, nobody else offers me something like that anymore. [laughs]

OL - Even though you were lovely in your *Sigismondo* DVD, I particularly disliked that production due to its stereotypical depiction of mental illness, with all the people drooling and twitching, given that I'm a psychiatrist. Any comments?

OP – I thought it was interesting, because *Sigismondo* has a really strange libretto. Who is who? [laughs] And why did the stage director decide to do it in a madhouse? I think it was because in the first aria, Sigismondo sings to somebody who is not on stage, who is not present. He ordered someone to kill me because he thought I was not faithful. And it was not true, of course, and I was very faithful, but I was not killed because a good man saved me. For fifteen years I was somewhere else, and then I came back. That's strange. That's really strange. So I thought it was quite interesting to make it in a madhouse. Psychologically it was interesting, but of course in terms of singing, when I saw all those people there acting crazy, they were not quiet. During my beautiful aria at the beginning there was this madman and he was yelling quite loudly while I was supposed to sing my beautiful line, piano piano. Then I yelled at him, "can you stop it?" Then I had to talk to the stage director and say that it wasn't possible. Of course, sometimes it is difficult when they want something that doesn't match the music, but we should speak with them. I had no complaints. I just told him about my doubts. I said, "I can't do that. Why should I do that?" But then he explained his thoughts and his ideas to me, and convinced me. If I wasn't convinced, I wouldn't have done it. In this case, it was a nice production. It was very hot. In Pesaro in August it was 35 degrees Celsius, which is how many, 100 Fahrenheit? [laughs] My costume was made from wool and it was so hot on the stage! During the dress rehearsal I lost my eyelashes because I was sweating so much, it was like I was in a shower! Ah! [laughs] But I like this production, because that's how I met my husband! [laughs]

OL - Your *The Tzar's Bride* at La Scala was in a very modern production, rendered as a TV studio. What did you think of the update?

OP – Oh, that production I liked very much! Tcherniakov is a very intelligent stage director. He convinces you, really. First I did it in Berlin, and then at La Scala, almost with the same cast. In Germany, you know, Regietheater, they are all used to see this stuff, and that was very interesting.

The idea was that everything happens right now. He made it very contemporary. I liked it very much.

OL – But the public at La Scala is very traditional, so how was it received there? When they don't like it, they boo.

OP – Oh yes! Oh, yes! The singers, they received us well, but the stage director was booed so much, you can't believe it! Tcherniakov's *Traviata* was booed too, to open the La Scala season. Actually it is suicide to take such a production of *Traviata* to open the season at La Scala! From the beginning, it was clear that he would be booed! [laughs] So it happened again with *The Tzar's Bride*, but in Berlin six months earlier it was a great success for him. You know, it's a different public.

OL - Tell me about your CDs *La Bellezza del Canto*, and *Arabesque*. How did you select the tracks?

OP – *La Bellezza del Canto*, they wanted to make this mix of everything. It was my first one, so I think it was good to present me from different sides. *Arabesque*, I liked it very much. I'm quite pleased with the result. Of course I wanted to show Mozart, because I do a lot of Mozart. There was some bel canto for sure, and the French repertoire that I put there, is actually the direction I'm going to, because for my voice it is perfect. It was a mix as well. It was Sony's strategy; they wanted something like that.

OL - Tell us about your personality and your take in life.

OP – I'm very positive [laughs] as you can see. I try to live every day and enjoy every minute of it, because life is long, but it is also short. My grandmother is dying at this moment. We should be grateful for everything. If you aren't, you start to be arrogant. I try to sing every performance as if it will be the last one, and that's exactly the way I think about my life. Live today!

OL - What do you like to do other than classical music?

OP – I like to read. Actually my life is what I always wanted it to be. I'm always on tour, and every two months I am in a new country, a new city, a new life. I can take it like this, and I'm doing what I love to do. Singing is what I wanted to do, and I'd like it to last for a long, long time like this.

OL – You don't have children yet, right?

OP – No, I don't.

OL – So probably it will become a bit more difficult, when you do.

OP – We'll see. I live today. When it comes, it comes. Then, I'll think about how to manage everything.

OL – Well, it's exactly the time you said you had to leave, and we got to the last question!

OP – We were perfect! [laughs]

OL – Thank you so much, it was very interesting.

OP – I thought so too! Thank you!

Jessica Pratt, soprano

Opera Lively has interviewed over Skype back in June 2013, up-and-coming British-born, Australian-raised, Italian-trained soprano Jessica Pratt, a high-quality young singer who is making a big name for herself in Europe. A bel canto specialist, her discography is growing, and having seen some of her recorded work, we are impressed! For such a young singer, it boasted already nine items at the time of this interview (more by now). Ms. Pratt is not only an extremely gifted singer, but also a very intelligent and articulate young woman. Her interview is courageous. She doesn't hesitate to speak up about controversial issues such as how opera houses and big agencies sometimes don't have a singer's best interest at heart. She majored in Psychology to better understand her characters, and it shows - she has interesting insights to share about some of opera's most intriguing figures.

Opera Lively – Thank you for doing this. I've just watched your *Ciro in Babilonia*, and oh my God, you are so good!

Jessica Pratt – Thank you!

OL – I watched your *Adelaide di Borgogna* Blu-Ray disc as well, and it's wonderful. Congratulations. People here in the United States don't know you as well as in Europe, and I hope this will change and your career will explode over here.

JP – Well, I've only been working for five years now, so it's not been very long that I've been performing. I had my debut in America last year.

OL – Right. We'd like to begin by talking a little about your background. You were born in England and grew up in Australia. Can you tell us what role music played in your home when you were growing up? Your father Phillip Pratt was a tenor; was your mother also a musician?

JP – My father was a tenor, and my mother is a visual artist. So we were exposed to both, visual arts and music, in every sense when we were children. My father would sing us opera arias when we went to sleep, and he would tell us the stories of the operas rather than regular fairy tales; and my mother would paint our bedrooms; she would paint all the walls with our favorite characters and whatever else we wanted. So I studied sculpture and enjoyed painting and at the same time I studied music. The thing was, when I went to university it was to do my art, but I had issues with selling my artwork. I didn't want to sell it because it was mine, so you can't have a career like that. [laughs] I continued to sing all the time, and I remember when I went to the interview at university I told them that I wanted to be both a visual artist and singer, and they said "you can't do both, you have to decide" and I said, "oh no, it's not like that, I'll do the art in the day and I'll sing at night." As time went on I realized that you really can't have that much time; you need to be one or the other if you want to do it well, so I chose singing.

OL – How old were you, then?

JP – When I started studying singing seriously, I was eighteen. I always wanted to be a singer because that's what we did in my family, but my father refused to teach me until I was eighteen. He wanted my voice to develop naturally. He said I had to play a wind instrument for at least ten years first, so I chose the trumpet. I played in an orchestra and a jazz band as a teenager, then when I was old enough to start singing he said I could start, so I stopped the trumpet and started singing.

OL - Before you went to Europe to study with Maestro Gelmetti and Renata Scotto, you began your voice studies in Australia for one year at the conservatory. What made you leave?

JP – The conservatory can be good and it can be bad. They certainly have a very good system in Australia as opposed to what I have found in Italy, talking to my colleagues. In Australia for the Opera Course in addition to the vocal coaching and lessons we had classes in Yoga, Dancing and Movement, Alexander Technique, Spoken Language courses in Italian,

French, and German and Singing Language courses for pronunciation separately. They were good courses. In my case, I went for about a year and then when the option to continue my studies privately in Italy came up I felt that would be an opportunity not to miss and I left the conservatory and chose to explore further studies in Europe.

Before my studies in the conservatory I trained personally. I would get up at six in the morning and work as a secretary until one in the afternoon and all the money I earned I spent on private teachers. If I went to a concert and liked the concert I would find a way to contact the conductor and ask if I could study with him privately. I had lessons in dancing, conducting and stage directing. I also studied Psychology and Drama in an Arts degree with the Queensland University because I thought that would help me to understand the characters and so on. When I moved to Europe I continued this manner of study, I feel it is more time efficient having personal lessons with select people.

OL – Oh wow, you studied Psychology. I'm a psychiatrist myself during the day, and in evenings and weekends I do opera journalism. It does help to understand the psychology of the characters, definitely. But back to your teachers; Madame Scotto was one of the great sopranos during the second half of the 20th century. How was she as a teacher?

JP – When I went to see Renata Scotto, she wanted to work mainly with the interpretation and the vocal line, that kind of thing. She didn't want to work on technique, because she felt that by the time a singer was with her they had to already have the technique ready. She was a good interpretive teacher because she is a very intelligent person. She is very good at telling you exactly what she needs and what she wants, whereas I think a lot of famous singers perhaps don't know exactly why they did what they did. Teaching and performing are two separate skills. She was actually very good at teaching as well as at performing.

OL – Nice. Have you stayed in contact with her since establishing your own international career? If so, do you ever ask her for advice?

JP – Yes, every now and then.

OL - And what about your studies with Maestro Gianluigi Gelmetti? What specifically did you work on with him?

JP – Maestro Gelmetti heard me in a competition in Australia and invited me to come watch performances and rehearsals in Italy, so that's what I did.

I came to Italy and spent six months at the Rome Opera Theatre, where he was the musical director, watching performances and rehearsals. He wouldn't let me take time off. I had to be at the theater before everybody else and leave the theater after everybody else, so it was quite intense. It was good. I remember one time when I asked him if I could go and study Italian and he said, "no, you have to learn it here at the theater." When I went back to Australia I was speaking Romano, I was speaking with an accent. [laughs]

OL – So, how old were you when you went to Rome?

JP – It was nine years ago. I was twenty-four.

OL – Was it difficult to leave Australia and go to Europe and be there by yourself?

JP – I think singers are a bit of an odd group of people because we do things without thinking about it. We take big risks because we don't see them as big risks. I remember doing an interview in Australia once when someone asked me how much money I spent on lessons and I had no idea, because I would spend my money until it was gone. There was no thought of "I'll spend a thousand a week" or any sort of planning. For me it wasn't spending money; it didn't count. It was the same thing with coming to Europe. When I first came here it was because Gelmetti invited me. I won a competition as well so I could come over but the return plane ticket was for a set date so I could only go back to Australia after eight months. I cried the entire way on the plane because I was leaving my family, everybody and everything I knew and then I got used to it. The first couple of weeks I was sad when I was on my own, and then I was fine. That's what happens, humans are adaptable, with time one can get used to anything. Plus we are very fortunate now as singers as we cannot only speak to our families on the other side of the world, but we can see them too via video calls.

OL - Likely your teacher Lella Cuberli who is a bel canto specialist is instrumental in your training. She is American. Tell me about her.

JP – Lella is a very good technical teacher. She helps me a lot with my technique and of course we sing much of the same repertoire. She really helps me with understanding different belcanto techniques and she is brilliant in interpretation and fraseggio. Apart from that, she is a really, really lovely person. Her being American and having moved to Italy and worked a lot in Italy, she understands a lot of what I go through. Without her the last few years would have been a lot more difficult.

OL - In a recent interview with the magazine "Opera Now," Kiri Te Kanawa mentioned how much the role of the singer's agent has changed since she began her career. She said that, at that time, agents really developed and nurtured a singer's career. For example, she said her agent made sure that she auditioned with the right pieces at the right places that suited her as a performer. But now, she says, agents only take care of a singer's bookings. What has been your experience in this regard?

JP – Yes, I think what I see in general with the agencies is exactly what she says. It's very much about booking; the secretarial work rather than actually creating and planning a career, there are so many young singers and they are so willing to do anything now… I remember in the beginning I would fight a lot with agencies, preferring to stay home for six months rather than accepting jobs that weren't appropriate. Then hopefully you get to a point where you begin to have a decent career and you can find an agent who will start to take you a little more seriously.

I think that singers tend to suffer a lot in the beginning – especially when they go into a big agency. Often the agency will just book whatever for that singer until they get to a point where they have some sort of name and then maybe the agency will be interested in creating something or sticking with it, unless you have a good agent, or you are lucky like I am now to have an agency that is actually interested in you as a singer and as an individual.

Unfortunately in many cases it is simply a game of numbers, an agency can choose to take one singer who wants to preserve their voice and sing for forty years, keeping to a specific repertoire and choosing carefully their productions and with whom they work or an agent can take on a series of young singers who will sing anything under any conditions for five to ten years before they burn out. Taking an example of 20 years, a singer who wants to preserve their voice might choose to do only five or six productions a year, on the other hand an agency can choose to take on four young singers who are willing to do ten productions a year, but will more than likely throw them away after five years. They make more money with the four short careers, than with the one who will sing less frequently for twenty years.

OL – That's sad.

JP – Yes.

OL - Along a somewhat similar line, Wolfgang Sawallisch told an interviewer from the magazine "Opernwelt" that the cultivation of an opera house ensemble played a much more important role in postwar Europe than it does today. He mentioned that singers like Dietrich Fischer-Dieskau or Leonie Rysanek would have firm, long-term engagements as an ensemble member at a particular opera house, and that the Intendant or General Music Director would then work with these artists over time and assist them in the development of their careers. Today, things are very different.

JP – Ah, this is a similar situation, having a permanent job in an opera house, now. What I've seen with my colleagues – I haven't done it myself – is that very often the house does not care. They pay you every month and you have to sing whatever they say, and if that means ruining your voice, you ruin your voice. They just don't care. There is no building up of singers or creating artists which takes time and energy and isn't financially rewarding for a house or for an agency. So it's really up to the singers to defend themselves and decide what they want.

And it is not easy, because you have a house that will come to you, like with me, and they'll say "we want to put on such and such for you, we know it is traditionally a role for a much more lyric voice but we are going to do a bel canto version, it's going to be light, it's going to be this and that," and they offer you a lot of money, and you have to say "no" to them. And your agent says, "try it, it's only one production and then we will put it away for five years," but it is not, because as soon as you do that one production and it goes well enough other theaters will ask and before you know it the offers have changed and you may find yourself being offered only this repertoire which you would not have willingly chosen. I felt like it was me against the entire world in the beginning – against the theater,the conductor and the agent – they all said "well, it will be great, we will be very careful, and we'll do this…"

And it's not the case at all, because I've seen it, I've seen other singers, especially in these productions that I've refused, and I've seen the productions, and they weren't light productions. It's been a normal production where the singer that is too light for the role just goes under. And of course, when they crash and burn, nobody is there saying "oh, sorry, we'll do something else." They just pick up the next one.

OL – Oh wow! That is a pity. Now, about your own career; you've sung many bel canto roles. But at the end of last year, you sang Donna Anna in Don Giovanni. This is a role that is usually sung by a spinto soprano, by someone who also sings Strauss and Wagner. Are you interested in singing more Mozart roles, or do you think your voice now is developing in a way that will lead you to heavier roles?

JP – I've very happy with the repertoire I'm singing. I felt very comfortable with Donna Anna, but I certainly didn't sing it like a Wagnerian soprano; I sang it with my voice. I think it depends very much on the size of the theater that you sing in, the rest of the cast, their timbre and vocal weight and so on. No, it's absolutely not an indication of a change in my career.

OL - Of course, there was another great Australian soprano who specialized in bel canto roles, but also sang Donna Anna, and even Turandot: Dame Joan Sutherland. Do you see yourself following a career path similar to hers? Just listening to your great bel canto delivery in *Adelaide di Borgogna*, I wonder if people in Australia have already started referring to you as the new Sutherland, which of course might put unwelcome burden on a singer. Any comments?

JP – Australia has produced many wonderful singers including great coloratura sopranos like Dame Joan Sutherland and Nellie Melba. Dame Joan Sutherland had a voice that was completely unique and extremely special, a voice like hers is born once every few hundred years! She's a big inspiration, certainly not a burden. I think it's normal; it's human nature to box people into things. You know, when a dark haired Greek dramatic soprano comes on the scene I'm sure many people are hoping for the next Maria Callas; when you say you're a tenor immediately people think Pavarotti, Domingo, that's just the way it is.

It's typical for us human beings not to look at people as individuals. It's what we do; we think "she was the last great soprano to sing this repertoire, is this the next so and so?" rather than saying "this person is a different individual with a different set of chords, training and life experience." I listen to Dame Joan Sutherland most days; I find her incredibly inspirational, especially when she sings the mad scene for Ophelia in *Hamlet*; there isn't anything more perfect than that; it's exquisite.

OL – Nice answer, I liked it. You are a light coloratura soprano, at this time, right?

JP – Yes, exactly. I'm a coloratura soprano.

OL – Which you do very well and I hope you preserve it, and don't let those agents ruin it.

JP – No, I'm lucky. My agent is good with me. They know my opinion and they are very careful with me as well; they are very supportive.

OL - Dame Joan was also a great Baroque stylist. You've sang back in time as far as Mozart with your Queen of the Night in Covent Garden. Do you have any interest in exploring the truly Baroque repertoire, such as Handel?

JP – I'd love to sing some Baroque, especially for example Cleopatra which would be really interesting. Most of my career has taken place here in Italy and they don't put it on so much. Emotionally I really feel at home with Bellini; I love his legato and his language, his sense of emotion. I adore the music of Donizetti, Thomas, Halévy and Rossini. When I listen to opera I tend toward belcanto, I'm very fortunate as I am able to perform the music I adore listening to and so I'm happy with what I have. But absolutely, if I got offered something Baroque as long as it is appropriate for my voice, I would accept it.

OL - You're scheduled to sing Inéz in *L'Africaine* in November 2013 at La Fenice, and Meyerbeer's music does have Italianate influence especially in the vocal parts, given his time in Italy with Rossini. So, it doesn't seem to be a very significant departure from bel canto, or is it? Can you tell us more about singing Meyerbeer versus singing bel canto?

JP – I don't know yet, I'll have to tell you after I've sung it. [laughs] Because one can study an opera, but you never really know what it is like until you perform it.

OL – Typically, you start studying a new role like *L'Africaine*, how many months in advance?

JP – It depends on the situation, because for example when I debuted *Roméo et Juliette* I only had three weeks to learn it. I was asked to come and sing it as a favor, because there had been a cancellation. In a similar situation I had to debut Eudoxie in *La Juive* and so while I was rehearsing *Lucia di Lammermoor* all day in the evenings I was studying Eudoxie. I mean, I can learn an opera in two or three weeks, but it's not ideal; you can't do your best. I took a month off in March / April between *Guillaume Tell* in Lima and *I Capuleti e i Montecchi* in Reims to be at home because I had to study my next three operatic debuts before my next break in August. First I debuted in *I Capuleti e i Montecchi* in April, then Rossini's *Demetrio e Polibio* in Naples in May, followed by *Rigoletto* (an opera I have already performed) in Sevilla with Leo Nucci and I will have my debut as Giovanna d'Arco by Verdi at the Valle d'Itria Festival in Martina Franca in July. So I didn't take the month in March / April so much to study these roles, but to sing them with my teacher because otherwise when I'm always on the road I don't get the chance to go and see her. This year because I'm debuting six operas, I have taken three months off, not continuously but three weeks here, four there. While I'm singing an opera I'm studying the next one so that when I get home I have it ready to go to lessons.

OL – Do you go to the literary sources as well, when they're available? Do you read the novels or plays?

JP – Yes, of course! It's often very different, for example in Sir Walter Scott's novel *The Bride of Lammermoor*, Lucia's brother is a little boy, it's her mother who manipulates the situation, whereas in the opera by Donizetti the librettist Salvadore Cammarano portrays her mother as dead and her adult brother is the manipulator. It is very important to read as much as possible on the subject, not only the direct sources, but also other literature on the subject or of the time period or the emotional state. For example, for Lucia, *Tess of the d'Ubervilles* by Hardy creates fantastic imagery and more of a sense of the desperation of a woman who has been pushed to her extreme. Lucia is pushed to her extreme as well in Sir Walter Scott's novel, but with Hardy's novel, he really gets inside Tess and you feel for this woman who is completely sane but years of continued pressure and horrible injustices, societal constraints and circumstances finally push her over the edge and she commits murder and loses her mind.

I think it's important that we don't only read the books that the opera is based on, but we also read other novels. They can be modern, they can be historical, but they give us an idea of that emotional state. It's also important to simply read – for me anyway – period novels constantly, in order to keep a fresh idea of what it was like when people couldn't shower, they didn't bath, women didn't have the right to be in a room alone with another man. People would think a lot about what they wrote to one another in a letter, because it may be the only opportunity they had to communicate in that month. Today with all our ease of communication sometimes I feel that we do not give enough attention to the words we use. We live in a throw away society where everything is easily replaceable, even relationships.

Three hundred years ago people couldn't get on the internet and straight away have 20 options for a new partner; they had to work it out with who they had as the option to leave a marriage was not an easy one. For example, Dona Elvira in *Don Giovanni*, she doesn't have a choice. He married her in front of the entire village. She was a rich woman and now she has to go to a convent. It's so sad, I think she chases him and tries to get him back to being her husband so that she can simply continue to live her life as a married woman in her own home. I mean, we see her as some crazy lunatic, but she is not; she is reacting to the circumstances and trying to make the best of it.

OL - Let's talk some more about some of your major roles. Lucia di Lammermoor: Do you think she's emotionally unstable from the start, or does her brother's treatment of her – and maybe Edgardo's treatment of her – pushes her over the edge mentally?

JP – It think that Lucia is suggestible; in her opening aria she describes seeing a phantom in the fountain, she is definitely attracted to death and to negative things right from the beginning and demonstrates obsessive behaviour in regard to Edgardo. She has already been attacked by a wild boar but she goes out unprotected in the night anyway to meet Edgardo. She's definitely in love with him, unhealthily in love with him. Also Edgardo throughout the entire opera is not necessarily a nice guy. Straight away, during the duet he flairs into anger at the slightest indication of rebuke and switches between being loving and being quite aggressive and attacking her and she thrives on that, perhaps because her brother is also like that with her as well in his duet.

I think she is probably used to this type of relationship with a man. The men in her world are generally aggressive and closed and only occasionally open. She finds the same type of man in Edgardo as she has known in Enrico, in my opinion. When she is forced to marry somebody else, she resists until she believes that Edgardo does not want her and then in my opinion decides to sacrifice herself for the sake of her family, perhaps she thinks she can just die internally and go through with it, but when she sees Edgardo at the wedding it is too much for her. Everybody has to have their own idea; I have mine. I think she probably goes to the bed chamber with the intention of killing herself with the knife, and then when Arturo approaches her and tries to have his right she kills him in self defense and that sends her over the edge.

OL - Then there is Elvira in *I Puritani*, who also goes mad – though, unlike poor Lucia, she eventually regains her senses and gets to marry the man she loves. Modern medicine might diagnose Elvira's "madness" as severe depression rather than actual insanity. Would you agree with this?

JP – Yes, I think Arturo ends up with a really fragile wife. I always imagine them in their middle age with her sipping Valium all day long. This is a girl who lives completely on her own with nobody her age around, no young people, few women in the castle, just one maid and her daydreaming of Arturo to keep her company. All in one day, she discovers she doesn't have to marry another man anymore and she will marry the man she loves, Arturo returns to the the castle bearing wedding gifts for her, then while putting on her wedding dress and preparing herself for the ceremony she comes out to see him running off with another woman in the wedding veil he presented her with hours before with no explanation. This would cause depression in most people I know! I don't think she is crazy; like you said I think she is depressed and extremely confused. Even in the Mad Scene, she is not mad, she just sings "please come back, please come back." She doesn't recognize Riccardo when she sings "chi sei tu?" She is just gone into her little world, doesn't really cope with what is going on around her.

OL - Some of your heroines also find themselves in situations that modern audiences may find hard to understand. Gilda is one example; Amina from *La Sonnambula* is another one. Social mores have changed so significantly in the past 50 years that many people seeing these operas for the first time may wonder what all the fuss is about. I suspect many women wish Amina would tell Elvino to get lost.

JP – Yes, I think this is the problem with audiences today, they don't have the understanding that the women in these situations didn't have much choice; once they were found in a room with a man they had to marry that man or go to a convent or worse. It's not a problem that has disappeared all together because there are still places where girls are forced to marry when they are still children, and there are still societies where girls are not allowed to be alone with men and have to be accompanied by male members of their families, so it's certainly not something so far in the past that we couldn't imagine it. It's just not necessarily part of Western society, in America or England.

OL - How do you create empathy for these characters and help modern audiences understand them?

JP – I love these characters. I'm a bit old-fashioned myself, so I totally identify with them. [laughs] I feel that another problem today is that we're so distracted twenty-four hours a day; we have to respond to people immediately with the Internet, cell phones, Instant Messages and what not. We have free access to so much communication, and with all this easy and free communication it becomes worthless the real communication that we could have with each other, you know? Ten years ago when we were having a conversation with someone on the phone we would end by saying "good bye" and wouldn't expect to talk to that person for at least a day. Now when I'm with my friends and the phone cuts off we just continue to do our things and it's not an issue because we can then text to each other and so forth.

We are losing a lot of formality in the way that we speak and conduct ourselves. The idea of writing a letter and waiting… When Callas was with her husband she would write a telegram and wait an entire day for a response. We couldn't imagine that now. But I think in that telegram there was a lot more meaning than in the text messages we send today.

That's one of the problems we have, and we also have the problem of a shorter attention span. Our attention span is constantly getting shorter and shorter. With television and cinema, they constantly flash different images and camera angles to access the primal part of the brain that is attentive when something changes in the perimeter. We in the opera theatre don't have that, so we are asking a public to go from being attentive to their environment, to sit quietly there and watch us sing. It's not an easy ask for a public of today.

Another important thing; empathy is something that seems to be lacking more and more in society today, and it's crazy because today we see so much and we hear so many stories, that one would think that our empathy would increase, but actually in my opinion it is decreasing between people, and I think music and theater have a responsibility to develop and encourage the public's empathy for the characters. When La Traviata was written it was a scandal because the protagonist was a prostitute and they couldn't deal with that, they didn't want that. The reason why they didn't want that was because when they came out of theater they felt empathy for a dying prostitute. Before they went in the theater they may have felt that she deserved to die of consumption due to her trade.

To give an example of a lack of empathy for a certain type of disease in more recent history, in the early 1980s many people did not feel empathy for people who contracted AIDS as it was associated with homosexuality and with drug use and there was a great lack of empathy for people suffering from the virus. Society needs to constantly develop understanding and empathy, it is too easy to just discriminate against what we don't understand. Hopefully the same people in the 1980s who were homophobic and might have said that a gay man deserved to die of HIV with education and exposure to gay people will realize that there is nothing strange or wrong about being gay and that no one deserves to die or be ill.

So, I think it's really important for opera and all the art forms to present and to help to develop certain ideas for people, so that when they are in the theatre, they relax, their emotions are accessed and as they watch the opera they start to reflect, hopefully, about things. I think the music helps us in that respect, to slow things down a little bit. It is no coincidence that one of the first things a political regime tries to, control, suppress and manipulate are the arts.

OL – Interesting answer! Has there ever been a character with whom you found it difficult to empathize? Or are there any roles you don't think you would sing because you dislike the character and would find it difficult to find some aspect you could identify with?

JP – No, so far no, but for example Norma is one that I wouldn't tackle, at this point I don't have the life experiences to attempt to understand where she is coming from. I'm not saying that we have to experience everything that we portray onstage; we have to be able to exaggerate experiences we've had and create a web of our own experiences and others' experiences that we may have lived through with them which can serve to interpret the character we are playing and I think that's also where reading can really help. I think reading is more important than watching cinema or television. Cinema and television are helpful but at a certain stage the problem with television is that it is a passive medium; it gives you images, you don't have to create them, whereas if you're reading, there is much, much more information in a novel than in a television adaption or a movie about the novel.

Also reading you develop your imagination and your ability to create pictures and so on, and I think it's really important for us to be able to put ourselves in that situation and fill it in with emotions. So if your role asks you to kill another character, we could take emotions from experiences we've had and just say, "OK, this is similar, this is not similar, if I exaggerate this ten times, it might feel like I was killing this person."

I haven't found a character that I dislike, and I feel very, very protective of the characters I do like. Lucia is very important to me, as is Elvira. I feel protective of them as personalities, I'm not quite sure why. I feel very cranky when I see them played like idiots that giggle, I'm not saying mad people don't laugh but the intention behind the laugh or the calmness that is contrary to the circumstance is what creates an atmosphere of madness for me. This little shallow girl that giggles is done by people who probably haven't experienced firsthand depression or madness in their lives, because they will go for very simplified versions.

For example, an aria I saw several years ago performed by a woman. She sang "Pleurez, mes yeux" [cry, my eyes] – her father has been killed, and she sends someone to kill her lover even though she still loves him because he killed her father. And she says "now I can cry" – so this girl was being a bit hysterical, throwing herself around the stage, but it's not like that, when someone is really at the very very end and they're really depressed they are very still and empty and solid. So you can see what people have experienced and what they haven't, to a certain extent when you see them on stage.

OL – That's right. That's pretty much what I was thinking when you said it was too early for you to sing Norma – not only vocally. She is quite a different sort of person than Elvira or Amina, and maybe requires more gravitas, and is more suitable for a bit older performers – maybe you're too young at 33 for Norma?

JP – Hm, hm. Exactly. She is thinking about killing her children, and I haven't even had any children. [laughs] With Norma, there are so many different problems. One, it's one of the Callas roles, so you are really asking for it, if you are singing it. Two, the problem of young singers singing it, it's not a question of whether you have the voice to sing it or the physical ability to sing it; it's whether you have the ability to control yourself, because she gets so angry and it's all central when she is angry; it's aggressive and you need to be able to sing that, to project that, without trashing yourself. I'm certainly not at a stage when I can do that, because I get way too emotional, still.

And I think that's why it needs to be tackled later in your career when you learn to pace yourself more and to control your emotions when you are performing, and to find that balance between giving emotion and not giving everything. Also, with Norma, it's another of those roles that once you sing it, then they ask you for that all the time, because there aren't many, so it's a bit of a misstep. If you are happy with what you are singing, why would you then go and sing a role where you are going to lose some of the things that are lighter? It's a role that once you go to it, you don't go back. And there is so much to sing in the repertoire that I'm in right now, that I don't see the point.

OL – Right. Now, if we could talk a little about your schedule and your plans: You live in Como, and you sing at many Italian opera houses, including, of course, La Scala. Do you consider yourself based in Italy?

JP – I'm a resident in Italy, so, it's my home. [Laughs] My dog is Italian. Absolutely, I live in Italy for my life and my career, and I like that. There is something good about living in Italy. When I moved here I was very Australian and I had the opinion that operas were exaggerated, and then gradually learning the language and living here where people are much more flamboyant and much more open and much more passionate… It's not that they are more passionate, actually, because the Germans are just as passionate as the Italians; it's just that an Italian person is much more comfortable with showing it. And they have faster emotions, more violent emotions, whereas a German or an Australian or myself might take a number of years to develop the emotions that an Italian will experience in a couple of months.

So it's good to feel part of it, because I sing the Italian repertoire so I need to speak the language. In Italy I can have a career singing exclusively belcanto operas. Works that in America are considered rare belcanto in Italy are standard repertoire for most theaters so there are just more options for me in Italy. I also feel that the orchestras in Italy play this music very differently. There is more respect in general for this type of repertoire.

OL – How so?

JP – There are differences between their pizzicato and that of other orchestras; just the way they play is different, they are not bored by it. With an Italian orchestra that knows how to accompany a belcanto singer it feels like they carry you along and you are floating on their sound below. Here they talk about the differences between Donizetti, Rossini, and Bellini, whereas maybe in Germany where they perform so many different operas they are talking about the differences between German repertoire and Italian repertoire – you know, much larger differences.

An orchestra that plays Mozart and Strauss all the time is not going to play Rossini and Bellini brilliantly, just like an orchestra in Italy will not play Auber, for example; these are specialised repertoires. It's not because they are Italian. It's because they've been playing it the most, for a long, long time. With this crisis in Italy, if they close down an opera theater and a musician goes to find work elsewhere which is perfectly normal, you can't then put together an orchestra in five years and expect that they will play this music brilliantly like before, because it's not going to be the same. This type of playing and this type of emotion is passed on from one player to the next over the years, so if you interrupt this tradition, you'll lose it

OL - I interviewed Anna Caterina Antonacci recently, and she said that Italian operatic productions are frozen in time, and while they were theatrically compelling a decade ago, now they're falling behind those of other countries. However I've just watched your blu-ray disc of *Adelaide di Borgogna*, and the stage director Pier Alli made compelling use of backstage projections, and I thought that the production was very good (not to forget, you sang angelically!). So what is your opinion of Italian productions, these days?

JP – I disagree. Personally I really, really love traditional productions, so, that's one of the reasons why I work in Italy. I don't see the point of another *Don Giovanni* in which the entire cast is having an orgy. I really dislike this. I love the fantastic costumes that they make in Italy and the stagings, and that's how I see opera, and I don't think that just because it's a period costume and a period production it doesn't have to be relevant, because these emotions are relevant in every century. We work with the same emotions – love, hate, jealousy, happiness, sadness; that is always relevant. So no matter what you put on stage or around the stage, you should be able to act these emotions for the audience.

I think that modern productions are also great; they can say a lot, they can add to it and so on, as long as they have a good reason – it can't be just because someone wants to make a show of themselves, and then they put naked people on the stage so that people talk about it. Or, you have to sing a scene on stage while dancers are doing all the 'acting' and you are just immobile in the corner – I've seen this many a time – and the paradox is that the director puts the singer on a corner because obviously he thinks that the singer is a bore and has nothing to say. And it's not true.

I think a lot of the time people don't trust in the ability of the music to slow things down for the public to be actually able to understand the underlying feelings. They need to let it be, to let the music come through on its own. And there is some fantastic poetry as well; we are not just talking about music, we are talking about language and stage movement. The singers should be able to move themselves in a way that is graceful inside their costumes and so on, and that can be very fascinating for the public.

I remember – someone a few years back asked me where I was singing because they wanted to go and see an opera; they had never seen an opera in their entire lives and they were really interested. They went to the theater to buy tickets and they found out that it was a modern opera set in the 1980's, so they didn't buy tickets because they said they didn't see the point of seeing an opera in the 1980's; they wanted to see real opera. And that was a general public person.

You know, this whole obsession about making opera relevant to the public of today by putting people in underwear or modern costumes, because they think that that makes it more accessible to the public, they are making a big mistake. Because the public can turn on the television and see that, and they can go to the cinema and see that. They want to see something different if they are going to pay all that money; they want to see something special.

OL -Well, Italy has other difficulties now, with budget crisis, old theaters with poor acoustics that aren't being renovated, and chaotic administration of opera houses. How is the experience of singing in Italy, these days?

JP – As I said, I've been working for six years, mostly in Italy and it's always been like this for me. [laughs] So I have no idea if it was different before. One knows that when one is singing in one year, maybe the contract will be cancelled, maybe there will be strikes, maybe they won't pay you for six months or a year afterwards. But for me it really doesn't make a difference. I don't care. I mean, I do care if they are taking advantage, if they are doing it on purpose, then I'll argue myself. But in my case I've been very lucky; I haven't had any productions cancelled in six years, I have never had any contracts cancelled, and I've been paid by every theater I've sung in. Two or three theaters have taken six months to pay, but that's all. And I knew that before I went there, and this was discussed, because they had problems.

I don't think one can go to work thinking that the money is the important thing. One has to take care of oneself, one has to be able to pay one's bills, it's absolutely true, and the theater shouldn't be taking advantage of a situation, but it's not the primary reason to decide if you are going to do a production or not, especially if the theater is honest with you and tells you that they have problems.

In Italy most opera houses are not renovated so the backstage areas are like they were fifty years ago – I find it kind of romantic, I like that. The administration is frustrating in most cases, because they won't tell you if you are singing first or second cast, when you'll be singing, they change the dates, that kind of thing. There is this opinion in Italy that if you sing in an opera here, the opera house has the right to your entire life for that six week-period, and they will tell you every day what you will be doing next without giving you any kind of schedule.

I suppose because I've always worked like that I'm OK with that and I don't have issues. But the more I work outside of the country the more they give me a schedule and they give me days off, and I don't have to work for fourteen hours a day, I start to think that it is actually quite nice to work outside of Italy. [laughs]

OL – Well, I don't want to appear like an Italy basher, because I'm actually a dual citizen; I'm Italian as well, so, I love Italy. I just wanted to discuss the situation there, a little bit. Not to forget that Como is such a beautiful region, so, you're privileged.

JP – Oh, that's the thing, in Italy you walk out of the theater and you are surrounded by what you sang about. Verona is still like it was. You get a real feel for how people lived, especially in Venice. For example, you walk in Venice once all the shops are closed and it's night time, you can imagine that you are there three or four hundred years ago. Where else can you do that? It's incredible.

OL – Right. Let's talk about that *Adelaide di Borgogna.* I think it is a good showcase for bel canto soprano arias, and there are some very good duets with the trouser role of Ottone. However I found it a bit un-theatrical, and less imaginative than other Rossini scores – of course in Rome at the time all recitatives were secchi, which can be a bit monotonous. This opera wasn't successful in its premiere, and never gathered much of a following. What is your opinion of it?

JP – It's not Rossini's fault, it's the way the drama was. Ottone goes out and comes back five minutes later, having won a battle that would actually have been something like a couple of days on horseback just to get to! It's obviously difficult for the stage director to do something about that. But I enjoyed the production, I really liked it. I liked the costumes. I think the libretto is a bit lacking, you can't do much with it. There are some great moments, musically. I enjoyed it, I might sing it in America; we'll have to see.

OL - Now, *Ciro in Babilonia.* You did it twice, first at the Caramoor Festival in a semi-staged production, then at the Rossini Festival in Pesaro with almost the same cast, the same conductor and stage director, this time in a fully-staged, charming that also had rather interesting projections, nice period costumes, and some neat tricks like the chorus looking like spectators in an antiquated movie theater, in more modern clothing, mixing up two timelines. Not only this is another example of a compelling and modern production, but also, I like much better *Ciro* as an opera, as compared to *Adelaide.* What are your memories of that production, and your opinion of this opera? Any plans to release that compelling production on DVD?

JP - I really loved the costumes in that production, they were just gorgeous. It will indeed be released on DVD/Blu-Ray, on the Opus Arte label. *Ciro in Babilonia*, I really enjoyed it. Yes, it functions a little better than Adelaide *di*

Borgogna in the dramatic sense. Davide Livermore, the director did a very good job with *Ciro*, splitting it up and using the period costumes, and then the cinema to kind of help the production through, because it is another one that is lacking in terms of dramatic sense. I had a great time; The performance at the Caramoor Festival was my debut in America, so that was moving and thrilling for me. The conductor Will Crutchfield was great, and my colleagues were fantastic. It was amazing singing with Ewa Podleś.

OL – Wow, isn't she great?

JP – She's incredible!

OL – Michael Spyres is a sweet one as well; Opera Lively interviewed him in person for almost two hours, and he is such a nice guy!

JP – He is a great guy, he is one of my closest friends, since we did the *Otello* by Rossini in Bad Wilbad. He is like a brother to me. It was lovely to be able to sing with him, because he was there with his wife soprano Tara Stafford-Spyres, it was just a lovely summer month hanging out with friends. It's a real treat when you get to sing with friends. And Ewa, apart from being a big inspiration as a singer, she is just a really great person. It was a lovely and really enjoyable experience.

OL - In May you did another relatively obscure Rossini opera – *Demetrio e Polibio* at the San Carlo in Naples. Would you please tell us about it?

JP – It was the same production they used in Pesaro three years ago. For me personally it's really important to sing at least one Rossini opera a year, so when I had the opportunity to sing this role in Naples I really jumped at it, unfortunately it's not easy to sing Rossini outside of a festival unless it's *Il Barbiere di Siviglia.* Until Naples I've only actually performed Rossini's Opera Seria in festivals; I did the *Armida* in the Garsington Festival, *Otello* in Bad Wildbad, and then the other two I did in the Rossini Festival in Pesaro, so for me it's important to sing Rossini in a theater, as part of a season, as well.

OL - You've also sung at many of Europe's leading international houses: Covent Garden, the Deutsche Oper Berlin, Vienna State Opera, Zürich, and Antwerp, just to name a few. In the New World, you've sung at the Caramoor Festival in New York, and in Peru. Do you have plans for debuts at any of the major U.S. or Canadian houses? I know that this year you're not scheduled for North America, but I heard that you'll be in Washington DC at some point for a concert. Can you tell us more about it? If you can't discuss specifics, can you at least tell us if you are in discussions with any of our houses?

JP – In Washington DC I'll be making my debut with the Washington Concert Opera, I think in 2015; they saw me when I sang Lucia in Berlin last December. About other houses, nothing I can announce as yet, I haven't really looked for work in America. I'm not a very ambitious person, in that sense. I'm not one of those singers who calls up the agent and says "I want to sing in here, and here, and here." As long as I'm singing things that I'm happy singing, I'm happy.

OL – But we want to see you here!

JP – [laughs] I would love to come back! I would also love to sing more in South America, to go back to Peru; I had such a great time, there. I told them "I'll come back any time." I think we are going to do *Lucia* there, because it is just such great fun! I certainly did like to sing in America, because I had a great time there. But my agent is Italian. [laughs]

OL - And what about Australia? Are there any plans for a visit home to sing with one of the major houses there? I realize it's a very long flight from Europe to Australia and that you lose a considerable amount of time just traveling. But are you able to go back to Australia occasionally to see family members?

JP – No, I don't go back. Last year I was able to go back after five years away, I had two and a half weeks off between Venice and New York, so I went back to Australia because my sister had a baby, and I wanted to see the baby, and that was the last time I went back, last year. I tend to fly my family to wherever I'm singing, because I find it easier. I don't have that much time off, it's a long lay-over, it is not very feasible to go home and hang out. It would be lovely, but it is not realistic.

This year I'm flying my sister and her husband to Spain, which will be great because her husband is from Chile, so he speaks Spanish, so I'll rent a big house! My father comes over when I make major house or role debuts. For him it's very important when I sing at Covent Garden or La Scala or Pesaro; he comes and sees it. And my mum comes once a year, but we try to make that when I am free or at least at the beginning of rehearsals so we can have more fun together.

OL – But what about the opera public in Australia? Are they following your career? Or is it hard to be a prophet in your own land?

JP – The fans write to me on Facebook and they ask when I will come. It's not just a question of wanting to go. I want to go, but to sing something that is good for me. I have waited a long time but I will finally make my debut in Australia in May of 2014 with my role debut of Violetta in *La Traviata* with the Victorian Opera in Melbourne.

OL -Let's talk some more about your recent experience at Ópera Perú in Lima, your first Matilde in *Guillaume Tell.* First of all, were there any striking differences regarding performing in South America, in a developing country, as compared to venues in Europe, and North America?

JP – The Gran Teatro Nacional in Peru is state-of-the-art. It's fabulous, it's new; they just built it. It's shockingly good. Amazing acoustics, all the stage machinery. Maybe the audience is more enthusiastic than an Italian audience might be. There were standing ovations every night and all that kind of thing. I think there are a lot more fans there, not so much that they are obsessive or anything, but they like the artists, there. I had a great time. I found the singers much more relaxed than in Italy, anyway. We went out a lot to dinner and so on. It was a really enjoyable experience, lovely performances. The orchestra was made of particularly young people who came from disadvantaged areas of Peru [Orquestra Juvenil Sinfonía por el Perú], so that was really interesting to work with them as well.

OL – Wonderful. Do you have any plans to sing at the Colón in Buenos Aires or the Municipal in São Paulo?

JP - I certainly do hope so. Some people from those houses came to see our performances and to talk, so I hope something comes from that.

OL - Tell us about singing with Juan Diego Flórez, in his homeland.

JP – Juan Diego is really cool. He is a really, really nice person, and it was just so fascinating to watch him sing, because he has this incredible technique and complete control. It was one of the few times when I sang with someone and felt that they inspired me to work that much harder. Because when you sing with someone who is really good at it, you think, "oh, I wish there were more hours to my day to figure these things out." It's really inspirational. He has complete control of his voice. He never pushes it, he never exaggerates, he is very graceful and elegant about the way he sings, and he is really good on stage. He is always able to be in the role, because he doesn't have to think about his technique, because it's all done, you know? You can see that he works hard and it's all under control.

Another thing I really liked about watching him is that he has this ability to pace himself, to keep everything under control, which I haven't learned yet, myself. So I watched him singing, especially in the last night, from the wings, and it was really amazing to watch. And of course he is a big star there and has lots of fans. And he is really nice, he helped everybody, did everything he could to help me, to help the chorus, and the orchestra. He is a great colleague.

OL - *Guillaume Tell* is an opera that is difficult to produce, given its length. It's hard to put it all on stage, but it is also hard to cut. How did the Peruvian crew go about it?

JP – I think they did their best. We didn't have much time to rehearse. I could have used an extra week, personally. But it really went well in the end. I think they were lucky with the staging. We had Massimo Gasparón, he is really good, and has been working in Peru for eleven years doing productions; he is used to them and they are used to him, he is very good at pushing things along. It came out pretty well at the end. [Editor's note – we learned that there were very discreet cuts, just some repetitions of cabalettas and some choral music were cut, but everything else including the ballets was preserved].

OL - And then, tell us about singing alongside a great veteran like Leo Nucci. Did he give you any guidance?

JP– Leo Nucci, it is so easy to sing with Leo Nucci and to pretend that he is your father in *Rigoletto*! I had this awe for him. Gilda is Rigoletto's daughter but she doesn't really know it because she is brought up in a convent, then she is taken out of the convent and brought home by this person who is her father. You can imagine she is all the time at this convent thinking about her father and her family, and she finally meets him, but he is so far away, still. He makes such an impression on her.

So there is this awe of his figure, then this wanting to be accepted, and in this case the character and the performer overlap a lot, because with Leo Nucci there, I think as a young singer, when you approach a singer who's had such a great career and sings in such an incredible way, you also have these feelings of awe and respect and wanting to be accepted, and he is of course such a lovely person; he does everything he can to help you. He is funny and easy to get along with, outside of the theater as well as inside. So it's really great, singing with him. And when you perform *Rigoletto* with him in Parma every night you repeat the Vendetta because the public won't let the opera continue without a bis, it's very fun and exciting.

OL - On the 8th of May, you have been awarded the prestigious La Siòla d'Oro - Lina Pagliughi prize (in the past awarded to sopranos such as Luciana Serra, June Anderson, Joan Sutherland, Mariella Devia, and Patrizia Ciofi). Tell us about it.

JP – It's a big honor to receive this award. It's incredible. I'm very excited about it. I don't know what else to say. All the singers who have won it are singers that I really admire, so that makes it even more important for me. In addition to the diamond broach in the form of the Siola I have also received the Medal of the President of the Republic, a very high honor in Italy.

OL – And it's great that you're getting it in your fifth year of professional singer.

JP – Yes, I'm really proud of it.

OL - You've also sung with some of the world's leading conductors, such as Sir Colin Davis, Nello Santi, Kent Nagano, and Christian Thielemann. In addition to your teacher, Maestro Gelmetti, have there been other conductors who played an influential role in your career?

JP – I think every conductor plays an influential role, either if they are a great conductor, or if they are not, because if they are not, you learn to be auto-sufficient, because otherwise, what will you do? The most influential conductor in my career has been Daniel Oren who basically took me all over the world with him. With him, when I perform I sing much better than I even imagine I can sing, and I don't know why. I still haven't figured out what it is. He is an absolute genius. He just changes everything, he changes the orchestra, and the mood, and he changes it according to how you are.

I remember one time when I was singing Lucia and I was unwell, so in four performances out of the five, he changed everything so that I could get through the performances – and not just get through; he made me sing well, and it was a great show. For the last performance, I didn't say that I had recovered, but I had recovered. And within two bars he realized it, and he changed everything. He made me hold all the high notes for a very, very long time. He made me repay everything that I hadn't done in the first four performances, you know? [laughs] So, he is really special as a conductor. And as a person, he has really helped me a lot.

OL - Tell us about Jessica Pratt the person. What do you like to do outside of opera?

JP – I like to go to walk in the hills, and nature. I think it is very important for us to be in touch with nature, and to spend time with animals. When I was in Australia I was a volunteer in a veterinary hospital; I took care of koalas and kangaroos. Two years ago I adopted a little dog. He is missing an eye. He is thirteen years old, and he's got a dislocated hip because somebody had beaten him up. He comes everywhere with me now, in Italy. Now he's got lots of hair, and he runs around on three legs, and he is perfectly fine.

And I think it's also important that people realize that dogs who lived ten years in a cage are perfectly capable of changing and living happy and healthy lives. He's never given me any problem, he comes in the train, he is a little dog so he goes in a bag, he sits in the theater and waits until I'm done with my show. He is incredible. So I have him, and every now and then we go on protests about anti-vivisection or anti-fur etc. I like cross stitching and I read a lot.

OL - What kind of person are you – outgoing, or reserved, etc?

JP – You know, I'm both, because I'm very, very reserved, but you can't be very, very reserved when you go on stage. I had a really hard time getting over that, because as a child I would not go to parties, I would not go out. If I had to go to a party I'd find a cat or dog and I would sit in the corner with the cat or dog until the party was over. And now I find myself not only having to go to the party, but I have to be the one in the middle of it, so that was very difficult for me to come to terms with in the beginning. I also had a hard time with the applause at the end of the opera. I used to be embarrassed.

In the beginning I didn't know what to do. I remember, my colleagues would count for me. I could hear them behind, saying, "stay there, stay there, one, two, three, four, five, OK, now you can come back." So, I'm getting better at it, I'm getting used to it but my colleagues still tell me I run away too quickly from the applause. Now I have these moments when I am very introvert, but also others when I'm very outgoing. But generally speaking if there is no pressure on me I'll just choose to stay at home and read or wander around the streets with my dog.

OL - What are some of your goals in life, in opera, and outside of opera?

JP – In opera, I'm achieving the goals that I've set, always have, maybe because I don't set goals that are impossible. Because I don't think in opera one can set a goal like – "I'm going to sing at this place, I'll have this career." One should set goals that one can achieve, which means setting goals that you have some sort of control over, such as how you sing, and how you practice. So my goals are more about improving my legato, being able to do good staccati, and get to a point where I can express emotion without being a slave to that emotion; being the puppeteer, not the puppet, as my father says. I'd like to raise awareness about animal rights, try to help as many people as I can, buy a house one day, and I'd like to have a family, and be happy. I think these goals are achievable.

OL – Very good. I loved this interview, it was a lovely one.

JP – Thank you.

OL – I hope you come to our opera houses, eventually.

JP – Me too! [laughs]

Melody Moore, soprano

This interview was done at Glimmerglass on the occasion of the very well received Francesca Zambello production of *The Flying Dutchman*, in August 2013. Again, Wagnerians will love it given that the experienced American soprano Melody Moore is also very intelligent and has some very good insights about Senta and other characters.

Opera Lively – Let's start by talking about Senta, the character. The idealistic young woman in love is a recurrent character in the history of opera. What makes Senta special for you, and how do you read her psychology?

Melody Moore - There are a lot of young girls in opera who fantasize, but Senta is non-typical because her obsession and her fantasy that this Dutchman will in fact end up at her port, fall in love with her and make her his bride, actually comes true. And it isn't that farfetched when you think about this story - she's been told her whole life about this Dutchman; she has set herself up to be ready for him when he arrives. She had an idea and she saw it through all the way, to the end.

Psychologically, she is obsessed, she is possessed, she is not living in the form of the reality of her town and engaging with her surroundings. What makes her different is that she has never been one of the girls that sits spinning, waiting for the men to come home from the sea. She has never dated a man who is also a seafarer. She is dating the town hunter. So she is an outsider looking for another outsider, and she finds one.

OL – Very nice! She spends a short time with the real Dutchman although she has been dreaming of his picture, and this is enough for her to jump to her death in order to rescue him. Sure, as a romantic character, that's what is expected of her, but do you read anything deeper in her rescue/suicide?

MM - I do. I think she is lonely. They find each other and they are a good match. She doesn't just dream of his picture, but rather of him as a person. She understands who he is - a person who wanders looking for something that he cannot find. She has connected with him on the psychological level because she is doing the same - alone, perpetually different, looking outside of her surroundings, and looking for her match.

OL – Musically, what are some of the vocal challenges involved in singing this role? The duet with The Dutchman is quite difficult, isn't it, maybe more than your opening ballad?

MM - Yes, the most difficult musical part is the duet. The challenge in that is just to stay anchored and actually sing with beauty. When you got someone singing really loudly into your ear [laughs] and right in front of you there is a huge section of blaring horns, it's hard not to want to scream. But the harder we push our voice, actually the less sound comes out. There is a perfect pressurization that causes the voice to ring at its maximum resonance. If you push past that or if you under-sing you decrease your resonance. So the trick is to stay anchored in your technique during that time.

The ballad is easier because you can hear yourself, it's lyric, it's beautiful, the melody is sweeping, the orchestra is not overpowering, no one is singing with you. So you can kind of monitor it as you go along, and change a little thing here and there, color some phrases differently, and have a little fun with it. With the duet, you just have to sing, I mean, loud. [laughs]

OL – Interesting! What is the concept behind this staging of *The Flying Dutchman* by Francesca Zambello?

MM - Conceptually we are sort of always on a ship. Of course the Dutchman has his own ship; it is a ghost ship that hardly touches the water if it does at all, and it comes to different ports every seven years for him to try to find a wife that will be faithful to him. During this production we keep everything on the boat, because the entire opera happens in a seafaring village. So, everyone, all of the chorus, my father, the Dutchman, myself, and Erik are all sort of on a boat. All the action takes place on there, so anything that comes on and off of the stage has to be dragged on or off. Otherwise it's ropes and plain wood, basically.

I enjoy the concept. It's stark, so that all the action that takes place on the stage is more important than any visual. The lighting is beautiful. They have a cold, bluish lighting for some of the storm activity, and it can even be sort of frightening.

OL – Working with such an accomplish director as Ms. Zambello must be thrilling. What kind of advice did she give you – maybe acting coaching, or something like that?

MM - No, she is so brilliant because she is an actor's director. She allows you to play, and if something visually is not working or not reading to the audience, she will tell you, but she doesn't necessarily give you a lot of advice, because unless we inhabit the character as the actors, the character is nothing real. Nothing that a director can say or do to you or for you is going to make that character real. You must find it for yourself. So what I enjoy about Francesca is that she sits, thinks, and watches as the audience. She puts herself in the position of the everyman, and tries to determine what is working, what isn't, and most of the time she is correct. That's what makes her brilliant. She can see through the eyes of other people. She doesn't look through her own eyes as an accomplished and educated watcher - she looks through the eyes of someone who may be seeing Wagner for the first time. She is very detail-oriented but she doesn't necessarily get in the way of the actor's process.

OL – Do you feel that she also matches her visual concept to the musical and textual cues that we get from Wagner?

MM - Yes. Many, many times Francesca will point out words that are very important. Wagner does tend to use high German language; language that has concept. There is a word - Treue - which means truth, that comes up often in this opera. Now, being that the Dutchman is looking for a faithful wife, one would think that Treue means truthful and faithful. But it also has a deeper meaning - it's the deeper truth of fidelity, honesty, dignity - the deeper truth, period. Often Francesca will point out to us - "hey, this word has popped up here again; think about that; ruminate on that, see what comes out of that!" When she just alerts us to the musical cues often times another layer will be added, because we will notice something that we hadn't noticed before.

OL – How has been for you the experience of singing with your colleagues Ryan McKinny as The Dutchman, Jay Hunter Morris as Erik, and Peter Volpe as Daland?

MM - All three of them are accomplished professionals, however they love to have fun. What I have loved about working with each one of them is their ability to play. I can't think of any scene in this opera that we haven't tried three different ways, in rehearsal or live. Because they trust me and I trust them, we are able to do this. I can't say that I feel that comfortable trying new approaches or new responses with everyone. I trust Jay, he is constantly thinking. Ryan is so clear with everything that he does; every motion, every eye that is cast towards me is clearly read.

OL – Good. How special is singing this, during Wagner's bicentennial year? How do you relate to Wagner's music?

MM - It is special to me to be singing my first Wagner role in the bicentennial, but more than that, it's important to me to be doing my first Wagner at all. Of course we all know that Wagner was a beautiful music writer but had some troubled politics. [laughs] It is difficult to separate the artist from his beliefs and his politics. At the same time, when I was a younger singer I used to dream of any chance that I would ever get to sing his music, especially his *Wesendonk Lieder* song cycle and *Rheingold.* I hear stunning epic God-like beauty in his writing. It's almost perfect. I know that a lot of people speak about Mozart being perfect as well, and I do hear the clarity and the mathematical precision of Mozart, but what I hear in Wagner is beginning romanticism playing with tonality, using accidentals, using sharps and flats in different ways to color a chord, complicating the music in a beautiful way that is very human. I love his writing. I hope to continue to be doing his music. He was very special.

OL – Yes. This festival run is a long one, with twelve performances. Does it get easier as it goes, or harder?

MM - It's a very difficult role to sing and it never stops being so, but you get used to it. Maybe a marathon runner could understand what I mean when I say it. Running a marathon is never going to be easy, is it? But it is going to get more comfortable, the more you do it. In other words, maybe you are just more used to the pain. [laughs] I have become accustomed to the show, therefore it may seem a little easier as it goes on, but it is never easy.

OL – Is there any vocal fatigue that settles in with so many performances? You do sing with several days interval, right?

MM - Yes, most of the time we have two or three-day intervals. Twice this season there is a show, then one day off, then a matinee. One has already happened, and I'm glad that that is out of the way. I wouldn't necessarily want to sing this twice in a row. It's very strenuous. There are either eight or nine high B flats or high B naturals within about thirty pages of music. So… [blows a raspberry]… yes! [laughs]

OL - Are you enjoying your time in beautiful upstate New York?

MM - I am so pleasantly surprised by how beautiful upstate New York is! Anytime that I get one of those long five-day intervals I try and go see something different that I wouldn't normally see - I live on the West Coast, I don't get up here much if it's not Manhattan, so when I got here I had never seen the Adirondacks, or the Catskills, or Lake George. I go adventuring, so I've been to Mirror Lake, and Lake Placid. I stayed quite a bit of time there at the Catskills. I'm about to go to Lake George after tomorrow's performance. I've hiked and kayaked and swam, everything. [laughs] I went to Saratoga. So yes, I have enjoyed it, it is stunningly beautiful.

OL - Although I haven't seen it, I'm interested in *Heart of a Soldier* - on Opera Lively we like to focus on new American opera. You created the role of Susan Rescorla in the opera's world premiere, which must have been very exciting. Please tell us about this experience.

MM - The opera itself was such an exciting experience! We were work-shopping it months before we actually put it on, to make sure that everything was settled. We were all on the same page with the music, with the drama, and with what we wanted to do on stage. It was like a preview experience on Broadway, where you show parts of it to the public via press conference or via workshop, and see what reaction you get.

It was incredibly exciting to play Susan. I got to meet her; she is actually coming to the show on the 12th here. We have remained in close contact. It was an incredible honor, to tell her story and her husband's. He was a national hero who got over two thousand people out of the South Tower before the collapse, and then ended up dying himself. Every day that I open my mouth, I thank the universe for giving me this opportunity. She is a beautiful woman.

OL –Did the fact of meeting her in person affect your preparation to portray her on stage? Did you do any sort of role study?

MM - Yes, I read the book, of course, and the sections about her. Then when I met her we had several lunches. I didn't want to use them opportunistically. I wanted to, more than meet her, just listen to her, because humanly, we do our best work when we listen to another person, without necessarily trying to enforce any kind of change. So, instead of looking at it as a homework assignment, I just wanted to hear her story, and we ended up enjoying each other's company. I left the door open to observe her, but didn't treat it as an experiment. I tried to just be open, and as a result, I have a friendship with her now, so I'm happy that I treated it that way. We did spend a lot of time together.

Melody's personal picture, with the real Susan Rescorla on the left

OL – Fabulous! Please tell us about the Recovered Voices Project at LA Opera, where you sang in Zemlinsky's *Der Zwerg* (The Dwarf) and in Ullmann's *Der Zerbrochene Krug* (The Broken Jug).

MM - Yes, it is James Colon's idea of putting on stage survivors of the Holocaust who were also composers at the time, and who may have been lost in the shuffle of important compositional voices. It was a brilliant idea, especially the Zemlisnky, which was beautifully directed by Darko Tresnjak to mimic the 1656 painting by Velázquez - *Las Meninas* - which inspired Oscar Wilde's short story *The Birthday of the Infanta.* It was a dark piece. I enjoyed *The Broken Jug* as well. It was taken from folklore about a woman who is taken advantage of and is trying to speak her piece. It's about her dignity. But I really enjoyed *The Dwarf*. We had an incredible cast, it was a longer piece that one could sink one's teeth in, both as a singer, and as an audience member. It had more of a story line. I would love to continue to be a part of any Recovered Voices series, as I think it is important to recover the voices of these composers.

OL - *Showboat* in Houston must have been a lot of fun. What are your thoughts regarding singing musical theater as compared to opera?

MM - One needs to be careful when one is crossing over from musical theater to opera and vice-versa because they are two different types of singing. However *Showboat* has an operatic style and was written in a period when operatic singers were singing these roles on stage, and were not necessarily miked, since they could project in vaudeville theaters. "Can't Help Loving Dat Man" sits in the middle of the voice and you can definitely sing it with projection, and "Bill" absolutely sits widely on the sweet spot, to sing it operatically but with style. I could still use my singing technique and not have to belt and change the entire way that I sing, and be able to still portray Julie La Verne quite well.

It was one of the most fun shows I've ever done, and I would love to do it again. I loved playing Julie. I was raised in Memphis so I understood her, the story, the theme of racism. I understand very deeply the family unit of the story; I had to observe that in my youth.

OL - Please tell us about the experience of having been called to replace Angela Gheorghiu during a *Tosca* performance at San Francisco Opera, when you stepped in for acts 2 and 3 as your role debut - that must have been something!

MM - Yes, it was the most exciting day of my entire life! [laughs] I will never forget it, and I probably didn't sleep for a week afterwards. I did not expect to go on. There was no forewarning whatsoever. Ms. Gheorghiu had been fine. All through the rehearsal process there was no problem. I was sitting in this conference room where we can watch the stage on a closed-circuit television, and be prepared, but the covers sit up there, eat a Subway sandwich and work on music; we are not very worried, because most of the time we are not needed.

But this particular day on the opening night of Tosca I did sense that there was a problem. Ms. Gheorghiu did not look well and she was shaking quite a bit and seemed a bit weak. So I went and told my colleagues that I was going to warm up. I went downstairs and I heard my name called on the speaker system. They told me that there might be a problem and I needed to go into costume, and we waited almost all the way until the curtain was ready to come up, because I do believe that Angela wanted to continue on, but just wasn't able to. She was very ill with the stomach flu, and had to be taken to the hospital in an ambulance. So, the curtain was about to go up and I had about the time that it took them to get me into costume, make-up and hair, to warm up further and prepare myself to go on.

Everything in me was the most alive that it has ever been. I had never worked on that set yet. We had only one cover rehearsal in a ballet studio. When I stepped in onto the stage it was for the first time and I had not ever sung the piece with an orchestra at all. No pressure [laughs] but just stand up there and sing Tosca. [laughs] So I decided "you need to get out of your own way" so I just tried to inhabit the character the best I could, and there were moments when I was so far into the character that I believe I was thinking as Tosca, not as Melody. It was invigorating and exhilarating and the best night of my life, musically.

OL - You did Don Giovanni for Opera Colorado. Is it specially challenging for a singer to take on the high altitude and dryness of Denver?

MM - Yes, it was the first time I sang in altitude like that. I've done competitions in altitude, but that's just showing up the day before and drinking some water, sleeping, singing in the competition and leaving. This was different, because I was there for over a month. I never drank so much water in my life. The company gave us all humidifiers to put inside of our rooms, and I had the humidifier running almost 24 hours a day, and even so the humidity would be 27%. A dangerous level for human survival is 20% so that will give you an idea of how dry it was. And the altitude of course changes the pressure in your body, so there were times when I was singing like a god, and then there were times when I couldn't get my breath. It took a couple of weeks to get used to it, but it was an awesome production.

OL - Critics have said that your voice has spinto power but that you are also able to portray vulnerability in your characters quite well. Please tell us about your Fach, and about what you try to accomplish with your acting.

MM - I believe I am Fachless [laughs] because I've sung so many different roles… To give you a small example, I went from Tosca to Donna Elvira to Pamina in Bordeaux, and then to Senta. Now some of these vocally lie on the same range. A lot of good soprano repertoire will go rather down into the middle and low voice area at some point in the opera. It is not that the range is all that different. It's the quality of the character that is different.

Pamina is so different than Donna Elvira which is so, so different than Senta. I sing them all with the same technique, but it's the acting and the immersion into the character that is different, so what I have relied upon in this last year is my sentiment about the character which provides the energy behind how I sing. But as far as a Fach, honey, your guess is as good as mine. I sing everything from Mozart to Wagner. [laughs]

OL - This does sound like a spinto, them, because you can go to the more dramatic territory, and you can go to the more lyric as well.

MM - Yes, it sounds like I'm some sort of spinto soprano; I'm not quite sure. A dramatic soprano can often sing mezzo and so can I; I have a very low voice, but I also have the ability to project very high, with power. I will sing everything the best I can, until something shows me that I cannot sing it. So far that has not happened.

OL - Good. I'm sure you've been asked this before, but your first name Melody is a nice one to have for a classical singer. It was destiny, huh?

MM - Yes. [laughs]

OL - So, how did classical music come into your life, growing up?

MM -I had no idea what classical music was. I was born and raised near Memphis in a very, very small town called Dyersburg, TN. The population at the time was 8,000; nobody lived there. I went to an Evangelical church. We sang whatever hymns were popular at the time. I took a little bit of piano, my mom taught me some. I had a little bit of exposure to the early, early piano repertoire of the classical style such as *Für Elise* but there was no recorded classical music in our home.

When we moved to Texas, I had to go to a public school, and I signed up for the choir because I had always sung in church and I figured that it was about the same thing. I was shocked because it wasn't. The Texas State Choir is very big, well funded, very popular, and very difficult and competitive. Throughout the state of Texas they pick three hundred singers, all from different vocal ranges, and then they go to San Antonio and sing for huge audiences. I ended up auditioning for that choir and I made fifth, then second chair in the alto section. So it was clear that I had some talent, and that's how I ended up auditioning for Louisiana State University, and getting in on a full scholarship, and continuing on in my studies to Loyola in New Orleans on vocal scholarship, and finally ending up at Kent State University for my undergraduate, and Cincinnati Conservatory of Music for my graduate degrees.

But it was really through the kindness, encouragement, and musical knowledge of professors surrounding me that I am here. I did not even know what talent was, and I didn't know opera at all. I had no idea who the main opera composers were. So, I went to the library every night and checked out and watched an opera per night for the first few months and continued checking out operas over the next two years. I was there to try to catch up with what other people already knew. Thank God for the people who told me I had talent, because I didn't know.

OL - Huh, huh, interesting. So, what are some of your extra-musical interests?

MM - I cook all the time. [laughs] I love to cook, I'm sort of a wine enthusiast and snob. Well, I live near Napa, so I can't help that.

OL - I envy you. It's my second interest after opera.

MM - Yes. Living in San Francisco with all the food movement, we are so lucky. Between San Francisco and Manhattan, the best of the best comes out; you can try all kinds of new things and a new restaurant pops up every week, and I enjoy cooking for myself. I love to be outside. I love anything that has to do with nature - walking, biking, hiking, swimming. I'd say, I would probably be cooking right now, had those professors of mine not told me that I was a singer. I'm pretty sure I would have a restaurant at this point.

OL - Have you done the Finger Lakes wine trail?

MM - I still haven't done the Finger Lakes wine trail. This last year I've been traveling so much, I just haven't had a moment to just wind down and enjoy something. When I have had a few days off, I've just decided to hike, instead. Maybe one day.

OL - Yes, I've done it, it is quite good, actually, not so much for the red wines, but there are some white wines that are quite compelling.

MM - Hm…

OL - How are you as a person?

MM - I like my time to myself. I like to read avidly; that's the other extracurricular activity I love as well. Because our career is so outward, and what we do is so extroverted, and after a performance we do also have to be social and greet and meet people and talk to them about our process, when I have time off I enjoy being quiet. I love to research - I'm pretty in love with Physics, and the different ideas that are coming up in string theory, dark matter, and multiverses. I guess personality-wise I would describe myself as quiet and introverted, oddly.

OL - Interesting, and then you chose the career of a performer; that must be complementary, in a sense, right?

MM - Yes, I think I picked it because I wanted to say so much that you cannot necessarily say or experience in everyday common life. In opera you can talk about these concepts that we need to delve into, and we are so lucky to be able to play these parts and experience these things in front of an audience. When I want to speak, I want to speak loudly. But I often don't want to. [laughs]

OL - Thank you for a lovely interview.

Ginger Costa-Jackson, mezzo-soprano

This pretty like a top model, very young half Italian, half American singer has a lot of energy, courage, and commitment. With her lively personality, talking to her in person at Glimmerglass in August 2013 , on the occasion of Verdi's *Un Giorno di Regno*, was a pleasure.

Opera Lively - First, let's talk about this production of *King for a Day*. The physicality in it is enormous. You leap and jump and sing in all positions. How challenging is it?

Ginger Costa-Jackson – It's very, very challenging. I remember the first rehearsal. You just do one scene at a time, so you think "OK, I can do this." Then when we do the final dress rehearsal, we have to do it all non-stop; my heart was racing. We had five weeks of rehearsals. After a month your body gets used to it. I did some exercises, like riding my bike and singing at the same time, or running and singing, to get that cardio and your lungs ready to go. I grew into the role.

OL – Yes. I once interviewed Danielle de Niese [Volume 1] and she told me the same thing about the *Giulio Cesare* she did at Glyndebourne with so much dancing. Similarly, at first she thought she could do it, then her heart started racing, so she had to train on a treadmill while singing at the same time.

GCJ – Exactly. It's to strengthen the lungs, I guess, because what happens is that in opera it's all about the breath support. We spend so much time rehearsing and practicing the breathing! So if you are exercising and moving a lot, your breath becomes very high, and if you are gasping for oxygen you can't sing. Long distance runners learn to breathe very low and keep the breath controlled. The more cardio you do, the more you can control that breath.

OL –Yes. I thought your acting was first rate. You had sensational comedic flair and stage presence. Please contrast the acting on a comedy like this, with your tragic acting in *Carmen* last year, and tell me how you learned to act.

GCJ – I was a young artist at the Metropolitan Opera and we had two phenomenal acting coaches, Stephen Wadsworth from Julliard, and Dona Vaughn from the Manhattan School of Music. They did exercises that helped me be in tune with what you have inside. Singers act from instinct. We are very "feeling" kind of people. We can feel when our voices are doing what is right, and when to give in to the music. You practice so much with your voice…

When you get on stage, it needs to be about the words. Instead of thinking "how do I sing this line?" we have to think like Maria Callas who said "I am an actress-singer, not a singer-actress." It's the idea that you say what you want to say, so every night it's a little bit different. [She demonstrates two ways of singing the line "I love you."] You make the words come out; then the acting happens. If you only pay attention to the sounds and not to the words, you miss the feeling of the moment. It's instinct, but I also definitely had training that helped me a lot.

In terms of contrasting this work with *Carmen*, I actually think that *Carmen* is a lot less difficult. With the Marchesa del Poggio in *Un Giorno di Regno*, Verdi's second opera, he was still trying to understand voices, and he cast a mezzo-soprano but it sits very, very high. It has a lot of high notes, as you can recall. The challenge with this comedy is one – the vocality is very difficult for a mezzo because it is very high, and two, it is bel canto, so it's about the beauty of the tones and all of these interpolations and coloratura. *Carmen* musically sits lower and is easier to say the words; there aren't many difficulties.

But apart from music, the physicality of the Marchesa, being it a comedy, is all about timing. We work a lot on the timing. Comedy is also all about your colleagues. You are only as good as the person you are with. It's true of drama, but especially of comedy, because you need to play off of each other and you really need to be actors. If you miss the timing by just a little bit you won't get the laugh. You need to be very precise.

For *Carmen*, you don't try as hard with your body. You just stand there and look good, but you have ideas. Carmen is about inner life. She thinks a lot and doesn't move as much. The Marchesa del Poggio on the other hand, everything that she thinks is in her body. You see moving, running around, you see her react. Carmen takes a moment. Something happens to her, and she doesn't react right away. She thinks about it, is very conscious, and is in control. The Marchesa is not in control. She is a chicken with her head cut off. Something happens to her, and she wants to see her lover who is the king in decoy, and she wants him to tell her that she is really his first love, but he is playing this façade of a king, and she is running after him and still doesn't get him. On act 2 I finally get to be in the room with him but he will still not admit that he is my true love, so I get drunk, and try to get him to tell me what I want. In *Carmen* you play the person who is in control, and in this one, you play the person who is out of control. It's more difficult to play, because you have to do more.

OL – Talking about playing with your colleagues, what about that adorable colleague of yours, the dog?

GCJ – Oh my Goodness! The dog is interesting. It wasn't my idea; it was the genius of Christian Räth, our absolutely phenomenal director. He came in and said, "I think for this first aria you want to come in with a dog, and you want to use one of the company dogs." I told him, "actually I have a dog." He said, "really??"

OL – It's your dog??

GCJ – It's my dog! It's a poodle! My little toy poodle. He said, "bring her in! I'd love to see her!" And of course he fell in love with her the moment I brought her in, and we rehearsed the full five weeks with her. What a better way to set the stage? My first aria, I come in with my fur coat and my glasses, my beautiful gloves and earrings, I'm this diva – what diva comes without a dog? Maria Callas had a toy poodle as well; hers was black. Actually Christian sent me a picture of her with her poodle, and said, "look, it's the same scene!"

Yes, she is my dog, and she is not a trained dog. She is three years old. She had never been on stage before so I was a little bit concerned. She is my baby; I don't want to make her uncomfortable with the lights and having so many people in the audience. The first rehearsal I could feel that her heart beat was a bit faster, but after that there was no problem. I think she actually really likes it. Yesterday there was a show, and she was a little bit depressed. My mother and I got her cleaned up. My mother is here with me. So we groomed the dog, and went in and did the first scene; I put her collar on her and I could tell she was getting a little happier. She goes on stage and when she is done she is just so excited! OK, good, we have two divas, I guess, in this family [laughs] who love being on stage.

OL – Very nice. What did you think of doing it in English? You are a native Italian speaker. To be the Devil's Advocate, although I liked very much the work done by Kelley Rourke with this new translation, I wonder if it is really necessary. You know, operatic singing changes the phonemes enough that the audience needs the supertitles in English anyway, so why sing it in English?

GCJ – Vocally there is no advantage. As far as the technical training of opera, it's going to be easier to sing a Romance language. The language sits more forward. All the work that we do is projection of the voice. Singing opera is to get the sound forward and out so that everyone can hear it and it is loud. English is a very back language. It takes more effort to sing English and to project it the same way you would Italian, and it is never quite as beautiful. The English language is not as sonorous, versus l'italiano è molto davanti e c'è una bellezza. It has a beauty, Italian, even just speaking it. There is a disadvantage of singing in English, because frankly, it's not as beautiful. As far as the translation, I had learned it in Italian, and I have the DVD.

OL – The one with Anna Caterina Antonacci?

GCJ – Yes, yes, the one with Anna Caterina, exactly, and I love the Italian! But I'm completely enamored with the English libretto for this staging, for this production, because with an American audience there is a faster pay-off to have it in the native language. People who may be not as much opera goers, because it's not part of the American culture, it makes it more accessible to them. Maybe it makes opera less frightening, and people think "OK, it's in my language, I can understand it."

We set it in the sixties and it is so quirky. Her libretto is not a direct translation, it's an adaptation. One of my favorite lines is when I come in to the Kelbar house, who is my uncle, and I say, "uh, if it wasn't for you, my cousin, I would not step foot in this gawdy, guilded bungalow." It really adds to the flavor of the comedy of the era, because it uses the jargon of the sixties, the way they would speak. For me anything that keeps it real to the time, real to your character, I will accept it. It makes your character come alive in a different way. But would I love to do it in Italian at a future point? Yes, it would make it a little easier, vocally.

OL – So you watched Anna Caterina's DVD. I interviewed her as well; she is gorgeous. [Volume 1]

GCJ – Oh wow!

OL – Yes, when she was Cassandre at the Royal Opera House.

GCJ – Oh, I just covered at the Met for a *Les Troyens* role, not Cassandre, but the boy, Enée's son.

OL – So, did Anna Caterina function as an inspiration for you? Do you usually look at your predecessors for your preparation?

GCJ – It's interesting. When I studied *Carmen*, I studied from the score, but then I watched DVDs and had them in the background over and over, because learning music is about repetition. Sometimes it's boring to sit at the piano and continuously plunk notes. I had her DVD at the Royal Opera House, the one that Zambello directed with Kaufmann and Anna Caterina.

So the two roles that I've been asked to do at Glimmerglass, I learned watching her DVDs. I think she is great. But I really think that the moment they put this in English, I can't do anything. Sometimes you take a line that you would maybe sing the same way another singer would – the same kind of feeling – but the moment they put it in English, it's really hard to take inspiration, because it changes what you are saying, it changes the feeling, it changes also the musical lines, I take breaths in different areas than she would take them, because the phrases are different. So, she was more an inspiration for *Carmen*; not as much in this.

OL – Have you ever met her?

GCJ – No.

OL – Oh, she is so gracious; I think she'd love to give you some insights.

GCJ – Oh, I would love to meet her.

OL - You are a very young singer with a meteoric path. How old are you, now?

GCJ – I'm twenty-six.

OL - Let's focus at length on your career experiences. I understand you were born in Italy and came to America very young, and in a household with three girls, all three of you have embraced the arts. You started as a violinist. Please describe how this came to be.

GCJ – How did you know all this? [laughs]

OL – I did my homework!

GCJ – Both of my parents are very musically inclined. Neither had a career, but my mother when she was a girl in Italy attended conservatory and got a certificate in piano and voice. It was the same conservatory I went to. She always sang in the house and played opera. Being Italian, it is part of the culture. We always grew up having opera music around. On Saturdays she would play the Three Tenors CD, and she would get the up tempos on, and she would say, "OK, everyone, you clean to the tempo of the music!" So we'd hear "Di… Quellla… Pira…" [sings it with a very marked tempo] and we would scrub to the tempo that was being played. [laughs] So I grew up with opera.

And then from Dad – he is an American – he was in the Barbershop Quartet in college, and loved symphonies and musicals. When I was very little he would put all three girls to bed and would pick out the flute from among the instruments, and would say "OK, in this piece you'll see how the flute sounds like a little bird." He would play a symphony and we'd close our eyes, and he'd ask "what instruments do you hear?" We watched musicals, *Music Man, State Fair, My Fair Lady, South Pacific, The Sound of Music*, we'd watch every single day and my sisters and I would dance to it, choreographing things and singing together. At one time we videotaped ourselves, because we made up an opera. Even at that young age, I played the prince, not knowing that I would be a mezzo and do pants roles. My sisters were the princesses and I would gallop on our fake little horse to save them. It was part of our culture growing up, so it was almost inevitable that all three of us became singers.

OL – How old were you when you made up that opera?

GCJ – Miriam was 11, the youngest, who is a coloratura soprano. Marina was 12, and I was 13. We made an opera DVD. I have to find this home video. Marina, my second sister, is starting her second year at the Academy of Vocal Arts in Philadelphia, and it's so funny because she is doing *Così fan tutte*, she plays the role of Fiordiligi, and I'm going to the Met to cover Dorabella, so when we are together we study the music and sing along, it's so fun! Miriam would make a beautiful Despina; she is in Utah right now and is married; she is actually currently pregnant, so she has her baby listening to opera.

OL – So maybe one day the three of you will perform together.

GCJ – That's our great hope. It would be inevitable for Marina and I. We are both East Coast. That would be the best thing I could ever do, more than any dream role, Carmen, Dalila, to be able to sing with my sisters. It's interesting because when we sing together, the voices blend very well. I don't know if it's because we are family, or it's the way we speak the vowels. We have these overtones when we sing together that don't happen with any other soprano or when I do duets with a man. Whenever I come to her apartment in Philadelphia, she has a long stairway going up, and I start singing her name from the bottom, and I hear her responding [hums the music]. Music is just part of our family.

OL – Super nice! So, how did you switch from violin to opera?

GCJ – We were listening to a lot of musical theater in the house. I was in Utah. We were raised predominantly in Utah. Our public elementary school offered orchestra. Nowadays it's not happening as much, in the educational system. They had people come to our school, maybe in fourth grade, and they brought four instrumentalists, and they had us all in the gymnasium, trying to recruit people to come to the orchestra. They had a lady playing the violin, and a viola, a cello, and a bass. When the bass was playing you could feel the vibrations in the ground. I remember thinking, "this is so amazing!"

I came home and said, "mama, I want to be part of the orchestra." She bought me a little violin, and I played it all into high school. I was the first violinist for the orchestra. The violin is actually the closest to the human voice. I didn't start taking singing lessons until sixteen or seventeen, but it really helped to facilitate being a singer. I took violin, Marina wanted to play cello, and Miriam the viola. We all had an instrument, growing up.

OL – Did you dream of performing in concertos as a violinist, or did you always want to be a singer?

GCI – I loved playing the violin, but I didn't want to be a violinist for the rest of my life. I loved doing it. I was a very straight-laced student. I was never tardy, never absent, and had a 4.0 GPA. I loved to do the very best in everything I did. Violin, I just saw it as another thing I wanted to be very good at, but I never wanted to continue on. I wanted actually to be a professor of English Literature. I was a studious person and loved reading.

I wanted to become a singer for the first time when Miriam started taking voice lessons. She was 12 years old. I'm two years older. She took voice lessons for a year and a half, off and on. When I was sixteen, finally, I decided that I wanted to take voice lessons. I remember one night I was in my bedroom and I was laying down; Miriam was in the kitchen, and she was singing "Chi il bel sogno di Doretta." I remember her singing the very high notes.

OL – It's not easy.

GCJ – It's not easy. She is very good; has a G, an A, an extreme top. For her those notes were nothing. She has a natural ability to do these piani that are very piano, like Caballé. I remember hearing that in my heart and I was thinking, "that sound is flying, I wish I would do that." Little did I know that it would be a long time before I ever learned how to sing high notes, because I'm a mezzo. One, I would never sing that song [laughs], and then, when I first started taking voice lessons, I kept cracking, almost like a boy who is having a hormonal change of voice. I wasn't very good, and I remember my mother asking – "Are you sure, Ginger, that this is what you want? Because you are good at everything else; you excel at school and with the violin; are you sure this is the path you are going to take?" But I was very determined, and said, "no, no; this is what I want to do."

OL – You've been described at one point as a contralto. I'm not sure if the journalist who said that was accurate. But you do seem to be a dark-voiced mezzo. What roles do you think will fit your voice?

GCJ – It's interesting, because I just finished doing *Francesca da Rimini*, where the role of Smaragdi sits very low. I remember this article saying I was a contralto. Now, this role of the Marchesa sits very high, and the maestro added two high Ds to spice things a little bit. And now, all the articles say "soprano Ginger Costa-Jackson." People become maybe a little confused, but I don't think there is anything to be confused about. A mezzo-soprano should have that range. Every singer should be able to extend both high and low. The difference that makes you a mezzo, a soprano, or a contralto, is where the changes happen, the breaks in the voice. I'm very happy knowing that I am a mezzo. If things change, they'll change, but for now I have a deep chest voice, so that's why people think contralto. But I do have the high notes.

I would say that I will go on to sing mezzo roles that are dramatic, like Verdi, in the far future, but for now I'm just keeping things very bel canto. Also, I'll be doing a lot of Carmens this next year. You have to sing each role with your voice, and pay attention to the size of the house and the size of the orchestra. Singers are very limited nowadays. They try to put you in a box; they say "this is who you are," and I don't believe in that. Someday I want to do a *Rise and Fall of the City of Mahagonny*, do a Jenny. You look at someone like Maria Ewing, for example, she did the Carmens, the Rosinas, but then she went on and did Salome, and Tosca! People try to limit artists, but I'll want to say, "no, you can't limit me." So, the short answer to your question is, I am a mezzo but I have a top and I have a bottom, so whatever roles fall in between, don't be surprised if I do them. [laughs]

OL – There's nothing wrong with that, as long as you keep your voice healthy. So, you made a very bold move, dropping out of high school at age 17 to go to a conservatory in Palermo, Italy. Please tell me about this experience. Was it psychologically hard to have the courage to do that and go away from your nuclear family?

GCJ – When I was sixteen I took voice lessons, and that summer we had planned a trip to visit family in Italy – all my aunts and grandparents and cousins. That summer, they were holding auditions for the Conservatory Vincenzo Bellini. I wasn't taking lessons for very long and wasn't very good, but I auditioned. I think they saw the potential, the dark tones. I was one of the nine that were selected out of three hundred people. In Italy it's free through the government, for citizens. My father is a high school teacher and my mother is a stay-home mom, we would never had the funds.

It was hard for them to let their sixteen and a half-year-old daughter go. Luckily I lived with my aunt who is a second mother to me; she is my mother's sister. She has two children, my cousins, and I had my grandparents. I wasn't alone. I definitely had the support of family there. I did two years there, then the Young Artists Program at the Met saw me at a competition and invited me to come audition for James Levine. Life just took off. I removed myself from the high school system in America but I continued high school through correspondence. I actually finished high school; I just did it while I was in my conservatory studies. They sent me the books and the tests. I had to teach myself but I got through it. Now I'm in this crazy career.

OL – Then you went to BYU but you didn't like it.

GCJ – Yes. [laughs] After being in Italy for a year and a half I was very homesick. I had my aunt and my cousins but there is nothing like your mom and dad and your sisters. To be separated from them was a big thing. I really wanted to be able to do school in America and continue my career, so I went to BYU for a semester. BYU has an amazing program with people who are doing very well, but for me it didn't fit at the time. After one semester my gut told me, "the training you need is where you were in Italy – you need to go back; you need to do it the way it feels right to you." So I left, after a semester, and went back to Italy. [laughs]

OL – Did you leave when you auditioned for Levine?

GCJ – I auditioned for him afterwards. I was 19 when that audition happened, and I was 18 when I went to BYU for a semester. It's college. In the conservatory you study solfeggio, voice, music appreciation; you are immersed in music all day long. The problem is, I went to BYU and had all these general credits that I had to fulfill. I was taking physics, history, math, eighteen credits, and I was being burned out, doing all that homework, and only had one music class which was group voice lesson at 8 AM in the morning. I thought to myself "this is the path if I want my degree, but this isn't helping me as a singer; this isn't furthering my talent or teaching me acting and how to sing." I was getting mono, because I am a perfectionist and was trying to get 4.0 GPA so I was studying up until 5 AM and never had time to practice singing.

OL – You did a short circuit, a fast track, going from that to the Lindemann, bypassing for example the National Council Auditions. Was it very surprising for you that you were accepted into the Lindemann?

GCJ – It was very surprising. I was doing a competition in Rome, the Ottavio Ziino, and Lenore Rosenberg was in the jury. I made it as a finalist. I didn't win, though. I was backstage feeling pretty poorly because I didn't win anything, and she gave me her card and said that they would be interested in having me sing for James Levine. She said she was very impressed, hearing me in the different rounds. She said they would fly me in December for a private audition.

I remember auditioning for James Levine, and he had just come from a concert. He was late, because there was traffic. He finally came and sat down and put his hands over his eyes and his head down. I guess he had a headache. I came and sang my two songs. I sang "Va! Laisse couler mes larmes" and "Di tanti palpiti" and I remember being so nervous! But when I sing I give my emotions over to the music. You have to think "what am I saying?" because people want to be moved. If you are saying what you want to say with the voice, normally people will like the singing. Don't worry about making the sounds.

Anyway, I just gave everything I had. He didn't look up once. He didn't look at me at all. He just sat there like this with his head down. I walked off, and thought "this is not good. I didn't even get him to look up once; this is not going to happen." So I went back to my hotel room and was so nervous, but I thought, "if this is the path that God wants me to take, it will open up." I tried to keep a good perspective. The next day I was flying home, and was at the airport about to board the plane when I got the call from Lenore saying "we are very delighted to welcome you into the program." I guess he was listening. I remember, I immediately called my parents, and everyone was in the plane, and I said "just wait a minute; Dad, I got in, I got in!" I didn't want to have to wait to give him the news. The airplane had to wait. [laughs]

OL - As a young artist you debuted at the Met main stage, if I'm not mistaken, in *Thaïs* with the great Renée Fleming. Did she mentor you? Did you get advice from her?

GCJ – She is so sweet! Every time we worked together she's been gracious and kind. The biggest lesson for young singers is just hearing voices and seeing what these great artists do when they are at work, in the rehearsal process. To my embarrassment when you first sing opera you sing with all of your sound and you think you have to push. I was nineteen and a mezzo and I thought I had to make big, big mezzo sounds [she says it in a low big voice]. I remember hearing her singing in the practice room, and she had a beautiful voice, but I thought "oh, I'm louder than her!" Right? I was singing with this "booo" [makes again a big low voice] and then there comes this person with perfect technique with a very sharp sound that almost sounds quiet in a room. But then when you go on stage, because they are creating overtones, those carry straight into the hall. The person who is singing with the big voice on the back of their throat, sounds big in the bathroom, but on stage it doesn't carry.

I was thinking, "wow, that's how loud she sings? That's not very loud!" And then we got on stage… [laughs]… my voice was left behind, and she was this easy singer. She is one of the most natural singers I know. She doesn't contort her face. She sings and the air just comes out. You need to play with the air gracefully. When you are young, you think you need to do so much... That was the greatest lesson from Fleming to see her voice in the hall go "voosh" and mine... [laughs].

OL – Yes, I saw a master class with Frederica von Stade and she was stopping the young singers all the time, and saying, "no, no, no – do this pianissimo! You don't need to belt and shout and yell!"

CGJ – Yes, she's definitely taught me that. I have great respect for her. She is such an amazing person!

OL -It's very nice for a young singer to have had parts in three Met DVDs already – *Nixon in China*, *Thaïs*, and *La Fanciulla del West.* Please describe the experience of being in *Nixon in China.*

GCJ – *Nixon in China*, I don't even know where to begin, there. The music is challenging because it's repetitive and stretches me as a musician, but I actually really, really loved that opera. It's so jazzy, almost! Even when I jog, I listen to the aria "News" [sings it, snapping her fingers to mark the rhythm]. When you first hear it, it's not what you are used to. I've done it now at the premiere in New York, and in San Francisco, always in the role of First Secretary to Chairman Mao, Nancy Tang. Now, it's one of these things... the music is really in me. And the history... this is actually what happened. It's just so compelling when you put yourself into the words and know the feelings of what happened.

And it was with Peter Sellars, he is so moving and gets so much of you. Did you see that DVD? [I nod yes]. Under Communism, all our movements are choreographed. We are always together and doing a lot of hand gestures. Having to do that while singing is almost like Yoga. You are singing and then your arms and your body are doing different things. I loved it; it was very fun.

OL – And it is amazing to be part of a world premiere.

GCJ – Yes, it really is. There is a feeling about it that is electrifying. And then, to have John Adams conduct you in his own music! He is so cool! He would come in with Star Trek T-shirts. [laughs] He is so intelligent. These people who are geniuses, they look at you and you can tell they are thinking a thousand things. They are not always with you; they are a little spacey. He is such a sweetheart!

OL -You got two principal roles at Glimmerglass, and now I understand you're slated to cover Dorabella and Meg Page at the Met.

GCJ – There were some other offers but I turned them down because I had the opportunity to do *Carmen* twice this year, in Tri-Cities Opera, and also Opera Hamilton in Canada. These contracts are being signed as we speak. I turned down a Bersi in *Andrea Chenier* at the Met. I would love to do that, I love Patricia Racette who will be singing there, but to be able to do *Carmen* again…

OL - How do you see the future of your opportunities at the Met? How hard is it to make it to the bigger parts?

CGJ –I've been at the Met for a very long time and I love it. When you are on that stage, it's amazing. But for any artist, it will always be more gratifying to do a bigger role than to cover a role. When you cover you are not able to make your art; you are sitting all the time. You are watching and you need to be ready to go but most often you don't go on stage. As far as doing lead roles at the Metropolitan Opera, that would be absolutely amazing. If that happens in my life, great. If it doesn't happen in my life, as long as I can make my art…

OL – Yes, but the cover roles… there are many stories, including that of Maria Callas, of singers who were covering and then stepped in and had a big break.

CGJ – Yes, that is true.

OL – So being there can be exciting.

CGJ – No, no, of course. I mean, it's the Metropolitan Opera, the biggest opera stage in the world. And you have HD broadcasts… it's such an exciting place to be. I'm a very simple person. Give me a role and I'm happy, as long as I can sing.

OL – In this video media era, singers now are required to have the right look on top of the voice, and you do.

CGJ – Thank you!

OL –You also have a beautiful voice. What does it take, to make it and maintain it, in this competitive career?

CGJ – I don't know what it takes. I was very fortunate to be a Young Artist at the Metropolitan. I have had opportunities because of it. Who you know, counts. If people don't know who you are, they are not going to hire you. It's been very good for PR. The Met put me on stage, and people look and say, "hah, that's who she is." Then you are already in people's minds and radars. My mother always said, "talent must always come forward." If you are passionate in what you do and you take great joy in it… Yes, it helps to also have connections, but if it is destiny, it happens. If it doesn't, it's fine, as long as you are happy doing what you do.

OL – Would you like to have a career in films or musical theater, or do you want to remain in opera forever?

GCJ – I would love to do some musical theater. I would love to sing cabaret music, or jazz. I grew up listening to musical theater. I would want to do everything – a one-woman show, cabaret, jazz… there is the Lotte Lenya Competition and I've done it a couple of times now. It's so much fun to sing Kurt Weil's music! He is actually one of my favorite composers. He is so real, with the quality of the music that he puts out, and the words are so heart-wrenching! I just love anything that you can sink your teeth into it, and become the character. All his characters are pirates, or whores; I tend to be typecast for that, so… [laughs].

OL – That's the destiny of mezzos anyway…

GCJ – I know… it is; it is!

OL -Psychologically speaking, is it hard on such a young person to be engaged in this kind of fast track? Are you prepared for the hardships of this life?

GCJ – Yes, you take everything one day at a time. Any career is difficult. Opera singing comes with its own particular baggage. You are always on the road and you can't always be with your family. You are being judged not on an instrument that is outside of you – like the violin – but you are being looked at. You are your own instrument. People are going to judge you every night based on what you do. You are alone on stage. There is no one who is going to come and help you, if half-way through a phrase you have no more breath. You have to make it happen.

But honestly… we had a show yesterday in matinee, and I'm so happy on stage! I love it when I can see the audience's faces. I love the idea of doing recitals because I love to engage with the audience. People come to the theater and it is a therapy. It is to laugh, to cry… it's an entertainment but so often in hearing a singer sing, it evokes some of your own emotions and thoughts and you can feel that you can relate to that character on stage. You can say "ah, she is crying; I know, I also have something in my life that is similar to this." You can mourn with them. It's an amazing therapeutic thing. There is such a symbiotic relationship between me and the people that come to the show! I need them, and they for that moment need me to play a character. I love doing it.

OL - What are some of your extra-operatic interests?

GCJ – I love to draw. I draw little caricatures and cartoons. I would love to write a children's book. My father is a very good writer. We are working on a couple of books that he is writing. We spin ideas on each other and I illustrate. That's very fun. I love to dance. I don't know if I'm good at it. I love to watch TV and read and dance and bike and hike and be in nature – you know, the normal things. At the end of a long day of work, the best thing is to sit in front of the television on your couch and watch Bravo – mindless television! [laughs]

OL -Please describe your take on life and your personality.

GCJ – I heard – I don't believe in Astrology so much, but I'm a Virgo – that I'm very, very perfectionist. I believe all the artists are like this. You are never happy with what you do. You always feel "I could have done that much more!" I'm a little bit hard on myself; not on other people, just on myself. I love people, in general. I love getting to know people. Even when we had donor events, this doesn't sound so funny, but I like interacting with someone else. Later on, you may play that character. I like to analyze other people.

About my take on life, that's a very complicated question. [thinks] I believe very firmly in God. I'm very religious. I wouldn't be where I'm at, if it weren't for Him. When I was sixteen, I listened to my sisters' voices, and I remember praying, "Heavenly Father, this is what I want to do; please help me." I believe very strongly in a superior being. We are all here on Earth trying to do good. We are all brothers and sisters. I think that's why I love singing on stage because you can relate to people. I feel that we are all related, anyway. So why be nervous? We are all family.

OL – That's all I had. Do you have anything to add?

GCJ – You were very thorough and had a lot of interesting questions.

Thank you so much! I also talk so much! I get that from the Italian side. I guess I could add that my mother was my first voice coach. My greatest fan is my father. He does my website. Everything I do, my father thinks it's amazing. My mother, I think she is my greatest critic. But she takes me through vocalizes. If you don't have the support of your loved ones, you can't make it. My father doesn't make a lot, but he was able to support me through living all those years in Italy. Everything he makes, everything he has in the bank including retirement funds, is to help his daughters. He never wants anything in return. He thinks, "these are my daughters' dreams, and I want to help them."

OL – That's nice! OK, thank you so much!

Jill Gardner, soprano

Jill Gardner is an Opera Lively favorite, having been featured in Volume 1 with her serious research and original take on each of her roles. This is the kind of very cultured and smart regional singer who could perfectly have been an international success given some luck. Sometimes wide fame is a question of being in the right place at the right time and great singers remain regional when they don't happen to get that big breakthrough. We talked to Jill again, in January of 2014, for her Trittico at Opera Carolina.

Opera Lively – It's nice talking to you again, Jill. Have you had a chance to look over the draft of our questions I sent you?

Jill Gardner – Yes. I love how passionate you are. It's really wonderful to go through your questions. I love to delve into them along with my process, too, because in my own research for a role it is very nice to be able to use your questions to figure out my thoughts about it.

LG – Thank you, it's very kind of you to say so. OK, let's go, about Il Trittico.

JG – All right!

LG - Puccini had great trouble keeping his *Il Trittico* together, since public and critics have always liked *Gianni Schicchi* more than its companions, and starting with his own publisher Ricordi, people such as opera house managers have been tempted to separate the three components. Something can be said, though, for Puccini's initial intention of presenting several facets of the human experience in the same evening. The composer himself did not hesitate in calling the idea of separating his operas "a real betrayal" as he had planned the three operas as an arc – *Il Tabarro* for Hell, *Suor Angelica* for Purgatory, and *Gianni Schicchi* for Paradise. What is your opinion on the advantages of performing all three operas together?

JG – There is this Dante reference that you talk about, of Hell, Purgatory, and Paradise. In Puccini's life, after the mature works of his lyric writing, which were *Manon Lescaut, Bohème, Tosca* and *Butterfly*, the later works that he did were *Fanciulla del West, Rondine, Trittico*, and *Turandot* right before he died. What was interesting about the *Triptych* was that the he was trying to create a completely different evening of dramaturgy for the audience. He researched a lot of different things to build this idea. The reference to Dante was one of them, but he also traveled a lot to go to the theater – not just the opera – all over Europe. He had a huge interest in French literature and theater. I personally think that this *Triptych* was highly influenced by the Grand Guignol theater in the Pigalle area of Paris, where short plays were often produced in this kind of contrasting styles in an evening. When you went to the theater you might experience one or two or even three different short plays in one evening, and often one would be a comedy and one would be a horror play. The Grand Guignol theater specialized in Gothic horror.

OL – Yes, *Il Tabarro* is based on a Grand Guignol stage play originally presented there, with two murders instead of one.

JG – That's exactly right. I'm intrigued by that. I haven't figured out exactly the timing, if Puccini would have seen it, but I can't help but think that he did. There are Massenet influences as well. You were saying that *Il Tabarro* represents a stronger violent vibe, then there is the sentimentality of *Suor Angelica*, and the comedy of *Schicchi*. This is the kind of thing that was presented at the Grand Guignol and Puccini wanted to recreate a similar type of evening experience in the opera theater. Musically he was experimenting, and continuing to grow, compositionally. He wanted to present three different works, all with contrasting colors, and contrasting orchestral flux, meaning how he used the orchestra in the evening throughout the *Triptych*. He was clearly trying to continue to develop stylistically.

For the *Triptych* he was particularly inspired by the theater, like he was for *Tosca* and *Butterfly* which were also based on actual plays. He wanted to channel that dramatic expression in his very unique way through his four mature works. I personally think that the *Triptych* musically and dramaturgically can be seen as a zenith for Puccini.

There was a tradition in the German repertoire of presenting one-act operas. You think of Strauss, with *Salome* and *Elektra,* then *Daphne* and *Capriccio*, or even Schoenberg's Erwartung which was recently presented at New York City Opera before it went out of business. So the Germans had this idea of the one-act operas, but apart from *Cavalleria Rusticana* and *Pagliacci*, the use of this within the Italian tradition was not as developed. So I think he saw this as a means of personal expression which I see as extremely unique.

OL – Yes, people think of Puccini as romantic and melodic music, but he was a great innovator. He was original and pushed music forward.

JG – That's what I think he was. This Giovane Scuola that he was a part of, the school that came after Verdi, started to create this veristic tradition. He was the biggest innovator, and the most inspirational veristic composer of that time. He wasn't just growing as a musician, as a romantic lyricist, but he was truly trying to meld the theater with music, and create the most compelling dramaturgy that he could, which is why I think he also had controversial and confrontational relationships with all of his librettists, because he was very specific about what he wanted his texts to be, to be able to design the music to support the text in those dramatic situations.

OL - Let's start by talking about *Suor Angelica* in which you'll be singing the title role. What is your opinion of this opera? In spite of it being Puccini's favorite, it is certainly the least popular of the *Trittico* operas, and it is rarely a stand-alone like *Gianni Schicchi*; sometimes it gets omitted, and unlike *Il Tabarro* which is sometimes given with, for instance, *I Pagliacci*, it is rarely paired with something else. I confess that it is indeed my least favorite *Trittico* opera. I guess what I like less about it, is the fact that it is an all-female opera – I like the contrast between male and female voices. But if you do love it, please defend it for us.

JG – I can totally appreciate that you would say that *Suor Angelica* in many ways could be your least favorite opera within the *Triptych.* When you see *Il Tabarro*, the first work of the evening, you are very impressed by this. My sister saw the 2006 production of *Il Trittico* with the Hawaii Opera Theater, in my husband's Jake Gardner's debut with the company singing the roles of Michele and Gianni Schicchi. Even in that particular evening, my sister loved *Gianni Schicchi* but her favorite of the three was *Tabarro.* But I personally love *Suor Angelica.* I think that more than, shall we say, the least favorite, it can be the most misunderstood of the three.

It has to do very specifically with this woman that has been banned to this convent so you are relegated like you were saying to an all-female cast of basically fifteen voices. There are extra choral voices that are added at different moments in the evening, but basically you have fifteen nuns who are living together. You are dealing with this particular life in the 17th century, in that normal practice, shall we say, of having a Catholic church within your community with people going into the convent and taking the veil. That practice in modern culture has become less and less a career path. [laughs] The issue for Suor Angelica, similar to Gianni Schicchi which also deals with all these family dynamics, money, and greed, is that you have this very particular situation of a woman who has been banned to a convent, which is harder for modern audiences to identify with. It's very unique within the *Triptych*, and it is one of the reasons why it is sandwiched between the two.

It was Puccini's favorite. It has more to deal with this person of Suor Angelica and why she is there, what her life is about, and the real tragedy of it, that is overcome through the grace of God. Faith plays a very significant part of the telling of Suor Angelica's story because she truly relies on the grace and goodness of the Virgin Mary to assist her in her daily life, but there is also a real woman there. She is one of the most significant characters of the *Triptych*. I can say that because I've been developing that. What is the challenge of developing that role? You have to really show a real woman that is living hidden underneath this vow and this veil within this convent, because she is there against her will. That's the challenge for the performer, in order to be able to do credit to the work, otherwise it can come off quite stale. Does it make sense?

OL – Yes, it does; interesting answer – as usual. I love your answers!

JG – [laughs hard]

OL – You are very well informed. You are an interesting singer, Jill, you really get into your character. We can tell your passion for all the aspects of the operatic art form. That's great. So, the opera is often dismissed as overly sentimental. Have you encountered much of that prejudice, or had to address it within yourself?

JG – This continues what I was saying. I think what makes Suor Angelica so unique, is that one has to clarify the essence of sentimentality. For me, rather than it being a sentimental depiction or presentation, the point that lies at the heart of Angelica is that she is so misunderstood! She is the real subject of the abuse of power. She is an unwed mother. We just passed through the season of Christmas, so like Mary, the mother of Jesus, she is also an unwed mother, but unlike Mary she is banned to this convent for her sin, that sin being that she had a baby out of wedlock.

Clearly also within the story as you learn, not necessarily first hand or first person from Suor Angelica, later we learn from the nuns and from the big duet that she has with her aunt, the real circumstances of her life. The nuns say early on when they are talking about Suor Angelica that she clearly came from money, that she came from nobility, and has been living now for seven years in this convent. She is not there because she chose to take the vow, but as a mean of punishment. As it often happens in monastery life, her secrets, she holds to herself. She's taken a vow of silence. It's a very oppressive environment. If you portray this character well, you understand that there is a level of paranoia, insecurity, guilt, shame, and it has all been imposed on this young woman by her family. We latter learn that her parents were dead.

OL – I wonder if her parents died of shame; if some other sin when she was younger would have played a part in her parent's death (or maybe her mother died of childbirth), which would bring even more guilt associated with the later sin of Angelica birthing a son as a single mother.

JG – That's right! We learn in the Aunt's monologue that Angelica's parents died over 20 years ago, probably when Angelica was very, very young. Angelica's Aunt, her mother's sister, was then responsible for raising her. And ultimately, Angelica horribly disappoints her guardian aunt by having a child out of wedlock. Thus, her punishment to save the family was to enter the convent. For me as the performer as I develop roles, these are always the questions that I ask. For me, theatrically, and for the standpoint of developing the character, I always try to find the conflict, because that's where the real motivation is, the seeds for every character. Whether it's a conflict that I've personally experienced in my life or not, you have to be able to get in there and start asking those kinds of questions.

When I was learning the role, I couldn't help but think of that horrible scenario in Cleveland where that man by the last name of Castro held those women prisoners for all those years – granted that that was a much more violent and subversive role that he played. I think of those girls' lives, and that's the level of suppression and repression and oppression that Suor Angelica is living in this environment. But it is personal; it is not overt in any way. It's just where she is in this particular day that we go to this convent and see this life. This is when all these interactions happen. The fruition of her wanting to know about her family and specifically about her child, which is her big secret, we get to see. And then there are choices she makes from that, which are huge.

OL – In the opening scenes about desires, all they can come up with is food, and getting to know about her family, and soon enough there is the issue that nuns should not have any desire whatsoever. Of course the big elephant in the room is sexual desire, which is what the scene is about. This is completely suppressed and overlooked, right?

JG – That's exactly right, and leads into the second part of your question. This is my first Suor Angelica, and in the process of learning this role, I pay attention to what is beautiful about her. It's similar to the character Marguerite in *Faust*, and even to a certain extent Manon Lescaut. With Manon Lescaut it is more difficult because she completely goes on the wrong path due to her desire.

OL – She is not as innocent.

JG – Exactly, she goes on a different life path due to her desire. Clearly Manon Lescaut is being sent to the convent for a reason. [laughs] When you bring up sexual desire, I think this is so important for us to deal with, because it talks about sexual need and falling in love and being able to produce children, to bear fruit. Clearly Suor Angelica fell in love. In her heart she is so go good. Clearly she had a relationship with a man and had a child out of wedlock, and her family which is aristocracy or nobility could not stand her open femininity, which many of us women are now getting more and more of an opportunity to communicate. In the end, she is there in this convent dying to return to a life of normalcy and be with this man that she loves, and above all with this child.

Another interesting thing we learn in the convent is that she is smart and very resourceful. Whether she came to the convent knowing the skill or not, she became a highly developed herbalist. She learned how to make remedies from flowers and herbs and was able to offer her expertise to her sisters. She is a person of a good heart. That's why she goes on to help Sister Clara when she is stung by bees. She says "I am here to serve."

Yesterday I was looking into this and confirming it in the score. I think there is a personal sadness which she feels about the earlier death of Sister Bianca Rosa that they are remembering, and which later they sing the "Requiem Aeternam" for her. In my imagination, Suor Angelica probably tried to help her. Unfortunately the type of medicine that she could provide her could not help her. There is a personal sadness that she also feels at that moment, which links later to when she listens to the Requiem Aeternam that is being sung for her- but from this remembrance, Angelica is bolstered to say "I'm ready to meet my fate," to have this confrontation and this dialogue with her aunt.

Of course that leads to the unraveling of her. The convent has been basically a prison for her. There is a level of daily silent oppression in all those years she's lived there, and she has a huge desire to hear from her family. That's why she sings this very beautiful arioso about this. She is basically saying then that the Virgin Mary will clench those desires, and we should yearn for this no matter what the outcome should be. This is the other part of living with any kind of religious faith. People in those religious communities or confines do live within this concept of death. But she lives with a very deep psychological conflict that rose in this duet with the aunt. When you peel the layers of this onion, that's when you start to see how deep and how huge, portraying this kind of character is.

OL – With the final redemption scenes, basically a divine being is forgiving her, but her family is not. This is akin to being more royalist than the king. It makes it even more tragic.

JG – That's exactly right. That's a beautiful way to say that. That's what Puccini is often trying to show here. I do understand what you mean by the sentimentality of the piece, but I think he really is trying to deal with the idea of grace and forgiveness within this kind of miracle play. The aunt is the most significant contralto role Puccini ever wrote. Within this world of the convent and all these female voices, she definitely in my opinion represents the male Yang energy. She is there to represent power and therefore it is abusive power.

Clearly this sister that Suor Angelica has, Anna Viola, is the favorite, either to the family or to the aunt. That's what I think is so interesting: when the aunt comes there, she says 'I'm here to do the bidding of your parents; they told me to oversee the estate. I came to ask you this favor. The reason I came today is to ask you to sign this document' – which basically gives away Suor Angelica's rights – 'so that your sister can marry.' When she tells her that, it's when we see Suor Angelica's purity and the goodness of her heart. She is so happy for her sister. Just to hear from her family is graceful in itself; it's a real gift in that moment, considering how long she waited to hear anything.

But then it becomes about 'you need to do this because the only way for her to get married is for you to do this, because you've shamed the family.

We have to take you out of this picture in order for your sister to find her ultimate happiness.' The interesting thing for me as I play this is that in these moments Suor Angelica definitely has two or three strong lines back to her aunt. This was because that was the nature of her family, too. She is a good, good girl, but she's got a fiery spirit within her, which is probably why she did this irrational thing of falling in love and having a baby out of wedlock. Then when the aunt demands that she does this through guilt and shame and she has to repent and offer everything over, that's when Suor Angelica comes forward and says, 'OK, I offered everything over to the Virgin, but one thing I will not offer, is not to know about my son.' She is the one who brings up the son. I think that if the aunt could have had the signed paper without any resistance she would never have told her that her son had died. The principessa lives in this state of judgment that 'who cares? You did the wrong thing and it is best for everybody and for the child that he died.'

OL – Right. The signing out of her rights is a complete annihilation of her as a person. It's like deleting her.

JG – Correct! It's a very medieval approach to this miracle play but it is relevant to my culture, now. That's why it is very important to show these human responses, these human situations. I mean, Luiz, look at our world now! How many unwed mothers do we have? How many people are not living within societal norms? People process that all the time, currently. But I still think that in a human level, these same emotions, these same judgments and attitudes, the same practices like the aunt takes with Suor Angelica, still exist and are used today. It's a very clear example of abuse of power trying to subjugate this natural, beautiful, good-hearted woman.

OL – Yes. I'm starting to like *Suor Angelica* more…

JG – [laughs] Yes, this is what the next month will be while we prepare this; that's exactly this kind of character that I think that she is. When she realizes this horrible thing that has happened to her, her only hope is to be with this child. Then she needs to deal with the ultimate choice which will allow her to be with her child which is suicide.

People today still have very difficult issues with suicide. Some cultures accept it more, like the Japanese culture does – we see it in a character like Butterfly who in the end returns to her family roots. She is living within this confined society of Japanese culture and life, and she is trying to get out of that and to be in love and have this relationship with this American and go on to leave her culture. But in the end when she faces shame and disgrace she then returns to her roots and takes the path of her father, and kills herself in order for her child to go on, whereas Suor Angelica in her mind and her heart, she wants to die. She says at the beginning, 'O sorella, la morte è vita bella' - death is the beautiful life. She wants to die in order to be with him.

LG – Very interesting.

JG – And yet, she realizes that again she's made a choice that is very similar to the earlier one: an irreversible choice. The only thing in that moment is for God to forgive her, which goes back to what you were saying. That's where she ultimately experiences forgiveness and grace. That spiritual experience is what we are trying to portray.

I will humbly say that it's going to be very hard. I love that Jay Lesenger with whom I've worked in the past will be directing this Trittico. Leave it to a wonderful Jewish man to be able to portray a beautiful Catholic miracle. [laughs] I do think it's very hard. That state of ecstasy is going to be challenging, but I'm very up to the challenge because in the end, I love this woman. I had similar moments in my life to deal with that are very personal, similar to Angelica's plight. I feel like it's an honor to be able to try to portray that through Suor Angelica.

OL - Each time I remember that *Il Triticco* had its world premiere in America, precisely at the Metropolitan Opera House on December 14, 1918, I think that it is important for American companies to continue to carry it on. But it's three hours, three operas, and a lot of casting and different sets; it is taxing, for a company.

JG – Yes, you are doing three one-act operas. You are not doing three acts of one opera. What Puccini did within each opera is very similar to what he did with *Tosca* and *Butterfly*. The idea of the *Triptych* is to be able to show in a few hours within each opera – and in this sunset time setting - how the present circumstances which these characters are going through, are transformed into the future. Within each of them there is a dream or a state of bliss that is trying to be achieved.

What is also interesting is that there is a reverse time order. *Tabarro* takes place in the 1890's Paris. *Suor Angelica* takes place in the 17th century, and by the time you finish the night you are at the farthest point in the timeline, which is 1299 Florence. If the production is done well, you will have time traveled. Within each of them, you have these very human people, which is ultimately what the arts express – the human predicament, our greatest strengths and our greatest weaknesses - and how their choices either undermine them or bring them redemption. This is the ultimate vision of the *Triptych*, which is why I admire any company that does it.

LG – That's what opera must do.

JG – Exactly; that's our present day conflict within the opera world, of how to justify our existence, how to prove that this is important and why we need it. It's not frivolous and not relegated to entertainment like you could experience very cheaply through other means. There is no judgment there by saying that. I'm not passing judgment on someone who partakes in as much entertainment as possible, just because I'm fascinated with opera. But this is the point, the Gospel, shall we say, of opera – that it is truly trying to present the human condition at all times. You have theater with music to support that. It's not just film, just music, just TV; it's the live experience of seating there in a theater, being within this larger circle of a stage and an audience. We have to go back and justify our means like the Greek tragedists had to do moons ago.

OL - Did you watch the 2007 Met production, which moved *Suor Angelica* to 1938? What do you think of the practice of updating the time signature of an opera? And what are your thoughts about the way different productions handle the ending – should we actually see Angelica communing with a beatific vision, or just staring ecstatically into space, or (in the ROH production) clutching a little orphan boy in the mistaken belief he's her lost child?

JG – I have not seen the 2007 Met production. About the way different productions handle the ending of *Suor Angelica*, should we see her ascending to Heaven, or should we actually see the materialization of her vision? It is difficult to create, display, or show this mystical experience of death she is going through, and sometimes that's where people try to change the time setting of the opera. What's wonderful about opera is that these very real moments get suspended in time. Even though someone is dying, you may have someone singing an aria about it or having a whole ensemble responding about this death. It's actually taking quite a few moments for this person to die. [laughs]

OL – I thought that puncturing a lung through stabbing someone would disrupt the breathing for the singer, but apparently not, because they can be stabbed and they continue to sing and sing. [laughs]

JG – [laughs] For me, Angelica's extended death experience she is going through is in part brought about by this hallucinogenic poison that she took, with that flower concoction that is going through her body. My question that I will take to the stage direction is, 'how do I show this, physically?' We have to show this huge desire for dying. Then, everything she goes through – the pain when she starts to feel the reality of the potion, and the thought that this is an irrevocable sin – indicates that she doesn't want to be damned and die in this way. That's when she starts praying to the Madonna to save her – 'Salvami, salvami.' Then there is this final chorus scene with a fantastic, beautifully lyrical moment that Puccini has written to display the miracle. You feel that there is ultimate release for her from the pain and psychological suffering, that she is forgiven. That's the miracle that we want to show. And you can't be afraid, either personally or in the production itself, to show this miracle actually happening.

You mentioned the ROH production; I read many things about that. I also saw a specific production of San Francisco Opera with Patricia Racette where they had them living within this charity hospital. There is a lot to be said about that effort, it does work for this piece. This piece is esoteric and deals with forgiveness and sin, first of all, and staging it in a convent seems so far removed from the current public! So this ROH and this San Francisco production put it in a more contemporary setting, like a charity hospital. But she is still a female victim of oppression, and she experiences true forgiveness and true love, and that's what you still have to see, or you miss the point of the piece. I appreciate the effort of directors and designers to try to put a story in a different timeline. I've done that with *Tosca,* actually. But the characters are still living the same existences and conflicts. You still have to show the same emotional panoramas. Showing the feeling of salvation is the point.

OL - Let's talk about the music in *Suor Angelica.* Some call it cloying or saccharine and not as innovative as that of *Il Tabarro* and *Gianni Schicchi.* Others however point to how Puccini's musical portrait of Angelica's aunt, the Princess, is an artistic masterpiece – the only important alto part he ever wrote – transferring to this female character the characteristics of his threatening male characters such as Scarpia, like you have acknowledged when you mentioned the male Yang. How do you feel about the music in *Suor Angelica*?

JG – All of the music in *Il Trittico* is some of Puccini's most experimental and truly inspired. In his later period of his life it is very clear that he had already been through that peak of fantastic romantic lyricism in *Manon Lescaut, Bohème, Tosca,* and *Butterfly*. He also displayed incredible orchestral depth and economy of means. He learned through this period how to get the best bang for his buck, not only orchestrally but in his musical language.

When you think about that, when he started to deal with his later works *Fanciulla, Trittico,* and *Turandot,* he is getting to means that are really theatrical, so he saved his majorly lyrical romantic moments for the power moments of the opera. He uses alternate means, in more truncated and less conventional moments, to really depict the dramatic situations.

In *Suor Angelica* he achieved beautiful transparency in the orchestral writing. Sometimes he uses very brightly colored orchestration, like in Sister Genoviffa's little arioso about sunlight. That is so beautifully descriptive, particularly through the use of the woodwinds and the strings in that moment! The level of transparency he achieved early in the piece with this contrapuntal, ancient style, in the Ave Maria prayer, continues through the piece with a predominance of modality. Even the Principessa's entrance is completely modal. Her entrance is in C sharp minor, and then he lands on D minor, and E minor.

He is relegating himself to this modal, tonal writing, which depicts the kind of music for a convent at the time. It reflects the transparency of the situation, I think. He is so brilliant, so inspired! He uses leitmotifs – we associate them with Wagner but they are so much part of Puccini too! He has themes in every opera of the *Triptych.* In *Tabarro* we have an adultery theme between Luigi and Giorgetta. We have the cloak theme that comes later in the duet between Giorgetta and Michele. We experience the theme of the water in motion that begins *Tabarro.* We have the same thing in *Suor Angelica* and later in *Schicchi.* Not only he has these leitmotifs, but he uses them to demonstrate the different conflicts that come along in each piece.

He is also highly influenced now by Impressionism, with the use of sevenths and ninths in the chordal structure throughout each opera. I could write a dissertation on it. The opening prayer in Suor Angelica starts with the bell, in a very modal entrance, then the nuns start singing and the orchestra comes in, and stays very pure and holy. By the time Angelica comes in, he introduces intervals of sevenths and ninths to create this impression of a time warp, when the organ comes in. It's a discreet but extremely inspired use of Impressionistic harmonies. Then by the end of that prayer he has totally taken them out, and he does these very normal cadences and we move right along. He is just brilliant, in that way. I can't speak highly enough of how he uses the music throughout this entire thing.

OL - Your main number is 'Senza mamma.' Would you please comment on this piece? Any particular difficulty?

JG – Yes, 'Senza mamma' for those of us who know and love Puccini is a very inspired moment of romantic lyricism, as only Puccini could write. In the context of this piece, particularly comparing it with Giorgetta, this moment is similar to what 'È ben altro il mio sogno' is for Giorgetta. It's their big lyric outburst. But, 'Senza mamma' is the most private moment any of Puccini's women have. I can't think of any other aria with this kind of solitary grief. It's delivered from a complete and utter state of total grief and shock, like a coma-like state. She's learned that her son she's been living for, and dying for news about, has died. So, there is a total detachment from reality. I think of it as the greatest representation of Hell, specifically for her. It comes out of this incredible confrontation with her aunt.

Puccini used for this aria the purest modal harmonic juxtapositions. Then, the aria has such a huge transformation! There is a personal movement from the beginning all the way through this hallucinatory state, when she starts to remember and be taken over by the representation of the physical form of her son. It's what brings the transcendent departure that she is on. These are the beginning moments. She starts with grief and by the end of the area she is on a path of bliss, trying with every power to reconnect with this son, and therefore with this symbol of love. It's so powerful! It has to be sung solo, but has to also show and reveal all those layers of desire within her, that cause her to make all her choices.

She goes on to sing next, one of those beautifully lyrical moments – 'La grazia è discesa dal cielo' [grace has descended from Heaven]. That music is completely inspired, with the choir of sisters singing behind her. This is truly what she wants to experience: this state of grace with her son. She will do anything for it. The progression that you need to achieve while you are singing this, is the challenge.

OL - There is a quite modern aria for Angelica with polytonal implications, that is often cut. It's rarely seen in recordings – there is one in 1920 with Lotte Lehmann in which she does sing it. I'm not sure if it will be part of the Charlotte show. It's 'Amici fiori, voi mi compensate.'

JG - It won't be in this production, no.

OL – Let's move on to *Il Tabarro*, in which you'll be singing Giorgetta. First of all, Is it difficult to sing the two roles in the same night?

JG – This is my debut of these two roles. I performed Lauretta separately in another configuration. Is it going to be difficult, these two roles in the same night? Well, we will see! [laughs] Because, it is my debut of these two roles.

The beauty of this and the reason I am a Puccini singer – the perché, the why? of this - is that I am a veristic singer. This is the true nature of verismo singing: being able to balance the heightened emotional states of these characters while maintaining beautiful singing and creating an entire palate of vocal choices that serve these emotional moments. It's a huge challenge.

This is what I'm paying for. I'm currently studying with Diana Soviero, who was one of the greatest veristic sopranos of this repertoire. We continue to address the technical issues that these roles bring forward. I'm particularly mentoring with her because of the density of this repertoire. To be a real verismo soprano you have to go to the people who sang this, because there was a specific technique and a specific approach. You work with someone like Diana, you listen to someone like Renata Scotto… Teresa Strattas also had a huge effect on these pieces. She wasn't completely of a veristic vocal style but had a commitment and a level of depth that allowed her to sing *Il Tabarro* and *Pagliacci*, It's hugely informative. That's what I do to prepare myself to sing this, and I have high hopes for it. I think it is going to be a beautiful production, and it is right where I need to be. This is the music I need to sing, this is what I am on the Earth to sing.

OL - Now, I like Il Tabarro very much. It has a cinematic quality; its score sounds like a film score with a lot of tone painting, and it is one of the quintessential verismo operas. Like you said, there are echoes of French impressionism with dissolution of the usual harmonic outlines. There are leitmotivs such as the one for the river Seine. What do you think of it, musically?

JG – What is beautiful about this piece is that he very much starts to show these kinds of themes, contrasting the river with the relationship that Giorgetta and Luigi have, and the relationship that Michele and Giorgetta have. You look at the score, and he has this river theme, then he introduces a drinking song when the stevedores have come up from unloading the goods. Then there is a dancing song, with an organ grinder. The sheer variety of ideas and themes Puccini produces just within *Il Tabarro* alone, is amazing. It is seen not only in the orchestral colors but in every moment, and that's why I think you referred to it as cinematographic. When you watch a movie they punctuate subliminally what is happening, and Puccini does it completely, in this piece. He keeps referring back to these themes, in different moments, so that you get that subliminal connection. It's really well done.

OL -Now tell us about your lyrical outbust 'È ben altro il mio sogno.'

JG – What is beautiful for me is that the other female character in *Il Tabarro* is the mezzo Frugola who is married to Talpa. 'È ben altro il mio sogno' which is an aria for her is also punctuated by all these interjections from Luigi, because a part of why they were drawn to one another, is this background that they have, having grown up in Belleville together and knowing that Parisian suburban life, and they talk about this.

But prior to that aria, Frugola has also talked about her passion, her fixation. Giorgetta says: 'E la tua fissazione, la campagna!' and then Frugola goes on to sing her one-note melody about living in the country and having the little house that she and Talpa have lived in, which has four little walls and is surrounded by palm trees, with a little garden, and their little cat. It's their dream, their *sogno*. And Giorgetta says, well, I have a different *sogno*. Then she goes on to describe what she and Luigi are united in. It's a reference to something that is unattainable. It's not just harkening back to where they come from and the beauty of what unites them, but it is particularly in reference to this life that she is living now in this boat with Michele. It's about a bygone time. While she yearns for what the magic was at that time, there is an aspect of it that is truly a *fascino*. It's unattainable, and that's the beauty of it.

OL - Unlike Suor Angelica (and like Gianni Schicchi), Il Tabarro does have a literary source: Didier Gold's play *La Houppelande*, a dark drama written in the spirit of Emile Zola and in the Grand Guignol tradition with its double murder, which is softened in the opera. Have you explored the source?

JG – Yes, I have explored that source. Puccini and his librettist Adami maintained many aspects of that *pièce noire*. The other murderer you are talking about in the play is Tinka. He murders his wife in a bar because he finds out that she is having an affair. Between Michele and Giorgetta, when he does discover that she is having this affair, unlike the Canio-Nedda relationship in Pagliacci, where Canio not only kills Silvio but he kills Nedda as well, in this situation Michele kills Luigi, and the opera ends by him displaying the dead body from his cloak, where he and Giorgetta used to embrace. In the play, he takes her face and pushes her into the face of the dead Luigi.

OL – Yes, this macabre element is very much into the Grand Guignol tradition.

JG – That's right.

OL – Someone asked Puccini, 'aren't you overdoing this, by pushing her face down?' Puccini said, 'No, that's how is must be; trust me, I know what I'm doing.'

JG – Yes, that's right. There is a 20, 25-year difference between Giorgetta and Michele, which is also the case in the play. I keep thinking about what happens to them next. Does he go on and kill her? Do they stay together? At the end of *Tabarro* when she comes out of the hold after he has killed Luigi, I tend to play her as truly coming there to fix some kind of reconciliation with him. Do you agree?

OL – Yes, she is starting to regret the affair and trying to reconnect with him, yes.

JG – That's right. That she considers ending her affair with Luigi shows the complexity of her life. She has this relationship with Michele, and she loves Michele. It's unfortunate that this child died, that they had. Nedda loves Canio even though it's a very difficult relationship. These young women… I know that, because of my relationship with my husband Jake who is twenty years my senior. I love to say jokingly that I married my father, but in many ways there is an aspect in women who are in a relationship with an older man, that they are seeking a father, they are trying to deal with something in themselves. There is something to be said for being in a relationship with an older man. My mother said she wasn't surprised at all because she thought that I was always an old soul. I think that's what characters like Giorgetta are finding in these relationships. These men have saved them, and they don't hate these men.

OL – He does call her a whore. I'm not sure he would be willing to take her back.

JG – He does. Correct. That's exactly the way I think about this. But you see, I think it's because he is so tormented! Earlier in the opera as you see Giorgetta and Michele fighting, in the whole beginning of the opera all that they are doing is that they are having a spat. Eventually even before the duet starts, she is saying 'you know, if you need to let anybody go, you need to let Tinka go because he drinks too much.' He says 'he drinks too much because his wife is a whore.' 'Una bagascia.' Later he calls Giorgetta 'sgualdrina' [both are Italian for whore].

These men are tormented by this, because they themselves think they are less; they are wondering 'what is wrong with me that caused this beautiful young woman who loved me to go away from me?' You are exactly right; it's doubtful, whether or not he can find that time of reconciliation that

Giorgetta in the very end is coming out of the hold of the boat to try to have. Because I think that she is a good girl. It's the feminine condition, the Yin principle, the less dominant, the part of ourselves that is always trying to find reconciliation, the humble aspects; that's what these women are representing, in these very strong past historical moments. I agree with you; whether Michele can find that with her or not, is what the ultimate question is. In my mind, I don't think he kills her. He is a much more brooding character than Cagno, who is too out there, passionate and extroverted.

OL – Probably Michele will just withdraw within himself even more and things will fall apart, if the story is continued.

JG – Correct.

OL – Let's go back to this: we can feel some sort of thread in the three operas, addressing different social classes – here we are talking about proletarian life in a big city. Also, there is some symbolism, in the fact that the piece progresses from daylight to darkness. It just gets darker and darker, this true *pièce noire*. Any comments?

JG – Yes, and I think this is an aspect that is overlying the entire *Triptych*. In *Tabarro* these people are seeking their *sogni*, they are seeking their dreams. It's all about dreams. In *Suor Angelica* it's about being able to find this grace, this blissful state. Giorgetta and Suor Angelica are bound together by these secrets. These women have these secrets. Giorgetta has fallen in love with Luigi and she is having this adulterous affair with him, and she is tormented about it, and knows that if Michele finds out about it, he is going to kill them. She is very much afraid of him.

OL – *Gianni Schicchi* also has a secret: that the old man has died, and the family wants to keep it a secret.

JG – That's exactly right, and where I was going to ultimately go with that; this secret of how this fortune is going to be divided. Schicchi is the greatest schemer, and he does it for his daughter, so that she can go on and live her dream. There is death that is involved throughout the entire *Triptych*, the secrets that all those people hold, the dreams that they hold. The reason why he ends it with *Schicchi* – you know, *Tabarro* is the darkest of the three pieces; the story would probably go on like you said to Michele going deeper into his brooding and pushing Giorgetta away and it all falls apart, and everybody goes on to the road to ruin. In *Suor Angelica* he manages to find hope and forgiveness and grace. In Schicchi, through the humor of it, here is this old man trying to find reconciliation. He is not such a vengeful person, but is putting forward the law as he sees it, so that his daughter can live her dream.

OL – So, what you are getting at, is that there is optimism in this arc. Puccini starts from the darkest parts of the human soul, progresses through grace, and then he opens up to the fulfillment of dreams and to happiness, with these two youngsters being able to marry.

JG – I think that's it. This is a big part of what the emotional human context is. In the end, artistically and in every way, the arc of this is that Puccini is trying to balance this relationship between Yin and Yang, always.

OL – There is also an element on humanism, of kind belief in humanity, when Rinuccio in his aria 'Avete torto' describes Florence like a flowery tree made of different people of all backgrounds – what makes of a city, a city. At the end, Puccini seems to be saying, 'there is something to humankind, after all, and things can work.'

JG – That's exactly right, and it's what I'm referring to. He is drawn to trying to find that balance, both individually as a human being, and as a culture, as the human spirit, as humanity within itself. This is very clear, the more you live with Puccini's works. His musical language illuminates it completely, and that's what is behind his leitmotifs.

OL – Wow, fabulous, this was a very compelling interview. I remember when we were making editorial decisions at Opera Lively about what interviews should be included in our book, and one of our senior staff members was saying, "Jill Gardner's must be in; she is great, look at all the insights she had about *Tosca*; I had never thought about some of those aspects, myself."

JG – Lovely. That means so much to me, Luiz, because this is my vocation, my calling in life. That's why I do it, and it is so important to me as an artist to be revelatory. I love what I do and I think it is important; it's a much bigger job than just singing.

OL – Absolutely. At year end we think of how to allocate money for charity and all that, and I think it is important for people to realize that donating to opera companies fulfills a societal role as well, just as important as the role fulfilled by other charities. Opera companies bring music to inner city schools, for example, and this can do a lot of good.

JG – Absolutely, particularly as our culture changes, when more and more we have people who are not exposed to the arts. Even people who are not disadvantaged are not being exposed to the arts these days and have little notion of why this is so important and why we need it. As Jake says: 'you know, this is our Western civilization.' We are talking about the best of the human spirit, and how it is expressed. The arts put the mirror right up to our faces, not only as individuals, but as a species.

OL – Yes, I recently interviewed the artistic director and principal conductor of the Greek National Opera, Mr. Myron Michailidis, and in this interview [here in Chapter 7], this was one of the things he was saying. Greece is in the middle of a horrible economic crisis, and with all the funds being cut, he was actually successful in telling the government that opera should not be cut because it represents Western civilization, a value that Greece as the cradle of this civilization must uphold. He said (I paraphrase), 'Greek theater started it all, the Italians picked it up and created this art form, and now we must carry it on because it is essential, and in a moment of crisis when our people are in distress, we need more opera productions, not less.' He actually increased the number of productions by his company, instead of cutting them.

JG – Oh my God, that's brilliant!

OL – Yes, he said, 'now that the nation is in turmoil, our people need the arts even more than before. While they are saddened by all the hardship, we can deliver to them an opportunity to stop and think about their humanity, and be together, and be inspired by the arts.'

JG – Yes, people attending opera are being inspired by something that is bigger than themselves. I reject the idea of opera as elitist. I think particularly the composers understood that opera was for all humans. Now we have so many forms of entertainment, but we should wake up and realize that we shouldn't try to become like everything else in order to attract the public. We should try to be like we are supposed to be, and therefore be different.

OL – Yes, I don't like the efforts that try to popularize opera by compromising its artistic integrity. People will come, if our companies present the best possible artistic product.

JG – Absolutely. One of the most innovative jobs in an opera company is director of marketing and development, and it is not just a business job but is rather a very operatic one. When companies put together the best artistic performances that they can, then it belongs to the director of marketing to show to the people why they need to come – again, the *perché* : why should you need to come and see this? If this is done well and with true operatic spirit, people will say, 'wow, I need to come and see this!'

OL – You made me thing of an ad that the Royal Opera House put together, where two young women discuss the plot of Don Giovanni – have you seen it? It's so interesting! Oh my God, two hours! That's the longest Opera Lively interview, ever! [Certain parts were cut for this book]

JG – [laughs] Yaaaay! I get the gold medal! Thank you!

Elizabeth Bishop, mezzo-soprano

While our interview with Elizabeth Bishop in January 2013 was nice, it was of only regional interest regarding a Wagner concert for NC Opera. Over here we will keep only a few of her answers, about the Liebestod, about opera's budget crisis and how someone develops a taste for opera (we loved that answer), and about how Susan Graham guided her through a last minute Didon substitution when she was covering for her. The full interview can be found on our website at www.operalively.com.

Opera Lively – How is the concert shaping up for you, with the first act of *Die Walküre* and the other excerpts?

EB – The only excerpt I'm in besides the Act One Sieglinde is the "Liebestod" from *Tristan und Isolde*, which is an aria that I sang once in concert with the Atlanta Symphony about ten years ago, and have been begging to get to do it again, ever since. It's one of the most glorious pieces of music I've ever heard. It's just outstanding.

OL – It is! And it is long and difficult.

EB – Hey, I'm almost hating to have the concert come, because then I won't have a reason to sing it every day. [laughs]

OL – What are the challenges you see in singing it?

EB – The "Liebestod" is difficult because it simply never stops. It just grinds on and on and on. There is no resting point and there is no hiding place. You have eight minutes of just singing. It's like running a marathon uphill, but on the most beautiful hill you've ever imagined.

OL – Not to forget that the orchestra accompaniment is rather loud during the "Liebestod" and you need to pierce through it.

EB – It is. You do, you have to pace it well, and there are a lot of difficulties with it. The pacing and the tessitura are the most challenging. Isolda is typically done by a soprano and I'm a mezzo-soprano, so it has an added flavor of danger [laughs] to it, but my voice tends to sit very well with the German soprano rep. I hope it comes out as well as it feels to me to sing it.

OL – Yes, you sang Venus in *Tannhäuser* and Kundry in *Parsifal*, and sometimes we see mezzo-sopranos singing these roles, but it is less common for Sieglinde and Isolde.

EB – Yes. I've seen mezzos doing Sieglinde before, but it is very unusual. It's all the sufficiently stocky mezzo types like Christa Ludwig, although I don't know if Christa ever did it or not [Editor's note: apparently not; she did Fricka and Waltraute in *Die Walküre* but not Sieglinde]. Waltraud Meier can hop up and sing it, but it's usually done by a soprano. It is, I think, just to balance it out. You have one crazy dramatic soprano, and that's Brünnhilde; and then you have a crazy, relatively high mezzo, and that's Fricka; so I think that Sieglinde is supposed to be the nice fluffy filling in this crazy sandwich.

OL – This week, you're conducting a master class at Duke University. In March, you'll be conducting another master class at Georgia State University. What do you see as some of the greatest challenges facing young singers right now?

EB – For singers, the general difficulties never change. You have to overcome your inexperience, you have to build a reliable technique; some of those things never change from generation to generation. Just becoming a singer in general requires an incredible amount of discipline and delayed gratification to play it smart. In today's world, the extra challenges that we face are of course that there is very little money left over for the arts, at the moment. Orchestras and opera companies almost everywhere are so squeezed financially that it is difficult to get into any company, because things are squeezing from the top down. The Met cuts back shows, which means that a lot of these singers that normally would be working at the Met are now looking for the jobs elsewhere, which displaces the next tier of singers, which displaces the next. It's squeezing a lot of the people who are in their late twenties, early thirties, post-program, pre-big career, pre-steady career. I think it is very difficult to get your foot in the door.

OL – Interesting enough, I was reading some stats a couple of days ago, and it looks like the number of people going into vocal training is actually increasing, in the United States.

EB – Well, is it really? That's a surprise to me. I didn't know that. That just goes to show you that hope springs eternal. [laughs]

OL – Yes. [laughs] I guess that what we are seeing is part of the international economic crisis but opera will bounce back. Those stats I was reading show that decline for pop music concerts is actually steeper than the decline for opera. I think we are still resilient.

EB – I do too, I'm one of those people who believe that everything is a cycle. Everything is like a pendulum, it will come back around, because this art form has survived so much, relatively intact!

OL – That's right.

EB – If you look at the way pop music has changed throughout, just the last few decades, and then you look at the changes in opera, we are the stable ones. So much of classical music in general is an acquired taste! You have to be introduced to it, then you have to realize that it is OK to love it, then you have to realize that you do love it. And then you start going. Pop music has the benefit of being a "wow" right out of the box for most young teenagers because it's what all their peers are listening to. But I think that when we find an audience member, we find a much more loyal audience member. When someone falls in love with Verdi's operas, it's a longer relationship than when you discover Lady Gaga.

OL – Right. I love this answer, wow! So, you recently sang two performances as Didon for the Met *Les Troyens*. What can you share with us about that experience?

EB – Well, that was terrifying and exhilarating. I had three rehearsals total. [laughs] I had never done the role before, it was a role debut.

OL – Wow!

EB – I know! The covers at the Met had done what are now typical cover rehearsals but we hadn't had a rehearsal in weeks. I had been going through it on my own every now and then. Susan [Graham] was doing fine. She is a friend of mine. And then she calls me and says, "You know what? I'm sick." And I'm, "No, you're not!" She goes, "Yes, I am" and I go, "No, you're not, because I don't want to do this!" It was so intimidating, in short notice. And she goes, "No, I'm really sick!" And she was, so they called me from the Met at about ten o'clock in the morning, I marched over to the Met and put on the costume and tried my best. And it went well. It went very well, actually, both times.

OL – Very nice!

EB – Susan was awesome. Susan rarely cancels. When she does, there is no question that she is not feeling up to it. But she is so wonderful as a colleague! That morning, when I was going to sing it that night, she actually talked me through the music, and said, "Watch out, the conductor does this here, and he tends to slow down right there, and blah, blah, blah" so she really gave me little extra hints when I went off to do this.

OL – That's nice of her.

EB – Yes, she is awesome.

OL – Thank you so much for the interview!

EB – Thank you, it was a pleasure to talk to you!

DIVISION TWO – EMERGING, REGIONAL, OR YOUNG SINGERS

CHAPTER SIX – MALE SINGERS

Michael Spyres, tenor

This interview done in person in November 2012 is dense and long (Michael is quite the talker), but worthy of careful consideration given how it shines a candid light into a singer's life and mind. This young American tenor was already growing in fame with four opera recordings and a solo CD at the time, and he has ever since become even more of a household name in Europe, having been featured as the title roles in two important DVD recordings, of *Ciro in Babilonia* at the Royal Opera House, and *The Tales of Hoffman* alongside Natalie Dessay at the Gran Teatro del Liceu .

Opera Lively - You grew up in a family of musicians. You are named for your uncle who sadly died at a very young age, right? He couldn't pursue his intended own career as a singer. Can you tell us about your background growing up in this musical environment?

Michael Spyres – Yes, definitely. In my small town [Mansfield, Missouri], we were the entertainment. My mother and father were my band, and choir, and drama teachers, and they switched back and forth in different years. If there was a funeral or a wedding, it was the Spyres family. We were basically the Hillbilly von Trapps… [laughs]. All of us sang together as a family from before the time I could speak. They had old recordings of me when I was two or three years old singing with my family and we just grew up that way.

My parents [Eric and Terry Spyres] really instilled in me this love of music; music being a huge part of life and something that enriches you and helps other people in a very real way - not just in an abstract way, but in getting people together to sing in choirs.

The town where I came from has roughly 1,400 people. My mother and my father didn't know many people in the area, but they knew that they had music, and they knew that they were going to be the ones that people thought were a little weird, so they started making friends, and made them all join music groups and put on plays. They started this thing called the Ozark Mountain Players, and thirty of them would do melodramas three times a year in this small town just as something to get together and have fun. In a town that small, there are not a whole lot of social events other than Church, and a lot of time churches have a tendency to be rivals with each other [laughs], but music was one thing that everybody could agree that it is something that everyone lives with. People listen to the radio, and love to be together.

My town is quite well known because there is a famous writer named Laura Ingalls Wilder, and she wrote *Little House on the Prairie* books and they are world famous, and it is wonderful because everywhere I go I tell people about it. In German I say, "have you heard of *Unsere kleine Farm*?" "Yes of course," they say, and in Italian it is *La Piccola Casa nella Prateria*, and everyone knows *La Petite Maison dans la Prairie*, all of them, and I tell them, "well, that's where I'm from, little Mansfield. " When Wilder was about 27 years old she moved to the town and lived there for 64 years, and was a teacher and part of the community and wrote these books, and we still have this small house that her husband built for her, which lots of tourists come to see. My mother was a curator at the museum and she and her best friend wrote a musical that now has become quite a tradition; it's in its twenty-second year. From when I was nine my whole family did this musical that my mother wrote together. My father and all of us helped build sets and we played instruments and sang and dressed up in folk costumes. We did this every single year for about two months out of the year and it was a fantastic way to grow up because I was always performing. We did sports, and music, and we were so active. When I went to college it was bizarre, because I started realizing, "wow, I don't remember much of my years growing up because we were so busy." I was having a chance to perform two or three times a month every single year, because when you live in a family that is that dynamic and full of music where everyone looks to you to sing in their weddings and funerals, music becomes very much a part of your life.

OL – And what about classical singing; when did it come about, and operatic singing?

MS – Well, my uncle whom I was named after, died when I was I believe one year old, and I grew up with this story of him wanting to be a famous opera singer. He was a bit mad from what I hear [laughs]; his only possessions were about thirty records of Enrico Caruso and Mario Lanza, and a record player, one chair, one table, a mattress on the floor, and a couple of sets of clothes. He would spend all of his money on voice lessons and trying to figure out 'The Voice'. I still have his books and drawings and sketches and his ideas about singing. We grew up with this story, and my parents always had in the house so many operas! We loved music in all aspects but especially classical.

It started to become a part of my life when I was in junior high, probably, when I could fathom the idea of how complicated classical music is. In college my mother and father were in multiple operas and operettas; they were both in *The Pirates of Penzance*, they did lots of Gilbert and Sullivan, and *La Bohème*, and *La Traviata.* They were very aware that classical music is a huge thing that takes a lot of practice and thinking ability, so they weren't pushing us and making us listen to classical music all the time when we were children; we listened to all types and we sang folk music, and bluegrass. My sister played classical violin at the age of three, and then when she was six she started playing folk music, and switching back and forth. Around ten or eleven I started really wanting to know what these singers were doing because I always wanted to be a cartoon voice-over person. Mel Blanc was my hero. I'd just imitate and make sounds, and once I started hearing classical singing and really hearing it, I was thinking "I want to do that, it's the most amazing sound, I want to figure out how they are doing that."I would imitate and just sing baritone arias, because the idea that I was going to be a tenor took many years of struggle [laughs] so I thought, "I want to be a baritone, it's so much easier."

OL – But the tenor gets the girls!

MS – Exactly, but you live on the edge as a tenor; we don't know most of the time if we are going to hit the right notes, because it's really not natural to sing all the time in the passagio, but that's how it is.

OL – Listening to your CD "A Fool for Love," [Delos catalogue number DE 3414] I had the impression that the lower range is more comfortable for you.

MS – Definitely.

OL – So you started singing baritone.

MS – Yes, for about three years. Well, when I started my studies I was eighteen. I went to school for two and a half years. I had a teacher – he is now an agent and a really nice guy named Robert Mirshak, and he was one of those natural tenors, a smaller guy who had this pinging tenor voice. My speaking voice was like this [makes it very low], so I thought "there is no way I'm a tenor." And he said, "no, no, no, I think you can do it, I think you can try it." He just helped me start thinking about preservation of the voice and direction and healthy techniques and all that, because before that I was just like any kid that doesn't know. I knew about breath and I knew about diction and these things because I grew up singing so much choral music. My parents, being choral teachers, would talk about proper stance and vocal production, but to really go into classical singing, you have to learn first of all the old technique, the positioning, and you have to understand how the breath works with the tiny vocal chords. My teacher opened my mind up to the fact that the more effort you give, the less sound you produce, because the sound waves stay in your body, so you need to be as effortless as possible and be in the right position and let the sound go, let the waves go out into the audience rather than staying in you. Singing should be about the audience, and not about "this feels very good to me, it's wonderful". They are not going to get all the sound or feel good if all the sound waves are stuck in your jaw or your throat.

It was that switch that started making me realize that I love to sing. For me it's a form of meditation because I'll want to sing for hours and hours a day. But in order to do that, you have to really, really concentrate, and think, "how much can I give and do I want to give?" Classical singing is not only about the love of music and what you are willing to produce; it's trying to get other people to love the sound that you produce, and bringing them together. It's a difficult balancing act because if you don't like your job, the audiences are not going to like you, and if you like what you're doing too much, they are not going to like you either, because they can see that you are only doing it for yourself. So there is both that kind of openness and holding things back emotionally in order to get the emotion to other places. It's a really interesting flux of emotions that has to happen when a singer is doing it for the right reasons.

Singing is so difficult. That's why I love choral music, because I grew up singing in choirs and bands and doing things in group together, and that's why I love Rossini so much, because Rossini and Mozart did these ensembles. In ensembles you have to be a real musician, because you can't have four people who are shouting together and then the harmonies don't pop up where they should. That's something I really miss, though, when I'm the soloist, the center of attention, because I know that the pressure is all on me rather than on us as a group. [laughs]

OL – Let's backtrack a little bit, and ask you a sort of psychological question. Could it be a burden for you as a child, to say, "OK, you've been named after your uncle who wanted to be a famous opera singer, now you have to make it, you have to succeed, you have to be famous" which you have done. But was it scary in any way, to have that fate, that mission put on you? Was it troubling?

MS – It's all in how your parents raise you. I took that on myself. My parents said "you're named after him," so there was some pressure, but there wasn't anything that I really took on as a negative impact. It felt like I could do something that someone else couldn't do, and I never even thought that I was not going to be a singer. I've always done many, many things in life. For years I was a construction worker, a part-time teacher, and a waiter, but while I was working in construction, people would ask me who I was, and I'd say, "well I'm an opera singer, I'm just working in construction right now." "What, you're an opera singer?" And I'd say, "yeah, yeah, I am, I promise you'll hear me someday." To me it was a really anchoring effect, because I wasn't scared of the burden of carrying this torch with me; it was something of a goal to look forward to. My parents were really great. My mother and father come from absolutely different worlds. I came from this schizophrenic lifestyle if you will, because my father grew up very militaristically; everything was in its place, in order, very Midwestern, while my mother grew up basically a vagabond; she went to sixteen different schools. My grandmother raised three kids on her own, and my mother grew up in bars and casinos, and moving all the time. Seeing these two people come together and make it work, made me really realize that I can choose my path, and make what I want of it without them putting pressure on us. Neither of them ever said "you're going to be a famous singer," it was just something that I love to do and I took that upon myself as a child.

OL – Do you have a clear recollection of the first time you attended live opera?

MS – Yes, I was ten years old and I went to my mother's alma mater, in Branson, Missouri. I got to go backstage and watch this university production of an opera. It was such a fascinating thing because it was what we were doing in our small town, performing for people, but with real costumes and an orchestra, so it was so amazing to me, and especially because I had been to lots of musicals in our area. I played Kurt in *The Sound of Music* when I was 10 years old, so I was able to sing with an orchestra, and I loved that feeling. But opera was something different; to me it was the height of music. I think that's what opera is: the collaborative height of dance, acting, singing, all of the arts put together in one, and you rarely get that chance in life to bring it all together, and that's why opera is so important. Unfortunately singers get all the glory, but we are nothing without the others; we may be a very strong arm, but there's a huge body we are connected to.

OL – So, let's talk about training a little bit. You went first to a school here before you went to Vienna.

MS – Yes, I went to a school here in the States at MSU, Missouri State University, in Springfield, Missouri, and I had this voice teacher for two and a half years. My choir conductor there, Dr. Guy Webb, is a very prominent choir conductor and he is an amazing singer on his own right; he went to Juilliard back in the forties, and he conducted in a style that matched how he would sing. He would stand in the perfect position, and go oooohhhhhh [sings] when he conducted, and you would see this perfect model while he was conducting. Then my voice teacher was telling me all of the things that I was asking, like "why does my voice go ahohahohah? [sings with unstable pitch] on this part"? And those two people taught me so much during the two and a half years that I was there! I just couldn't stand being in a university anymore, because all I wanted to do was sing full time. I didn't go to classes except for music; I just sang for six hours a day, I'd go to the rooms and just sit there with a piano. The Tenors' Greatest Hits Book has some thirty arias, and I would make it my goal every day to sing through every aria. So I was singing lots of inappropriate things, but still it taught me something so interesting. Every repertoire teaches you about your voice, because almost every piece was written for a different singer, and was written for the strengths of the singer. It might not be right for you on stage or anything, but it will teach you completely. When you are twenty, nobody should really be singing heavy Verdi or Puccini or Wagner, but you should sing through it in order to learn about your voice, and realize, "huh, that's weird, it makes me sing higher in a different way than I use for Rossini or Mozart," so you have to switch your technique around. Anyone who says "technique is technique" is being too close-minded; you have to change your technique slightly for every composer and even every role. With certain composers, especially bel canto, it is not extremely high tessitura. Most of the time it lies quite low, but then you have floating melodies, and it doesn't stay with E, F sharp, G, as a lot of the dramatic repertoire or say Mozart does. Switching back and forth teaches you so much about your instrument, and I find that it is such a pity that so many people stick to just one form of repertoire. Pavarotti only did a few roles in his entire career and he was amazing, but if you read his bio, for literally years, all he did was work on sounds, work on vowels, work on vocal production, thinking all the time "what am I doing here, ah ha ah ha, oh, that's what I'm doing". I think a lot of singers unfortunately get into this groove of going to a teacher, and then finding the next teacher. It's great to have teachers with good ears, but most of the burden should lie within ourselves to figure out our instrument. Most singers, because it's so scary, won't take on that responsibility of doing all the research, reading all of the old books, figuring out why techniques have changed, why people were writing in a different way before Caruso, and why audiences liked the style – that of Jean De Reszke, for instance - rather than the visceral high C from the chest. Thinking about those things is what I do in my days; I'm obsessed with sound, so when I hear a bird or a squirrel, I wonder how their vocal tracts work, I think "ta,ta,ta,ta, does that work for me?" I put all these things in the context of fascination with sound and instrument; I think that's the most important part about singing, and especially about technique.

OL – You had Dr. Webb and Dr. Mirshak, right, and then lately you haven't been working with a voice teacher; why is it so? It's a bit unusual, among the people I talk to, so, what made you go solo on the training lanes?

MS – Well, when I was twenty-one, I quit college when my teacher moved away to New York. Then I realized, "I'm going to have to do this on my own," so for five years I really didn't sing anywhere. I was just doing odd jobs, and I was involved in this choir called The World Youth Choir, and that was about the only thing that I did. It's a choir that meets once a year in Europe for two weeks and then performs, so in those five years this was about the only singing opportunity that I had. The rest of the time I was thinking about technique, and thinking solely by myself. Then I went to Vienna, I did auditions all around, and I was accepted at the Conservatory there. It was great, because I didn't have to do a lot of the course work. I was twenty-six, and they needed a tenor for the opera studio, because tenors are scarce everywhere, and fortunately I had the technique to sing a lot of things, so I got to perform. The conservatory in Vienna really shaped me into a more well-rounded singer. I already had a good understanding of vocal technique, but all the diction coaches in the conservatory, who also work in the Staatsoper and the Volksoper, gave me invaluable coaching. Even though they were not giving me voice lessons they were giving me vocal technique; they were teaching me about phrasing and shaping. Having a lieder teacher really helped me understand the intimacy of sound, and realize that singing is not about shoving as much sound into an audience as you can; it's about making them perk up and want to listen to you.

OL – Was Vienna before or after you attended the Saint Louis Young Artists Program?

MS – That was after. Saint Louis started when I was twenty and went on for two years. My first Rodolfo was at twenty-two, yes [laughs], and it is still a tough sing, actually. But I was fortunate because I got to start with Saint Louis. The people there are incredible; it's a really high level of artistry. I was fortunate enough to work with Stephen Lord as well as the late Colin Graham. The amount of really, really good art in Opera Theatre Saint Louis was invaluable for me in the two years I was involved with their young artists program. It broadened my mind about what it means to be an opera singer.

OL – So that was simultaneous with your college period?

MS – Yes.

OL – And then, was it a difficult time between twenty-one and twenty-six?

MS – Yes. Definitely. [laughs] Very much so, because all the burden was on me to do what I said I was going to do. I was so fortunate, because my parents let me move back to their place rent free and they had a great piano and I would come back after work and just sing until one or two in the morning, and they wouldn't care about how much sound I made; because they told me that they knew that I was going to make it!

OL – And so, how did the decision to go to Vienna come about?

MS – It came about because of my ex-wife who was a singer as well – she is Serbian. She and I knew that we couldn't live in Serbia and we couldn't live in the United States, because we didn't know anybody in New York or Chicago and because of visa situation, it was very difficult to find a place to live. We thought of Europe because we had a few friends from our World Youth Choir days; that's how I met her, and we went and auditioned for four or five different places. Fortunately we had friends from the choir in Vienna, and they said "If you come to Vienna, I'm sure you can get into the Conservatory and you can also get into the Arnold Schoenberg Choir," because I was so used to choral music. So while in Vienna both she and I sang in this wonderful choir, and that's how we were able to make enough money to live on.

OL – For how long did you stay in the Vienna Conservatory?

MS – I believe it was two full years.

OL – So what happened next?

MS – While at the Conservatory I was basically singing all day in the choir, sometimes six hours a day. [laughs] Many people say about choral singing, “Oh, it will tear your voice up.” It will, if you are not conscious of what you are doing. It was very difficult for me, putting myself in the challenging situation of having to sing choral music for many hours everyday. You have to force yourself to understand vocal production or else [speaks in a small hoarse voice] you lose your voice and you can’t sing. And then you start thinking, “wait a minute [vocalizes with a small, controlled voice], that’s the tone you want, and not [vocalizes with a forceful, loud voice].” Having to be restrained in the choir is what really helped me think about vocal production a lot. While I was in that choir I was doing audition after audition and getting nothing because I still didn’t have connections. My German was still improving, I could speak it, but it takes years. Everyone I talked to agreed that unless you are an exception it takes three to five years, whatever country you are in, in order to work full time and try to figure out how this society works and who is going to help you and who is not, and how you are going to fit in. So that’s what I did, just audition after audition after audition, and finally my big breakthrough came through at the Rossini Festival in Bad Wildbad in Germany. That’s when I got into this bel canto repertoire that I always wanted to, especially this baritenore repertoire that feels so comfortable for me. Because, especially with Rossini’s *Otello*, you have to have this baritonal voice, but you have to have flexibility to sing florid passages and sing up to high C’s and C sharps, and then down below A’s, and that to me would just fit perfectly with my understanding of the voice. That’s where my career started changing, and people said, “Huh, that’s an interesting voice,” there’s not too many people who can do that, and of course there is a great tradition of Americans doing this type of repertoire, like Bruce Ford, Rockwell Blake and Chris Merritt. People love associations, so they started hearing me, and they thought “Oh, another American Rossini tenor, that’s what we need”. You have to find your niche somewhere. [laughs]

OL – That led you to your La Scala debut, right? As Belfiore in *Il Viaggio a Reims.*

MS – Yes.

OL – By the way, I love that opera. It's not really an opera, it's more like a showcase for the singers; it's like a concert because there is one aria after the other, after the other, one for each singer.

MS – Yes, exactly. He wrote it to have a good time and just for people to get together and show off their talents. They all come together and make fun of each other and they are all having a good time.

OL – So this is a very good debut because it gives you opportunities to show yourself in that setting, right?

MS – Yes, definitely.

OL – So, then you did Arnold in *Guillaume Tell*, then the comedies, so you started with Rossini. However you do have some thirty-five roles that you've sung, and you're working on getting to forty-nine, huh?

MS – Yes, exactly. The last one I did was *La Damnation de Faust*, that's actually my forty-fifth role, including character roles, all together, a lot of them in these past seven years. But I had a great situation being from Springfield, we had the Springfield Regional Opera, and by the time I was twenty-two I already had six roles under my belt, because I was doing small parts in this regional opera company. When I moved and talked to friends in New York and Chicago, they said "Wow, this is really rare, you had a local opera company and you got to perform in it?" Most of these friends at twenty-five had never even done one role, while I was able to have stage time in that small environment. I loved it in Springfield because we had an opera, and a ballet, and two symphonies and two chamber orchestras. I think there are twenty-two different theaters in a town of a hundred fifty thousand people so there is a lot of art going around.

OL – So I hear that in European houses these days it is easier for them to hire Americans and Eastern Europeans, than the local people. Because first of all they think Americans are very well trained, and second, since the fall of the Iron Curtain the Eastern Europeans are coming in force. Did you have more facility with your career in Europe? Because it's only now that you're coming back to the United States. Can you tell us a bit more about this conundrum? In the past that's what people pretty much had to do, they had to go to Europe to train. But then we got our strong conservatories and universities, and regional opera companies… I think we are pretty much a force in the operatic world, now.

MS – Completely.

OL – But still, the Europeans have the tradition. But we might say that you are on the other side of history, right?

MS – Yes. Exactly.

OL – Can you tell us a bit more about all that?

MS – Yes, definitely. One person that I like to quote a lot is Jonah Lehrer, a young neuroscientist, who gave a speech about the virtue of being an outsider, and to me that has been an incredible help, being an outsider, because it forces you to look at all of society and what you are doing in a different way. All my friends and people I grew up with said, "OK, if you are going to do opera, you need to move to New York, or move to Chicago or Seattle or San Francisco; there is only a handful of places, maybe five, that you can go to, do your studies, and then get into the opera world and make a living." But in Europe I saw all this opportunity; Germany alone has something like three hundred opera houses, compared to ten big houses that everyone is trying to get into in the United States. I decided I was going somewhere where I could wait, because I knew it was going to take a while, and I really needed to learn languages, because when I moved there I didn't speak any languages whatsoever. Because of my skills of imitation, I could sing and had good diction in four languages, but I didn't understand a word of what I was singing unless I would write it down. Now I speak four languages, just because of being immersed in the society. For me it was just a logical decision.

Going back to what you were saying about US singers, they have to work harder than the European ones, who are singing in their own language. In the US there are so many really good singers, and it is really hard to get work here. When you go to Europe you've already had the training of the schools and the professionalism which is the most important thing that is taught here in the US. Every US person that I sing with in Europe, we are usually looking around and saying, "How do people show up for rehearsals and not have their music memorized?" Especially in Italy people are used to someone teaching them the role during rehearsal periods. And it just makes no sense to me, but that's how it was, that's how the system used to be set up; you would have six months with a maestro, and the maestro would tell you about tempos, and talk about meaning and so on. Now the world is going faster and faster, and with the US and Eastern Europeans and also all the Koreans and Chinese, all the jobs are going to the people who want them more, and really feel that they need to make it. Like any job market, the people who are the most qualified get the jobs. Sometimes unfortunately you are not exotic enough. That's one of the problems that I was having, I would do auditions and I wasn't getting much work, and I didn't know many people.

OL – Do you mean here or there?

MS – Here, here. So I moved to Europe and it took me a couple of years, but people said "Ah, the American kid, yeah!" I'm an exotic person over there. Europeans come here, and a lot of them are getting work if they are well prepared [laughs], but they are getting work because they are exotic, and it's just that people like this exoticism.

OL – What would you say to young singers, what advice you have for them, for someone who is coming up the ranks? You had this unusual path but you made it. I guess it's not the wisest advice to give, to tell them to follow this unusual path. I'd think it was harder for you to make it through this convoluted path than for most people, so what do you think people should do these days, when they are starting their undergrad studies and thinking about operatic singing?

MS – I don't know, because for me it just seemed logical that in order to make it in any business you have to be really good at what you do and really well prepared, and the burden is going to be on you. Definitely universities and singing teachers are very important, but out of the forty or so young artists friends that I had at Opera Theatre Saint Louis, there are 5 or 6 that are making a living singing to this day, and that's only been ten years. The main problem is that when people get into this mentality of "I've got to follow this path in order to make it", it closes in their idea of what making it is. I had to give up a lot in order to be in this position. I had to move to Europe with the money that I was given – a thousand dollars, and a suitcase. It sounds like a cliché movie but I was willing to give up everything, go to a society where I didn't speak the language and I didn't understand the culture. I knew I needed to learn languages so that's what I did. For younger singers, they need to be willing, to understand what it means and what they really want. Do they want a life of being a star? It's just like people who want to be a politician or an NBA basketball player: about one percent make it in the world. That one percent that does make it, they are the ones that are truly obsessed with the singing, obsessed with music.

OL – And driven.

MS – Yes, driven, exactly. They are really driven. And a lot of people do it for the wrong reasons. It takes five years before people either give up, or they don't [laughs]. It's all about analyzing why you want to go into music and especially singing. If you are doing it for the love of it and for the interesting cultural aspects of being able to see the world in a different way and expanding the mind and trying to make the world better, do it. But don't go into opera thinking that you are going to make a lot of money and be a star, because stars fade, stars go bright and just die out. If you really want to look up to someone who is very important, to me it was Nicolai Gedda. He had a singing career for sixty years, and he started out as a banker, and did all of the work that you are supposed to do. Everyone thinks that you are supposed to get famous when you are in your twenties and have this great, great career. If you look statistically at what happens, same as in any professional sport, people do it for about three or four years then they start to get worse and worse and worse, because they are not doing it for the right reasons, for the love of the game, or the love of the arts. What I would say to young singers is "you have to get in your mind that you are a singer. Even if you don't have work now, you still have so much work to do". By the time I'm sixty I hope to be fluent in ten languages. It's just constant learning, constant openness to change; that's what an artist is supposed to be.

OL – Thinking of Gedda and his sixty years of career, and Domingo going for more than that, probably, do you worry about your own longevity? In terms of all this diversity of roles, and your start with choral music, are you worried about damaging the voice?

MS – I'm not, personally. Of course one always thinks anything can happen, which is true [laughs]. But look at singers, people like Jean de Reszke. That's what made me realize, "Wow, you can do lots of varied repertoire and be quite successful, but you really need to be really smart about it." Some people argue that de Reszke was one of the singers who did the *voix mixte* a little too much, but he was able to have this really wonderful career, and I remember looking at a Met log, and Jean de Reszke was doing Rossini and Wagner and Bizet all in one week, and people were thinking, "what, you'd never do that." No, you would, and that's what keeps my voice really intact. Because if you stay in one way of singing and only do Wagner, only do Puccini, only do Rossini, you really start getting lazy. I think you need to have this very varied repertoire in order to have different vocal positions and think in a different way. The more varied the repertoire, the better you understand your instrument, because you are forced to. That's how it's been for me.

OL – So now you're moving to light Verdi roles such as Alfredo, and the Duca, and you're about to do Hoffmann in Barcelona, right? But interestingly enough, you are preparing for Oberon, which is a part that is usually for a spinto or a juvenile dramatic tenor, right?

MS – Yes, I did study the opera *Oberon* and was preparing to perform the young lyric role of Huon and not the darker more dramatic Oberon though. With Oberon there is the darker, older tenor who has the more dramatic voice. Unfortunately nowadays people usually do not cast the correct voice types for the voice it was intended for. [laughs] When you are doing obscure repertoire it costs so much money to put these productions on. You need to get the top of the top. Usually you need to get someone who is going to really excite the ears and unfortunately most of the time this means this loud dramatic spinto kind of tenor, even though most spintos now aren't true spintos. For me Aureliano Pertile was one of the greatest singers of all time, because if you listen to his voice he had this massive instrument - people said it was the biggest voice of all time - but he could sing *pianissississimo* – you could hear the control that he had. I just can't even think of a spinto who is singing now who can actually sing dynamics. And that's the tragic part: so many people are so focused on sheer volume of sound that they are not realizing, "no, no, no, you don't need that much sound all the time." Everything is turning into a mezzo-forte to fortissimo. Dynamics is something people have forgotten about.

OL – Absolutely. We had a discussion recently on the website; people were saying, "that's because the audience expects it; they are listening to opera CDs on their car stereos, they go to the huge cavernous opera houses like the Met, and it's not the same sound." And I was thinking "it is not the same sound, people shouldn't be shouting all over the place."

MS – Exactly!

OL - [laughs] If you can't tell the difference between your car stereo and the live opera experience, you shouldn't be there in the first place.

MS – Precisely, yes!

OL – What are you doing there anyway?

MS – Exactly. Right now one of my really good friends, Bertrand Delvaux, is in York in the UK; he's a physicist and singer as well, and he is doing his PhD combing fluid mechanics and the voice. He and I are collaborating. He is going to be taking an MRI of me while singing, this next year. I'm very interested in the scientific aspect of vocal production, especially acoustics, because a lot of people don't understand overtones and vocal performance; they don't grasp the concept of sounds being physics. In order to go over a specific volume you need to make a certain frequency that can cut through an orchestra. One of the funniest things to me is that what people think is a big voice, is actually not if you record it and look at the decibel level. For instance, Pavarotti. A lot of people say he didn't have the biggest voice, but if you look at the frequency levels and the decibel levels you heard him always, no matter what. You would hear that frequency that would cut through the loudest orchestra. Most people aren't even thinking about that; they just think "Oh, it's this huge voice" because people are hearing timbre and confusing it with decibel level and sound. Just because someone is going "aahhh" [vocalizes] doesn't mean they have a small voice, it means that they are trying to find that specific sound that is going to cut through. It's true you want this big sound, but people need to be flexible in their ideas of what is right for the voice and what is right for an audience. It is our job as artists to cultivate other people's ears and make them want dynamics, make them want to sit on the edge of the seat and think "oh my gosh, that was one of the most beautiful pianissimos I've ever heard." And also be taken away by this beautiful forte. It's all in a gigantic palette that needs to happen, but when you have everything at mezzo-forte…

OL – Right. I'm learning from what you're saying, and I think I can now understand the experience I had yesterday. I was introducing opera to one of my Psychiatry students, because I think opera is a great tool for Psychiatry, actually, because it touches the human experience all the time. So I was telling my student about several singers, and told her that on Opera Lively we voted Waltraud Meier as the best current singer from the technical standpoint, among all singers who are currently active in opera houses. The student wanted to listen to her singing, and I played a video clip of the "Liebestod." There was this huge Wagnerian orchestra with this huge sound, and Waltraud was cutting through it, without being louder than it. She was piercing through it. I was myself mesmerized. I had goosebumps. I wanted to demonstrate to this young person Waltraud Meier's singing, but I got the full impact myself; I thought "Oh my God, how does she do it, how does she weave through this huge sound of the orchestra?" We could hear her crystal clear, but she wasn't shouting or anything.

MS – Exactly, and that to me is the mark of a great singer. Same thing with one of my colleagues, she unfortunately passed away last year, Elizabeth Connell, she was one of the greatest singers of all time, and people need to know her name if they don't already, because she had one of the most varied careers ever, and she was the height of technique. She started out as a contralto and ended up as a dramatic soprano which is very much in the opposite order that most singers tend to go. She sang for over 40 years moving into all different types of repertoire and she was singing Turandot very healthily just last year when she was sixty-five. I was fortunate enough to be the last person to sing a duet with her on stage. Though it's not the right repertoire for me, I did Verdi's *Otello* duet "Già nella notte densa" and she was Desdemona, and despite me being a true lyric tenor and her being a dramatic soprano, we found a way in order for our sounds to blend and find that place that is tasteful.

OL – Where do you see your voice going? I was thinking about this *Oberon*. There is *Der Freischütz* – Max might be another one of those, right? What do you think you might be singing next, and what are your goals?

MS – It seems right now that I'm going to be singing a lot of *Damnation de Faust*, a lot of French, because I'm doing four different *Damnation de Fausts* in the next three years. [laughs]

OL – This is one of my favorite pieces.

MS – For me too. Fortunately enough I just sang it in this revolutionary production with Terry Gilliam as director, but French repertoire for me specifically is that right balance of dramaticism coupled with intimacy. I think it's probably also because I love the times when people didn't have a set idea of which era they were in, and so for me the 1830s into the 1860s people were composing and trying all those things out. I love that period of writing like Auber, and Meyerbeer; and Berlioz was the end of that period when all of those people were doing these amazing different things with orchestration. Wagner also is absolutely incredible. Wagner wrote these huge long phrases and these beautiful melodies, and people think you have to have a gigantic voice to sing Wagner, but that's absolutely untrue, because if you ever go to Bayreuth about half of the orchestra is covered up and it's all about the blend and gravity of sound and the effect, and not the sheer volume. That's the one thing we have to start doing because it's detrimental to audience's ears, and singers' years of singing are cut short simply because everyone thinks that the audience wants volume, so we better give them what they want. No, no, the audiences want to have their hair stand up, to become alive and see something that is going to change their lives.

One of the most maddening things to me is that people aren't putting things into context. We go to a competition, you'll hear some of these incredible voices and they sing wonderfully two arias that will blow your mind, but when you see them doing an entire opera after an hour it's the most boring thing in the world. You hear it come out and you think "wow!" and then five minutes later, [sighs] "so boring, so boring." It's all one sound. People aren't being artists like they should, because we are all trying to give people what they want rather than what the composer wanted. We need to get back to why the composer wrote something in a specific way, and we need to get used to the fact that people think differently now, but there is no shame in going back and realizing that "Oh, maybe there is a reason that Verdi wrote the B flat at the end of 'Celeste Aida' triple pianissimo, and it's OK to go into *voix mixte*, that's why he wrote it, he was so specific." But now you hear everybody sing triple forte, because, "Oh, the audience wants to hear something loud." It's making all of us dumber for not willing to follow the composer's wishes.

OL – Well, we interviewed Dr. Philip Gossett from the University of Chicago.

MS – Wonderful man.

OL – Yes, wonderful. And he is working a lot on this, trying to restore the right dynamics on the critical editions and trying to see that people pay more attention to what the composer wanted.

MS – Yes, I've been fortunate enough to work with him three different times, actually. When I did my debut at La Scala in the *Viaggio a Reims*, he was giving us ideas and helping us especially with cadenzas and things like that, and then I worked with him again in Chicago when I did Rodrigo, the smallest part in Verdi's *Otello* with Muti. There is a reason why someone like Muti is up there, because he pays so much attention to detail and he won't let anyone get away with things and he'll just start laughing at you if you are singing forte for no reason. [Unfortunately we interrupted him and he didn't tell us about the third occasion].

OL – OK, let's talk conductors, we have one of the greatest right here, right? John Eliot Gardiner. How is it, to work with him?

MS – It was quite nerve-wracking the first time I auditioned for him, because he is one of those legends that I grew up with, along with Riccardo Muti and Alberto Zedda. Those three guys were the pinnacle of conducting, and they are all very different, but there's something about them. When I auditioned for Gardiner for the first time, he was so down-to-earth, and very intellectual, and he put me at ease, because he wasn't unimpressed, he was staring me in the eyes, going, "Hm, I like what you're doing, it's really interesting, but let's try something else, see if this works." I really enjoyed working with him. He is very meticulous and very adamant about musicality and doing everything for a reason, and he has the capacity to do it. Some conductors don't. Some conductors are doing conducting just for themselves. And you can tell – "look at me, everybody look at me!" But he is just like what a conductor should be, looking at everything and hearing the whole sounds. The main part of a conductor is making sure that music is flowing in the proper way and that art is being made. When you hear Beethoven's Ninth a million times, there are some good recordings out there, but to come and hear him and be able to sit there and watch the rehearsal like we just did, I was just on the edge of my seat listening to how every single phrase, something that you've heard a hundred times, can be made new. When you have a true artist at the helm of the orchestra and it's never exactly the same, that's the great thing, it depends on a gesture, it depends on the feeling, but it's always based on what is written and the phrasing, and that to me is the mark of a great conductor.

OL – And there is also the question of period instruments, a bit controversial. There are those who say like Sir Colin Davis, "Oh I don't like this thing that they are doing because they are pushing us out of the Baroque repertoire." [We are paraphrasing] I interviewed Maestro Botstein [Volume 1] from the American Symphony Orchestra…

MS – Yes, a marvelous orchestra.

OL - … and he also said, "You know, I don't think we really need to be doing all this soft sound and so forth because there is a place for the full modern orchestra as well." [We are paraphrasing] Now you are doing the Ninth with a period orchestra. How do you position yourself in this discussion?

MS – I think there is a time and place for everything. This orchestra is perfect for this sound. We are doing original tuning in A430, so that's a little hard to get used to, because when you are used to singing everything in 440, you have to be slightly flatter than you normally would, because it's not a full half-step. It's just a little bit more rounded. Yes, it is quite different, but I absolutely love it, you just have to take things into context, because with the modern orchestra the problem is that it is this exciting huge sound and people forget that "OK, there is this huge amount of sound coming out so I need to be delicate but broad and grounded." The problem is that a lot of people are either / or, and I've never been one of those persons, I'm either and or. I like to have the full spectrum of everything. It depends on the hall, that's a big thing. I'd love to hear this orchestra in a massive hall. You do have to watch for and listen differently than you would with a big orchestra, but I think both sides need to realize that there's enough music out there and enough places to have both. We live in modern times, I have a lot of scores, and all my music is on my Galaxy tablet, and I do all of my learning from it, and I have so many friends who say "No, I just can't get used to electronic music!" Why not? I have both. You can have this rich existence in both sounds, both orchestras, and it is not that controversial. It just got to be right. Maybe you'll not like the sound as much but you can't deny the beauty of old sounds.

Today we were having a problem with pitch a little bit, because some of us singers were realizing that something is wrong, because the orchestra is in front of us and we are not hearing their pitch at 430. What we are hearing is the sound that is bouncing off the walls and coming back to our ears, and we are hearing something that is slightly different, because we are behind where the sound is. Sometimes just because of aesthetic purposes you don't want the singers to be all singing in front, but it's almost physically impossible. [laughs] But one aspect that I really love about John Eliot is his ability to realize that choir, singers, orchestra, conductor, we are all one body. So we are not more important than the orchestra, the orchestra is not more important than him, he is not more important than anybody else. He is the one who is keeping us all together, but he doesn't have such a massive ego that "Everyone watch me at every turn" – all of this is a give and take and a realization that we are all working together and that's what I absolutely love.

OL – About stage direction. I read in one of your interviews that you like very much Thaddeus Strassberger, right?

MS – Yes.

OL – And we've just interviewed him too.

MS – Oh, really?

OL – It was one of our most spectacular interviews ever.[Volume 1] I really loved him, and I went to see one of his productions, *Le Roi Malgré Lui*.

MS – Oh, you did, at Bard? Great. I just saw some of the production pictures. We talked about it, yes.

OL – Great. But you are mostly based in Europe and America is a different place. I was just talking to Maestro James Meena from Opera Carolina, and they had over there this beautiful, visually striking staging of *Madama Butterfly*, with a production by Katano, a visual artist. And Maestro Meena told me that they had to do a very traditional *Tosca* because a lot of patrons complained about the Katano production, and I found it so incredibly beautiful! His patrons said, "Oh, wait a moment, we don't want, we don't need this!" The next production, they had to go back and rent very traditional sets for *Tosca*. So there is a difference in culture. Here we have some trouble accepting the novelty of Regietheater and all that, right? Personally the jury is still out for me. I like some of those director-driven productions, but some I think go a little overboard, over the top, so what do you think of this?

MS – Yes, I'm of the same nature, I love everything that is well thought-out and well presented. The problem is when someone is trying to do a revolutionary production and a lot of time they aren't taking into consideration the demographics and the likes and dislikes of a community. If you are going to do something really inflammatory, it's your job also to educate people, to go out there and hold extra conferences and talk to the donors and the people and say "this is why it is so important and so crucial that we do something different, because this is what opera is about." For instance, in Vienna most of the time the productions are of an older nature but when they did this *Don Carlos* that I got to see a couple of times with Ramón Vargas, the French version with five acts, it was funny because it was semi-traditional and then they had little parts that were newer and set in the fifties, they had a little Hausfrau and the people were so enraged and yelling and booing the production. But to me that is the core of opera; it should be this revolutionary thing. You can't make everybody mad because you still need audiences and you need money to come in, but to me that's why art is so important; it should be this revolutionary thing that just gets you mad and you start talking about it, like "That was total crap". After you do that, if you really care about your project, you should have question-and-answer situations, and if people are really mad at you, you have as a director to be able to say, "Well, I see your point, but the reason I did this is because I thought that the traditional values have changed." You just need to have a discussion.

Most people want to see operas with people in traditional costumes like in the movies. I'm all for traditional opera, but I don't want it to be stale and boring. Some composers have written really time-specific operas, and that's a hard stretch to do, but I have no trouble with newer productions, it just has to be presented in the right way. These revolutionary ideas are what everyone is after, but some people are just not subtle enough with their ideas. Calixto Bieito is the height of what people do not like in the States, and with a lot of his productions, I think they are a little too… in your face for the wrong reasons. I enjoy the thought process that goes along with it, but I think a lot of directors now aren't musicians, and they are not taking things into consideration.

Thaddeus was amazing, because he wasn't himself a musician, but he started realizing, "Hmmm… why can't the singer do this? Maybe there is some kind of technical reason, so I'll let them do that, but they want to move here, so…" It takes so much thought in order to make everyone happy, and I think especially Thaddeus, and Terry Gilliam did an amazing job too. With him at first it was a little difficult to get him to understand the concept of opera timing. If you are singing [sings] "I looooove youuuuuu" and you want this big gesture to come out during "you" he would get all upset and say, "no, no, that's not visceral enough and I need you to say I love *you*" and we'd say, "OK, you said that, and I do believe that, but there are six seconds of music between the action that you want, and the next word; we can't do it the way you want it…" and he'd say, "wow, I see what you mean". The action and build-up to the climactic moment takes longer and is more drawn out in opera than in movies or other mediums.

You need a director that is really taking everything into consideration, especially all of the words. I've worked with some directors who are working from a translation, they don't even know the original language that they are trying to direct in, and sometimes you say "Huh, I can't put my arm up here because there is absolutely no reason for me to do that, because I'm trying to say I love you" and they're like "Oh, huh, I didn't know that." There have been many cases like that, because people get so driven on their own idea of their revolutionary thing, the concept they think the whole thing is going to fit into, but they are not taking the composer's wishes into the context of their new brilliant idea.

The successful directors are those who have a real broad aspect of what an opera is supposed to be, while still catching all the things that the composer wrote specifically for it. I don't think that there is anything wrong with modern stagings, in fact that's what is going to propel opera into the next level in the future, because I don't think that opera is this stale form of art. It's just that we don't have many ambassadors that are willing to say "OK, opera needs to be revolutionary, but very well learned and traditional in that sense," and people have a hard time taking new and old ideas and perpetuating them. It's either… "No, I like it how it always has been" or "No, I want something crazy and new and different." There is a way to get it all in there; you just have to be really sensitive. Most directors, though, can't be bothered to put the time in, because we live in the fastest world. What I think that is going to be really interesting is newer technologies, especially electronic projections. They've done these art installations in different places in Europe. The first place I was aware of it was in Berlin, but I got to see it live for the first time in Barcelona. There is this new type of projection that they started to put on outside Gaudí's house, they turned it into a movie screen. They had really good sound and really good projections. So the house came alive. The house was singing to operatic music.

OL – That was a production of what?

MS – It was just an art installation. They were doing just art for art's sake and it was only a ten-minute thing, but this got me really excited thinking of the possibilities for opera. It's already hard to be a singer with all the art you put in, and now you'll need to do the same thing with these new technologies. I had a fantastic time doing this obscure Baroque opera in Lisbon, *Antigono* [1755] by Antonio Mazzone.[1717-1785] It was the first time it was being performed since the great Lisbon earthquake back in the 1700s. We wanted to do it very traditionally as far as staging went, because the music was just so absolutely hard, it is one of the hardest operas. The old Baroque way was to come out and stand there and really sing, and there wasn't so much action, but the great thing is that we coupled this with a very good visual artist who was working with us from a digital pad for the two weeks we were rehearsing. He was drawing in real time the entire set, ideas for the background, so while we were singing he was projecting what he was drawing and you could see him right next to the conductor just watching and feeling and moving and creating art at the exact time, and making flames shoot out from people's heads, while we were standing there and singing our hearts out.

OL – Have you seen the DVD of *La Pietra del Paragone* with the blue men and the pancakes flying?

MS – Yes, yes! Of course! I just think there is room for it. People just need the education, they need to understand that this is the only way they are going to propel opera to a newer generation, because I'm sure you know in your profession, people's attention spans are getting shorter and shorter, and you need to get the endorphins to come out faster. The amazing thing for me is that the more you can educate someone, the less they have to have instant gratification and they can start to read. Our brains work differently when we read books and excite parts of our brains, and we can put the brakes on a little bit. With classical music and especially opera we can have the best of both worlds, we can have the open, crazy, in-your-face kind of moment and after a couple of seconds you need a little downtime and not everybody is going to be exactly on the same wave length, but there needs to be variation, just like with the dynamics we were talking about. There also needs to be dynamics in acting, because there is so much acting involved in our newer operas that people are forgetting that there are physical limitations. If you want to have a really good sound, that pure, pure legato, you probably shouldn't have your singer doing cartwheels or having a physical fight. There is a way to do it, but it is not going to be exactly correct, if you have someone fight while singing [sings], it just looks awkward. [laughs] Most people are just not willing to put in the time.

OL – What about contemporary opera, any interest there? We were talking about projections, I was thinking about an experimental opera I saw. It's hard even to call it an opera, it's more like electronic percussion / visual effects musical theater with projections out of a pad, by a Portuguese composer called Miguel Azguime, it's called *Itinerário do Sal*, I don't know if you saw that.

MS – No, but I have friends who told me about it.

OL – So, that is very radical, but I loved it, by the way. Then you have the famous machine by Robert Lepage at the Met for the *Ring*, have you seen that?

MS – No, I haven't seen that yet.

OL – Because that is also controversial, with all the use of technology, what does it do to the staging? I thought that the stage was a little cramped and the machine didn't give as much space for the singers to act. I value blocking and dynamic use of space a lot.

MS – If you noticed that they don't have a lot of room to act, that to me is the same situation of directors having a beautiful idea which is not working out in real life because they are not realizing that the most central thing about opera is human expression. It can't be just about one centerpiece or how amazing a mechanical arm is; it has to be the assimilation of humanity and technology. Most people go with one idea and they don't take things into consideration.

OL – But let's talk about true contemporary opera. Any experience singing it, or plans to?

MS – Yes, actually when I was in Vienna that's what I did; I was singing a lot of different contemporary chamber operas. It was really eye-opening. I did this opera called *Scherz, Satire, Ironie und tiefere Bedeutung*, and it's by this incredible composer named Detlev Glanert [Ed. Note: from the play by Christian Dietrich Grabbe, premiered at the Komische Oper in 2001 with a libretto by Jörg W. Gronius]. I think he wrote it back in 85 or 86; it's so difficult but he is such a smart man. Some composers compose [sings a 12-tone scale] these twelve-tone situations which are amazing but don't take into consideration the physics of the voice, but he specifically did. I did another one called Die Sühne (The Expiation) [Ed. Note: Josef Wenzl-Traunfels, 1883-1955, premiered in 1937, a chamber opera in one act, based on a work by Theodor Körner] which was an opera that was composed back in the 1930s, very much like a mixture between Schoenberg and Richard Strauss, and it's absolutely incredible when you have a newer composer that is doing something different with harmonies and rhythms and words. But the main thing, just like with directing, is that you have to put everything in context and realize that people love melodies; that's what sounds good to our ears, it's pleasing to hear chords once in a while. You can't just go on your own way unless your entire idea is to make people frown. Sometimes that's good too, but it all has to be in context; everyone needs to realize that modern opera really has its place as well, because it's very scary sometimes to be watching a modern opera where there is no life, there is no happiness, and everything turns into this post-apocalyptic terrible world. That's OK for an effect, but that's not what the world is, the world is getting better and better, look at longevity of life and health worldwide. Yes, it's getting worse in some places but overall the quality of life is getting better. Modern opera is missing sometimes a lot of the romanticism that is around in this world; there are so many good people and wonderful things to be seen and new revelations to be had, but a lot of the time unfortunately the niche for modern opera is just showing the bad part. [laughs]

OL – You are getting back to something you'll probably enjoy a lot, *Die Fledermaus*, because with your family background in musical theater, are you looking forward to the operetta genre?

MS – Yes, very much so, and also because when I was in Vienna, I did a lot of tourist concerts, and I had to sing a lot of operetta. It was great for me because operetta has its own specific style. A lot of people don't quite understand the double entendres that have to happen, especially with the language, and fortunately in Vienna the operetta culture is still just really vivacious. The Volksoper is always doing operetta. For me it's a charming moment in musical history and I love it because you can be funny and romantic and it is all a little bit more lighthearted.

OL – I would assume – I haven't had the pleasure of seeing you on stage yet – that you are a good actor, with your background, right?

MS – Yes, I love the acting aspect. That to me is just as important as the singing, because if people just want to hear a voice, let's just do a standing recital. This is opera, it's alive, and you are supposed to use your entire body. For me that's why this operetta is going to be so much fun, because I love acting, I just love it.

OL – Combining the French repertoire with that, maybe you'll want to do the operettas by Offenbach, not just his *Hoffmann*.

MS – Yes, I love *La Péricole* and others, what's the one, La Belle…

OL – La Belle Hélène.

MS – Yes, I might be doing that in a couple of years as well. Yes, I just think that all of this repertoire has its place, and we are so poor if we only think of opera as just what the Met is doing at the moment. [laughs]

OL – I'd like to end with two aspects. One is your CD. I actually have it here and will ask you to sign it for me.

MS – Of course!

OL – I have one small criticism to make of the track selection.

MS – Yes.

OL – Because I see all this incredibly diversified background that you have, I thought you were not as adventurous as you might have been, when you selected the arias to include in your CD. And of course, it's your first one and you need to really place it, and people want to hear those famous tenor arias. But do you feel that you'd want to go off the beaten path for a future one?

MS – Definitely. My goal is to have different types of CDs. For this one I ended up switching gears, because I initially just put forth a CD of all of my obscure loves, and tried to put them into this idea, but they said "Huh, we are not going to put out a CD like that, because it is just not going to sell, nobody knows you, it's your first CD, it's not going to work, so you'll have to rethink." Which was good, because it did force me to realize that I want to reach the broadest audience, not just opera snobs or the obscure crowd, but then I don't just want the greatest tenor hits, you have to get a bit of everything in there. And I wanted to go a lot more obscure but my wife and other friends said, "Perhaps that won't be the best way, because you are not taking into context the rest of the listening crowd." There are two songs that each of the groups will like, I think. But yes, going more obscure will be for when I have my own record label someday. [laughs]

OL – Just listening to you and noticing your background and the way you were driven to succeed and did so many interesting things, you seem to be a happy man. I've talked to many singers who love the art form but feel very burdened by its demands, to be on the road and in hotels all the time, away from family. It looks like you found solutions for this. You've remarried, your wife is a singer as well [Tara Stafford-Spyres], you go places with her, it's probably less hard on you, although I'm guessing a lot here.

MS – Yes, I've been through a lot of things. The funny thing is that people say, "Wow, you are so upbeat" – that's why *Candide* is truly my path; I love *Candide*, because I came from this small area and then I got to see all of the world. From my diverse background in terms of my mother and father, I was forced to not look at the world through one eye. A lot of people end up doing that; it's just human nature, we only go to places that we want to go, and my parents forced me, because of their different backgrounds, to constantly go into places and situations that were going to be difficult. I don't really revel in that but I know that there are certain things in life that you have to go through, like love, and loss, and moving to a place to where you've never been before, and seeing new cultures and being an outsider. Being an outsider is such an interesting thing to me, because it's helped me realize that the world is much more open and a loving place than a lot of people give it credit for.

Of course we can't control the world, but… my mother has a really great saying, that you can't carpet the world but you can wear slippers. That's truly my belief too in life, that you have to protect yourself for the long haul, but only in the last couple of years I've found this balance of happiness, just simply because I started looking at my life and seeing all the mistakes that I've made in the last ten years, personally and family and all of these things, and I started to wonder if what I really want out of life is just trying to get famous and just trying to do this job? What am I doing? And fortunately once I started to question everything I started to say, "Wow, I'm getting more and more work, now that I've become more comfortable and happy," because everyone wants to be around people who are nice and happy.

Sometimes you have to smile and act like you are in good shape. For me positivity is the only driving force in evolution, it's realizing that a situation hasn't happened yet and thinking, "well, maybe this is going to be good!" Maybe it will be bad, but it is better to think positively and be happy about a situation, because – you know this better than anybody – the brain has thought patterns and we develop these neuropathways, and it's so familiar to us. But when you go somewhere else like a new city, or learn a new language, it throws you off, and you have to start creating new neuropathways. In the last ten years I've lived in five different countries, I've had an ex-wife, I've had friends die, friends go to jail, family that almost broke apart, but then came back together, but I wouldn't be here without it. I don't look at any of this like horrible, fearful times; there were some times that were bad, but fortunately they are in the past [laughs] and I'm looking forward to the future, because the more that I start thinking about myself, that's when I start realizing that, "oh, the world is terrible." And then I watch things like TED conferences, and talks about amazing kids that come out of poverty and are changing the world, and it just makes me open up and think "oh, gosh, the world is getting better and I need to be a part of this incredible positive force for change." We need to always look forward to the future and be happy that we are alive. Because we shouldn't even be here by all accounts. [laughs] One of my favorite quotes comes from a great musician named Andrew Bird: "ask our esteemed panel: Why are we alive? And here's how they replied: You're what happens when two substances collide and by all accounts you really should have died. " Why are we alive? Nobody knows, but it is amazing that we are here, so, let's just make the most of it - that's what I say - while we are here. [laughs]

OL – I guess we shouldn't spoil this great answer by following it up with something else.

MS – Thank you so much! Are you going to be able to come to the concert tonight?

OL – Yes, I will.

MS – Wonderful! It will be an amazing experience.

.

Paul Appleby, tenor

We met in person in Santa Fe in August 2013 this very friendly, charming, knowledgeable and intelligent young American tenor who was the lead male role alongside Susan Graham's Grande Duchesse in Offenbach's operetta. A winner of the Met National Council Auditions, his career continues to grow. His enthusiasm for his art is contagious.

Opera Lively: Let's start by something that is certain to put you in a good mood… It's what your colleague Susan Graham said about you when I interviewed her last week [we quoted her interview that opens this volume, when she talked very favorably about Paul.]. So first of all let me give you the opportunity to respond in kind. How is it for you, working with Susan Graham?

Paul Appleby – It's a little surreal, still, because I have been a fan of hers and listening to her work, her records, and videos of her performances for fifteen years or so, now. Since I started studying this kind of music, a lot of what I know about Reynaldo Hahn songs and Ned Rorem songs was from her CDs and recitals of that repertoire. To be close to her and to work side by side with her now after admiring her and learning from her from a distance for so long, is a little strange but it has also just been a lot of fun, which you can imagine, with the personality that she has. But more than that, to really see how this art that she's created, the process through which she goes to that end result that has made her Susan Graham has been really instructive. It's so many things: little details about how she uses the French language – I've learned so much! – or shadings of vowels, parts of the voice, her comic timing, but more than that, it's also seeing her interact with people from the opera company – everybody from the choristers to the stage hands. These aspects of the professional career are very important. The public doesn't see how it manifests itself, but that grace and humor and professionalism ties in with the artistic part of the career. It's a blessing to be a part of it and to watch her.

OL – Tell us about this production of *Grande-Duchesse de Gérolstein*, and how you relate to your role.

PA – I have to give to our director Lee Blakeley a lot of credit for imagining the arc of the character in this version of it. When I looked at the score I had read Fritz more like the leader of the pack; a rebel pushing against authority. Lee's take is that he is more of a slob. He is the last guy picked for the kickball team. His issue has to do with confidence and the lack thereof. When the Duchess for some reason picks him as the object of her desire, very quickly he goes from total lack of confidence to artificially bloated self-confidence, and then there is a needle that pops the balloon of that false inflation. That has been a really fun avenue to explore, and a much more interesting way to tell the story. Lee and I worked together to shape the shade of that character.

OL – There are some really comic scenes, like that one with the guardhouse.

PA – A piece like this is not exactly Stravinsky or grand opera at all. Embedded into the way the music is written and the nature of the piece, the comedy and the gags are really important. It is challenging to do this kind of work, because it is so silly, and you want to respect its silliness, but you also want to have the story of the characters and the emotional part behind these people, to make them more real. In our production, I'm proud of the fact that we have managed to embrace the silliness completely, but Lee came up with very clever little gags like the guardhouse becoming our little tent for our nasty business, while at the same time creating fuller characters who have vulnerabilities as well as just outrageousness.

OL – I liked the update with references to "A Fish Called Wanda." I couldn't stop laughing.

AP – There is a tradition in operetta of adapting it to the culture of the location and to some closeness to the time period. The liberty we took with the dialogue, there is historical precedent for it.

OL – Yes, that's what I said in my review. I usually don't like alterations especially when they modify endings, but in the case of operettas, it's what the composers and librettists wanted, that the public would relate to them in their time and would understand the gags.

PA – Absolutely.

OL – Is this your first time in Santa Fe? What can you say of the environment, here?

PA – There is something special that I can't quite put my finger on. I can tell you about the different parts that appeal to me. For one, I love the climate. I was just back in New York last week and it is disgusting this time of the year. The presence of art everywhere seeps into you. In every restaurant you walk into there are these great paintings and sculptures; even in stores and homes. I start seeing the architecture around here in a much different way that ignites my creative mind. The people here are incredibly charming and gracious and welcoming. The opera company has been the same way, very well run, very supportive. My wife was here, visiting me for a week and we started going to open houses, because we were so struck by the beauty of the place and the people. We are not in a position to buy anything, it's more of a fantasy [laughs] but it's a very compelling place. It's very fun to be here.

OL – What about singing at this altitude and dryness; is it vocally challenging?

PA – Yes. When I first got here it was a little difficult; the altitude primarily, and the dryness as well. In our production we jumped in at the first scene, the first day of rehearsal, and it is quite physical. I was gasping for air, desperately, the first day or two. But once you adjust, it's very manageable.

OL – Is it harder to project the voice in the open air theater?

PA – No, surprisingly not. I was a little dubious at first. I don't know what the acousticians who built that place did, but it worked really well. I've now watched several shows from several locations in the house and I'm always amazed by how clear and well projected the sounds are.

OL – Let's switch to your next major engagement: *Two Boys* by Nico Muhly, in the role of Brian. Please describe the opera to our readers.

PA – The opera *Two Boys* which was premiered at the English National Opera two summers ago is based on a true story that happened in Manchester, England to two teenage boys. I play Brian who is the oldest of the two. The younger one – he is 13 years old, and Brian is 16 – creates all these online personas that the older boy believes to be real people. The younger boy has some sort of obsession or crush on the older one. He creates a girlfriend and a very elaborate scheme of people, involving the Secret Service; pretty unbelievable and laughable things when you look from a distance, until you get into it, and this happened in real life.

It's structured as a murder mystery. The younger boy gets stabbed. The older boy is accused of doing it, although he denies it. The opera tells the story of the detective investigating this situation, unpeeling the layers of this very mysterious thing. It's sort of an Internet murder mystery, in a way, but it is very socially relevant and contemporary because of how the Internet is affecting our society and the social lives of especially young people who have never known a world without the Internet, and how it affects our idea of self. At the same time, it is traditional storytelling and in fact Nico the composer says that it is his version of the *Maskarade* opera. People can conceal their identities by creating these avatars and living a fictional life. It is germane and specific to our contemporary society but also historically informed and traditional in storytelling.

OL – Tell us about the psychology of your character Brian.

PA – It's very mysterious and shocking when you read about the real story. It's hard to fathom how someone could be taken in by this seemingly ridiculous ruse. There were thousands and thousands of pages of transcripts from chat rooms. The elaborateness of this scheme by the younger boy is overwhelming and daunting. It's easy to forget that the mind of a 16-year-old is malleable and vulnerable. With the Internet interaction, people are becoming more isolated, it seems to me. They have their iPads and laptops and iPods. We are increasingly surrounding ourselves in this bubble of media and narcissistic self regard. This mystery of the digital age, I can't pin it down to describe it to you. The genius of the opera is that it doesn't explain, but depicts how this plays itself out. It addresses critically how as a society we engage with each other in this new world with vast amounts of information that gives us access to so many things, but at the same time can be very limiting for personal interactions. Come see the opera!

OL – Yes, it sounds very interesting. Sometimes I have to text-message my son to get him to respond, across the table, when he is on his iPhone. If I say something he mumbles, then if I text-message, he replies.

PA – How old is he?

OL – He is 21 now, but it has been like this for a while. OK, you are doing a lot of Britten, in this year of his centennial of birth. Is this a repertoire that has always interested you, or is this more because of the centennial?

PA – Both. As a tenor I'm a beneficiary of Britten and Pears' relationship. There is an unbelievable repertoire that Britten wrote for Peter Pears. I just did *Les Illuminations* back in Woodstock, New York at the Mavericks Festival, which was such a joy because I love Britten. I really enjoy singing it, because the way he wrote for Pears, as unique and specific as it is, suits my voice pretty well too, and it's always a really helpful exercise to navigate that very specific way he writes that is very passagio-centric. The colors and the ways of approaching phrases are very unique so it's always a challenge but a rewarding one to do. *Les Illuminations* particularly was charming because unlike a lot of Britten's music which tends to be very inward-looking, very concerned with heavier, darker issues like war and death, *Les Illuminations* is about a young person in love; it's just bubbling with this enthusiasm and embrace of life and love.

Those sides of the Britten repertoire particularly I'm fond of, but at the same time I'm also performing *The Serenade for Tenor Horn and Strings*, which I am doing for the first time with the New York Philharmonic in November, and I'm also doing it in recital here in Santa Fe, with a string quintet and a horn. That is such a masterpiece, and it is a little daunting to approach it because it's so well known; it's such an important, canonical work! Britten in this piece slowly reveals layers, and it is really joyful to get underneath what is in the surface and understand how he is interacting with the text, and how he chose the text that he picked. In the *Serenade* there are these wonderful classic British poets and Britten makes them come to life with his very unique voice.

OL – Please tell us how this affinity for the French language and repertoire that Susan noticed, came to be. First of all, is it true? Because I see your repertoire as quite varied.

PA – It's very important to me, but everything I sing is important to me. Because I studied French pretty extensively when I was in college and spent my sophomore year abroad in a French-speaking country, my brain works a lot better in French. I can comprehend the language and I can think in French a little bit. People who hire young tenors for French repertoire can recognize that my ability with French is perhaps a little more advanced than other people of my age. That I think is one of the reasons why I've been called upon or hired to do a number of French pieces, and yes, I love singing in French. It is at the same time the hardest language to sing, because the specificity of every syllable is really a challenge to get just right and be authentic. There are vowels that we don't have in English, and things that you have to do with your tongue…[laughs].

OL – Is it harder than German?

PA – I think so, absolutely. For me as a native English speaker, German is a lot more similar in its expressiveness. The way one expresses emphasis in German and English is similar. You sing the first consonant of the word you want to get out really strongly, and if you want to make a point, you use these consonants. That's what we do in English. But in French and most of the romance languages, it is more allusive, because it's about vowels; it's about elongating and shaping and coloring the vowels, which is not as natural to a native English speaker. On the other hand there is variety within French. You have a lot more choice in a way, on how exactly you want to color the phrase. There is the *accent d'assistance*, where you can, as opposed to the natural flow of the French language, stop and emphasize an initial consonant of a very important word. Even then it functions differently in French, so the expressive possibilities are immense but they are also very challenging because they have to be very precise.

OL – *Les Troyens* – the role of Hylas has only one song but it is oh so beautiful! How was it for you, to perform it in front of a worldwide audience for the Live in HD broadcast? Was it nerve-wrecking?

PA – I've been very careful about this whole HD thing, which is to say I try to completely ignore it. There is always a performance or two in the run of a show, especially in a place like the Met, that gets the most attention, whether it is opening night when all the press is there, a radio broadcast, or whenever the critics are in the house. This happens here in Santa Fe as well. This week in Santa Fe when all the shows are running, it is Press Week, and the psychological burden that comes with that is somewhat unavoidable, so I approach the HD the same way that I'm trying to approach those performances when you know that people are watching and taking notes [laughs]. My approach is that I just try to do every show as if it was like that. So I try to bring the same preparation, and have a very routine approach to the way I warm up, the way I eat whatever I eat that day, the time I go to bed, little things like that. I try to be very consistent so that the added pressure of that moment is not too overwhelming.

OL – Comic roles vs. tragic roles – do you have a preference?

PA – I prefer tragic roles that are really funny [laughs]. You need to approach tragedy with a comic mind and comedy with a tragic mind. You have to serve the characters, the ideas, and the libretto with the same thoroughness and the same attempt to realize the character in a very full human way. The trap in comedy is of course to play funny which is never funny as we all know, but it is a lot harder to find a way to get the humor across while also being true to the character and not just displaying the funniness. Being funny is a lot harder than showing that "this is funny." And similarly, you can't play a serious role or a tragic role with this heaviness constantly, or always with the end of the opera in mind. Like Susan says, in *Iphigénie* she never smiles once in that role. [laughs] There are occasions like that. But for me, for example the role that I enjoy the most, and that is closest to me and I'm most fond of doing, is Tom Rakewell in *The Rake's Progress*. That is undoubtedly a tragedy, what happens to that young man over the course of the show, and yet it is also at times hilarious, and that's for me why I enjoy that show and why I think it resonates with people to this day. Things like the charm of the Nick Shadow - the Devil character - and the word play, the youthful exuberance of Tom, all these things make the tragedy at the end all the more bitter and touching and moving and relatable. These variations reflect life more than they would have, if the entire piece had a constant tragic tone.

OL – *Così fan tutte* in Boston, directed by Sir Thomas Allen – does it make a difference to be stage-directed by a former singer?

PA – Absolutely. The relationship between the director and the singer is always unique. Every director is very different, every singer is very different and especially in a show like *Così fan tutte* which is such an ensemble piece, the relationship of the director and the cast is essential to the tone of that piece. In *Così* it is important to collectively decide on how to tell the story and what the gradations of the comedy and tragedy should be. Tom is as we all know one of the greatest singing actors of his time. He has done *Così* countless times. He is familiar with the text and with every little shading of characterization. The consequences of each of those choices as an actor have a ripple effect throughout the whole piece. Something that Don Alfonso says in a recitative in the first act has resonance in the Ferrando and Fiordiligi duet much later. Tom is very aware of the piece and understands these details. He brought this wealth of experience into the room with him and made us all really pay attention to every detail. So, it was pretty amazing.

Most directors are very preoccupied with other things. The work of a director is incredibly difficult. It's a huge task, because the staging and the details of what the actors and singers are doing are a small part of what they do. So it's nice to have someone like Tom whose priority really was with the singers on stage. That was really fun and rewarding.

OL – Nice! Your European operatic debut at Oper Frankfurt was as Tom in *The Rake's Progress* – how was that experience? Not just from the standpoint of singing the character which you've just mentioned as one of your favorites, but also considering yourself as an American in Europe, singing an American opera (well, by a Russian naturalized American). I like to think of it as an American opera.

PA – I do too. I mean, it was written in California, and the librettists were English, right? And Stravinsky is Russian, and yet it is so American, I think. My experience in Frankfurt was terrific. It is a great company as well; it is very similar to Santa Fe in the way that it is very supportive of the artists and it really puts the art first.

That production was very specifically American in a way. That show was very relevant to contemporary society, again going back to this idea of the digital age and this celebrity culture that we are a part of. We framed that production as Tom being someone who wanted to be famous. "What do you want to be famous for?" "Well, that's not important, I just want to be famous. I want to be known." This is a very common aspiration of young people these days, just to be famous. People wish to be a famous actor or a famous chef, to be known and enjoy the privileges of that.

Frankfurt is also a very international opera company, so, there were singers from all over the world in that cast. Although it was a German director, it was very inclusive of all of our ideas and just a wonderful experience. You hear horror stories about Regietheater, and there is definitely an aesthetic in German opera houses. I saw a lot of shows there as well, and the aesthetic is different, even visually, the way the sets are designed. But this particular production and the majority of productions I saw, although they take different slants on things, were very respectful of the piece and really paid very close attention to the text. As long as that happens I have no problem being a part of it, and that was the case in Frankfurt.

OL – Yes, I was about to ask you to contrast your experience with Oper Frankfurt with that of singing in the United States. Looking at your schedule it seems like you're busier this side of the Atlantic, but you do have that European experience, so they have the hired personnel; it is very different from the seasonal approach here and so forth. Can you talk to us about the differences?

PA – Absolutely. One of the striking things I found when I was in Frankfurt which has an ensemble of singers who stay there and sing various roles over the course of each season, is that the focus is a little less on the singers themselves, on the individual performances, and more on the interpretation of the piece. The public there has a lot more exposure to opera, it's safe to say, than American audiences typically, so because of that greater familiarity with the repertoire the engagement with the pieces themselves is a little less reliant on telling the story, which is where the various degrees of Regietheater come into play, in trying to refresh a story that everybody knows, whereas in America I think economically the margins are slimmer. They have to work a lot harder to get audiences to come to the piece and also have to introduce these audiences to a lot of the repertoire that they don't know as well as in a place like Germany.

Those differences are pretty much immaterial for me. My training in America has been so thorough and so great that I'm always doing the same approach. I strive for the same degrees of accomplishment as a vocalist, a linguist, and an actor, no matter where it takes place, in America or Germany. As long as the director and the cast have done their work and really know what is happening in the libretto and in the score, a lot of actions are available, and I'm very open to all kinds of interpretative choices as long as they are informed and very well thought out.

OL – How do you see the situation for young singers today, in terms of challenges – agents interested in quick profits, lack of protection against predatory companies and agents, too much competition? In the past the agents would shape a career; would be advisors. Today we see sometimes quite the opposite: people being thrown at roles they are not prepared for, build up some idolization, make a quick profit, the singer then damages his or her voice. Who cares? We'll get the next one, and so forth.

PA – I don't have too much to say about the industry at large and the tendencies in there. I think it's driven mostly by economics, I'm sure. I can't elaborate much more than that. All I can say is that I feel extremely fortunate and blessed, just the way my career to this point has been unfolding. My educational opportunities were just as wonderful as you could possibly hope for. I didn't go to a conservatory for undergrad, I went to the University of Notre Dame, and I was an English major with a secondary degree in music. That experience really was vital to what I am doing today. Being an English major is actually important as a singer, because you are dealing with texts virtually every time you sing. To have a better sense of yourself outside of the industry and the discipline of music, before really jumping in, is a luxury for singers, unlike say a pianist or violinist. It's very competitive when you have to basically be ready to launch an international career by the time you are twenty-one or so if you have any hope to succeed as a pianist, whereas as singers, especially a male voice, it takes a lot longer to mature and reach that level.

It was a bit of a luxury for me to get to do something like biding my time while at Notre Dame. But then from there I went to Julliard and to the Met Young Artists Program. Again, I was very fortunate. I have a wonderful manager but I also have from my time at Juilliard and at the Met a whole cadre of advisors and coaches, mentors, and teachers to whom I can always turn for advice and who also have clout. So I can say James Levine doesn't think I should do this right now, and people pretty much back off when I lay that one on them [laughs] so I'm in a really enviable position in that respect.

For me it's very obvious. There are lots of young singers I know who have a lot of potential and very exciting voices. They are the ones who are in much more danger of vocal damage. I'm very fortunate in terms of my Fach because the repertoire that is out there for me to take is for the most part very healthy. It is easy for me to accept those and I have had enough opportunities to do those. I'm not torn about singing an Alfredo in *Traviata* too soon or something like that.

OL – What are you trying to accomplish in this stage of your career?

PA – Having earned a liberal arts degree as well as having had the very intense conservatory training at Juilliard, I'm in a position to focus on things other than just opera. For example I'm very committed to my work as a song recitalist. That's actually the thing that I enjoy perhaps more than anything else. I love to be programming recitals and spending time on that. It's hard to get opportunities to perform because the markets for such performances seems to be shrinking but again my educational background and my connections there in New York have allowed me to focus on things that are conducive to my growth over the long haul.

OL – Then, what comes next?

PA - It is fairly obvious to everybody who hears me that for the time being Mozart is the center of my repertory. Not for everybody, but for me certainly, it is the perfect thing to sing; it is very healthy and it suits my voice very well. There are four or five Mozart roles that I started to do now: Ferrando, Ottavio, Tamino, Belmonte. I'm focusing on these for the foreseeable future, for the next five years. Then, I may stretch a little bit in any given direction. I would love to do Nemorino someday soon, and Fenton in *Falstaff*, roles like this that are in the lighter side of the lyric repertoire.

OL – Let's switch a little bit to a more psychological approach. You've been very successful; your career is really picking up. Does the hectic life of a successful opera singer frighten you?

PA – No. [laughs] It doesn't. It suits me very well in a lot of ways. I really enjoy the experience of that first ever rehearsal with a new company and a new group of singers. It's kind of like the first day of school. It could be a little nervous, but it is really exciting and fun. I'm still early enough in my career that I haven't been to a lot of these cities that I'm singing in for the first time, so there is a real sense of adventure. I can definitely foresee a time when the novelty of that will wear off and I'm sure that it will be an issue before too long for me, especially as one tries to balance having a family and the stability that it provides. That will be a struggle, I know; but for the moment I have a very supportive wife and what I've been doing has just been a real joy. Ask me again in five years; I'm sure I'll have a different answer, but for now it has been pretty exciting.

OL - What are the unglamorous parts of being a performer?

PA – There are several, but I don't consider them that unglamorous because the payoff is so great. To get to do what I'm doing and get paid for it, I'm still pinching myself a little bit. I have confidence that I can sustain this thing over time.

There is another aspect I learned from Susan, this summer. Performances can be rewarding and fun, especially if you can find a really magical moment where you just sense a connection. You are performing well and the audience perceives it, and you have this very satisfying moment. However, these moments are too few and far between to truly sustain the demands of this career.

The greater joy for me is in the process of doing it in itself. I really like practicing. I love for example coming with song programs and researching them, and reading about them. I just read Benjamin Britten's autobiography. If you can find genuine pleasure and joy in that part of the career like Susan does, then you can manage it over time.

Anyway, you have to keep studying. I had this silly idea when I first started at Juilliard – "OK, I'm going to study singing for the next three, four, five years, and then I'll be a singer, and then I'll go sing." [laughs] It's so funny to me now, because I realize that there is no point in which you are a singer and your work as a student is done. You have to constantly be adapting. Your body is always changing, your strengths and weaknesses shift over time, what was easy for you when you were twenty-six is a lot harder for you when you are thirty-five, but then again you are also a lot better at other things. So, you are constantly having to adapt to the demands of different roles, to the repertory, to your voice changes over time, and it takes a lot of dedicated work. What I said about Susan is that to have her voice in the shape that it is in, after all these years of doing what she has been doing, has taken a great amount of focus, discipline, and commitment to the art. So for the time being I enjoy that discipline and I look forward to continuing to grow throughout my career.

OL – *The Enchanted Island* – how fun was that?

PA – That was so much fun, especially because the cast for that show was just phenomenal! It was a great group of individuals. I got to know Luca Pisaroni and Joyce DiDonato and David Daniels; like Susan, these are people I have been looking up to and studying their work.

OL – Danielle de Niese…

PA – Oh my God, she is incredibly intelligent, actually. Because she is so very beautiful, she doesn't get credit for her brains [laughs] but she's got those too! It was a huge amount of fun, and the production was very clever. For me as a young artist at the time at the Met, the role was very manageable. It was not too challenging, and there were ten performances of it, so it was really an important run for me because I could really focus on the various aspects of performing, especially in a space like the Met, without being too over-concerned with various vocal challenges and what not, so that was a really rewarding experience.

OL – So, you're passionate about art songs? What about American art songs?

PA – Totally. I do feel a certain degree of responsibility to American composers. There is a fair amount of anxiety among many people in the music industry and the audiences as well, about the future of classical music, opera, and art song.

I did a Q&A event with Nico Muhly in the spring about *Two Boys*; I sang an aria from the piece and he answered questions. He got a version of this question a number of times: "how are you going to save the future of opera?" They were kind of saying, "it's your responsibility, you know?" [laughs]

What Nico and other American contemporary and 20th century composers have done, is that they have written pieces like *Two Boys*, which is of great quality and substance, really thoughtful and accomplished. That's what we need to do to sustain the art form, is to create the art continuously, and to support it, perform it, and put it out there into the public's ears and into their minds and intellects.

I identify with the composers that really speak to me, particularly when they pick poetry that really speaks to me as well. I find of all the things I do, a sense of responsibility to diffuse this work. In the near future I have plans for a recital with songs, among others, from many American composers.

One of the great things about being at a place like Juilliard is that there is a lot of activity of new composers around there. I got to know a lot of great people. For example, I premiered a song cycle by a guy named Harold Meltzer who was a Pulitzer Prize finalist a couple of years ago. It was rewarding for me to be a part of that, because he wrote it for me, and I was able to give input during the process of composition. It was exciting to participate in the creation of something new. I am not saying I wrote it, but I was able to ask him to shape it to my voice, and I also taught him a little bit about how singers approach things like this. I feel a duty to do this, and I look forward to being a part of new pieces for as long as possible, whether operas or songs.

OL – Yes. I always had a feeling that the prophets of doom who yell "Opera is dying, oh my God, what will we make of the future?" are groundless. I just interviewed George Benjamin, and his new opera *Written on Skin* is brilliant.

PA – I haven't heard the whole thing but I heard sections of it.

OL – I just read a journalist who wrote a headline for it: "Opera's New Masterpiece: If opera is dead, someone forgot to tell George Benjamin."

PA – [laughs hard]. It seems to me that there has been a perennial fear that opera is dying, and of course there are legitimate concerns about economics, but I think we are in a very exciting time, too. Back to the Internet age, it's going to take a lot of really creative young people, and they are starting to create totally new organizations, new platforms, and new ways of presenting music. That is really exciting. I don't know where this is going to lead us. It's not my gift to imagine those new forms and the new media through which we create and disseminate new art, but I think yes, I agree.

All those – I don't want to call them Cassandres, because they are not right, but as you say - prophets of doom should focus instead in understanding that the old way of doing things may very well be dying indeed. The way things were funded is not there any longer. These big institutions may not be able to function on the same level they once did; that may be true. But creatively I see a really bright future ahead. It's just that the future is not entirely clear, but I think it is very hopeful, because there are great artists like George Benjamin, Harold Meltzer, and Nico Muhly, who are writing pieces of great quality and substance, and as long as that happens, artists and business people will find ways to get that up to the public. The public yearns for it and wants it, and will come to it.

OL – I love the answers that George Benjamin and Joyce DiDonato gave to this issue. He said that opera will never die because there will always be people willing to tell a story and sing to each other, and Joyce said that we should stop apologizing for opera. We have this great art form, it is relevant, people will continue to acknowledge it, as long as we keep doing it well – that's what she said.

PA – I couldn't agree more. In fact I think in this age of increasing isolation from each other, the experience of being in the opera house is more and more of a rare opportunity. Just the acoustic physical presence of a human voice unmitigated by any kind of technology, just waves coming from one human being and hitting another one, is a phenomenon that is essential to human need. Singing to people and being sung to, is how we teach children about language and everything, and I think, that will never go away.

I feel that there is a movement of sorts, a backlash against the digital age where everything is ones and zeroes. I have a lot of friends who now engage in old fashioned pursuits like crocheting and pickling, because there is this essential human need to participate in the creative process in a very fundamental un-technological way, and so the experience of opera is so unique and so primal that absolutely there will always be a need for it. As Joyce said, it is our responsibility to do it with excellence, and if this is the case then it will thrive.

OL – How was the experience of singing at "A Prairie Home Companion"?

PA – That was really cool. I've been listening to Garrison Keillor a lot longer than I've been listening to opera. [laughs] I remember driving with my family, sitting in the back of the minivan, and I would totally fantasize about singing with Garrison some day. And it happened kind of out of the blue. He happened to see me perform in New York and the next week he invited me to come down and sing. It was very special because it was the childhood dream come true that I didn't even ask for or didn't seek out and it just came, and it was such a beautiful fun gift to be able to be a part of that.

I enjoyed seeing him create the show. He is pretty amazing; it's all him; he writes everything. We had a couple of rehearsals and he ran off stage to go to his laptop and rewrite some sketch. To top if off I got to sing and harmonize with him. In fact in the first rehearsal he said, "can you sing harmony? Really?" I said, "yes, yes, yes!" I didn't know if I could do it or not. And we started and we were singing like "shall we gather at the river together" – successfully harmonizing with him, and he said," it's like we are brothers," and I just… oh, man, when he said that in rehearsal, that was pretty cool. So that was really satisfying to be a part of.

OL – Notre Dame, Juilliard, National Council Auditions winner, Lindemann – that's a rather prestigious track. Were you a teen-prodigy?

PA – [laughs] No, definitely not. I have to give a lot of that credit to my parents. For one, my father is a professor at the University of Notre Dame, so me going there was a kind of no-brainer, because I could go tuition-free. It's an amazing school. The education I got there was so important, even if it didn't directly correlate to my profession now. It was sort of the formation of my mind and of my social skills, and things like that are really important.

And again, my parents have always been totally supportive of me, and never questioned when I said, "yes, I think I want to sing opera and Schubert." And they said "oh, great! What's that? Tell me more!" Over the years going to conservatories and meeting other young people who wanted to be musicians, it never occurred to me that somebody's parents wouldn't be totally supportive, but I guess not everybody had my luck. My parents never said "you should get a business degree as a back-up." They never said things like that. Maybe they were foolish, I don't know. [laughs] I have to give them total credit for who I am in terms of the educational pursuits I have had. Just loving the process of learning is something I learned from my parents, and that is what sustains me and creates the opportunities of these really incredible institutions that I've been very fortunate to be part of.

OL – How did you get to love opera, growing up?

PA – Well, I didn't really have much exposure to it. In my household, we listened to a lot of music, but it was mostly pop music. My grandma thinks my namesake is actually Paul Simon, not Saint Paul as my dad will tell her. But I took piano lessons from the time I was six years old, and when I was in high school I was in theater and I did musicals. I was fifteen years old and I was going to sing *Joseph and the Amazing Technicolor Dreamcoat* – which was a big deal for me, my first big leading role in this sort of summer school district-wide production.

So I wanted to take some voice lessons, and there was a guy that a friend of mine told me about, who was a voice professor at Notre Dame, who also taught privately. I went to him and said "teach me how to sing this role of Joseph better" and he said, "I teach classical music and classical technique;

you can use that and apply it to anything." But pretty soon within a few weeks he was giving me the old Italian songbook, some Schubert songs and things like that. I had enough exposure to classical music through my piano lessons. Not that I was ever any good at piano, but I knew Bach and Mozart and things like that, so once I started working on things like Schubert, Schumann, and maybe an aria or two at that point, I was just so taken with that whole world of music!

I was always very fond of languages and interested in the fascinating history of classical music. I don't need to tell you; if you like Schubert you know what I mean; falling in love with it is a pretty instantaneous thing, so that's how I got started. I just kept going along that tract, and by the time I got to Notre Dame, that's when I started doing operas. It started as this hobby that I loved, and I just kept doing it, and becoming more and more invested in it, and I'm still going. [laughs]

OL – What are some of your non-musical interests?

PA – Well, I guess my biggest hobby outside of music is food. I really enjoy cooking a lot, and reading about cooking, and restaurants and all that stuff. I was just reading yesterday in the new New Yorker, this article about Daniel Boulud, have you read it?

OL – No, but I've been to his place.

PA – Me too! Well, there is this article by this writer Bill Buford, who wrote a book called *Heat: An Amateur's Adventures as Kitchen Slave*, about when he left his job at the New Yorker and worked in Mario Batali's Babbo kitchen and then moved to Italy and learned Italian cooking. Now he is studying French cooking. That is the kind of thing that really excites me, reading stuff like that. They made these really old fashioned French recipes together and he wrote about it. Cooking is really important to me.

I like the Saint Louis Cardinals a lot. In fact funnily enough, Kevin Burdette and Aaron Pegram who are in this show as well [*The Grande Duchesse de Gérolstein*] both happen to be Cardinals fans. We had a lot of fun this summer just following the team. They just slipped out of first place right now, it's a little stressful.

The other thing about being on the road is that I got to read a lot more. I hadn't been reading for fun for a long time. When I was an English major in college I read a lot. That was often an assignment, and then I was in music school really very busy with that. But being on the road, you might have a number of days in between performances. If it's a city I've never been to, getting to travel and explore the city to learn the history of the place is very fun. And then, reading is the other part of it. I've been reading a lot of fiction lately. E. L. Doctorow is my favorite writer right now; he is unbelievable.

OL – There is a disciple of Daniel Boulud here in town. He has two very good restaurants, where I ate the day before yesterday, and yesterday.

PA – In Santa Fe?

OL – In Santa Fe.

PA – What are these restaurants?

OL – Coyote Café and Geronimo.

PA – Oh, I didn't realize they were owned by a disciple of Boulud. I'm going to eat at Geronimo tonight for the first time.

OL – Yes, in my review of La Grande Duchesse I put the pictures of a meal there at the Coyote Café, because I was saying, "come to Santa Fe, folks, there is opera, and there is also this." So, you are going to Geronimo tonight; you will enjoy it. The staff is very friendly. I was talking in Italian with the waitress who wasn't even Italian but could speak the language, and I was thinking, "oh my God, this is a really artsy town, you know? Where else your non-Italian waitress speaks perfect Italian?"

PA – Sure. This is a great thing about Santa Fe, the number of incredible restaurants per capita.

OL- Now, let's talk about something else. Are there social problems that you feel touched by and would like to help?

PA – Absolutely, I've been really thinking hard about that question. Since I'm sort of emerging out of my educational phase of my career, and becoming more known in the public eye, I've been thinking about that question a lot. For me one of the most important things is children's welfare. I worry about things like literacy, food and hunger issues, children under the poverty line, or who are victims of abuse. I'm concerned about access to music and better education, especially in the last five or six years with this economy. Of course the first things that are always cut from schools are the arts. I'm trying to find the right platform to address these issues and be a positive force in that way. That's where my heart is drawn to.

OL – Nice. So, Susan said you are funny in a subtle way, with dry humor – does it define you well?

PA – I'm very flattered by that, because I'll tell you what, the thing about rehearsing operas is that it is a very intimate thing, and it can get very intense. I come from a family that is a very witty family and we often exchange barbs, and teasing is a way of expressing affection. Over the years I've learned that most people don't come from that [laughs] so I had to sort of train myself to subvert my more natural inclinations of joking around or teasing in an affectionate way – or at least what I perceive as an affectionate way. So I guess I'm trying to do it, and I come out a little more dry than I would natively be. I'll take it, I'm glad to hear that, I guess I'm doing OK. As long as I'm still supportive and being a positive member of the troupe, that's what is important to me, so yes, I guess that's what I've tried to mold myself into.

OL – What about fearless? And down to Earth? How do you see your personality?

PA – This is again something I learned from my parents, which is that you need to treat the busboys as well as you treat the opera intendant. The importance of the dignity of every human being is something that I try to live out every day. I'm really flattered by being called down to Earth, that's most important to me of any compliment or nice words said about me. What I take by that to mean is just respecting everybody. It's really unappealing when people will treat a low-level person without the same respect, and then all of a sudden someone who may be able to hire them shows up and they turn around and all of a sudden are very gracious and humble. For me I try to treat everybody the same way.

Fearless? Yes! I am fearless, I guess! I mean, again, I'm in a very privileged position with my educational background and the amount of support I've received throughout my whole life. I'm just a very privileged person, so I can stand on all that and move forward with confidence and a conviction in what I'm doing, and experience joy in it. I guess I wouldn't call myself fearless. It's just that I'm extremely well supported by a huge number of people. I'm just a lucky guy, instead of fearless.

OL – Great, I think that's about what we had. I loved the interview.

PA – Oh, thank you. I loved this opportunity to speak in greater length about the artistic aspects of life!

Massimo Giordano, tenor

Mary Auer, one of Opera Lively's journalists, interviewed Massimo Giordano in October 2013. The increasingly successful singer has a nice personality and was charming in this pleasant exchange.

Opera Lively - If we may, let's begin by talking about your new album, "Amore e Tormento," which was released on the 6th of May. This CD is your first recording since you signed with BMG Rights Management as their first classical recording artist. Can you tell us how your signing with this label came about?

Massimo Giordano - I have always wanted to record an album and waited many years to do so. Finally, when I thought it was never going to happen I met a woman named Ashley Bettis who told me about BMG and what they call their " Master Right Model". It works in the reverse way of your usual record deal. The core focus of this model is to give the artist pure artistic freedom. For a classical artist this is something that is very fundamental. In October 2012 I signed the deal with them that would allow me the freedom to choose everything from what arias I wanted to sing to how I wanted my album cover to look. Every detail I can more or less make the decision. It is almost like working in a structure of an independent label but still by benefiting from the strong brand name of Bertelsmann Music Group. I really think it's the business model of the future.

OL - How did you develop the themes for your album? And how did you select the arias that you've included here? Some of these are from roles you haven't yet performed onstage.

MG - When I chose the arias I did not want to follow a stylistic or chronological logic but convey to the listener the emotion of tormented and suffered love, which is an emotion we all feel in real life at least once. For this reason I have chosen arias that even in their sequence tell the evolution of love and suffering related to it even though I have never sung some of them and some I will never sing in the theater.

Also, I always loved arias like "Come un bel dì di Maggio" or "Non piangere liù" and to have the chance to record those arias for me has been a challenge but overall a great achievement because some of these operas will belong to my future repertoire and I wanted to prove to myself and to the audience that I was able to fulfill this challenge.

OL - When you record arias, does it help to have sung the role in a staged performance before? Or does it make little difference in your interpretation of the aria?

MG - Of course it helps to have sung the role in a staged production. Naturally, if it is an aria that I have rehearsed over and over again, it makes it a bit easier technically to sing. However, if it is a role like Mario Cavaradossi that I am singing over and over again I have to really think how to make it special and unique so that it does not become too sterile.

Also, since I have performed it before the recording it gives me a lot more confidence versus recording an aria that I have never sung in a theatre. In fact, I also choose arias that are not in my repertoire but will be in the future and on the contrary I choose as well arias that I will never ever sing in a theatre, which was the greatest of all challenges. I really wanted to overcome this challenge and prove to myself and to my audience that I can really do it.

OL - You've also recently made a music video directed by Marisa Crawford, which was filmed in Naples and off the coast of Amalfi. Can you tell us about how you came up with the idea for this video, and your choice of music for it?

MG - I have to say, filming this video was great fun and a very memorable experience for sure. I collaborated with my co-producer, Ashley Bettis who introduced me to Marisa Crawford, a very talented fashion film director and photographer. Ashley and I really wanted to create something that was as "close" to me as possible and therefore we chose to travel to Naples, near where I was born. I love the old films like "Dolce Vita" for example and I wanted to make a music video that was a representation of real southern culture and cinematography and avoid a "commercial" approach.

In the old Italian films from the 60's its not always about the architecture of the cities but rather a representation of the people that are brought to life as well as cinematography that shows off their way of life. We all worked very diligently to also translate the text of the aria into beautiful imagery with a real story board like you would see in a film or in the theatre. I wanted it to be almost like it was the soundtrack for my own film and to translate it through film.

OL - The German journalist Stefan Kruecken has been working on your biography, called "The Miracle of Boscoreale," which is going to be released this year. How did you meet Herr Kruecken? What did you think when he suggested the idea of a biography?

MG - I was introduced to Stefan Kruecken by Ashley Bettis. She always told me I had a beautiful life story to tell, so she said to me "why not have someone write it." I have to say I was a bit uncertain at first because sometimes you don't realize the life you have had until you see it through someone else's eyes. In fact, I better understood her vision only after I travelled with Stefan Kruecken to my birthplace, Pompei. We spent about four full days in Pompei and Boscoreale where he followed me around. I showed him all things belonging to my youth including a local bar where I went with my father during the FIFA World Cup in the 80's. It had been such a long time since I was there. We also travelled to the village of Boscoreale that was the village I actually grew up in.

To travel back to the area that I come from and see the poor living conditions of the people and the debris all over the place with Mount Vesuvius in the horizon brought back so many memories and naturally stories to tell. After this experience of sharing my life story with Stefan I realized sometimes it takes seeing it transposed through a writer on paper to grasp that - my God! I come from a place and a life so far from the glamorous world of the opera!

OL - You've sung at major opera houses around the world, and many of them have been in Germany and Austria. Those two countries are well known for their avant-garde opera productions, the so-called Regietheater. What are your feelings about this?

MG - To be honest, I have spent the majority of my career on the stages of Germany and Austria so these opera houses and their audiences are very dear to me. I am completely supportive of modern productions and I am by no means a purist in this aspect. However, I do think that often in " regietheater" there is a miscorrelation of what is "modern". To create an entirely different story completely out of context with the libretto does not make it "current". There is a very definitive line between what is "modern" and what is a completely made up story by a director. I remember I was once told by a director- "Massimo, it does not matter where things move – as long as they are moving." In my opinion, are these discussions about the productions really constructive?

OL - These types of productions are less popular in Italy and the United

States. What other differences have you observed in the countries in which you have performed? How different are audiences in Italy from those in Germany or Great Britain, or audiences in France or the U.S.?

MG - Interesting question. I would say worldwide audiences are enthusiastic and supportive of the artists. I feel like worldwide where I have sung all audiences respect the musicians. There is not one country I prefer to perform in over another. I think the differences I have seen in my career are more about the audiences and their reactions to the actual production itself.

I would say Germany is by far the most liberal audience because of the topic of the previously mentioned Regietheater. I would say in Italy, they are the most conservative audience as Italian opera belongs to our culture and therefore the audience wants to see the roles and Regie presented and interpreted as the composer wanted. In my experience I would say Italy has the most " pure" audience and this is something that I can appreciate and respect as opera is something that belongs to our country throughout history. I think the American, British and French audiences are the most "easy going" audiences. They like to be entertained and do not get so caught up in the discussions of the stage direction, but rather just enjoy the performance, the music and an evening at the opera.

OL - You make extensive use of online media: Facebook, Twitter, your web site, even your own YouTube channel. How important are social media for your career?

MG - To be honest, I never used any social media until I knew I was going to release an album. I manage my own Facebook, Twitter and Youtube even if at the beginning I was a bit " slow" to understand how it works. It is important to me that I use it personally and that I do not have a PR agency or Marketing firm do it. I decided if I was going to use social media I wanted it to be really me, Massimo. I think social media is the future to market yourself as an artist. Honestly, I did not realize I had the large fan base I have until I started using Facebook. It used to be that people would send you "fan mail" by the regular post office; now it has turned into a "Facebook wall post". Who would have ever thought it? I used to take time answering fans by a simple letter; now it has turned into a 5 second response through the Internet.

I think its also a great tool to keep your fans close to you and to easily engage yourself with the click of a button. Most importantly, it is a nice way to share personal things with your fans that before was not possible unless it was some kind of feature or interview in a print publication or the television. It is really the best way you can interact directly with those who support you in your career.

OL - You really try to stay in touch with your fans. What is the most valuable feedback you receive from them?

MG - I think the most valuable feeback I have received from them probably is their beautiful words of encouragement and appreciation. To be an artist on the stages is also a very demanding job and sometimes the critics can be very tough. In addition, you spend so much time on the road away from home... This also makes this job difficult and tiring. It seems like such a simple answer, but I have to say that I think it's a good feeling to know that they are there to support you regardless of what the critics may say. At the end of the day the audience is the most important because you are the one who is there to share your music with them and make them happy by doing so.

OL - When we look at your roles, we see that they are concentrated mainly in the Italian and French repertoires, yet they still represent a rather broad vocal range. You sing lyric parts such as Rodolfo in *La Bohème*, Alfredo in *La Traviata*, and Gounod's Roméo, but you also sing spinto roles such as Don José, Cavaradossi, and Don Carlo. How do you see your voice developing?

MG - I started with Mozart and then did a lot of singing in the French repertoire - *Roméo et Juliette, Manon, Faust...* I love the French repertoire. It is very intelligent, refined, with profound roles, as they are not often found in the Italian repertoire. I would like to sing these roles more often. And what I really regret is that I have sung so little Mozart. But it's like this: Italian tenor - Italian repertoire. And you have to sing what's perfect for your voice. I started with *Falstaff* and *L'elisir d'amore.* Then came *Traviata, Bohème, Tosca*, and now the heavier parts open. As a singer it takes a kind of journey through the repertoire. That is fine for me; I just miss Mozart. Giacomo Lauri-Volpi said: "the perfect tenor develops from *Otello* and *Falstaff*" - and that would be to reach the goal in my life as a tenor.

OL - When you sing a role frequently, such as Cavaradossi, how do you keep it fresh and from becoming routine?

MG - This is really tricky. I can say that especially after this past 2012-2013 season as I sang so much Mario Cavaradossi, it is really so difficult. I have to say that sometimes when you would think that it is easy because it's always the same music over and over again, it ironically becomes the most exhausting. I think in order to keep it fresh you must not focus so much on the technical side, but rather on the interpretation that comes from deep within the soul. I think to sing from the soul is the only way to truly avoid something becoming too stagnant. When it comes from the heart it is never the same and this is the most important thing if you are singing it all the time. If you just focus purely on the technical aspect then you for sure will have a superfluous sound.

OL - How do you see the character of Cavaradossi? It seems he and Tosca both have trouble trusting each other.

MG - Mario Cavaradossi is the perfect romantic hero: he is an artist, a revolutionary rebel and overall he is in love! It's a very intense and lively relationship of two very young people, I don't think they are more than 25 years old. There is a great element of joking between the two of them: Tosca plays to be jealous and Cavaradossi pretends to be annoyed and teases her. But there is great tenderness between these two characters and when the circumstances require they are ready to sacrifice themselves for each other.

OL - *Don Carlo* is sometimes sung in four acts, sometimes in five; sometimes in Italian, and sometimes in French. Which version of this opera do you prefer, and why?

MG - Don Carlo is a very demanding role irrespective of it being sung in French or Italian, in four acts or five. I always say I am never going to perform another Don Carlo again, then somehow the occasion to sing it again always arises. After I performed Don Carlo in Berlin is 2011 the opportunity came to sing it in the Netherlands. Then here I am again just recently singing Don Carlo - the five act version - in Florence. I would say only because of the of vocal endurance I prefer to sing the four act version otherwise I have to say the music of the five act version is so beautiful! It is sad to not sing it despite the fact that is so technically difficult.

OL - You are scheduled to sing Maurizio in *Adriana Lecouvreur* next February at the Vienna State Opera. Will this be a role debut for you?

MG – No, this is not a role debut for me; only a new production with Angela Gheorghiu and the stage director David McVicar.

OL - What are your thoughts on the character of Maurizio? He's intentionally maintaining romantic relationships with two different women, one of whom is married.

MG - Maurizio of Saxony is a character who really existed; a great historical character. The Colautti libretto doesn't do him justice. Already the play of Eugène Scribe and Ernest Legouvé was problematic, and the collaboration between Cilea and Colautti was not the happiest. Luckily in the opera there is the marvelous music of Cilea to balance everything.

Maurizio was the illegitimate child of the king of Poland, and really the wish to regain the kingdom led him to entertain the relationship with the princess of Bouillon for motives of political opportunity. It can seem a cynical and calculating aspect, and probably is, but we also need to compare it to a very different epoch from ours (although these things, and even worse, they happen today as well). He strongly belonged to a sexist society. In the opera he says to Adriana that he wants to marry her, asking: "Do you accept my glorious name?" This is an affirmation of an unbelievable machismo, but those were the times.

Maurizio was famous for his courage. He was almost reckless in battle. He was a famous leader, but also an enlightened strategist and his treatise on the art of war, although it diminishes the importance of firearms, has some aspects that even today are advanced. In short, he was a complex figure in a very complicated historical period. He was also a Don Giovanni; was a handsome man, famous for his physical strength, and sowed illegitimate children around Europe. His love, however, was certainly Adriana, who is also famous and revolutionary in a way that forever changed the art of acting.

OL - If we could now, let's talk a little about your background. Though neither of your parents was a professional musician, your father had a beautiful singing voice, didn't he? How important was music in your home life while you were growing up?

MG – Yes, my father had and still has a wonderful voice. Unfortunately, he did not have the opportunity to ever study music or pursue a musical path in life. Music was a large part of my life growing up but only in the conservatory in Trieste where I studied the flute, but not at home, unless you want to count me practicing the flute for my parents, which I have to admit that I seldom ever did. However, I do remember my grandfather, who had no education at all let alone a musical education, listening to records of opera from his chair in the living room. Actually, it was not just a record player, it was a phonograph. This was the only time I can ever recall hearing opera as a child.

OL - When you were a teenager, your taste in music tended toward hard metal rock. When did you develop a serious interest in classical music? I know that when you were eight years old, your family moved to Trieste, where your father took a job at the G. Tartini Conservatory. You enrolled at the Conservatory yourself, to study flute.

MG - I was a very very rebellious teenager. Although I studied the flute in the conservatory, I was not well behaved enough nor did I have the temperment to practice the flute and really study it outside of the conservatory.

OL - What made you decide to study flute? Were you thinking of a career as an orchestra musician at that point?

MG – When we moved to Trieste the only job my father was able find was a position as a janitor in the conservatory. Because my father secured a job at the conservatory, this allowed me to attend school there. I entered into the classroom for flute only because there was no space in the classrooms of other musical disciplines. At the time all seats were filled in all of the classes. I never even liked to play the flute as I always wanted to play the guitar. I think when I was a child, I wanted to be some kind of rock star. I definitely never thought of or had interest in being an orchestra musician; I just wanted to sing and play the guitar and listen to rock-and-roll.

However, upon graduation from the conservatory for flute, I entered the school again to study voice. I met a teacher named Cecilia Fusco who really helped guiding me and training me vocally. I would say it was when I met her that I really took an interest in classical music. From that point on, I listened only to classical music on my cassette player. Around 19 years of age I really became serious about learning, and completely submerged myself into listening to old recordings.

OL - How old were you when you attended an opera for the first time? Do you remember which one it was?

MG - I was 19 years old when I saw my first opera. I remember I went together with my father Alberto to see *Don Pasquale* in Trieste.

OL - After your singing talent was discovered and you entered the Conservatory's vocal training program, you went on to have a very successful career as an opera singer. You didn't really like the flute. Have you ever played it again?

MG - I have not picked up the flute and played it in many years. Maybe I will one day. I still have my flute at home and sometimes my daughter on occasion is playing it. Maybe my son will play it one day. However, he is still very young.

OL - When we think of a tenor who is also a flutist, we naturally recall Benedikt Schach, for whom Mozart wrote the role of Tamino in *The Magic Flute*. Schach actually played the flute himself when he sang this role. If you were offered an opportunity to sing Tamino in a production where you would also play his flute solos, would you consider it?

MG - This is a role that I would one day love to sing! Of course I would consider playing the flute solos! I would just need to train and study as much with a flute teacher as I do with my vocal coach! But yes, absolutely, I would love to do this!

OL - You made your opera debut as Mozart's Tito Vespasiano. You said that you regret not having sung more Mozart - do you plan to revisit this repertoire, somehow?

MG - I would love to sing more Mozart and the time that I did sing Mozart was much too short. I have not performed Mozart since the early days of my career. In fact, I do not sing Mozart anymore. Like I said, I think because I am Italian – I quickly received roles in Italian repertoire early on and pursued Italian repertoire only to help advance my career. However, I deeply regret not singing more Mozart because I really truly love his music.

OL - At the conservatory, you studied with Cecilia Fusco. Over the course of your career, you've sung with many famous conductors. Which persons do you consider to have been the most important influences in your career? What did you learn from them?

MG - Cecilia Fusco taught me the basics of the art of singing. But I also remember Maestro Aldo Danieli. He continues to teach me all the operas. During my career I have had the honor of singing with almost all the greatest conductors in the world and each of them gave me something, enriching me as interpreter and as musician. In the early years I owe a lot to Gianluigi Gelmetti, who wanted me to inaugurate twice the Rome opera season, including in 2000, the year of the Jubilee. Thanks to a hearing with Claudio Abbado, I sang in Salzburg in 2001 in a memorable production of *Falstaff*. Zubin Mehta, Riccardo Chailly, Yuri Temirkanov and everyone else... I really do not want to hurt anyone by failing to mention him. Each one of the greatest I've met has taught me something, allowing me to mature and grow, a path that certainly does not feel exhausted.

OL - Of course, your career keeps you very busy, but when you do have some private time, I understand you love to play chess. Do you find this relaxing, or do you like the mental concentration it requires?

MG - I find chess very relaxing. Yes, it does require mental concentration. I know when I can no longer focus on a game of chess on the computer that it means that I am really tired. It is relaxing for me but is also a sign that I am in need of a good rest!

OL - Another one of your interests is classical paintings. Some of the world's greatest artists came from Italy. Who are your favorites, and what about their paintings appeals to you? Do you paint yourself?

MG - No, I don't have this talent, but painting is an art that literally magnetizes me. When I am able I always try to visit the museums of the cities where I sing, and also with my family we love to do it in our free time. I remember at the National Gallery in London to have been in contemplation of "The Ambassadors" by Holbein the Younger for a long time. I was completely fascinated. Recently the same thing happened to me at the Uffizi in Florence, in front of the paintings of Leonardo da Vinci. I know, I'm talking about some of the greatest masterpieces of world art; it may seem banal, but when I am impressed with a painting the thrill for me is really strong. Unfortunately I don't have specific preparation to appreciate the art of painting - it's more a matter of skin feelings. I always try to visit the museums within the limits of the little time I have available, and at each visit there are always exciting new discoveries.

OL - What else can you tell us about your personality and your interests? What kind of person are you?

MG - I think I am pretty easy-going and simple. I am interested in paintings, chess and most importantly just spending time with my children since I am away from home so much. Nothing is better then time at home with my children.

OL - You and your wife have two children, and you live in Trieste. Do your parents still live there as well?

MG - Yes, my father and mother both live in Trieste as well as my sister Marilena with her husband and children. We are one big Italian family.

OL - How old are your children? Do they have an interest in music, or have you ever taken them to operas in which you're singing?

MG - My daughter is 13 and my son is turning 5 soon. My daughter is very creative and has a really good eye for photography and design. I think my son has a bit of musical interest. He currently is taking piano lessons and is really focused even for a 4-year-old. Time will tell as I think that he is still a bit too young. My children do travel often with me, but rarely actually sit and watch the opera. I do not think they have much interest in it and I do not force them. I just let them be kids.

OL - Thank you for a fascinating interview, Mr. Giordano!

Ryan McKinny, bass-baritone

On the occasion of the Glimmerglass Festival in August 2013, Opera Lively interviewed in person the excellent young American bass-baritone Ryan McKinny who gathered excellent reviews from critics everywhere for his great rendition of the title role in Francesca Zambello's production of *The Flying Dutchman*. Our readers may recognize the singer from his participation in the DVD *The Audition*, a documentary featuring the 2007 Metropolitan Opera National Council Auditions finals. It is good to see that his career has developed quite nicely.

Opera Lively - Let's start by talking about your title role in *The Flying Dutchman*. What do you think of this production?

Ryan McKinny – It is a great production. Very often you see stand and sing versions of this piece, with everybody stationary on stage. Instead, we worked very hard in creating relationships between the characters. Francesca's ideas of using one platform and having all those ropes signifying various symbolic elements worked really well. Working in this production has been a pleasure.

OL - What advice or direction did you get from Francesca Zambello?

RM – When Francesca is directing a show, we sit around a table and talk through the entire libretto, in original language and in English. We stumble on some ideas all together. We used extensively her notion that the Dutchman is burdened with guilt. All the women who had tried to save him in the past had failed and were damned with him. He has a long list of people he has hurt. Even when he thinks Senta might be the one, he still hesitates about whether or not he wants to put her through this, because he has found his own feelings towards her. This helped me in trying to find a real human character in the Dutchman, and not just a scary ghost.

OL – Yes. I did notice that in your characterization of the Dutchman, you made him feel scary and dark, while at the same time withdrawn, almost shy, and ambivalent.

RM – Yes. There are many different ways you can go with a role like that. It was essential for me to convey that he cares about Senta. The fact that she has right away so much empathy for him is different than what other women he has met have demonstrated. While the others would say "I'll marry you, but only because you have all this treasure," Senta is the first person who has understanding for his pain. This was important to him, and their resulting connection is something that I adore.

OL - What are some of the vocal challenges in this role?

RM – It is very difficult to sing. It sits in two worlds. It is Wagner, and it does have some classic Wagnerian moments, but it is also bel canto. You have many long phrases sometimes high in the voice, but also down low, and the orchestration can be quite loud. You have to sing big a lot of the time. Also, it is a long role in some of the scenes and an endurance challenge even though the opera is not quite long. It gets to be very fatiguing after a while. I'm lucky in that it fits my voice quite nicely. As long as I sing the way I know how to sing, it works out pretty well.

OL - You are developing an early career rich in Wagnerian roles, having done now your first Dutchman, and having been engaged in two productions of *Tristan und Isolde* – and you even won the first Birgit Nilsson prize for singing Wagner or Strauss at the Operalia. Although you've done plenty of other repertory from Baroque to contemporary, sometimes I've heard from singers that once you get into this path, you can be typecast and only be invited to do Wagner – which of course is not necessarily a bad thing. But how do you see your relationship with Wagner's music evolving with time?

RM – Yes, that's a great question. I worked very hard with my manager to schedule enough Wagner that I keep developing in that repertoire, but not so much. I don't want to be typecast as you say, but more important than that, maybe, is that doing too much of that kind of heavy repertoire all the time can be really difficult on the voice, especially for a young singer as I am. I also think that to have the potential to become a great singer in those types of roles, it takes many, many years of practice and performing them, to reach the peak of your abilities. So, I'm happy that I'm able to start these roles at the age that I am, and I'm very mindful to try to keep my repertoire varied. I have a lot of Britten coming up, and some Italian pieces, some Mozart, and musical theater in there too, but my overall focus in my career is probably going to be in the German repertoire.

OL – Yes, embracing Wagner fully at your young age can be concerning for the health of the voice.

RM – Yes. The most important issue is that you have to sing well, and you can't be tricked into trying to sing loud all the time, which can be detrimental. You look at the great Wagnerian baritones - somebody like Hans Hotter, Jim Morris, or George London; they don't sing loud all the time. They sing beautifully, in a way that their voices cut through the orchestra. If you look at the score, especially in the later Wagner operas, he is very careful about the orchestration, so if you are mindful of that you are not yelling the whole night long. A lot of this is pacing. You need to worry about how many of these roles you do in a row in your career, or in a season. It is a challenge.

OL - Tell me about being a member of the ensemble at Deutsche Oper Berlin. How was that experience, for you?

RM – I moved to Germany so I could learn the language. I knew I wanted to sing a lot of Wagner and Strauss. Being at Deutsche Oper was an excellent experience for me. They do so many different kinds of repertoire there! I was around many great singers. I saw my first full *Ring* cycle there. Working with Maestro Runnicles was great. I made connections and good friends in Germany and really enjoyed living there; I like that country. The Germans get a bad reputation but are not actually unfriendly.

OL – Is the ensemble work with all the variation in the repertoire, very challenging as opposed to being hired by an opera company and spending several weeks preparing for a single role?

RM – In a lot of ways it was very similar to my experience in a Young Artist Program at the Houston Grand Opera Studio. At that time I was nearly in every show that they did, often in very different kinds of repertoire. The fast situation in the German company is comparable: you are doing a different opera every day. That can be very difficult especially if you are singing bigger roles. But you get used to it, and it is a good experience. Here in the United States you get five or six weeks of rehearsal and everything is very put together. Often in Germany we would have maybe a few days of rehearsal. You learn to be on your feet and be ready for anything.

OL - Your career has been very much split between Europe, mainly Germany, and the United States. Is this challenging? Would you want to focus more on one side of the Atlantic, or is it just the way it goes for young singers these days?

RM – Oh, I think it's the way it goes. Ideally we try to split time, and be up in America as an American singer. I enjoy working over there and I enjoy being here as well. My next few years will be mostly in America but I have a few things happening over there. If you spend too much time here or there, you get forgotten by people. It's something to watch for, but so far it has gone quite well.

OL – What about the hardships of frequent travel?

RM – Traveling is definitely difficult. I often travel with my wife and my two children, so going back and forth to Europe can be trying. I've been lucky that I spent long periods of time there, and then long periods here. If I had to go back and forth every few weeks, it would have been more challenging.

OL – Once your children get to school age, it could get worse.

RM – Yes, we now do what we call travel school for our eldest daughter. It's basically what we would call home school in America. We have a school in Houston where we live, and when we are at home, Emma our daughter spends a few days a week there, and then when we are on the road we teach her. So far that is going well, but we'll see for how long we will be able to keep it up.

OL – How old is she?

RM – She is seven.

OL – It's good for you that your wife can travel with you. It must make it all a lot easier.

RM – Yes, I am very lucky. As a singer, it can be a lonely lifestyle. I feel very, very fortunate that my wife is able and willing to travel with me and that I have a family. After a performance, good or bad, singers talk about going to a hotel by themselves and getting a little bit of a letdown. For me it is nice to go back to people I know love me, no matter what. [laughs]

OL – You get to center your core and recharge your batteries.

RM – Exactly, yes!

OL – Good for you! You sang in a broadcast performance of Schubert's *Die Winterreise* for Australia Broadcasting Corporation. Was it difficult to learn?

RM – I've sung the *Winterreise* cycle three times now, and I'm doing a fourth one this season for Wolf Trap Opera in the spring. The first time I learned it, was when I did it in Aspen. It is quite difficult. It is much like learning a Wagnerian role, honestly; practically like singing a one-person opera. It is one hour and twenty minutes of singing straight through, but I love that piece.

OL – Yes, it's very beautiful and poetic, but singing non-stop can be killing, right?

RM – Yes, it is very intense. You have to learn to pace, so that you don't lose your voice by the end. And just for your concentration, it takes a lot of mental focus.

OL - Tell me about the psychology of the character Nathaniel that you sang in the world premiere of *Der Sandmann* by Andrea Scartazzini.

RM – That character is one of my favorites. He is a struggling writer, and depending on your reading of the story, he is either schizophrenic – he hallucinates, he is crazy – or there are some kind of ghost characters. I play him from the perspective that he is hallucinating his father who has already died. He has these fantasies about what his life might be like if he was a famous writer, or if his girlfriend looked and acted differently. There was an intense rehearsal period. Christof Loy was the director. It's a great piece, actually. I really enjoyed doing it. He was also the director of the *Tristan und Isolde* I did in Houston. He is really a fantastic director.

OL – What about the vocal challenge of contemporary music?

RM – That was quite difficult, with *Der Sandmann.* It called for a lot of screaming, with very high and very low singing and extreme intervals that were not tonal, most of the time; but I enjoyed that kind of challenge. If you have a solid vocal technique you can use your voice in many ways. We had to be careful because we had several performances. As anyone who spent some time in a football game will know, you can lose your voice pretty easily if you are screaming for hours. But mostly, like in Wagner, you sing with your own voice, with the way you know how to sing, and that keeps you safe.

OL - You chose an aria from Rachmaninoff's *Aleko* for the Met 2007 Southwest Region Competition--I believe it was "Ves' tabor spit". That was taking a big chance, wasn't it? How did you go about picking that particular aria to audition with? Were you at all afraid you might end up a casualty of it?

RM – [laughs] That aria I first learned when I was in California, before I went to Juilliard. It is a beautiful aria. The opera isn't done very often but the aria is sung fairly often. I had a good Russian coach so I felt pretty confident about my Russian. That is a good piece to show. I knew that my voice had the potential to sing some more dramatic music at that point – I already thought that I'd be singing some Wagner some day. But I wasn't quite ready to sing something like the Dutchman's aria in audition. So, that aria was a good way to show that kind of singing, while being a little bit safer.

OL - In many ways, the Met 2007 Nationals was a defining moment for you. You sang well and certainly the video [that contest came up on DVD] shows that you acquitted yourself well with an excellent on-screen presence. How did these auditions change your personal and professional life?

RM – I can be quite a perfectionist with my own performances. I'm not ever completely satisfied. I was frustrated with my performance in the Finals because I felt I didn't do my best work. I often think about that. But it taught me lessons about how to prepare for something, how to pick repertoire, and also taught me about competitions. Nearly all those people who were in those Finals - whether they won or not - are having careers. Competitions are a way for people to hear different kinds of singers and to support young singers who need some extra exposure. But you don't really compete with those people in the opera world. My friend Jamie Barton who is a dramatic mezzo, she and I are never going to compete for the same role in an opera company. [laughs] So sitting in a competition next to each other, is interesting for that situation, but it doesn't mean you are better or worse. But a lot of people saw that, and many of them started to sort of follow me from that point on, so I think that overall, it's been very helpful for my career.

OL – Yes, I do feel that in your last number you didn't do very well, and apparently you agree.

RM – Yes, yes. I didn't really know what to be singing, honestly. I started looking at singing some Wagner pieces. If I was doing it now, I'd be singing the Dutchman or Amfortas, and that would fit a lot more. I didn't quite have the right repertoire. And also, I just wasn't as good a singer as I am now. It takes time.

OL – Did you have a coach, trying to help you through those auditions?

RM – Oh yes, I'm sure like everybody else there, I had coaches trying to help me. It is important to understand about young singers in these competitions or in singing roles, that through your twenties and even your thirties, your voice changes, while career events are happening quickly. When you hear people in that phase of their lives, it is good to follow them and not judge too quickly what you think they might do with their careers.

OL – Let me address now a more psychological aspect. You are heading for to the Met in a Britten opera in his centennial year in a comprimario role. Theseus is silent for two acts then has some recitatives. The experience of being in such a prestigious stage for a young singer trying to break into the bigger roles but only getting a small part must be psychologically daunting. How do you feel about that?

RM – It is and can be daunting. It is difficult when you don't have a lot of time to show what you can do. In my case I'm lucky that they know who I am there, and they like me and want to see me progress. I don't have to stand out in the sense that I'm not coming out of nowhere. I just want to do the best that I can do for that piece. So my goal is just to sing Theseus as well as I can and be part of the drama of the production as well as I can, and not really worry about if I get noticed, or if I get some career boost from it. Mostly, I'm there to do my job. If I do my job well, I expect that they will notice that, and will want me to come back again.

OL – Good attitude! Well, you are getting a good boost from this Dutchman. You've been getting very good reviews.

RM – Yes, definitely many people came to see the Dutchman here and they had very nice comments. It is good for me because I've been focusing on this repertoire for a long time. People have wanted to wait and see how I would handle a lead Wagnerian role. So far, the experience has been very successful.

OL - I've observed that you have had very tragic roles, and just the occasional comedy. It may have been a matter of opportunity, but is there anything else that explains it?

RM – I enjoy doing comedy. I think what my voice does best is probably why I've done more tragedies. My voice seems to match that music a little better. I think I excel at characters that have some kind of pain or anguish going on. I'm not quite sure of the reason for that. [laughs] But I also enjoy comedy and I will do some more in the future.

OL - Please describe your encounter with opera, growing up.

RM – Both my parents were classical guitarists when I was a child. I sang in some choirs. Most of my introduction into vocal music was through choirs of one kind or another. I sang a lot of musicals when I was a kid. When I was a teenager I started going to the opera. I had a choir director who was also a voice teacher who gave me some lessons and suggested that I might be interested in pursuing a career in opera. I started collecting all the recordings I could get. There is a great public library outside of Los Angeles that has loads of recordings, and I just checked out everything I could. I remember one of the first great operatic baritones that I could not stop listening to was Leonard Warren. I was listening to his Rigoletto, and I just fell in love with it, pretty much right away, as soon as I was exposed to it. Then I started going to operas as often as I could, in Los Angeles and in Orange County, and it went from there.

OL - Please describe your training path – I know you're a Juilliard graduate, but what came before and after?

RM – When I finished high school I wasn't sure of what I wanted to do with myself, so I went to Pasadena City College. I was mostly interested in choral music. I had a teacher there who was very supportive of me as a singer, so I spent three years there and I transferred to Cal State Northridge. I spent one year there and felt that I could be more challenged. I got serious about this as a career, and I thought I had a good chance. I auditioned for Juilliard, and for Manhattan School of Music, and for Mannes College The New School for Music, because I wanted to move to New York. I was accepted at all three and I chose to go to Juilliard. I moved there and worked very hard the three years I was there. I spent a summer at the Aspen Music Festival. From there I went to the Houston

Grand Opera Studio for two and a half seasons, where I finished my training and began my career.

OL - What are some of your non-operatic interests?

RM – I really love other kinds of music. I am very interested in bluegrass. I like to play bluegrass guitar, and to play golf once in a while. I really like to cook. I cook for our family all the time.

OL – Oh, that's a very nice Dad. Do you sing to them?

RM – [laughs] Yes, sometimes I sing to them. My eldest likes to come to the opera. She came to *The Flying Dutchman*, actually. She thought it was pretty neat.

OL – How old is the youngest?

RM – The youngest one is three. He doesn't quite have the patience for an entire opera, but he likes to listen to pieces.

OL – I'm surprised that your 7-year-old does.

RM – I know. I am, too. It's impressive, actually. [laughs]

OL – Anything else you like to do?

RM – Yes, I read a lot. But what I do besides singing is that I'm a Dad. [laughs] And it seems like sometimes I'm a travel agent, because I'm working on our travel schedule so often.

OL - How do you describe your take on life and your personality?

RM – When I talk to young singers and they ask me about how to have a career, I tell them that you have to separate things into the ones you can't do anything about – if someone likes the sound of your voice – and the ones that you can do something about, like show up on time, learn your music, be a good colleague, learn the languages, study, practice. It's kind of my take on life too, which is that there are many factors we can't control, and then there are a whole lot of things we can control, and if you take advantage of these, you might find that you can reach your potential as a person, maybe. I'm still working on that. It's a question I often think about, especially in terms of opera – what's the point of opera? Why are we doing this? I think it is a connection to other people. We stand on stage and sing without any electronic amplification, and you as an audience member can hear what I am going through as a person. You can hear that in the air, and we can all experience it together; and hopefully that creates some kind of empathy, and we understand each other better as human beings. It's my outlook on life.

As for my personality, I'm mostly a pretty calm person. I'm sort of subdued, until you get to be better friends with me; then I can be kind of goofy sometimes, and silly. I like to laugh a lot.

OL – Anything you'd like to add?

RM – You have covered most of it. This was very interesting, thank you.

OL – Thank you.

DIVISION THREE – THE CONDUCTORS

CHAPTER SEVEN - CONDUCTORS

Marco Armiliato

Opera Lively met in person the convivial and personable conductor on March 22, 2013, in his room at the Met right before he conducted Zandonai's *Francesca da Rimini.* Maestro Armiliato came across as a really nice and passionate man who loves his music, his singers and instrumentalists, and the culture of his country. His thoughts are very entertaining and talking to him was extremely pleasant. It is easy to understand why Maestro Armiliato is unanimously beloved by his musicians and singers, since he is such a pleasure to be around, with his contagious smile and friendly demeanor.

Opera Lively - I was told by a conductor friend of mine: "Some critics accuse maestro Armiliato of being unimaginative…

Marco Armiliato – Yes, maybe, why not? [laughs] I'm human!

OL - … but in my view, it's because they don't really understand what bel canto opera is about. Marco Armiliato does."

MA – Yes!

OL - My friend said that there is a specific rubato for bel canto, and profound differences between conducting, say, Italianate and French operas. Would you please elaborate on this, and tell us what makes of you such a good bel canto conductor?

MA – A bel canto conductor, you know, it's a crazy definition, because what is a bel canto conductor? Is it one who follows well the crazy things that the soprano and the tenor do in bel canto music, and he is happy with that, and just keeps the orchestra quiet? Or is a bel canto conductor someone who supports the singers and give them space to breathe, and to work on the musical line while they simply sing? Bel canto is definitely not difficult music to play that would require difficult techniques. The way to play Bellini, Donizetti, etc., is to have the vision of beautiful legato, of phrasing, and to allow the singers to be comfortable, to be able to breathe and do all that they need to do. One needs to express each note in the orchestra while making musical sense of the totality of the piece.

OL - Also, I've heard from different singers that you are the best partner a singer can have when singing bel canto…

MA – That's good!

OL - …and that you are a really "singers' conductor." People seem to love to work with you. I'm sure you won't want to toot your own horn, but it seems to be a consensus.

MA – It's like a collaboration.

OL - This conductor friend of mine was saying that you are very able to adapt to the lead singers, and that this is one of your strengths. I mean, when you are conducting Italian Romantic opera, especially bel canto, but also Verdi, verismo and, to a lesser extent, Puccini, most of the opera is there, in the voices. The singers should be the real stars of the performance, if you are shooting for a really great show (and have available great singers, of course). The conductor, in this case, needs to put everything into supporting the singers, adapting the orchestra to them, not the other way around. So, we'd like for you to explain to us what exactly a "singers' conductor" is, and what makes you so special for the singers.

MA – Yes, absolutely. The goal of the conductor in bel canto is one of not bothering the singers. The voice is what is important in this style, and the orchestra needs to be the pillow that provides support. A "singer's conductor" is someone who really loves singing, loves the voice, and understands what the voices need to perform their best. For me, if you want to conduct opera, you need to love voices. If you don't love the voices, it won't work, because you'll probably want your orchestra to play too loudly, and to make your own show, when definitely opera is a collaboration between the orchestra and the singers. The orchestra is at the service of the voices. Opera singers are people who can understand the moment and pick up on the fact that they are supposed to be number one.

OL - I am impressed by your prodigious memory, and the fact that you conduct most operas without a score. Before I ask you how you do it, let me be the Devil's advocate a bit. Again, that same conductor friend of mine who always makes sure he has a score in front of him even for operas he knows by heart like *Norma*, was telling me the advantages of having the score there. He said "You need to take care of so many things: the right tempi, the way the string section is always entering a little bit too slow in that part, remember to subdue the horns here, give some breathing space to the singer there... When the score is available, most of the time you don't even look at it, just move it mechanically forward when you reach the end of the page, but it *is* there."

MA – Yes, your friend is right, the score is there for security, maybe. You probably don't need it. You skip twenty pages at a time.

OL – Yes, he said, "you don't need to worry you will just forget something, because you can always look at the score. You are free to take care of those other things that are really your job. You can also be more responsive to anything happening in the pit, or on stage, because you don't need to worry about remembering the score." So, given this opposite viewpoint, what would you say about the advantages of conducting without a score?

MA – OK, the fact of conducting by memory or by heart provides such freedom, if you really trust yourself and your memory! When I started to play piano as a kid, my teacher wanted me to learn in a few days some huge amount of music, at the time. This was a very good work-out for my memory, for my brain, to just memorize those pieces right away and keep the music inside me, and have the vision of the page in front of me. I can't tell you what kind of memory this is, if it's here [points to his ear] or here [points to eyes]. I don't know. But in my personal experience I feel more comfortable not having the score, because I like to look in the eyes of the people who are playing and singing. If I have the score there I'm going to turn the pages, I'm going to get distracted and lose the connection that I really want to establish with everybody. It's just what is most comfortable for me, but it's not important, each conductor must do what feels most comfortable.

OL - Let's talk about the score for Zandonai's *Francesca da Rimini*. It is complex. Zandonai was quite ambitious in it, and seems to have crammed into it different styles. He apparently wanted to carry forward what Puccini set up to accomplish, and wanted somehow to marry Romantic melodies with modernist harmonies. Please tell us about the gems you find in this score.

MA – It's complex, very. Ambitious, true. It's romantic and modernist music at the same time, exactly. When they asked me to do *Francesca da Rimini*, I had in mind the glorious production from the Metropolitan in the early 1980's with Plácido Domingo, Renata Scotto, and the fantastic James Levine conducting. It was recorded on CD and DVD and was one of the masterpieces of the Metropolitan Opera. That recording traveled around the world and everybody was listening to it. Of course I was one of those, and I watched that video a billion times. So I knew the piece very well. The problem is, of course, that we are going to be compared to them, in this production. Since I started to study this piece, I decided that it was impossible to emulate them because they did a fantastic job with this opera. So I had to make of it some other version. It's the same production but with different singers thirty years later. Everything has changed, here. Almost all the members of the orchestra have changed, and all the choristers. Just a few members played in that production thirty years ago. Only the set remains the same. So, it's a new piece for them; it's fresh.

My goal was to bring as much as I could from the score, because it is so full of things! Zandonai's writing is very interesting because it is a mix of different styles. In one night, you can listen to it from the standpoint of the German school, and another night, you can pay attention to what comes from the French school, from the Russian school, and from the Italian school including verismo and romantic. Of course, for a conductor, this is beautiful because you have a palette of colors to show, and lots of feelings to express during the opera.

This is all helped by the beautiful text of the libretto. These words in Italian are difficult even for me. I'm Italian, but the d'Annunzio play revised into a libretto by Ricordi is very complex. It's in old Italian. I admire people like Eva-Maria [Westbroek]; she is Dutch and she learned the sense of the words and the sense of the phrases so well! I was really amazed, I said, "wow, I'm really surprised!"

OL – Yes, she is great.

MA – She is very intelligent and such a wonderful person. I love her. Everybody falls in love with her, because she is not only a very good singer, but she is also a fantastic human being; so professional, and really nice!

OL - Please tell us about what advice you gave to your singers for this opera. What did you tell Eva-Maria and Marcello Giordani?

MA – Well, Eva-Maria did this role before. She knew the role already when we started the rehearsals here. She sang it in Monte Carlo last year. Actually I was just in Monte Carlo last month, and everybody was talking about her, how great she was. However, the Monte Carlo version had lots of cuts, so Eva-Maria had to learn a lot of new music. The time we had for rehearsals wasn't too long. We had to get ready to go on stage, but she did a fantastic job; she took it so seriously; she stayed here after the rehearsals with the pianist, to study and practice her new music, and she learned it so quickly and so well! I was very impressed with her diction, and the way she absorbed the psychological traits of her character. Marcello as well, he did the role before. I mean, I know Marcello since I was a kid. I played piano for him in concerts in Italy, and had a long experience with him in so many roles, conducting him. So, it's not like these two needed a lot of advice.

OL - What are some of the pitfalls in singing this opera?

MA – This opera is not easy for the singers, especially in the beginning when it is rich in rather weird music. The singers need to understand the various different styles that are required. If you don't understand this, it is hard to put the vocal score together; it's quite tricky.

OL - Let's go back to your activity as a conductor. How do you prepare for a new opera? Do you listen to reference recordings?

MA – Yes, mostly, but sometimes there aren't a lot of reference recordings available.

OL - How long does it typically take to study a new score? How do you find your own interpretation of it?

MA – Whenever I have a new score to study, it's like opening a new book full of things that I don't know. I'm very curious about what is going to happen. Usually I start by reading the libretto, without the music. I want to get familiar with what is being talked about, with the story, and with how that story that I've just learned can be put into music. Once I know well the libretto then I play the score by myself in the piano. Next, if there are good reference recordings, I listen to them. Actually I listen to any recording that is available, just for information, to know what Toscanini did here, what Kleiber did there. I have great respect for my predecessors, of course. If I have something to learn from them, I'm very happy to do so. I must listen to them all. When I get a contract to perform something even if it is six or seven years down the road, I start to study the piece right away. Then, maybe I forget about it for a year, then I start again. It's a long process, to assimilate entirely the score so that when rehearsal time arrives, I'm able to explain to the musicians and singers what my point of view is, on that score.

OL – So, are you always constantly studying, several hours a day?

MA – I wish, but I'm very busy. Sometimes the only time I have to study a score is when I take it to an airport lounge and I read it in flight. Sometimes I'm waiting for a flight for four hours in an airport lounge, and I'm reading a score. I don't need a keyboard because I have perfect pitch. [laughs] That's good, because while reading the score, I know exactly what the music will sound like.

OL - You are also said to be very solid and strong on the planning stage with the orchestra. Please tell us about that process. We'd like to understand better the ins and outs of being a conductor, and what you need to go through to make sure the performance comes up right.

MA – Oh la la, that's a complex question. Because conducting an orchestra is something psychological, something that you have to catch in the moment. Sometimes we need to arrange the music for the musicians. A good musician needs to feel the music in order to give the music to the public. Sometimes when you don't get from the orchestra what is in your mind -- what you think the sounds should be -- then you have to change what they are doing, then and there in the moment. Maybe you need to make the musicians a little more reactive, you need to shock them a bit and awaken them. Sometimes you feel that you are losing control of some section of the orchestra and you, the conductor, need to wake up.

OL - A lot of your conducting activity has been as a guest conductor with some of the most prestigious orchestras in the world. You don't seem to prefer to settle down with a single orchestra. What are some of the challenges in conducting many different orchestras throughout the season?

MA – It is true. It has never happened to me, to have a static place. I've had so many requests in the past to take on a permanent position with an orchestra, but I always said to them that I prefer to travel the world. I've said that I'd only consider settling down when I get to the age of fifty. But now I'm getting close to that age so I'm starting to think about it. Maybe I'll need to slow down and settle down in a place and travel a little bit less. All this travel sometimes is my choice, but sometimes it has more to do with the demands I get. You can't always decide things in your life; sometimes they just happen to you and you follow. It's kind of a mix between the requests you get, and the things you want to do. For now, I'm happy, but maybe the time will come when I'll work with just one orchestra, and then I'll do it.

OL - You once said that conducting the Metropolitan Opera Orchestra is like driving a Ferrari. What is special about this orchestra?

MA – It is true. Oh, the Metropolitan Opera Orchestra! I said Ferrari, but actually, then I started to think about it, and I believe it is best compared to a Boeing 747. This engine sound that it makes is more comparable to the power of a Boeing engine than to a Ferrari. [laughs] It has this "whoooooooo" – every time I do my first downbeat here, I always gasp and think, "wow"! This orchestra has a great sense of sound. Only this orchestra has it. I know this orchestra so well, and I consider it my favorite orchestra. The relationship with them is 100%. I know them, and they know me. I admire them a lot, especially when they get into a *tour de force* like two weeks ago when they played *Parsifal* Friday night, and *Francesca* at noon on Saturday and another opera in the evening – they are always under this kind of pressure and they keep performing at the top level. This orchestra always plays well. They always remember the right style and they change styles so easily – they play German style, French, Italian, Czech, they are amazing, what can I say? I can just say "wow", they are the best opera orchestra in the world.

OL - Have you ever had any profound differences of opinion with a stage director? What is your opinion of the movement known as Regietheater?

MA – Yes, of course I've had these differences of opinion. Things have changed a lot since I started to do this job. When I started, most productions were classic; only in Germany they were doing something modern and weird and tentative, but now it looks like we're in Germany, everywhere. The directors took over the operatic art. They command these new productions, and sometimes they are good, but sometimes they are very bad [emphatically]. Some of the directors are geniuses. I can mention a few, like David McVicar who is always great; Laurent Pelly who is always fantastic. These are the kind of people who use modern techniques and modern mentality but respect the score and the music and make beautiful moments on stage. But I'm disappointed when I'm conducting and I look at the stage and see things that don't match the music, and unfortunately, these days, this happens many times.

OL – Do you try to influence the director, in this kind of situation?

MA – If it is a new production and you have your own say and you can fight with the director, yes. But when you're doing a revival, it's a *fait accompli*, you just have to go and conduct the score, and hope for the best.

OL – Has it ever happened that you declined to accept a job because you didn't agree with the staging?

MA – Sort of, yes. It has happened. I won't tell you exactly what directors I'm talking about, unless you turn off your tape recorder [laughs hard].

OL – I can do that! [laughs]

MA – Oh no, even so, I think I wouldn't say… [laughs] It's not a big deal. But yes, I have plain declined to go conduct in a specific production; it was actually a very important one for my career at that point, but in that case, I preferred to say "no, thanks."

OL - We would like to hear your opinion on playing opera with period instruments versus modern instruments, and on the modern versus ancient tuning of the A key for opera and its impact on singers (A440 versus other pitches that were practiced in the past).

MA – Yes, about that, there is a fantastic video with Piero Cappuccilli, the masterful Italian baritone in the last century. There is a video of one of his master classes he did in the 1970's, with two pianos. One is tuned to 440, and the other one to 444. He was singing parts from *Andrea Chénier* and *I Pagliacci*, and then he got to an aria from *Ernani*, and said "the baritone range here, for this piece that Verdi wrote, it can be sung perfectly with this piano; it matches my voice and my legato, and I can do a perfect passagio, but if you put the same aria in this other piano, then you have to change your technique to solve the passagio, and it is not anymore what the composer wrote – just a little tiny difference completely damages your technique." And this happens also when you go to different orchestras – in Vienna it's a bit higher, you go to New York and it is a little lower, you go to Munich and it is in the middle, and for the voice, of course, it is difficult.

With the modern instruments, especially after a while when the instrument gets a bit warmer, the pitch goes up. It's very difficult to keep the same note forever throughout a long opera. It's a big problem. The period instruments allow for a bit more control in this regard. But we have to be relaxed, and think about the pitch that was adopted by the composer. We shouldn't have one standard to fit all, but should rather try to be faithful to what the composer wrote.

OL - Please tell us about contemporary opera composers. Who do you see as possessing great talent?

MA – Heh!... [In what we interpreted as a sort of dismissive tone].

OL - We just lost one who was great, in my opinion, Mr. Henze, who died recently.

MA – Yes, you are right about this one, he was good.

OL - Do you look at contemporary opera with interest, and do you follow the careers of some favorite contemporary composers?

MA – Yes, of course. I have several composer friends, people for whom I have interest and I follow them. But it is very difficult today, to be a composer, as compared to the time of the great masters of the past. We already have a huge amount of music to play, so it is hard to be fresh. Like in this case of *Francesca da Rimini*, we haven't played it for 30 years so getting to it again feels new, and it's tough competition for those who want to truly write new music. When you have a new piece by a contemporary composer, everybody has this question – how will this sound like? It's interesting, because it could be a very great piece… or not! It's the incognito part. When can you be sure that you are in front of true talent? Time talks. It's only when a piece survives long enough that you can be sure of its value. Of course, you can gauge the ability of a composer to write for the orchestra and for the voice, but true talent depends on a complex combination of things; so, only time will tell.

OL – What do you think of Sciarrino, in terms of his ability to carry on, composing new Italian opera?

MA – Oh, Salvatore Sciarrino, of course, he is very good! He is very interesting, a wonderful composer! He is one that I'm sure will be famous in the future. There are a handful of those. You know, even at the time of the great composers, some of those premieres were disasters, like *Traviata*, and *Butterfly*, and *Carmen*, and then with time these pieces got recognized as some of the most beautiful operas ever, and today if someone says he doesn't like *Traviata* or *Butterfly*, people will say, "What??? It's a masterpiece" but the opening night was a disaster.

OL - You once, in February 2012, conducted six performances in six days. How did you manage it?

MA – [Laughs] Yes, I remember that, it was here, at the Met. You know, it was actually fine, fine.

OL – It wasn't exhausting?

MA – No, no. Music gives you energy. When you are on track, if you take it easy, one by one, day by day, you are fine. You live in the moment; that's my point of view: just be relaxed and just enjoy the music; enjoy the moment. In this way, you are calm and you can even do thirty operas a month… If you are in shape. The health is very important. If you are healthy, you can do it.

OL - Please tell us about your encounter with classical music at some point in your life. I imagine that as a young boy in Italy, everybody was crazy about soccer.

MA – Exactly, just like I am.

OL – Luca Pisaroni told us that his schoolmates considered him to be weird because he liked opera over soccer. Any interesting stories to tell us about your beginnings?

MA – True, the same thing happened to me. [laughs] At first, I was too young to understand what was going on with music. Then my dad decided to rent a piano for himself, so he put me and my brothers in the car and drove to the piano store. On the car radio, Beethoven's Moonlight Sonata was playing. When we got to the store, I sat in front of one of the pianos and played the Moonlight Sonata from memory, from having heard it on the radio minutes before. I don't know, I don't have a recollection of that scene, but this is what my brothers told me. [laughs] So, that was quite shocking for everybody. There were no musicians in my family up to that point. When my father heard me play spontaneously like this, he immediately found somebody to teach me seriously, and sent me to study music.

For me at that age, the piano was a toy and playing it was a game. But the lady who came to teach me was desperate because at the time I was more interested in playing soccer rather than playing the piano. [laughs] I was actually pretty good at soccer and almost became a professional soccer player, but I simultaneously kept playing the piano. At a certain point I realized that music to me was life, and soccer was just fun [laughs].

OL – So, you started with the piano. How did you decide that you wanted to be a conductor?

MA – I always wanted to be a conductor. I was considered to be a child prodigy because I could play the piano so easily, but in my head, in my body, I always wanted to be a conductor.

OL – Why?

MA – I don't know… because I was always fascinated by the beauty of making music together. It was not for the power associated with being a conductor. When I attended a concert I was always looking all the time at the conductor, watching him.

OL - What major influences shaped your training?

MA – I had a stint as a boy singer as well. When I was a kid in Genoa, Alfredo Kraus came to sing *Werther*, and I looked up to him like he was God. I was singing a small part for a child singer in act I and act IV. So I was listening to him from the wings during the other parts of the opera, and it was a fantastic experience. I also remember the first time I saw Pavarotti when he came to sing in Genoa, in *La Bohème*. I remember the feeling I felt that day, as a child, listening to Luciano's pure sound. I was sitting in the back of the opera house, and his voice was so well projected that I had the feeling that he was singing only for me – and I think everybody else was feeling the same. Luciano Pavarotti was the greatest; he was this kind of person who can go right into your heart and give you the right vibe to fall in love with this beautiful world of opera.

OL – How old were you when you sang in *Werther* with Kraus?

MA – I was about seven or eight.

OL – And when you saw Pavarotti?

MA – I was ten. I was lucky to have heard these people up close as a boy.

OL – Definitely. What opera you've conducted was the hardest one for you?

MA – The one I do tonight! I explain, I don't mean *Francesca da Rimini*, I mean any opera I'm performing a given night. [laughs] My first thought is, "Oh my God, am I able to do this?" But then I watch myself on the mirror and I say to myself: "Try it." [laughs] And then, I add the passion, and it works! But I always feel that the hardest piece is the one I'm doing at the moment.

OL - Please tell us about a couple of items in your discography that you are most fond of – if someone wanted to purchase Maestro Armiliato's recordings and wanted advice from the man himself, what would you say?

MA – Oh… it's difficult to answer. They are so different… It depends on the listener's tastes. Recordings are a little weird; there are two ways of doing them – in the studio, or live. Personally, I prefer live recordings, because it's more spontaneous. It's full of mistakes, but it doesn't matter, it's the reality, it's what it is, and it is more natural. In the studio you can say "that clarinet wasn't perfect, can you repeat it" and you can do it 21 times, and you can get the sound technician to work on things… But I prefer to make music, than to obsess about these things we do in studio recordings. But of course, the market asks for recordings, so, why not?

OL – I have one of your blu-ray discs, that opera gala in Baden-Baden, when Anna Netrebko was singing "Meine Lippen" from *Giuditta*…

MA – Yes, yes, and then she started to dance…

OL – And then, you started to look at her, not at the orchestra!

MA – Yes! [laughs hard] Anna sometimes does things that you don't expect! She starts doing some crazy things that we were absolutely not taught, and then we go, "Oh, OK! Why not?" [laughs hard]. I mean, how can one not look at a woman like Anna? [laughs]

OL – I agree! [laughs]. What is your opinion on the current state of opera, and its future?

MA – That's the main question… I'm afraid, because the way to see the opera world is changing, especially in the young generation. Certainly we are going to lose some of the tradition, because there is always transition, it's impossible to keep things as they are; this is what has happened to music since its start. So we have to have new developments. But I believe that one day we will go back to the old mentality. People will again want to see something more traditional. That's my point of view – that regardless of evolution and change, we also have to preserve the old world of opera – the one I fell in love with. I don't know if I would have fallen in love with opera the same way, if my first contact with it had happened in one of today's bad modern productions. I fell in love with Pavarotti singing *La Bohème*. And now we have this big responsibility of bringing opera to the new generations. It is not easy, because they are too distracted, now, between social media, and the Internet, and sports, and TV, and all those small screens.

I think one needs space and time, in life. When someone finds the time to sit in that space that is live opera, and takes the time of listening directly to it – not through the radio or broadcasts, but right there, with the orchestra live and the singers there with no microphones, with that combination of beautiful colors on the stage and beautiful sounds from the pit, and all the drama and the dancing and the story and the passion – death, fighting, love – if you allow this world of opera to get to you, you will find there the things that interest you and keep you alive. We must open the doors of this world to everybody, and get the young people to come for free to see the rehearsals. I believe that even today's distracted youngsters can be touched by opera, if they are given the opportunity.

OL - What pieces would you recommend for a young person's first contact with the art form?

MA – In generally, when people ask me "what opera is good to start with?" it is easy to say *The Magic Flute* or *The Barber of Seville*, because they are funny, have nice music, everybody recognizes the tunes from some commercials, but I don't know, I fell in love with *Werther*! [laughs] I think *Tosca* is one of the operas that are good for beginners, because it is not too long, you don't have time to get bored if you are going to the opera for the first time. *Bohème*, also. It depends on what kind of person you are. If you are a light person you may want easy music, but if you are a deep person you may prefer *Eugene Onegin*.

OL - What can be done to reverse the apparent crisis in popularity and financial support for opera in Italy?

MA – Heh, the problem is not only with opera, in Italy. The problem there is with arts in general. Right now we don't have the government behind us any longer. How can people not invest in art, in Italy? I mean, Italy became famous because of art! What is Italy? Pizza, Mafia, soccer, and especially, the arts! [laughs hard]. No, seriously, in the world we are famous for the arts, for what we were able to create in this small peninsula, this small piece of land, and we got arguably the best artists in the history of humankind! Italian history is in our hands, now, and we are destroying it! We are destroying the best thing we had, and it's a shame. I hope it will be fixed. Because we created opera, and we exported it around the world, and now if you think of La Scala, everybody dismisses it and says, "Oh, La Scala is going bad." And to me, unfortunately, I have to say, it is true! It is true, because compared for instance to the Metropolitan, La Scala is not on the same level, now. Today, the leading houses are the Metropolitan, Vienna, Munich, Zurich, London… I mean, come on, we need to do something about this!

OL - How was the experience of conducting for the Metropolitan Opera National Council Auditions? Any promising new singers we should watch?

MA – It was wonderful. I always love the opportunity to listen to new talent. In this competition, we work for one week with the finalists, and sometimes we discover people like Angela Meade. Now she has a great career. When she came to the competition, she said she would sing *Norma*, and everybody in the jury said "she is too young to sing *Norma*." I said, "guys, listen, she is something!" The same thing happened in Monte Carlo, when I listened to this fantastic young soprano called Sonya Yoncheva. She sang *La Traviata* there.

OL – Yes, and she is very pretty.

MA – Yes, and what a beautiful job she did with *La Traviata*! Oh my God. I'm sure she will make her Met debut soon, and will have a great career [Editor's note – she is scheduled to sing Musetta in La Bohèm at the Met in January 2015]. It's very interesting when you find somebody who could be the next star, and in fact is! Leah Crocetto is another one, she has a beautiful voice, I loved her in everything I've heard with her. When I talk about these young artists, I call them "my people," I'm very proud of them!

OL – Yes, when I interview them, I also get protective; I feel some paternalistic feelings, like they're my kids!

MA – [Laughs] Exactly, exactly!

OL – Do you have any specific plans at this point for the future of your career?

MA – It's not that clear yet. But probably, like I told you before, I'll take a position somewhere, at a certain point. It's been a lot of traveling, and it's hard, especially when you start doing too many projects at the same time. Here at least when I come to do a run like this one at the Met, I have my own apartment in New York City and I can relax a bit. But in Europe sometimes you have to conduct an opera in Vienna then you fly to Berlin to conduct another one then you go to Munich the next day, and you can't sleep very well and get some rest.

OL - Please tell us about Marco Armiliato, the person. What kind of person are you when you are away from the world of opera and classical music? How do you define your personality? What is your take on life? What are some of your interests?

MA – I think I'm a very pure person. As you know me, I am. I have no secrets. I live the life in the happiest way I can. I think this is thanks to my family, to my mom, to my parents who gave me the spirit and the joy to just enjoy life. I have a very important word in my life: it is passion. In everything I do I put all my passion, all of myself. It can be good or it can be wrong, but I always do it with all my heart. I believe in what I'm doing. We have to believe. But I'm not perfect, I'm a long way from being perfect, so I just try to do my best. This is what I try to teach my son as well: "whatever you do in life, do it with passion." Even if you do something wrong, as long as it's done with passion, it's not that bad. [laughs]

OL – How old is your son?

MA – He is 24 now, a big boy!

OL – Is he a musician?

MA – He is not but he loves music, of course. He studied music a little bit, for me, actually.

OL – So you like soccer!

MA – Oh my God, soccer, yes, it's the other part of my life!

OL – Do you root for Sampdoria? [Editor's note – one of the two main soccer clubs in Genoa]

MA – Yes, of course, I'm a Sampdoria fan! I root for my Sampdoria and I don't miss a game. I wake up at 6 AM to watch their matches if I'm in a different time zone. I do crazy things for soccer; I'm really fanatic about it.

OL – Me too. I'm a Rossoneri fan [Editor's note – AC Milan is known for the colors red and black and is called the Rossoneri by fans].

MA – Oh, OK, of course, you're Italian too. [Editor's note – the maestro had inquired about the journalist's Italian last name before the interview started, and got confirmation that the journalist is a dual citizen of Italy and the United States]. Then, you understand me [laughs].

OL – Any other interests besides opera and soccer?

MA – Many, but the problem is, I never have time for anything else. I'd love to have more time, to do stuff.

OL - Regarding your brother Fabio Armiliato and his wife Daniela Dessì – do you have any plans of engaging in any sort of foundation or teaching or some other project together with your brother and your sister-in-law?

MA – Not yet, but maybe… Why not? Of course. We may in the future do something like that, of course. It is very hard to plan on doing this sort of thing right now, because I'm so busy! I barely have time to go home and see my wife! But in the future, yes, for sure. I would like to start a foundation to benefit opera.

OL – I guess we are getting close to the performance, but we did well, we covered a lot.

MA – Perfecto, yes!

OL – Thank you so much, it was wonderful!

MA – No problem! My pleasure!

Yannick Nézet-Séguin

Opera Lively interviewed one of the brightest emerging stars of a new generation of conductors, French-Canadian maestro Yannick Nézet-Séguin. We met him on the occasion of his *Traviata* run at the Met with Diana

Damrau, Plácido Domingo, and Saimir Pirgu in March 2013, but we talked about many other topics. Maestro Nézet-Séguin is intelligent and articulate, and had some very interesting answers.

Opera Lively - You took over the Philadelphia Orchestra recently. What has that experience been like? What do you think is unique about the orchestra and the city, and what are your plans for the future of the orchestra?

Yannick Nézet-Séguin – About the Philadelphia Orchestra, when I first conducted them in 2008 there was something very special happening. It was as if we had known each other before, as if it wasn't the first time. Maybe we knew each other in a previous life or something. Now that I am the Chief Conductor and the Music Director, I feel this very special connection that allows us to already benefit, even if it hasn't been a long time since I'm at the helm. I feel that our work is already very significant, because I feel the style of the orchestra and what I want to achieve with it is becoming more and more impressive by every concert. It's a very special group of musicians. They are very great human beings, not only great musicians. They are very passionate and very dedicated.

My plan for the city is that more people in the Philadelphia will come and see our concerts, to reconnect. Because the city used to be very, very proud of its orchestra and maybe in recent years people were proud but they were not going to the concert hall. Now we want people to come back.

OL – A glance at your numerous recordings would appear to suggest that you have interest in both instrumental and vocal music. Do you have a preference between conducting symphonic pieces and conducting opera? What kind of different satisfaction a conductor gets from these two genres?

YNS – Opera and symphonic music for me of course have differences, but I would say that maybe unlike many others, I don't feel that there is so much difference between the two. I'll even say that I tend to conduct symphonic music more like opera, because I find that in opera there is always the conscience to be accompanying an instrument, or a group, or a voice – to breathe, in other words. To breathe is so essential to all of music, whether it's a Brahms or Beethoven symphony, or whether it's a Verdi or Puccini opera! For me it's the same thing, I have to make the orchestra flexible enough to always listen to what is the dominant voice, and this is why for me doing both is something natural.

Of course opera involves much more people - the set designers, the producers, the costume makers, the chorus, the lighting designers, and so it's a different kind of control than in symphonic music, but I really need both to live as an artist.

OL - Since our website is about opera, please allow us to focus on operatic conducting. You are currently doing *La Traviata* at the Met with Diana Damrau, Plácido Domingo, and Saimir Pirgu. Would you please tell us what is needed for a successful *Traviata*? Is there a way to describe in words your personal reading of the piece and to express to us how you go about it? What advice do you give to the singers of a piece like *La Traviata*?

YNS – *La Traviata*, Giulini used to say that it was the perfect opera. I always look at *La Traviata* as being this perfect opera; but until now I had never conducted it, so this is my first time. I realize that what is very special about it is that we have to have a great understanding of the character of the music and what it says beyond the words, between the singers, the conductors, and the orchestra. It's more like large scale chamber music. I find *Traviata* at its best when it's intimate, and that's when we accompany the duets and the arias of Violetta with all the delicacy that is needed. It's very important to have the tenderness, and the inflexions of the harmonies. Of course we have grand scenes and the concertati at the end of Act II; yes, we have powerful moments, but the most important thing is to be able to create something very intimate, and that was possible this time with the wonderful cast that the Met put together. We really worked prior to the performances to make sure that we would be very, very close to each other during the performances to make this chamber music effect.

OL – Yes, I attended one of the performances and noticed that in acts II and III the dynamics were kept very low. It was very intimate. Ms. Damrau was singing softly, which I loved. Was it your doing?

YNS – Yes, well, I accepted to do this production at the Met because I knew that this cast would be so wonderful! But this exceeded all my expectations. And the Metropolitan Opera Orchestra of course knows Verdi so well, and they react so well when singers are so intelligent and sing it beautifully and expressively; then the orchestra transforms automatically the way it plays. This is why it's really a dream.

OL - I'm curious about the opera scene in Québec. Is there a bigger space there for French opera as opposed to other Western countries where Italian and German-language operas seem to be more popular? For example, I'm extremely fond of Berlioz and I think he is underappreciated by the operatic public. Are his operas more popular in Québec than elsewhere?

YNS – I don't know really what it is that in Québec we have about the voice, but there is quite a long history with the voice and opera in general. There was Léopold Simoneau, of course who was this great Mozartian, then we had many people like Richard Verreau, and we had Maureen Forrester, English-speaking coming from Montréal, so, there is a long tradition, and now we have great singers like Marie-Nicole Lemieux, and also opera conductors like myself and others. I think it is probably because in Québec there is this fight always to exist in a more French tradition among all the English tradition in the North-American continent, and that creates this desire to express and be creative. Therefore it probably makes us accept some repertoire more easily than others. You know, when you talk about Berlioz's works, Dutois did a lot for making them appreciated in Québec. It is probably because of the language. The Montréal Opera, for example, doesn't do a lot of Wagner; it's not something that is necessarily so popular in Québec. Maybe we also have the same struggles and pains of everywhere else in the world but what is very distinctive, I would say, is the diversity of the number of people and groups – two symphony orchestras, two opera companies, many, many chamber orchestras, many ensembles of contemporary music, and this for a total of only seven million people; it's not very big.

OL – Yes. I love Léopold Simoneau's version of *Les Pêcheurs de Perles*, more than Alfredo Kraus' that everybody raves about – I think Simoneau did it with more elegance and delicacy.

YNS – [laughs, pleased] Yes, I would tend to agree with you!

OL - What do you think of critical editions of opera scores? Do you like to consider all possible explanations for different versions of a work that scholars come up with, or do you like to follow the living tradition of operatic performance more than the scholarly research?

YNS – Yes, I think critical editions are very important. It's interesting to look at what was the research and understand especially where the traditions come from, because in opera more than in other genres I think that the balance between what is written in the score and the many traditions is very interesting, and I'm not a conductor that says – "oh, we should get rid of every tradition and just play what the composer wrote." But it is very important to understand why there is a tradition to slow down here, or why there is this change in the vocal line, so in that sense, to be aware of the critical edition is important, but it shouldn't mean that we get rid of all the experience that the generations have accumulated, performing the opera.

OL - Opera recordings in studio are becoming rarer, while live recordings in video media are becoming much more frequent. Is this a reason for concern?

YNS – No, the video aspect of opera is not necessarily a concern. It's good news. Because video now makes opera more accessible, and more visual; it is true that people have more immediate access to opera everywhere in the world, especially younger people, and I think this is something we should be happy about, because that means it is an art form that is far from dying. However, like any new phenomenon, it has its own dangers. In that sense, maybe yes, there is a small concern about the visual taking the place of the musical aspects. Real opera for me must reach a perfect balance between the two. I think there is a place for recordings, and there is a special place for experiencing the intensity of the acting of the singers when we get the video. The series that I'm doing now with Deutsche Grammophon of the Mozart operas in audio only, almost studio-like recording of concert versions, I think there is also space for this because the recordings give us the opportunity to concentrate really on the beauty of the music and especially to understand that all the drama is within the music. But opera at the end of the day is this perfect union of both visual and musical aspects, so I think we should always be careful to keep the balance right.

OL - Could you give us examples of operas that people would assume are simple to conduct but aren't, and are, instead, surprisingly difficult? What about the other way around: operas that are seemingly complex but are easy to tackle?

YNS – Well, the first example I have is *La Traviata.* I think it is a little bit like in the symphonic world, talking about Beethoven's 5th. Everybody knows it; that makes it extra difficult to conduct, because first of all not only everyone has an opinion about it, but also there is always the danger of taking things for granted, for routine. I was worried about this here at the Met, because I thought, "oh, this orchestra plays it all the time." So it's very important to go back to the score and really work on not doing things automatically. That's related to my previous answer. In the end I find that the operas that are more difficult for me, personally, as a conductor, are the ones where we have to search really this delicate line and have the orchestra and the singers accept to sing more dolce and to express in a more intimate way, rather than for example *Turandot. Turandot* is the opera that I have most pleasure to conduct, and for me it is almost easy, because it's big, it has its challenges, but the more there are people, the more you can conduct in broad musical gestures, so I think the most difficult ones are the most intimate ones.

OL – Very nice answer, thank you. Do you have an interest for contemporary opera? If yes, what composers?

YNS – Regarding contemporary opera, what interests me is the process. I'm in discussion already with a composer who is about to compose her first opera, Jennifer Higdon, American composer; she will create her first opera in a few years in Santa Fe. [Editor's note: Higdon is currently writing an opera based on Charles Frazier's "Cold Mountain". It is co-commissioned by Santa Fe Opera and Opera Philadelphia and is scheduled to be premiered in Santa Fe in 2015]. I would like to be with her for her second opera. What I would be interested in, is to witness the process from the very beginning when the composer decides for a libretto and decides for the shape of the piece, and I would be involved in every step, to feel that there is a real sense of creation. This is what was the most wonderful about the creation of music. For us, interpreters, we always wish that we would have the red telephone line to talk to the previous composers who are now dead. It's incredible to think that we can have a composer working with us in contemporary opera, and exchange our ideas with these composers.

OL – Right. And do you have any favorite contemporary composers that you admire?

YNS – I have to say that when I saw Nico Muhly's *Two Boys* last year in London I was very interested in it. I think he is a composer who is able to speak a very different language, just because of the bridge he is able to make between pure operatic music and also music that is more influenced by a certain aesthetic of popular music. It's not the only way for me to do opera, but I think it is also very interesting that someone of this generation in the 21st century is able to make more bridges and more connections.

OL – Nice. Today's operatic environment is quite hectic. With conductors' and singers' busy schedules and all the flying around, sometimes rehearsal times are drastically short. Do you make a point of not accepting projects that don't have decent time allocated for rehearsals?

YNS – Yes, the schedules, yes. [laughs] I mean, my own schedule is one thing, because I'm a relatively young conductor, and I'm able to have a lot of energy and I'm able to focus very well when I am traveling. Of course my schedule is maybe the biggest subject of conversation that I have with my agents and people around me, just to make sure that it is still livable. But in more general terms, I think it's a big topic, because we have to distinguish whether it's stagione, or repertoire opera houses, which are different challenges. You asked about short rehearsals, but I find that much the opposite, now the periods for rehearsals are getting longer and longer because some directors with new productions think they need seven weeks of rehearsals, but I find that sometimes there is a bit of waste of time, because everyone now arrives more prepared, including the set designers, the directors, the actors and dancers when they join us, so everybody does more work in general, and when we put together everything with the singers, when everybody is ready, it should take less time for rehearsals. And then, this would enable the opera singers who are very much in demand, the opera stars, to all be there at the same time. Because sometimes what happens everywhere in the world is that because the rehearsal period is too long, the star singers will miss two weeks of rehearsals, and other singers will miss two other weeks, and we will end up with seven weeks of rehearsals, but only for the last week everyone is there, so, if rehearsals were shorter with everyone more prepared, and no permission to go away, it would be better. It's better to have two weeks with everyone ready and working hard, than seven weeks while having half of the people, all the time.

OL – I see. What do you think are the advantages and disadvantages of the stagione versus the repertoire systems? What is more conducive of good performances?

YNS – I think they bring two different aspects of what opera is. I think it is beautiful to have cities where all year long one can really go and hear in a nice theater good quality singers and orchestras, like especially in the German system, where there are all these ensembles of house singers who work very often together. I think there are good qualities to it. But personally as a conductor I prefer of course to be involved with only one team of singers and do it in a concentrated time, so I'm more for the stagione concept. Both systems have their own merits. It's a question of comfort and taste.

OL - What do you think of abridged versions of operas and of performing opera with heavy cuts to make it more palatable to the public or to comply with labor or budget limitations? We've heard of efforts like the recent 7-hour *The Ring of the Nibelung* in Buenos Aires, or the 2-hour *Rienzi* DVD... Is this a concerning trend?

YNS – Hm... you're talking about cuts, but you are also talking about Wagner. Wagner of course has his own space and time. While I believe maybe for some people it might be good to have a shortened version to get more at ease with the offering, OK, Wagner may be an exception, because in general I am very much unfriendly to cuts. I find cuts like an insult to the composer. I know that operas have very often been cut by the composer himself because of circumstances, having one scene less because of this singer or the other singer, because of demands of the theater… They could have this freedom. But I think that for us nowadays, we think sometimes that to cut an opera will make it seem shorter, but actually very often the cuts are badly done, and we end up with less harmonic diversity, and that means that in the end, for the psychology and for the ears of the people, it ends up feeling longer. I'm very, very careful about cuts. I can agree sometimes to cut a full scene or something like this, or when there is ballet music but there is no ballet corps in that staging, I agree, but to cut a few bars here and there, for me, it's not something I'm generally in favor of.

OL – I agree. What opera composers and/or works do you consider to be unfairly obscure and would love to help revive?

YNS – I'm interested in one day actually trying to do on stage Massenet operas that are not done a lot. Think of an opera for example like *La Navarraise* by Massenet. I think Massenet is a great opera composer, and *Manon*, yes, we do a lot, and we do *Werther* and it is beautiful. I know that by saying this I contradict a bit my attitude of the last few years when opera houses would contact me and ask me to conduct a lot of the French repertoire that was forgotten, even some Meyerbeer, and I decided not to do this for the moment, because I don't want to be typecast as a French opera conductor, because that's not what I feel I am in essence. But in a few years time, maybe in a decade or so, maybe I can use my own position as an opera conductor and then try to take on some lesser known French repertoire.

OL – OK, great. But when you say "that's not my essence," what is your essence, then?

YNS – Hm… my essence is that I need to conduct a lot of repertoire. I cannot be confined to any single one. I'm not a specialist, by nature. To me, to be able to do Verdi right, I need to do Verdi against Gounod, against Mozart, against Monteverdi, against Strauss, and then I'm able to understand more what Verdi's style is. I feel sometimes that people who do only one style, they try to put everything in the same style, instead of finding the differences. But this is a very personal choice. This is how I feel, and I think it is very good now that I have a more varied exploration of the operatic repertoire. It's not because I feel more Italian than German or French; I just feel more international! [laughs]

OL – I see. [laughs] While you were training, what were your major influences, and who functioned as a source of inspiration? We know about maestro Carlo Maria Giulini. Any others? Do you have some interesting vignette to tell us about some epiphany or encounter with a major source of inspiration, that helped shape who you are as a conductor?

YNS – Yes, maestro Giulini of course was my main inspiration. But many aspects of many other conductors have inspired me, in terms of their interaction with the artists. This is what interests me the most. Because it's so personal! Of course, the genius of someone like Giulini, or the genius of Toscanini, or Bernstein or Karajan, or the genius today of Claudio Abbado, for example, it's something nobody can imitate. We can be inspired by them but we cannot try to reproduce them. What we can try to reproduce in a way is that kind of interaction with the people. Because for us, conductors, the primary function is of course to be a musician, therefore, to be very true to the composer and the score, but the second most important thing is that we have to make the people around us do their best. The whole trick is how to achieve that, and I'm mostly inspired by people who, in concert, like Abbado or Carlos Kleiber, would leave people extremely free in the performance. But someone like Kleiber, what people don't always know is that he actually was extremely detailed in rehearsals. He would rehearse a lot in order to achieve that freedom. This is more what I'm trying to do myself.

OL - How did you get into classical music, as a child or teenager?

YNS – My encounter with classical music happened when I was five years old, and was playing the piano. But it's the combination with the singing in a choir, when I was nine years old, that was the real shock, when I became passionate about it. So, it started very early for me; as a child really, and I already knew that this was my goal in life.

OL – Your parents are not musicians, right?

YNS – No, no, they are teachers. They love music but they are not musicians.

OL - You are known for physical fitness and even got an endearing nickname by Ms. Joyce DiDonato – "Mighty Mouse" - that makes reference to your physical strength. Does fitness play a significant role in conducting? Is working out at a gym part of your preparation for conducting?

YNS – Oh yeah! (laughs hard). Yes, the fitness happened in my life because when I started to conduct more regularly ten years ago and more often, of course I started to have pains in my shoulder and some back pain, and I visited a few therapists, and they all advised me to just have someone who could help me develop evenly all my muscle structure. Because that is the problem with conducting; one always starts a lot of movements, but they are always the same movements, and it was important for me to get this balance, and eventually in my life it became a good way of resting my brain, concentrating on the body so that sometimes, a few times a week I could forget about music and give myself a little bit of rest for my brain. I think everybody needs that, and this is what fitness has done to me, combined with making sure I don't get injured. Since I started working out, I never got injured; I was never in pain in my muscles any longer.

OL – Nice! Outside of classical music, what are some of your other interests in life?

YNS – It's related. Apart from fitness which is my only time away from music, I think I still consider myself as completely dedicated to my art. Of course I have interest in movies like everyone else, in good wine and good food, and I spend a lot of time with my friends and my family; this is very important for me, having some holidays at the beach, you know, nothing very unusual. But even when I am at the beach music is always present somewhere, with some scores, and I'm perfectly happy with this.

OL – Oh wow, we made it through all the questions in the time we had allocated.

YNS – Yes, thank you so much for your good questions.

OL – Thank you for your time, Maestro! Good bye.

Myron Michailidis

Opera Lively traveled to Athens, Greece in October 2013 and interviewed in person maestro Myron Michailidis, Artistic Director of the very dynamic and resourceful Greek National Opera

Opera Lively - I have heard of a tribute to Maria Callas you have presented in five outdoor performances around the city, which drew more than five thousand spectators. Is the memory of Maria Callas very much alive in

Greece today?

Myron Michailidis – Maria Callas is a legend for Greece. She is one of the most important elements that connect our younger generations of artists with this historical theater. We work here with technical difficulties but historically we never forget that on this stage Maria Callas had her first steps. So every year we have some ceremonies and some concerts dedicated to her memory. This year we decided to insert these activities about her, in our general master plan for cultural activities outside the theater. We did a totally different tribute to Maria Callas. We organized this promenade in five acts. We started in the Acropolis Museum and then continued to the Herodes Atticus Odeon, then to central squares of Athens, and the final concert was in front of the National Archeological Museum, and in all those concerts more than five thousand people were with us.

OL – Five thousand in each concert?

MM – I'd say that they came together and followed us to each venue, since it was a promenade. This was something that had a very strong effect on our citizens. Our city, during the economic crisis, had a lot of problems. We miss our friends on the streets. They suffer from the crisis. And now, the live theater gives them the opportunity, to every member of society even if they are not rich, to be together and to pay together a tribute to a famous singer like Maria Callas.

OL – What about the new generations? Are the youngsters aware of Maria Callas as well?

MM – Yes. We believe that Maria Callas doesn't only belong to Greece. She belongs to the history of opera and to the world. Our singers, directors, and conductors when they study opera, have Maria Callas as the standard. The same is true for the younger generations: for them, Maria Callas is still alive.

OL – How popular is opera in Greece?

MM – In my opinion opera is very popular in Greece, and even more popular is the institution Greek National Opera. The GNO is a very popular institution. I don't know all the reasons for it, but I can tell you some of them.

The GNO started at the beginning of the 20th century as part of the National Theater. It became an independent organization during World War II. In those years Maria Callas made her debut. The GNO as an independent organization is about seventy years old. Opera is something that impresses the Greek friends of the arts, because it combines theater – and let's not forget, theater had a great tradition in Greece – with singing – and Greeks sing a lot. A big part of the repertory by Verdi and Puccini, and also the French repertory, is very similar to the Greek Mediterranean mentality. The Italian mentality is very similar to the Greek mentality.

Our numbers show that we have the possibility, in the summer when we do our eight open air theater performances in the Herodes Atticus Theater which is big and has a seating capacity for five thousand people, to have it full for all eight evenings. Only the Greek National Opera has the possibility of filling this theater for eight evenings.

The problem we have at the Olympia is that it is a small theater with about seven hundred seats. We are not happy because we are always sold out; we need more seats. We are very happy that we are moving into our new house; I will tell you about it later.

OL – Opera has suffered around the world for the last five years due to the economic crisis; not just in Greece, but everywhere. What is the situation for the financing of opera in Greece?

MM – It is very difficult. Before the crisis hit five years ago, our annual cost was of about thirty-three million Euros, and our budget fully met that cost. Then, because of the crisis, our debt grew, and at the beginning of 2011 we had a deficit of about 17 million Euros. When I was appointed as Artistic Director here two years ago, we started a recovery project to make the organization healthy. Today our debt is of 4.7 million, so to go from 17 million to 4.7 is very good and positive. We now have annual funding of about 16.7 million Euros – that's what we need to go ahead. Unfortunately all institutions had budget costs, and we are getting only 12 million per year.

This is a very big problem. We strongly believe in the last three months that the government will continue its support and will consider which institutions are functioning well and which organizations belong to the society and have already done reconstruction. We have already remade ourselves; to cut any further is just not possible. We believe that when we have something that is doing well, we should not destroy it. It's easier to keep a good thing stable for the future instead of trying to fix other organizations that are not functioning well. We are sure that the government shares the same logic in this.

OL – Other than the governmental subsidies, what sources of income do you have?

MM – We sell about 3 million Euros in tickets, and we get private sponsorships, but this past year was a disaster. Banks in the recent past before the crisis were strong sponsors for the opera, but now the bankers are very afraid. The businessmen from private corporations are now very afraid to engage in big sponsorships. We still get a few sponsorships for specific productions, and we get subsidies from the State Lottery. I hope that investors will understand that investing in cultural organizations could help them in coming out of the crisis.

OL – What about private citizens? Do they give money to the opera? In the United States a significant part of a company's revenue comes from individual donations.

MM – Yes, we'll be trying to find new ways, in our new home, to find possibilities for support of the GNO. We have a club called "Friends of the Greek National Opera". I think that sponsorships should go to support specific cultural activities but we shouldn't rely on them to pay the salaries of our personnel. The salaries are the minimum that the government has to ensure. We have a staff here which generates ongoing costs, and this cost should be met by the government, and then it will be up to us to use our energy to find sponsors for our activities.

OL – Do you have a fixed staff of singers, like the German model?

MM – We do. We have a relatively small staff of Greek singers and we also invite foreign singers. About ninety Greek singers are singing in our productions. We also have a very interesting program financed by the European Union, which is an interactive way of making an opera in primary schools. With this program we go to schools in the whole country and we give the students the opportunity to participate in a production by making the sets and the props, and singing as well. We are taking *The Barber of Seville* to schools. We send them the material one month in advance, then we go there the day before the show to train them, and the next day the opera is presented in the school auditorium. This system is a big success. We go everywhere, including the islands and small villages in the North and the South, and it's a win-win situation because not only they get to see opera, but we also get to hire young animators and choreographers, set designers and musicians, etc. This program which is going very well shows how popular opera can be in Greece.

OL – With the crisis, have you had to cut the number of productions?

MM – No. Our strategic plan was not to cut productions. Instead, we actually doubled the number of productions. We used to have one hundred productions – now we have 210 productions all over Greece. One can have very expensive productions that are not of good quality, but one can have very economic productions that seem rich. Instead of making very big and expensive productions, we are giving - an example for this is *La Cenerentola* - an opportunity to a very young director who worked for the Royal Opera House Covent Garden, named Rodula Gaitanou. She and the costume designer, Alexia Theodoraki, were able to recycle old costumes and sets we had from our past productions. We use many tricks to be able to make these productions. In this theater, on the main stage we have about 12 productions. Outside the main stage we also offer opera, operetta, ballet, and Greek operetta.

OL – How do you select operas to present to the public? Do you try to present operas that are outside of the usual standard repertoire, or do you need to focus on the more popular ones in order to put people on the seats during the crisis?

MM – Thank you very much for asking this which is a very interesting question. To make an interesting season, it's like a Sudoku game. We are the only opera company in Greece. We used to have a stagione company in Thessaloniki, but during the crisis it closed down. We are a national company and as such we have to present the repertoire. It would be a disaster if the basic repertory operas couldn't find a venue to be shown to the Greek public. We need to continue to stage *La Traviata, La Bohème, Il Trovatore, Tosca*… but we are trying to also present operas that are less familiar to the public, like *Faust* from Gounod which was last seen in Greece twenty years ago.

Our main productions in our main stage are either traditional or modern but they all respect the operas. We do have an experimental stage where we engage in more adventurous productions. In our plan we have Janacek, Wagner and Richard Strauss but we do continue to present the very popular Verdi and Puccini operas. This season we are doing *Werther* from Massenet which is a big risk for us. We are collaborating in this production with Spyros Evangellatos who is a very well-known Greek director.

So, a very popular work like *La Cenerentola*, we are presenting with a very young director. A very difficult title like *Werther*, we are presenting with a very experienced director like Evangellatos. So we are always trying to find viable ways to present these operas. Our *Don Giovanni* this summer is with Yannis Houvardas, another very important Greek director. He was up to two months ago the artistic director of the Greek National Theater.

I have to tell you about our Suitcase Opera program. We make a miniature of the opera and transport it to every place where normally they wouldn't be able to stage an opera. We transport the sets and lights and good singers. The Stavros Niarchos Foundation is sponsoring this program which is a big success. They are a private foundation, and they are building now a cultural center in the South of Athens, which will host our new opera house. The center is 170,000 square meters in a park full of trees, and will host the National Library and the Greek National Opera. It will be our new home in two years. It is amazing that during the crisis, a private foundation is building this enormous center. It will be ready by the end of 2015, at a cost of 566 million Euros. This private foundation is also the sponsor of our Suitcase Opera program – Opera Tis Valitsas.

OL – What about contemporary Greek operas – are there good ones, and do you present them?

MM – Yes, of course. Every year we have new opera productions in the beginning of the summer, and we work on it in two ways. One way, is that we have an opera competition and we invite young Greek composers to write one-act operas, and we present two of them on the stage. The other way is to commission compositions by very important and established Greek composers. Next year we will present the opera *Fonissa* based on one of our most famous Greek novelists, Alexandros Papadiamantis, and the composer is Giorgos Koumendakis, who organized the music for the 2004 Olympic Games opening and closing ceremonies. This will be a totally Greek production: a Greek title, a Greek author, and a Greek composer.

OL – Are there other important contemporary Greek composers that you would quote?

MM – Yes, we have Tsontakis who lives in the United States, Antoniou, Kouroupos, Tsalahouris, Christos Samaras. For example, Antoniou composed an opera named *Oedipus*, and we will combine his opera with Stravinsky's opera *Oedipus Rex*.

OL – Tell me about your Opera Bus program – is it the same as the Suitcase Opera?

MM – No, these are different programs but both are important cultural activities in our planning. We have a specialized team for the planning, and another team for the productions. We discuss about it almost every day.

The Opera Suitcase like I said, is a traveling program with small ensembles, sets, props, costumes, and a piano, which allows us to give shows in places that are not equipped for mega opera.

It's very important to realize that admission to these performances is free of charge for the public. The other project is this Lyric bus. In some cities and occasions, we show up unannounced, with no publicity, and suddenly we sing parts of operas in different places like a market or a subway station.

We do open rehearsals as well. You can find them on YouTube. They became viral; lots of people have seen them. We went to the Piraeus port and presented rehearsals for our upcoming season. This is the Flower Waltz from *Nutcracker* [he shows me the YouTube clip on his smartphone]. It is nice, isn't it?

OL – Yes. You have a very dynamic and lively company!

MM – Yes! This is also in our Facebook page. This one here is our Herodes Atticus Theater rehearsal for *Madama Butterfly* [he shows other clips]. This one was in the Acropolis, and this one at the Archeological Museum. This one here was a very crazy concert, in the Meat Market.

OL – What about this one here, the "*Manon Lescaut* Meets *Carmen*"?

MM – We did that as a street event in a subway station, the Monastiraki station. It was with singing and dancing.

OL – Do you engage in collaboration with sister institutions in Europe?

MM – Yes, we've had collaborations with the Royal Opera House, the Arena di Verona, and the Vienna State Opera. We are now discussing co-productions with them. In November we will have in Verona a co-production with the Arena di Verona, the Greek National Opera, and the La Fenice in Venice, of *I Capuleti e i Montecchi*. The production will be given first in Verona, then will go to Venice, and will arrive here in two years. Isn't it nice?

OL – Yes, it is. Tell me about the most successful Greek opera singers.

MM – There are many important Greek singers both here and abroad. Let me tell you some names: Dimitra Theodossiou, Alexia Voulgaridou, Myrto Papathanasiou… Of course there is Anja Harteros but she isn't only Greek. Other good Greek singers are Dimitri Platanias who was Rigoletto in

Covent Garden, Dimitri Tiliakos who was Macbeth in Paris, and Tassis Christoyannis.

OL – Ms. Vassiliki Karayanni is a very beautiful soprano.

MM – Yes, she belongs to our ensemble.

OL – How is operatic training in Greece? Do you have good conservatories? Does your company have a Young Artists Program?

MM – Unfortunately in Greece we don't have a National Music Academy. This is a very important shortcoming. We need one; we need to invest in one. We have some private conservatories. Some of them have good teachers but some others do not. Young singers need to choose the right teachers to improve their singing art, but it is very difficult to do so in Greece. The most important Greek singers often need to go abroad to finish their studies.

But yes, the Greek National Opera is offering a Young Artists Program. We have improved the program in the last two years. We are a very vital organization. We have now about fourteen young singers. It's a two-year program. They study with our artists. They learn singing, dancing, foreign languages, and they collaborate with the conductors and directors. At the end of each year they present a full production. This year we had Mozart's *La Finta Semplice*. It goes very well because some of them start to have small and even bigger parts in our productions.

We also have a Ballet School. Our ballet company is very good. The director is Renato Zanella who used to be the director in Vienna. We not only have the ballet company but also the ballet school for very young dancers. They are learning classical ballet. It's very important because we have only one institution in Greece offering classical ballet. Also, in September of 2012 we started a Children's Choir. We have 80 young singers and they sang in the ceremony of the passing of the Olympic flame to the Russians for the Winter Olympic games. Our Children's Choir is very good.

OL – To finish let's talk a little more about the history of opera in Greece. We all know about Maria Callas, but are there other important landmarks, important works?

MM – Our company has about 70 years of age, and we had not only Maria Callas. We had composers who tried to build a national school in opera. An important one was Manolis Kalomiris. He composed, among other works,

Protomastoras based on a work of Nikos Kazantzakis – you know him, I'm sure, because he is the author of Alexis Zorbas. We also have Spyridon Samaras, a very important composer, and Dionysios Lavrangas, who was one of the people who made this institution. They all composed operas. Spyridon Samaras is the composer of the Olympic Anthem played everywhere today in the Olympic ceremonies.

OL – Let's talk about the future of the company. You told me a lot about the current programs. What are your ideas for the directions you want the company to go into?

MM – Our planning for our next five years include two years of preparation to get into our new house, then one year to transport everything to the new house, and then the first two years in the new house. We have the following goals: first of all, to improve our repertory. On this stage because of technical difficulties we didn't have the possibility to present bigger works. We will present bigger and wider repertory. We will present operas that have never been performed before in Greece.

Second, we will try to bring the lyrical theater to the community, to continue this relationship between lyrical theater and society. This is very important because we strongly believe that the lyrical theater is rich in history and is not for just one segment of society; it is for the whole society. We will have to find special points for each societal category, but will also engage in projects that appeal to the whole society.

The third goal is to bring lyrical theater to the schools and families. Fourth, we want to reach the ages between twenty and thirty-five. Fifth, we aim at improving our relationship with other theaters abroad, so that the Greek National Opera will belong to a group of theaters – I will not say leading theaters because it's a very big world – but we want to be one of the most important theaters of the Mediterranean. Well, we also have a sixth goal, it is to improve our recordings. We have plans for our first DVD production, with *Faust* by Gounod.

OL – What about you; how did you come to opera?

MM – I was born in Creta. I studied piano in Creta and music theory in Athens, simultaneous with Law school – I hold a Law degree. After I finished my studies in Law, I wanted to be a musician. Somehow my piano teacher drove me to conducting. I started Orchestra Conducting in the Berlin Academy. Then I started to work.

I think this is the best experience for a conductor's training: the opera theater. I was a young conductor and started to work in various opera houses in Germany. I was in Germany for about 14 years, ten of these as an opera conductor. I had the honor to be nominated Artistic Director at the Thessaloniki State Orchestra, in Northern Greece.

It was a regional orchestra but today it is more than regional and became an orchestra of a very high level. We arrived to the point of making a discography, and we recorded Beethoven with the famous soloist Aldo Ciccolini, the 3rd and 4th concertos. After seven years in Thessaloniki, it was very exciting for me to come here to become the Artistic Director of the Greek National Opera and try to rescue it from the crisis. I've been here since 2011.

OL – As a person, what do you like to do outside of music?

MM – I like to travel, to relax in fantastic places in Greece like our islands. You can't imagine how many nice places we have in Greece that are not famous. The famous places are too full of people, you cannot relax, but Greece, don't forget, has more than 1,400 islands.

OL – I was in Santorini this past week.

MM – Santorini, that's right. I was there last month. It is one of the most beautiful islands. It is unforgettable, with that ancient volcano. So, I like to travel, to be with friends, to go outside and relax and hike in the mountains, alone in nature, listening to music.

OL – That's what we had. Thank you very much.

MM – You're welcome.

.

DIVISION FOUR – THE STAGE DIRECTORS

CHAPTER EIGHT – STAGE DIRECTORS

Laurent Pelly

Opera Lively is thrilled to present to our readers the words of one of the most brilliant operatic stage directors in activity, Mr. Laurent Pelly. His answers to our questions are very entertaining and enjoyable. He directs and designs costumes for productions that are often surreal, exquisite in taste and wonderfully imaginative in both conception and execution. We interviewed him in July 2013.

Opera Lively – So you are in Santa Fe for *La Traviata.* Please talk about this production that you are doing for them for the second time.

Laurent Pelly – First of all, I'm very happy about reviving this production, because four years ago it was the first time I staged *La Traviata*, and also the first time I did any Verdi. Usually we don't get too much of an opportunity to rework a production in a revival, because there is a need to be very fast in rehearsals and we only have the time to do exactly the same thing. In Santa Fe however I had the time to revise the second act completely and I was actually able to do a brand new design, which is quite rare. When you approach a masterpiece like *La Traviata*, doing it again and having the time to rework it is never too much, because for this kind of piece, the work never ends.

OL – Has the concept changed?

LP – No, I'm using the same concept, with a very figurative setting that is at the same modern and dreamy. I don't have any intention of doing this piece in a traditional way. Have you seen any pictures?

OL – Not really, but I'll see the production in person, next week.

LP – Ah, OK. What I used is a set of blocs that look a little bit like a cemetery. The opening scene is mirrored on the novel *La Dame aux Camélias* by Alexandre Dumas fils, because as you know the novel, unlike the opera, starts with Marguerite Gautier's funeral. Our cemetery is evoked but not realistic. The same blocs also look like a model of a city, and can function as furniture as well. Then, this setting is useful in all four acts. After the funeral opening, the set becomes a plateau where the party at Flora's home happens.

When I did the production in 2009, the second act, the countryside scene, had some fake grass and it wasn't really successful. Therefore, this time I decided to use the same blocs for the second scene, but they open up and change from looking like tombstones to being backdrops of the sky with clouds and air that evoke liberty and are much more coherent for the scene. I think this new set is dreamlike and poetic and more appropriate to the arc of Violetta's story.

OL – This sounds fascinating. It is true that the novel proceeds in the opposite chronological order of the opera, something that Verdi tried to acknowledge by doing his overture also in reverse chronological order, with the death theme right at the beginning; so it is very interesting that you picked it up in your staging. Now, we have a completely different cast from 2009, so tell me about it. Natalie Dessay is so energetic on stage; does it work the same way with a different singer?

LP – Yes, the cast is not the same. On one hand, certainly this production was conceived for Natalie Dessay, and Brenda Rae is very different. On the other hand, I've done many productions with Natalie that were revived by other singers, and they worked fine. Of course, Natalie has her own style and creates a whole universe. We have an enormous rapport – she knows very well what I love and what kind of style of movement I appreciate, and she adheres to this.

It is true that this production forces Violetta to be very physically active, especially in the first act, and I didn't alter this for this revival; I kept almost exactly the same physicality. We changed the costumes for the second act because the old ones didn't go well with the new sets, but we kept the other costumes almost the same. But Brenda's personality is very different; therefore even though we use the same costumes, having a singer with another personality affects the emotional perfection of the show a lot.

Michael Fabiano who is doing Alfredo is also very different from Saimir Pirgu, but the chemistry between these two young singers, Michael and Brenda, is fantastic. I'm very happy with this part, because the emotional exchanges between them are very strong.

They are not exactly beginners, but they are at the start of their careers and have a wonderful energy. I'm very pleased to be reviving this with them. When I got to Santa Fe, I was thinking to myself, "Oh my, I'll have to revive this production, it won't be easy" – but in the end, it was a real pleasure.

OL – Talking about Ms. Dessay's unique talent, I'd say that your *La Fille du Régiment* seems to fit her like a glove.

LP – Yes. The entire production was planned specifically for Natalie, and even the adaptation of the libretto done by Agathe Mélinand [co-director of the Théâtre National de Toulouse Midi-Pyrénées] took into consideration Natalie's personality. However later the same production was done with three different singers, Patrizia Ciofi, Diana Damrau, and Aleksandra Kurzak, and it worked, because we had very precise instructions for all the playful movements. The only problem might be the language, because necessarily in *La Fille du Régiment* when the singers are not French, it might be more difficult. But with someone like Patricia Ciofi who is also a magnificent actress, there is no problem.

I believe that Natalie Dessay has left a legacy in this regard, and now, more and more I meet young singers who are very interested in theatrical acting. Even though I say that it is the music that takes priority in my productions, the inner workings of a character can often contribute to the evolution of the artist's singing. When a singer is not just fixated on the musical line but also interprets and builds up the character, the interpretation influences the singing.

OL – Perfect! Every time I see one of your productions, I notice that the music is always in close relationship with the character. When you are the stage director, it seems like you are able to obtain from your singers a style of performance in which, for example, when they sing a coloratura passage, it's not just for the sake of decoration, but if feels motivated by a clear dramatic justification. I believe that you have the means to work with the singers in finding or producing this motivation that links the music to the dramatic elements.

LP – What you are saying of my productions is very kind and gives me a lot of pleasure.

OL – Oh, I really love your productions. I have many of your DVDs; you are great.

LP – Thank you.

OL – I imagine that unlike spoken theater, when you are directing opera you might encounter differences of point of view between the stage director and the singers. You were first a stage director for spoken theater. This aptitude for finding the drama in the music, does it come naturally to you, or is it particularly difficult and the biggest challenge in staging an opera?

LP – Indeed, I always say that I primarily stage the music. What interests me is to tell a story, to make theater out of the music, to turn the music into something as lively as possible. It works for certain pieces, but it works less well for others. We can't use the same recipe every time, because the pieces are very different from each other. I always consider myself a craftsman who is a servant of the piece; the piece is not my servant. This is very important. I mean by this that I do not try to forcibly introduce a concept into the piece.

There are operas that need a new concept because they are a bit dated and dusty. This is particularly true of comedies because they don't age well, given that the public is no longer privy to the same culture that generated those comedic moments, so sometimes we need to find different ways to be effective. But I never try to imprint a forced concept onto the work; it's rather the other way around: it is the piece that inspires me. Most often, the music inspires me.

I don't really like the idea of tradition. I don't experience a need to make something traditional, but I don't fear it either. One needs to always be as sincere as possible. I have read the questions you sent me for this interview in advance, and this is part of one of your later questions: I always think about the kind of public that doesn't have a frame of reference. I don't think about the opera connoisseur, those who know all the works by heart and have seen ten thousand versions. I rather think of the public that has never seen the piece and is coming to an opera house for the first time. This kind of public might think "this is old and dated and not something that interests me today." For the sake of this segment of the audience, I try to ask myself how to deliver the most sensitive, the most lively emotion, and how to turn it into something that is contemporary, but without forcing anything.

OL – So, you've been directing opera since 1998, after a remarkable career in spoken theater, which continues to this day, in your capacity as director of the Théâtre National de Toulouse. Recently, you have directed *Mangeront-ils?* by Victor Hugo. I imagine that there is much more freedom when you stage spoken theater, without the constraints of a composer's recommendations and the musical requirements. What are the differences and similarities between directing spoken theater and opera?

LP – First, I just want to make sure that it is understood that I am primarily a spoken theater director. Your question says "after a career…" which might imply that one thing took over the other, but I define myself as a man of the theater.

OL – Yes, yes, I know that you continue to do both.

LP – That's it. I share my life between the theater and the opera. For me, I think I'd have anyway a hard time doing one without the other. Certainly I'd have trouble doing opera if I weren't a man of theater. The spoken theater allows me to question my own work, to challenge myself. When we have such a magnificent tool like the theater in Toulouse with all the means at our disposition, we have the time and the ability to invent new forms and to create experimental things and take more risks than in opera, which needs to be more efficient. In opera time is shorter. I say that in spoken theater we can look for something while in opera we have to find it! In opera given the musical, technical, and time constraints, one needs very strict planning. But I love to take advantage of the constraints and make of them sources for invention. This is why I feel so good in opera.

OL – Very good. But singers, I believe, arrive with a more fixed idea about their roles, as compared to theatrical actors. Does it affect the relationship between singers and stage directors?

LP – Yes, it is at the same time pleasant and complicated, the fact that singers may often know their role and the opera better than the director probably does, by virtue of the fact that they have played the role two, three, ten times, whereas the director is usually tackling the piece for the first time. But most singers are intelligent and experience a need for new suggestions and for hearing new ideas and another viewpoint about a piece, therefore in general it all goes down very well. For me, working with singers who master a role and have a very well constructed take on it but are also flexible, is very interesting. Sometimes there is some tension and some difficulty because there are more risks for the singer, but it is possible to relax and share those risks.

OL – In spoken theater you have recently directed *Macbeth*. Would you like to also direct Verdi's opera based on it? If you were to direct the opera, it would be the same tragedy but in another genre – what would have to change?

LP – Regarding the Scottish play, I don't know very well how to reply to this question. The play is a piece that I love in the theater; I find it extraordinary; but I have never approached Verdi's opera as a director. It was rather the other way around. It was when I saw Richard Jones' production of Verdi's opera at Glyndebourne that I experienced the need to read the play again and approach it in the theater. *Traviata* was my first Verdi. The opera *Macbeth* frightens me a little; I don't know if it is for me.

What I found extraordinary in Richard Jones'staging was that it was simultaneously heavy and somber, but funny. There was an element of derision that was wonderful. I said to myself "oh, OK, we can dare to do this!" At the same time, it was very respectful, painful, and very musical.

OL – We have talked about the relationship between the stage director and the singers. Now, let's talk about the conductor. When you approach a new production, what happens between these two artists who are the principal creators who have control over the final product, the conductor and the stage director? How do you manage the issue of creative control over the product? Are there frequent conflicts of artistic vision? Are there conductors you prefer to work with?

LP – In general, it all goes very smoothly. My operatic career started with Marc Minkowski. My very first operatic production fifteen years ago, *Orphée aux enfers*, was with him, as well as the next two, *Platée* and *La Grande Duchesse de Gérolstein*. Marc is a wonderful conductor and a good friend. I trust him. He loves theater and makes music theatrically even when he is conducting symphonic pieces. *Platée* is an extraordinary work, an absolute masterpiece that is very complex, and Marc Minkowskyi was the one who taught me how to see what is in the music.

The relationship with a conductor was the starting point for me, in opera. Today most of the time this relationship goes very well because I am very respectful of the music. I don't ask singers to sing with their back to the conductor when I know that it is a very difficult passage. I know how singing works technically so as a result, when a conductor realizes that I respect the musical work, it all goes very well. There were a couple of occasions when it wasn't as smooth, but I don't feel bad about it. For me, a good relationship between the stage director and the conductor is essential.

OL – In my interviews, I heard from different artists – conductors, singers, video directors – that they love to work with you because you understand the musical side of the opera. Have you received musical education?

LP – Yes, I had a lot of musical education when I was young. I was a chorus singer for ten years, and an oboe player for five or six years. Later I took singing lessons – not that I consider myself to be a singer, but I wanted to learn how it all worked, so I took lessons for three or four years. Now I have no more time for lessons, but I would have loved to continue. I think it is important, and that's why things go well between the singers and myself. Today, for example, it's the general rehearsal for *La Traviata* and I have an appointment with Brenda Rae to talk about her character, not only from the standpoint of acting, but also from the musical standpoint, and I feel close to her because I'm able to listen to the music.

OL – So, as you've been saying, you approach an opera first musically, therefore the libretto is not your starting point, right?

LP – Certainly it's always the music that is my starting point. Anyway, there are certain librettos that are just impossible. In November I'm doing *I Puritani* at Opéra Bastille, and that libretto is atrocious. It is of such a degree of silliness! But the music is sublime. It is true that one needs to make use of the libretto to stage an opera, but I'm planning to approach *I Puritani* rather musically.

OL – How much familiarity do you need to have with an opera before you start to work on your concept for the staging?

LP – It depends. Certain pieces, I don't need to listen to them one hundred times before I get my ideas. Sometimes it all happens very fast, in an instant. Certainly one needs to know an opera very well, its history, and its dramaturgy, but there are occasions when it all falls in place a bit simultaneously.

OL – Let's talk a bit more about Mme. Natalie Dessay. Many of your productions have her as the leading singer. Is it just a coincidence, or do you personally invite her and you insist with the opera company management that they need to have her come?

LP – It's not a coincidence, it's a shared choice. It's a well-established relationship. For *La Fille du Régiment*, for example, she was the one who insisted that I should be the stage director.

OL – Interesting!

LP – Yes. On the other hand, there were productions like *Pelléas et Mélissande* where it was the other way around. I had heard Natalie, Laurent Naouri, and Stéphane Degout in concert in Bourges, I think, and I proposed to the Theater an der Wien to do *Pelléas*, and next I suggested to them that we needed Natalie, Laurent, and Stéphane. But frequently, singers are hired earlier than the stage director. Singers at this level are very busy people; busier than I am, and their schedule is established years in advance, so often the stage director and the conductor are hired last.

OL – Is she active in the realm of ideas? Do you discuss the production with her, in advance?

LP – No. Natalie doesn't have preconceived ideas. She is very much a listener. Certainly we do discuss a lot, but not necessarily in advance.

OL – She is saying that she is about to retire from opera. Do you see other singers with whom you'd have a similar rapport, in the future?

LP – No, it's true that it will be a loss. But I've been lucky to meet extraordinary artists like Natalie and Anna Netrebko, and several others. This is one of the best parts of my profession. It is true that she will retire from opera after the *Manon* we are doing at the Capitole in September, but we have other projects. We experience the need to do spoken theater and musical comedy together. I think she is a bit sad about it, but we'll continue to work together.

OL – Let's talk about revivals. One of our staff members at Opera Lively bought your DVD of *L'Amour des Trois Oranges* and then went to see it live in Amsterdam. She liked it so much that she saw it again twice more. So, while comparing these four performances – the one recorded on DVD and the three she saw live at the theater – she noticed subtle differences each time. So, to what degree does a revival enjoy creative liberty over the original? Do you ask your singers to come up with new ideas? Do you try to work on your revivals in order to always make something new out of them? I heard that you aim at making productions that can withstand the test of time. Several of your productions have been revived, like *La Fille du Régiment, Cendrillon, L'Amour des Trois Oranges, Hoffmann*... Do you keep thinking about your past productions in an attempt to make them evolve?

LP – Regarding *L'Amour des Trois Oranges*, it is a show that I love. Productions disappear, they get destroyed, but this one we were successful in getting it picked up elsewhere. So, seven years later, it necessarily changes. *L'Amour des Trois Oranges* is a masterpiece like *La Traviata*, so we can redo it without any problem, without getting bored. This is not the case for *La Fille du Régiment.* I have trouble redoing it over and over, because it is not a very deep and powerful work [he laughs]. *Cendrillon* is magnificent, and each time I work with the singers to change some small things. I realize that there were some details that weren't right at the time of the creation, or were a bit awkward because we didn't have enough time to work them out, which is often the case. So, necessarily, things change.

OL – So, let's leave the revivals behind and talk about new productions. How much artistic freedom do you have when an opera company asks you to do a new production? Is it important to have the most complete freedom, or do you make concessions? Does it happen that they ask of you something excessive, and you end up refusing to continue the project?

LP – Most of the time there is complete freedom, certainly. It's the only way I can work. We have discussions when I show the mock-up, and there are concessions of a technical and economic nature that need to be made because you can't just do whatever you want, but artistically, it is essential to have freedom. Luckily, now I often am the one who makes the initial proposition to an opera house even of what operas to stage – they ask me "what do you feel the need to stage?" so for me it has been like this. I can't say how it happens for other directors.

OL – I'd say that for opera companies and video recording companies, to have the name Laurent Pelly on the poster or on the cover is an indication that they'll do good business, so I understand that in this prestigious phase of your career you are given the liberty of choosing your pieces. How do you make this choice?

LP – I have a very curious nature. I like to work with some pieces that aren't very well known or have been a bit forgotten.

OL – I have noticed that although you've done some 20th century operas, you haven't done any contemporary pieces – and by this, I mean 21st century works. Would you want to create a world premiere of a new opera? You've recently created a recital *Parlez Moi d'Amour* with Dame Felicity Lott. Doing a brand new piece must be pleasurable in terms of creative liberty.

LP – I dream of directing contemporary opera. It's a matter of opportunity. I haven't had the opportunity yet. I'd love to do it. For example, right now there is in Santa Fe the new opera *Oscar* about the life of Oscar Wilde, and I find it great to be able to invent something completely new.

OL – I very much liked your Ravel double bill at Glyndebourne – L'Enfant et les Sortilèges, and *L'Heure Espagnole.* Do you have good memories of it to share with us? This production of *L'Enfant* is one of those that have survived, given that it will be given soon at the Saito Kinen festival, and will be revived at Glyndebourne in 2015.

LP – I love Glyndebourne. I am crazy about *L'Enfant et les Sortilèges.* I was the one who proposed it, because I think it fits Glyndebourne very well. I love places like Santa Fe and Glyndebourne because unlike at the large repertory houses, we don't need to work as fast. We have time. At Glyndebourne we get great young singers and the chorus is made of young soloists. The conditions for set building are great. Like many people, I heard *L'Enfant* for the first time when I was a child. I think I was ten years old; it was one of my very first operas, so it's very emotional for me, to be able to direct it. I also feel much honored to work with Seiji Ozawa to revive it at the Saito Kinen. I have done two productions with Ozawa, and when he conducts, he displays great technique, extraordinary sensitivity, and he has an eye for opera that is of great intelligence and purity, like the way a child approaches something. So, I'm very happy about reviving this with Seiji.

OL – Your productions have been acclaimed by critics and by the public, but some of your colleagues haven't encountered as much unanimity, especially those who belong to the Regie movement. I wouldn't want to ask you to talk specifically about individual colleagues which would be uncomfortable, but what are your general views o the Regie movement and its legitimacy?

LP – It is a bit difficult to talk about this. I admire very much certain colleagues of mine. I have already mentioned Richard Jones, who is someone I like. I adore Robert Carsen; I have never met him personally. I adore Willy Decker as well. On the other hand, what I don't like is what I mentioned a while ago, when we have the person of the stage director enter the work, when we forget about the music, and when we impose a concept too forcefully upon a piece. But at the same time, like I said I am very curious, so I like the idea of being bold and taking risks.

Sometimes I discuss these matters with some people – not necessarily about my own productions – and after the discussion I'm left with the impression that I'm not bold enough. I admire people who take risks. Sometimes, it works; at other times it doesn't work at all. Actually, often it doesn't work. But often when it doesn't work, it's not because of the concept that is being proposed, but rather because of a lack of understanding of the music; this is what I think.

OL – Now we got to that question you've already partially answered, about the role of the audience, but maybe you will elaborate a bit more. Do you make art for the sake of art and this is enough for you, or do you make art for an audience? If it is the latter like you've already indicated it to be, then do you adapt your work to the prospective audience? In other words, are you more conservative or more avant-garde depending on the audience that will be attending the show?

LP – Actually sometimes I forget a bit that I'm working for an audience. Like I said, I prefer to think of the audience as people who aren't jaded, who haven't seen it all. Besides, this is why it is difficult for me to approach works like *La Traviata*, *Carmen*, or *Le Nozze di Figaro*, because they get more complex for the stage director. It is absolutely necessary to find new ideas, something original, and when it is a piece that has been shown hundreds of times all over the world, it is not easy to find something new, and it becomes a bit oppressive and blocking. Now, would I do it differently for an audience that is more avant-garde? No. If you think like that, you're screwed [laughs]. It's not a good way, for me.

OL – By the same token, does the fact that an opera will be recorded on video media influence the way you stage it? I'd imagine that certain space considerations on stage and the blocking would have to be a bit different to optimize the work for the small screen. Do you work with the video director and change the way your concepts are realized, when it's filmed opera?

LP – It doesn't change anything for the production, most of the time. Many productions now are being recorded on video media, and I love to work with the video director. I've worked with people who are great film directors; others, less so. But yes, sometimes the video director even gets to change your view of a piece. I think that some operas on video are more successful than at the theater – not often, but it has happened to me, sometimes, when the video directors' view was so good that it changed the rhythm of the production and delivered to it a supplementary breath. This is why I like to work with them. It is certainly very important to have them present during the rehearsals.

OL – Can you give us examples of pieces that were more successful on video than at the theater?

LP – For example, I loved what François Roussillon did with *La Vie Parisienne.* At the time, we did the piece three times, and François filmed the first one.

He gave to it a supplementary rhythm, some sort of madness that we were able to use for the subsequent shows, and the third time we got it really right. I love working with François Roussillon; he did something magnificent with our last one, *L'Enfant et les Sortilèges.*

OL – Indeed, he is very good. We've interviewed him as well [Volume 1] and his words were very interesting. Now, usually we don't see stage directors also designing the costumes, but you do it often. Is it out of a personal interest , or rather because you see them as an integral part of your artistic vision? What do you try to convey with your costumes? For example, you had a rather provocative costume for Natalie Dessay as Cleopatra in your production of *Giulio Cesare.*

LP – I always design the costumes for all my shows, for spoken theater as well as for opera. Now I've been designing the sets too, mostly for theater but also for example for my next *Le Comte Ory.* For me, designing a costume helps me to get into the character's head and to have a clearer view of the character's history.

Regarding Natalie Dessay's costume, it's funny, because we read a lot about Cleopatra, and the answer is very simple: there isn't a single representation of her in the history of art where she doesn't have a naked breast. For this production, we wanted to mix ancient history and works that were contemporary to the real Cleopatra and Julius Caesar, with the 19th century artistic representations of them in paintings and sculptures. And frankly, for me the fact that she always has one of her breasts naked is important because it makes of her a provocative character – and she was one. So, the nudity is not gratuitous.

OL – Oh, interesting. We loved your *Giulio Cesare* presented like a night in the museum. It had a poignant quality, of these historical characters recreating their lives in the middle of marble statues and indifferent curators. This seems to appeal to the metaphor of the operatic art form itself, in its continuous effort to revive the ghosts of the past and present them to the public as something more lively and relevant than museum pieces.

LP – Yes, that's exactly it.

OL – So, your *Le Comte Ory* in Lyon in January 2014 and at La Scala in July will have sets designed by you. Do you feel that it is important to design the sets yourself, in order to have a more direct expression of your visual concepts?

LP – I've always been interested in set design and I adore working with the designers. I work preferentially with a couple of them. First of all, Chantal Thomas with whom I've done several productions, who authored the set designs notably for *La Traviata*, *I Puritani*, and *Manon*, which are my next pieces. There is also Barbara de Limburg with whom I did *Cendrillon*, and *L'Enfant et les Sortilèges.*

The set design for *Le Comte Ory* was actually a bit of a hassle, because neither Chantal nor Barbara where available and it is always difficult to find a new designer, because with the new one I won't necessarily have the same intimacy and I won't share the same vocabulary. While I was waiting for another designer, I suddenly found that I was having fun thinking about the set design and decided to do it myself, given that I love *Le Comte Ory* very much and it is a piece that I don't fear.

OL – How do you find inspiration for your productions? Do you start from some core idea?

LP – The inspiration comes from the music, from deep listening. Next, it's my personality. I love to tell stories. I love to have a view that has a certain dose of humor. I've always done it this way, but it is hard to explain. I'm also a big lover of theatrical literature and of prose as well. These have always nourished me, and have brought me a lot.

OL – You seem to have enormous talent for comedic opera. But you have also successfully directed some magnificent pieces of serious opera, like *Pelléas et Mélissande*, *La Voix Humaine*, and *Barbebleue.* What is your preference, and why? After a series of comedies, your *Pelléas et Mélissande* was very tortured.

LP – It is true that I prefer comedies. I love telling stories in a comic faction. But what interests me in comedy, is gravitas. It's the somber, dark aspect. For me, a comedy is only funny if it is black. And reversely, in tragedies what I find interesting is to look for not necessarily humor, but at least a certain critical view of things.

Pélleas, like *Traviata*, is a bit intimidating. It is heavy and affected me deeply. I would like to redo it, because these days I have a different view of it – not musically, but regarding Maeterlinck's black complacency. It's something I think about now, but hadn't noticed five years ago. That's why I'd like to redo it.

OL – One of your biggest successes with the critics was your production of *Les Contes d'Hoffmann* in Barcelona and in San Francisco. This magnificent opera can be called a mix of comedy and tragedy. Is it ideal for you, given what you just said?

LP – Yes, that's it. Indeed I adore *Les Contes d'Hoffmann* precisely because of this. It is the same reason why I adore *L'Amour des Trois Oranges*, because it is also a very somber comedy. *Hoffmann* is an extraordinary piece and I find something new in it every time I stage it. Offenbach's genius is in the mixture of gravitas and humor, and that's why I love him so much.

OL - *Robert le Diable*, on the other hand, had less favorable reviews. However, one of our staff members saw the production live at the Royal Opera House and loved it. I haven't seen it yet, but I'm planning to buy the blu-ray. It is rather rare to see a Laurent Pelly production that doesn't gather almost unanimous critical praise. It is true that one can't please everybody, but do you see something you'd have done differently, or plan to change in a revival? Or are you rather content with this production, and shrug off the criticism for the sake of what I've just said, that it is impossible to please everybody all the time?

LP - *Robert le Diable* did not achieve unanimity; this much is certain. We can't please everybody; true. For one, it's a very complex and heavy piece. It is very long and full of constraints, musically very difficult, and requires considerable resources to put on. Regarding the sets and costumes, the creative process was complicated because we did not have the means to do any more than what we did. I don't think this work can be shown today, as it is, at face value. I tried to have some fun with it and to work on another layer, with some humor, because this Nineteenth Century piece is very excessive and outdated. We can't take it seriously. I was rather surprised that people blamed me for my approach. After all, it's such a complex work, and for me certain scenes in our production were more successful than others, but often this was because of a question of resources rather than due to our artistic choices.

OL – You have focused most of your work on the French repertoire. Beyond the obvious fact that you are a Frenchman, what makes of this repertoire the ideal fit for you? Does your choice stem from some sort of mission to diffuse national culture, or from a special rapport with the literature, the theater, and the music of your homeland since childhood? Do you see any part of the non-French repertoire that you'd like to further explore in the future?

LP – No, it isn't a mission of diffusing national culture; it's rather a matter of choice or taste. It is true that I prefer to work in French because I believe I can contribute more to the singers and to the production. I have the impression that in French I am more able to do my directorial work, just like I do for spoken theater. I don't want to work, today, in a language that I don't understand. I could work in English but I haven't yet staged an English-language opera. I don't want to stage Czech works any longer. I personally adore Janáček and the Russian repertoire, but I don't want to stage their operas because I don't speak their languages. It's the same thing with Wagner. I don't speak German and I think that to stage Wagner, one needs to speak fluent German. For me, to work with a translation is frustrating. I love being closer to the words. It's a choice I've been exerting more and more.

OL – What is in the horizon for the near future?

LP – My next productions will be *Le Comte Ory* and *I Puritani*, then *Don Pasquale* in Santa Fe. I have a project of going back to Offenbach with *Le Roi Carotte*, which has a fairy tale quality. It will happen at L'Opéra de Lyon. Then, there is *L'Étoile* in Amsterdam. As for spoken theater, next season I have *Le Songe d'une nuit d'été*. We'll redo the Scottish play [*Macbeth*] in Paris. Then, I'll do a piece with Agathe Mélinand on Edgar Allan Poe. So, it will be a busy season.

OL – For the last few questions of this interview I'd like to turn to the man underneath the artist. How was your journey towards opera? Were you interested in opera since a young age, or did your taste for opera start later in life?

LP – I have had an interest in opera for a long time. Before directing opera, I did a lot of musical theater. Theater that includes music is something that has always pleased me. The idea of directing opera came to me from Jean-Pierre Brossman who was at the time the director of L'Opéra de Lyon. It happened fifteen years ago. I was the director of the Centre Dramatique National in Grenoble, and Marc Minkowski was – and still is – the director of L'Orchestre de Grenoble. Jean-Pierre Brossman had the idea of getting Marc and me together to do *Orphée aux Enfers*. This is how everything started. So, I have to thank Jean-Pierre for this.

OL – What are your other interests outside of opera, either in the artistic field, or in the realm of more personal pursuits?

LP – What I like about opera and theater is that these are universal domains, and more so than other artistic genres. In opera and theater we approach painting and history and philosophy.

I work a lot so I don't have much time to pursue other interests, and I'm lucky that my field does touch on other artistic fields because I like the arts in general. My biggest hobby beyond the arts is nature. It's a true passion. I love nature, hiking, and traveling.

OL – How do you describe your personality?

LP – Describing oneself is difficult. I have the impression that I love sharing. If I do theater, it's to share it with others and be part of a company. A stage director can't do anything on his own. What I love in theater is the team. What I find fascinating in opera is that when we work in a production of a grand opera with chorus, we have almost two hundred people who are together giving all their energies to the project. When we get to the point of showing the work to the public, it's wonderful.

OL – We've reached the end of our interview.

LP – Yes, I barely saw the time passing. I talk and talk, and it's been more than one hour!

OL – Perfect. I loved the fact that you gave us enough time to reply to all the questions we had.

LP – I thank you very much. When you come to see *La Traviata*, I hope you will like it.

OL – Yes, I believe it will be formidable. I've seen many of your productions and each time, they are magnificent.

LP – Aw, thank you so much!

Francesca Zambello

On the occasion of the 2013 Glimmerglass Festival in August, Opera Lively has interviewed in person the gifted American stage director Francesca Zambello, focusing on the company and how she put together the festival, as well as on her production of *The Flying Dutchman* and other aspects of her illustrious career. We touched a bit on her tenure at Washington National Opera as well since she also accumulates the function of Artistic Director of that company.

Opera Lively – Thank you for doing this, Ms. Zambello; I'm a great admirer of our work. Let's start by talking about your ideas for the Glimmerglass Festival, which you joined as the Artistic and General Director in September of 2010, in time to plan for the 2011 season. What has been your focus for each edition of the festival that you have directed, so far?

Francesca Zambello – My focus for each season was to experience, through our core repertory, different ways of thinking about the world, politics, and the human condition. In 2011, the main arc was the exploration of strong female protagonists. In 2012 it was social change. This season, we are celebrating the American Romantics.

OL – Is it important to have a concept that guides the festival?

FZ – It is. We don't need to be the slaves of the concept, but the experience is richer if there is a greater take away. So, we put on stage operas, musicals, and concerts, and we discuss the issues and ideas embedded in these works, in our "Meet me at the Pavillion" programs.

OL – How are you highlighting the American Romantics, this season?

FZ – Given the bicentenaries of Wagner and Verdi, we are honoring all the Romantics, not just the Americans, but I wanted our audience to see that we are part of a bigger historical and cultural movement, so we partnered with the Fenimore Art Museum in town, which is presenting a major exhibition of American Romantic painters, a majority from the Hudson River School. These painting reflect three typical American themes of the 19th century: discovery, exploration, and settlement, as well as the pastoral landscapes where people and nature coexist in harmony. The literature of idealism and Romanticism finds a voice in our collaborative literary series at Hyde Hall, in nearby Glimmerglass State Park, featuring writers like James Fenimore Cooper who of course came from Cooperstown, and also Nathaniel Hawthorne, Henry David Thoreau, Ralph Waldo Emerson, and Emily Dickinson.

OL – How did you pick your music for this Romantic-themed festival?

FZ – When you look to the Romantic era in music, two of the pillars are Verdi and Wagner. They revolutionized opera as music theater – with Wagner's Gesamtkunstwerk and Verdi's real and dramatically credible stories. I wanted to present two of their earlier operas, written almost at the same time. Then, I added the musical *Camelot* which makes reference to a place of idyllic happiness. The Arthurian legend is within the concept of Idealism and Romanticism. Our fully staged double bill called *Passions* examines the Transcendental Movement which is in many ways in sync with the core philosophy for the individual in the Romantic Movement, even though it contains older music like Pergolesi's Stabat Mater. The other piece is contemporary, David Lang's *The Little Match Girl Passion*, but it borrows the form of Bach's *St. Matthews Passion.* The piece was revised to showcase the talent of our Glimmerglass Children's Chorus with 24 local children.

OL – Why were you attracted to this theme, here at Glimmerglass?

FZ – I was first attracted to this region thanks to its idyllic ways. Culture and nature reside very harmoniously here, in this setting.

I have been long drawn to the art, literature, and music of the Romantic period. The movement places emphasis on feelings such as self-examination, awe, the importance of the individual, often experienced through the sublimity of untamed nature and its picturesque qualities. It all came together in our festival.

OL – Nice! Tell us a bit about the history of the company.

FZ – Its first season was in the summer of 1975, with four performances of *La Bohème* in a high school auditorium in Cooperstown. This beautiful Alice

Busch Opera Theater opened in 1987. The name of the company comes from the surface of the Otsego Lake, the "Glimmerglass" of James Fenimore Cooper's *Leatherstocking Tales*. Our theater was the first one built specifically for opera since the new Met opened in 1966.

Productions have been presented in repertory since 1990. At first the company did only opera and was called Glimmerglass Opera, then there was a musical added in 2008. Since 2011 we've been presenting three operas and one musical each July and August and we changed the name to Glimmerglass Festival as we broadened the offers. Now we offer more than 40 performances, each summer, and we sold 33,000 tickets in 2012.

OL – How much does it cost to get this all done?

FZ – Our operating budget is of about $6 million.

OL – Where does the audience come from?

FZ – About 70% of our audience comes from New York State, with 12% coming from New York City, and 50% coming from a two-hour radius of Cooperstown.

OL – What does it take, in terms of human resources, to run the festival?

FZ – We have a year-round staff of 20 people; then we get some 90 seasonal production staff and some 25 seasonal administration and operations staff, helped by 50 interns. We have about 50 guest artists and 40 young artists. Then, you need all sorts of other human resources, like 15 parkers, 25 concessions employees… Our orchestra has almost 50 musicians. We get visiting Master Teachers and Coaches, conductors, assistant conductors… not to forget the volunteers, who are more than 200 guild members and 180 ushers. We have to house some 240 individuals – we lease 65 properties and own 6 more.

OL – Wow! It's a big operation. Tell me more about the Young Artist Program.

FZ – It was founded in 1988 and it brings singers in the first stages of their careers. Each year we have about 1,100 applicants. The focus is on education through performance. They cover roles and perform roles, and receive musical coaching, attend classes in diction and acting, and are given instruction in audition techniques, role preparation, and the business side of managing a career.

OL – Now, let's talk more precisely about the operatic aspects, and your role as stage director. First, this production of *The Flying Dutchman.* You made the entire action to be concentrated on Daland's ship, and the ropes seem to acquire a symbolic weight. Please tell me about your concept for the production.

FZ – You are a psychiatrist, you certainly must know that teenage girls are obsessed. They have a fascination with Gothic, and suicide is unfortunately a sad part of many teenagers' lives, I think, and that's where my point of departure was. Wagner of course wrote that she is obsessed with the Dutchman, but I wanted to have it as a question: is this in Senta's mind? Is it always happening on the boat of her father? What is that obsession?

The ropes are many things. Of course, on the surface they are the ship, but they are also weaving; spinning, they are phallic, and eventually of course they are what she kills herself with. I just wanted a true line that was something you could see with a teenager today, even if we set the piece in something historical; the costumes are suggestive of the 19th century. But that was my reason, to make her a teenager like the ones we see today. That's the tragedy of a lot of youth. Look at things like *Twilight, Interview with the Vampire*, all of that is this same story.

OL -Melody Moore [this production's Senta] in her interview with us told me that you direct opera with an eye for what members of the audience who haven't been thoroughly exposed to opera are seeing or experiencing. If you agree with this characterization, please elaborate.

FZ – Yes, here and in a lot of places, it is our job to not obscure the story, but to make it as clear as possible. That may mean that we are interpreting the story in a certain way, but it's got to be clear for the public.

OL - Senta in your production hangs herself instead of drowning herself at sea. We talked about the symbolism of the ropes, but was there any other particular reason for your choice of how to stage the ending?

FZ – It has to be clear that she is saving the Dutchman. Her action is about him. He tells her, "don't come with me." She makes a decision to die with him. I wanted to make it clear that she is dead, and her death-fantasy, her death-wish is that she is reunited with him. That's why I had the double Senta and the Dutchman going up together on a ship. There is a lot about Daland, her father, and the Dutchman. Does she have father envy? What is going on? It's all part of it.

OL - You have directed both operas and musicals (*Showboat*, for example). How are these different in your experience? Are there things which are easier to do in operas than in musicals, or vice versa?

FZ – It's funny, because in some ways it is similar. Your job as a director is to tell the story, number one; then, create the characters, use the material, be faithful to the material. Sometimes the stories are clearer in musicals than in operas. The way that you work with actors is different than it is with opera singers. It's a different vocabulary, but the process is still the same – you're rehearsing. You are in a room all day, figuring out the characters and the story. In that way, it's connected. But the type of work is different because actors and opera singers are different, although opera singers are actors also, and sometimes actors are very good singers.

OL – Maybe opera singers have a different mindset already, because of the music? Do they resist more when you give them stage directions?

FZ – No, nowadays opera singers are very flexible. They want to be theatrical. I don't know any opera singer now – I haven't worked with any – who says "this is how I do it." In the beginning of my career, people said it more often.

OL – Yes, there's been a shift towards more flexible acting.

FZ – Yes.

OL - Glimmerglass is committed to featuring one grand American musical every season. I'll adopt the Devil's Advocate stance for this question. One might say that Broadway is doing very well, thank you. Why are opera companies and opera festivals often featuring musicals, instead, for example, of focusing on American new opera? I know you're doing both next season, but why do you really need to include a musical? One argument I saw you taking was that it broadens the audience. However Glimmerglass has pretty much sold out performances if I can gauge by the ones I've attended; is there really a need for including musicals?

FZ – Well, you didn't come in July, when there were nights when it was empty. I need to sell more tickets in July. I tell people, "if you want good seats, come in July. You can get ticket deals, and it is cheaper." August, it sells very well. Tell everybody to come in July, please.

OL – All right. But do you really feel that there is a need to expand into this repertory?

FZ – Absolutely. First of all, I think that musicals are our own American opera. They are not operas, but they are the equivalent art form that we invented. We made musicals. Italians made opera. Germans made operetta and Singspiel. The English made Gilbert and Sullivan. We made musicals. Every American opera singer – and we use 99% of American artists, here – when they were in school, the first music that they knew came from musicals, or church music. I want to see them in musicals, and they want to perform in musicals.

OL - As director of Glimmerglass and now as Artistic Director of the Washington National Opera, will you be engaging in any joint activities between these two entities?

FZ – Yes. Some of our young artists here will be coming to our Young Artist Program in Washington DC, and then they will come back here in leading roles. Some productions will start here and go to Washington.

OL - What are your plans for the future of WNO? Again, the Devil's Advocate might argue that WNO in the past has lagged behind other major national companies. I for one would love to see a strong renaissance (it's at driving distance from where I live).

FZ – Me too. My plan is to have more American performers, conductors, designers, composers over there: more American stars. I want more operas about a political connection, and more world premieres. I'm doing a lot of short operas premieres. I also want more operas in English, and productions that have a political feeling.

OL – So I gather that you are trying to make the quintessential American opera company, in our nation's capital. Is that what you are trying to accomplish?

FZ – Yes, exactly.

OL - You did a *Ring* for San Francisco in co-production with the WNO but the latter ended up not putting it on. A *Ring* can almost break the bank with LA's coming in at $32 million and the Met's north of $20 million. Any plans to revisit this, in the future?

FZ – Yes, we've scheduled it for April and May of 2016. We'll have three cycles.

OL - Let's talk about your SF *Ring*. I understand you focused on American history. Would you tell us more about your concept?

FZ – Well, myth, more than history. History to some degree, but more specifically I focused a lot on American myth and American imagery, because I wanted it to be more familiar to our audiences.

OL - What is involved in this massive undertaking of directing the full *Ring*?

FZ – Endless rehearsal, and I mean, endless; non-stop, for ten weeks.

OL -It seems like a pity that your San Francisco *Ring* isn't out on DVD. I'm no expert on the DVD market although we have interviewed some videographers in the past like François Roussillon. But I'd risk the guess that the *Ring* has such a worldwide following that the public is always hungry for seeing another DVD version. Have you thought of it, and what is involved in the decision of doing it versus skipping the filming of it?

FZ – I know François Roussillon. He was the producer of some things I directed. He is a nice guy. But it's just too expensive to produce the DVD, because of the unions.

OL – Will the revival in Washington DC be filmed for DVD?

FZ – I doubt it. It's too expensive. People don't want to spend that money. It's a lot of money, so the public will have to just come and see it.

OL - You are known for directing some of opera's great large-scale epics like Wagner's *Ring*, Berlioz's Les *Troyens*, and Prokofiev's *War and Peace*). What are the most important requirements for a director working on this scale?

FZ – Patience! [laughs] No, you have to have a clear sense of how to marshal everyone. The *Ring* is long but each scene is not big. *The Trojans* and *War and Peace* are big; there are a lot of people. Most *Ring* scenes have two or three people, except for *Götterdämmerung*, while *Les Troyens* has huge chorus scenes.

Those big operas, you really have to plan what you are going to do, how you are going to do it, and how it is going to look like, very specifically. It can change in rehearsal, but you need to have a plan. You need to know what to do when you have four hundred people like in *War and Peace*. It's a lot of people; you have to be clear about what everybody is doing, so I map it all out. Now, I like doing these pieces like the *Dutchman*, which are smaller. It's fun to do a big opera in a small situation like this; you really get at the relationships.

OL – Many of your productions are visually striking.

FZ – Good, thanks.

OL – Do you plan for this yourself, or do you rely more on your set designers?

FZ – I work with designers, but I usually have a clear idea of what I want to do, and how I want to do it. It's important to have a clear approach.

OL - Your 2000 production of Prokofiev's *War and Peace*, the first time the work was ever staged at the Opéra National de Paris, drew boos during the final dress rehearsal for its unflattering portrayal of Napoleon. Though you described the reaction as just "a joke," did you find yourself considering possible French audience responses as you staged this piece?

FZ – No! It was written by a Russian; of course he made Napoleon not a nice person! Yes, I forgot about that, oh God. You know, [sighs] the French are very nationalistic. So are the Russians. So are the Americans, but I think we have a little more openness. Prokofiev made Napolean a caricature, in the piece.

OL – What is your opinion of Regietheater?

FZ – If it is good, it is good. If it is bad, it is bad. You can't say "yes" or "no" to anything. I try to do Regietheater where we are really focused on the people. The people are the most important thing, for me.

OL -Let's talk about your ROH *Carmen.* That production really has legs. In my opinion it is one of the two best *Carmens* on video ever (together with Domingo's and Migenes'). Maybe the very best.

FZ – Thank you! Thank you!

OL - The stars really aligned with some great performances by the principals. What do you think is the reason why this atmospheric performance really captured audiences' imaginations?

FZ – Everyone thinks they know *Carmen.* Everyone wants to be Carmen, or Don Giovanni. You have to create the character so that the audience wants to go on her journey. That is what I worked on with Anna Catarina Antonacci and Jonas Kaufmann. It was their debut in these roles. You can't play the stereotype. You have to play the need - her need for freedom. "If it comes, it comes" – that's not the character. The character has an obsession, and a drive. It's the same with Senta. Every character has one central need. Figaro needs to marry Susanna. Rosina needs to make her husband prove that he can be faithful. The count needs to get in bed with Susanna. That's what I start with, in any show –what is it that everybody needs? You are a shrink, you know this. It's primal, right? What is the primal instinct of the character? You have to understand that, before you can do anything.

OL - Please describe your creative process. How does an idea start to germinate? Do you start from listening to the music, reading the libretto, testing a number of different ideas?

FZ – Everything. I read the source material, the libretto, I listen to the music, and I do it all at the same time, over a long period of time, like six months. I don't do it in a day. It takes a long time to absorb something. I ask myself what is the story I'm telling. What must we have, visually, to tell the story? *Butterfly*? We need a knife. What is the most important prop? We don't need a telescope but we do need a knife. You figure out what you really need, and then you build it up from there.

OL - How involved do you get in the process of selecting principal singers? Now that you are directing this festival and the Washington DC company, you must have a much bigger say, but how about before?

FZ – I pick them all, now. And in a lot of places that I worked before, I got to pick them all, as well.

OL - Do you find yourself doing anything different when you know that a production will be released on DVD such as your *Carmen* and your *Cherevichki*?

FZ – No, no. I mean, the TV camera is going to do what it is going to do. People know it is a performance. You can't direct it like you are directing a film.

OL -How did you get to love opera, growing up? Does it have to do with your Italian-American background?

FZ – Yes, it does. My mother loved it, and she brought me to the theater with her. I fell in love with opera. I fell in love with the trio from *Così*.

OL - What are some of your extra-operatic interests?

FZ – Outside of opera, I love nature, so I love hiking, kayaking, doing outdoor activities – skying, snowshoeing, tennis… that's it.

OL -How do you describe your take on life?

FZ – I feel pretty lucky. I'm very happy; I'm married. My wife went to Duke, she is an attorney. I think you have to have an outside life to be an artist. Some people who are artists think they have to suffer all the time. I don't want to suffer. I mean, I want to suffer, thinking, but I don't want to be in pain about work. I want to enjoy it. I love what I do.

OL – What about your personality?

FZ – I'm pretty outgoing, because I love what I do, so I try to convey it to people. I proselytize about it.

OL – Anything you want to add?

FZ – Just that I look forward to seeing your site. Thank you, it was nice talking to you.

OL – Thank you!

Christian Räth

On the occasion of the 2013 Glimmerglass Festival staging of Verdi's early comedic opera *Un Giorno di Regno* (King for a Day), Opera Lively interviewed in August the German stage director Christopher Räth about that production, and his work in general (Wagnerians will like his comments on the *Ring*).

Opera Lively - First, let's talk about Verdi's *Un Giorgno di Regno* (*King for a day*) which you are directing for Glimmerglass. We'll start by addressing the piece itself, before talking about your production of it. This first attempt at comic opera by Verdi was thought to be a flop at the time of its La Scala premiere, since Verdi was in no mood to compose a comic opera after having lost to disease his daughter, his son, and his wife in rapid succession. What is your view of the piece in terms of its comic success or lack thereof?

Christian Räth – When I was offered the piece I didn't know *Un Giorgno di Regno.* I think most people don't know it. I was, like everybody else, a little bit skeptical of the piece, but I actually found that it is a very light and pleasant piece that has many comic situations. It is very interesting from a musical point of view.

OL - You studied musicology, which is admirable and must greatly inform your work as an operatic director. So please tell me how you feel about the musical side of *Un Giorno di Regno.*

CR - The comic dynamic lies mostly in the music. You can hear influences of Rossini and Donizetti. The music already invites comedy. The music is interesting not only because of the influences Verdi at the time was taking like a sponge from the music he knew, but also because in many moments you can hear music that you will hear later in other pieces, in *Falstaff*, or *Nabucco*, or *Don Carlos.* So the genius is already there; it's just that it will take a few more pieces for him to completely develop his style. People who know all the later Verdi pieces will have fun discovering all the future references in it. The plot is of course typical for that time.

OL - What concept are you bringing to the production?

CR - I tried to pull this whole story as close as possible to us, nowadays, because I felt that the original story is a little dated. Part of the problem at the time when it was premiered in La Scala was that already people might not have the right references, because it wasn't a libretto originally written for that occasion. Verdi used one that seemed to be the least terrible, at the time.

We had the chance to write a new translation into English. At Glimmerglass, this is being performed in English translation by the dramaturg Kelley Rourke who is very clever with the language. She gave it a contemporary touch in the words that she employed.

I felt that for this story about a king appearing at this house where two weddings are about to take place, it would be nice to take a contemporary view on it. It made me think about how people nowadays are so fascinated by celebrity, how everybody wants to be a celebrity even if it is just for one day. If you look at reality TV today it's all about people trying to be famous, when in fact they are not. There are references that are contemporary in the large sense, reaching from the 1950's and 1960's until today. It's more an inspiration than an attempt to reproduce the 1960's.

OL - Please tell me about the cast of singers you got at Glimmerglass, and how they are reacting to your direction.

CR – Most of the singers in this production are part of the Young Artists Program, so they are all young and they are all having their debuts in these roles because nobody has sung that piece over there before. Three members of the cast are more accomplished professionals already. They are a great group to work with. They are absolutely 100% behind the concept and the style my collaborators and I were looking for - the choreographer, the set designer, and the costume designer. We really had a wonderful time working on this piece. They are all extremely talented young singers.

Also, something that is very special at Glimmerglass is the chorus. Although it's a small chorus of sixteen people, eight men and eight women, they are all young soloists, so they bring another energy to the performance as well. It made a big difference for the whole show.

OL - How is the working environment at Glimmerglass, in terms of the artistic freedom you were given to direct *Un Giorno di Regno* ?

CR – The environment is lovely. It is a very beautiful place. They have now just opened a big new rehearsal studio, which gives us the best conditions to work. There is total artistic freedom. I started to work in the project about a year and a half ago with the set designer, then the dramaturg came on board and we worked together on the English translation of it. We really had *carte blanche*, so to speak.

OL – Great, I'm excited about it, and look forward to attending the production. Let's switch now to other subjects regarding your career. An interesting angle of your work is what you did with a video artist for the Dallas *Tristan und Isolde*; please tell us about it.

CR – Yes, I collaborated for that *Tristan* in Dallas with a videographer called Elaine McCarthy, a quite well known video artist who has done a lot of opera and many shows on Broadway. She is visually a very inventive artist. This was given in 2011, and we worked for about a year and a half laying out a whole pool of images that I thought would go well with this piece. When we all got together in the rehearsals in Dallas at the new opera house, it got very exciting. It was a very satisfying experience.

OL – Talking about Wagner's pieces, you are no stranger to staging Wagner's *Ring*, since you collaborated with Francesca Zambello for the 2010/2011 complete *Ring* cycle at San Francisco Opera. This is a hot topic at this moment, with the controversy surrounding the current *Ring* at Bayreuth. Seattle Opera has arguably the last traditional *Ring* in the world and many companies have been so adventurous with it that public reactions have been mixed, to say the least. How do you think the *Ring* ought to be staged, today?

CR – That is of course a once-in-a-lifetime experience. As a director or associate director you don't get an offer to stage the *Ring* every day. We started working on it piece by piece. We prepared *Rheingold*, *Die Walküre*, and *Siegfried* a few years ago for Washington DC. The Washington National Opera was a co-producer and they were planning to present it but they had to cancel for various reasons, but San Francisco went ahead, and we did the whole cycle in one go, which is a big undertaking. It took a lot of very complicated planning; we had three sessions a day for three months every day to go through the whole material.

I think it was a very interesting production in the sense that Francesca's concept was to create an American *Ring*, and to use American history and imagery to retell the story for an American audience of today. I feel that this *Ring* worked because it really tried to tell the story through the people, through each character, rather than having a big technical toy, which obviously for financial reasons wasn't even possible.

For me the main issue in staging the *Ring* is to really allow the public to follow the story and to understand the psychology of all the characters. Whether it is a traditional setting or a contemporary setting, it doesn't really change the detailed work you have to do to stage it.

I haven't seen the current production at Bayreuth; I've just seen a few photos so I can't really judge it. I can't say if I personally like the production or not. As always, Wagner's operas and especially the *Ring* tend to be very close to people's hearts, so the reaction is always a little more extreme, I feel. Some people are kind of religious about it and they feel the need to protect the story the way they think Wagner would have imagined it. In general, as a director – at least that's the way I see it – you should always think out of the box; not to provoke the audience, but to tell the story as well as you can, the way you think it should be told in the world of today. Every production you do, you make choices, and they might please some people, while other people might reject them. The *Ring* is such a big work that it allows for different approaches, and then, it's for the public to decide whether they like it or not.

To do the whole *Ring* at Bayreuth in one go is a huge undertaking, but over the years of life of that production, usually the director gets a chance to rework some passages and to improve the work, so it may be too soon to judge this current production.

OL - What is your opinion of recent efforts to stage an abridged version of the *Ring*? We got a 7-hour version in Buenos Aires and a 4-hour version in Minneapolis. Do you see pitfalls in doing this?

CR – I don't really know the abridged versions – I know of them. I personally think it is a good way to present this work. If you are a Wagner buff and you've studied the *Ring* inside and out, of course you will want the complete version, but for an audience that is not as educated it's a good way to get to get to know these pieces and to open doors to discover parts of them, and maybe to get interested in knowing the whole cycle. As we all know, to sit through the whole *Ring* is a long commitment.

OL - Although I've never been to it, I've always been curious about the floating stage at the Bregenz Festival, where you've stage-directed twice. Can you tell us a bit about the challenges and advantages of doing a production there?

CR – I worked twice on the floating stage at Bregenz. I collaborated with Francesca Zambello in *West Side Story* and then another time with Robert Carsen in a production of *Il Trovatore*. Bregenz is quite an extraordinary place to work because of the breathtaking stage on the lake. It's unique in the world. The size of that stage is enormous. Usually you have to deal with about two hundred people on stage, including all the chorus and supers and dancers, so often times it is challenging to work there. What is so incredible about it is the nature around it, the lake. I remember a performance we had of the *West Side Story*, and towards the end of the piece before Tony gets shot, a big storm started, and it was pouring down. It was one of those moments you never forget. People were soggy but it couldn't have been staged better. In the pouring rain, nobody in the audience moved, because it was so special.

OL – Nice! I'd also be curious to know how a quintessential American opera, *Porgy and Bess*, is received in Europe, since you've directed it in Lyon.

CR – It was a production in collaboration with a couple of French choreographers and video artists called José Montalvo and Dominique Hervieu, who are very well known in Europe; maybe less in the United States. Their work is very unique in the sense that they use interactive video. They film the singers and the dancers in the pre-production period, and then they work with the video image and transform it in astounding ways, morphing and transforming one person into another, and then they actually have the filmed character and the live character interact, which is something very unique that I hadn't ever seen before. It was a completely original approach.

At the time we used a group of dancers with a mix of different styles – there were hip-hop, ethnic dances, capoeira, classic ballet, street dances, all kinds of dances that you would see today in the streets. That is what made it special and gave it that contemporary feel without betraying the story. All the singers who had sung the parts before in different, traditional productions, were very skeptical at first, because they couldn't imagine where this adventure was going to go, but by the end they were all enchanted with the whole experience.

OL – How did the public react?

CR – The public loved it. It was a big success. It was done again in Lyon, and it was revived at the Edinburgh Festival. People really responded very well to it.

OL - Please tell me about the differences you encounter when working for American companies like the Met, Santa Fe, and Glimmerglass, and your extensive experience working with European companies.

CR – The difference in general is that most European companies are funded by the State and American companies are privately funded. The role that money plays for them is different. Normally in Europe you have the luxury of more time for rehearsals. In Europe you have five or six staged rehearsals with the orchestra while in America you have maybe one or two. On the other hand I must say that the conditions of work in America are extremely professional. People are extremely well organized and well prepared. Knowing that the time is limited, people are just more aware of that and make a bigger effort from the very start, to be able to pull the production off.

OL - You've directed musicals, as well as contemporary operas. Please tell me about some of the challenges and excitement of these modalities of work.

CR – As far as directing a musical goes, it really depends on whether or not it is a new musical that has just been freshly written and has never been performed, in which case it is really a completely different approach. You have the piece at the beginning of the rehearsals but it is not the ultimate version yet. So you constantly try to figure out what is the best way to get the story told as far as the dramaturgy and the musical numbers go; whether they work or not. You work with the orchestra, the composer, the writer of the libretto, and having these people present in the rehearsal is a completely different thing than when you are working with an opera by a composer that has been dead for a long time. To have the opportunity to say, "OK, this part doesn't work dramatically; let's rewrite it, let's think of something else, let's make another text for this duet" is just something you cannot do if you are working with a piece by Mozart or Wagner, even though sometimes you would like to make some cuts – Wagner is very long, but you can't do that, of course.

The same thing is true for contemporary opera. It depends on the style of the composer, of the musical language. I've worked on contemporary pieces that are very approachable, where the narrative of the story is very traditional in the good sense and you can easily tell the story, and I've worked on pieces that are much more enigmatic, that refuse to follow a story in the traditional way and are much more experimental. So for these pieces obviously the challenge is to get hold of the dramatic beat, theatrically, and create something that might not be traditionally expected of an opera, but might be interesting and fascinating for the public – you can sometimes employ more visual tricks of theatre.

OL – Do you feel that because the opera audiences have this quasi-religious relationship with the pieces, musicals give you more artistic freedom and more flexibility?

CR – No, not really, I don't think so. Obviously opera audiences are a bit more conservative but I have always felt that even if you have a modern take on a piece or a completely unexpected take, people will accept it and will go along with it as long as they see that you respect the story and that you show them something that interests them, that is visually fascinating for them. Often I hear people say "I don't like contemporary stagings but this time I was surprised; I was happy and I could accept it." But just like for everything else, sometimes you succeed, and sometimes you don't. But that goes for traditional productions as well, I feel.

OL - How do you prepare for a new contract? What is your routine, if you have any, for starting your research and getting to your concept?

CR – First of all I try to listen to the opera as many times as possible without doing too much research about it, at the very beginning. For opera, my first approach is always the music – whether the music speaks to me emotionally, and evokes some images and feelings. That's my first step. Then of course I read the libretto once, twice, ten times, twenty times, to really get all the details and understand the story and think about the problematic parts of it. And then I personally like to go in all directions. I often ask myself, "What would this story be, today? What would the characters be, today? Do I know people like those characters? Do they resemble people that I see around me, or on TV? How do these characters relate to me, today?" At the same time I do all the historical research. That's the way I work.

OL – How long does it take to prepare a new opera?

CR – I would say, about a year and a half. You don't work on it every day, obviously, but it is nice to be able to start working a long time in advance, to think about it, let it sit for a little bit, then come back to it. Then you work with your designers, and they will have different ideas, and we put all those ideas on the table and discuss them together. This is a very important part of the preparation for the work.

OL – When does the conductor get involved?

CR – The conductor normally gets involved when we start the rehearsals. The usual rehearsal period will be four or five weeks. But before that, the conductor will usually be in touch with the director by phone or by email to talk about the version, the cuts, the musical ideas; but the details really happen when everybody is together in a room for four weeks.

OL – Does it happen that the conductor resists some of your ideas, and there is some conflict?

CR – Sure, of course. I wouldn't say conflict, but the conductor might have different views on some things. I have to say that in 90% of the productions that I've done the work with the conductor was very pleasant and productive. But occasionally it was not.

OL – I see. What are some of your other interests, besides the performing arts?

CR – I'm lucky to be doing what I am doing because opera and musical theatre have always been my hobby anyway, so I'm happy that my hobby is my profession. I love to go to the movies, I love the nature around Geneva. I love to go to the mountains. I swim every day and love sports. And I like to travel, although my profession sometimes results in too much travel all the time.

OL - Would you describe for us your take on life?

CR – I try to be laid back and to not panic when problems occur. I believe that if you have good humour and you respect people, people will respect you. You can always find a solution for any problem.

OL – Thank you so much, it was a lovely interview.

CR – Thank you, thank you!

OL – Are you going back to Glimmerglass?

CR – No, I have to go to Edinburgh today for a revival of a production. I would love to go back; I'm tempted, maybe I'll go back at the very end of the run.

OL – Well, have a safe trip, then.

CR – Thank you Luiz, and I hope you enjoy the performance. Maybe one day we will meet in person somewhere.

OL – I would love that.

DIVISION FIVE – THE EDUCATORS

CHAPTER NINE – MASTER CLASSES

Lawrence Brownlee

Gifted lyric tenor Lawrence Brownlee gave a lecture and a master class to voice students at Asheville Lyric Opera, hosted by the YMI Cultural Center in Asheville, North Carolina, on March 2, 2013. Opera Lively recorded the event. Given that these interactions with the outstanding singer went on for three hours, it would be too lengthy to reproduce it all. Therefore what we'll do with this material is that we'll publish a series of maxims and pearls issued by the artist, who had dozens of interesting pieces of advice to give to the young students, and will summarize the parts that were spoken in between these statements.

If you've always been curious about how a master class goes on and you have never had an opportunity to attended one, this is your chance to get acquainted with the process. The main lesson from it is the realization of how difficult the profession of opera singer is – they work over and over on a couple of phrases or even on a single word!

We can't render here the full impact of these lessons given that we are not listening to the voices of the singers and to the vocal demonstrations Mr. Brownlee does, but the readers will nevertheless be able to have an idea of this fascinating process of a master class. A brief Q&A when Mr. Brownlee answered to questions from middle and high school students who were in the audience follows the master class report.

Photo credit Opera Lively - From left to right, Darian Alexander Jackson, David Craig Starkey(director of the opera company), Caitlin Sands, Brett Pardue, Lawrence Brownlee and Verntasia Finley

"You assume that someone is a master, I'm not. I'm still a student of singing, myself. Master classes are always for me an opportunity to grow and learn from each other."

"In a master class you can't change the world, but maybe there are some ideas that we can share."

[A student from Brevard College, Verntasia Finley, mezzo, originally from Los Angeles, sings a Barber piece from *Vanessa*, "Must the Winter Come so Soon?"]

"We can't ever be in auto-pilot; we need to always be in the moment, because the truth about singing in a live performance is that we don't get a second chance. Sometimes we are affected by a number of things – fatigue, allergies, or your vocal mechanism is just not working one day. So what do you do? I always think that a singer has to be really in control and know what they are doing so they can make some audibles and do something that they haven't done in their practice or lessons. You may have phlegm or acid reflux – some days your voice just doesn't work. Sometimes your voice and your technique match up – some other times you have to lean on your voice, or lean on your technique. That perfect marriage when they meet up and do everything you want them to do doesn't always happen."

"Luciano Pavarotti said he had two perfect singing days in his life, and neither of those days were days when he had shows." [generalized laughs]

"I don't think we have to have some sort of abandonment and start throwing the technique out the window. We need to be in control of the situation. There are unpredictable factors in a live performance, such as, an instrumentalist plays the wrong note – you have to adapt."

"When you sing you need to want to say something. You have a big responsibility: you have to express something to the listener. In a piece that has the repetition of some lines, you generally need to give to each occasion a different color. There needs to be a voyage, an arc that happens from the beginning to the end."

"Breathing is free. Sometimes you have to take the time to breathe, to set yourself up. In some moments you have to steal a breath or do a catch-up breath, but if you are really in control of what you are doing you usually can avoid these by setting yourself up and take your breath in points where you won't need to steal another one, later on. "

[To the singer] "When you rehearse you need to look at yourself on the mirror because you are giving not only something to the listener, but also to the viewer. I need to see in your facial expression that even in the interlude you are engaged. "

"For anyone, high notes are important – mezzos, tenors, basses, it doesn't matter. You have to make sure that you prepare for a high note before you breathe. The listener shouldn't feel that you are having difficulty reaching that note. If the note before it has less bloom or specialness or spin, it detracts from that high note. "

"In my practice I always try to look at the music as a road map of what I am going to do before I get there, because knowing where you are going is part of the battle. You can't say "oh my God, here comes that high note!" What you need to say is "I know that in this measure I am prepared because the phrase goes to the high note." If I'm descending in the scale in the previous phrase, I have to make sure I have enough support to rise again. So it never happens in the moment: it happens because you make it happen. You need to make a choice, make a decision, and do something with the phrase. This is your job; this is your place to say something different. "

"If twenty other people come and sing "Must the Winter Come so Soon?" – what will you do to make yourself different and stand up? Everybody can sing the notes. Samuel Barber wrote them, and if you have basic theory you can sing them as written and even do the dynamics – but it will be cookie cut unless you make something special. "

"I can see that you are doing a crescendo and trying to do something special, but can you sing more piano?" [Mr. Brownlee asked several times the students to sing piano, making repeatedly the point that these days singers sing too loudly and it is less artistic and beautiful]. If you sing piano you can go the extra mile and make more of it. If you start piano before the crescendo you don't need to do the latter right away, you can stretch and make the transition more gradual. Take the time. The pianist will follow you. Well, they should, right? [laughs] They are paid enough money, yes? [laughs]."

"Sound prints are what gets remembered. I remember Marilyn Horne doing *The Italian Girl in Algiers*, it's a great recording but I remember one thing that she did, a little moment, a little nugget, something special. So when you sing this piece from Barber, this is your opportunity to make more of it. Go to the limit!"

[The singer follows Mr. Brownlee's advice; starts the crescendo pianissimo, stretches it, and the result is indeed much better! It is impressive to see how Mr. Brownlee makes the master class effective in clearly shaping up and changing the young singer's delivery]

[Next he works on eliminating her catch-up breath right before the crescendo] "You can do it without a breath if you put all your stock into the preparation. You don't need to do this [sings like she's been doing it, with a deep breath in the middle – then sings it in one continuous line]. You have two and a half bars before this crescendo, when nothing happens – OK, hook up the air pump! You are not spending air before, because you are singing piano. [She does it, and it is so much more beautiful!] See, you can do it! [the public breaks in applause].

[It is interesting to notice that thus far, Mr. Brownlee has only allowed the student singer to sing the first two phrases of the aria, always interrupting her to shape it all up. It gives the public an understanding of how hard it is to sing opera – one needs a lot of work just to get two phrases right!]

"These changes you can do to the musical line – such as singing these two lines without a catch-up breath – these are the small little nuggets of expressivity or colors or dynamic changes that you can add in any song. No song has to be boring! It won't be, if you take a chance and do something special. That was very good – and just two phrases!" [Wild applause, and he dismisses the first student singer and invites the second one to the stage.]

[A student from UNC Asheville, Caitlin Sands, soprano, born in Cary, NC, sings "Batti, batti o bel Masetto" from *Don Giovanni* – in a rather uneven and shaky way with too much staccato – Mr. Brownlee picks up on it right away]

"Mozart keeps you honest. You can't play around. It's transparent; it's something where you can't hide the notes. There are few things that can give you more problems if you are not clear when you sing Mozart. You can't fudge or smear it over. Start again and try to do more legato. Even if you need to peel them back at some other point, think of these phrases as long legato phrases, as opposed to staccato. Think of your breath and the way you support it – you need to sustain something here from beginning to end rather that this ta-ta-ta, but rather, like this [he sings the passage smoothly].

[The singer points out to the fact that it is hard to make it continuous like Mr. Brownlee can, because of the breathing].

"Yes, when I breathe I try to be like a balloon, stocking up the air, and using all nooks and cranes that I have. I don't hold my breath; I rather try to support myself into it. I'm engaged in pushing the air down if you will. It is hard to talk technique in a master class because people are different, even physically – some like to carry their frame like this [sticks his chest out], others don't. There are different schools of singing. But if your technique is solid, you can feel your voice as a mechanism that always works; you can count on it. It's not 'today I breathe this way, tomorrow I breath this other way, the next day I breathe this different way.' No, you need to find something that works for you and you solidify that technique, and start using it consistently. You need to breathe every time the same way in your mechanism, once you get to a technique that is solid and works for you."

[Next, he works on her body posture:] "Your arms need to be more composed. Think of it as if you had jeans and you stuck your thumbs in the pockets of your jeans. Your body needs to be engaged rather than your hands, OK?"

[She sings the first phrase – much better than the first time, but starts very abruptly. He interrupts again:] "I'd like you to start a bit less decisively, engaging into it rather than tripping into it."

[She tries again, he stops her in the first word] "No, you're not doing it yet. You need to signal to the pianist that you are starting, with a little waive of your hand, and get into it naturally. Give the pianist the idea that you are ready to go – but not until you *are* ready to go!

[She does it, and the transformation, just like with the first singer, is amazing. He lets her go on for three phrases, stops her again:] "You cannot drop the support in the middle of the phrase, since it's such a long phrase with these melismas. You need as you go down, to engage more and more your technique, otherwise the phrase ends prematurely."

"That's my opinion: any high note that you *think* you can't do, actually you *can* improve on it."

[Mr. Brownlee brings the singer back to the first word – Batti – and demonstrates a way to sing it dryly and abruptly – which is what she is doing – and another way to sing it as if begging, with committed emotion, lengthening the emission of the "a" vowel].

[He lets her go on for a while again, but notices that she is running out of air, and encourages her to take a very, very good breath before she starts. Then he notices that her tempo is a bit slow which is lengthening the phrase and diminishing her air capital, and encourages her and the pianist to accelerate a tiny bit – a very good insight]. "You need to keep in mind where the finishing line of these phrases is, and make sure you have something left to get to it. So for this, you may have to do the intermediate steps a bit faster. You may assume that the faster tempo is not comfortable for you, when in fact it facilitates the breathing. I mark my sheet music to delineate the stretches I need to go through before I need to breathe. Let's try again!"

"Every space that you have for breathing, you need to, but then every time you breathe, don't apologize for it. Just breathe! [She restarts, and he reminds her with shouts of "breathe!" at certain points – again, the improvement is notable!]

"This part of the phrase is the most important [sings it] so you can't put too much emphasis on these preceding parts [sings them] or else you won't get to the most important part in good shape. You need to lean a bit on this more important part, with more support, and slow down a little when you get to it so that it gets underlined."

[She sings again – he suddenly stops her] "I thought you were a bit tight there." ["I forgot to breathe", she confesses. Mr. Brownlee picks up immediately anything that is not right – it's quite remarkable the way he does it, and how gifted he in his teaching. He gets down to each note that she needs to sustain, stretch, and prevent from letting it drop, as opposed to the auxiliary notes that she can issue faster and then move on.]

"These notes are fast. Therefore you need to breathe fast, which is different. You need to think: 'when I breathe fast, how do I breathe? Because if you breathe fast you don't have the time to really inhale, so you need to know your own body and find a way to make enough air go in even when you breathe fast. You know the feeling when you take a long breath, how full you feel. You need to practice how to get to that even when it's fast. [He demonstrates to her some breathing techniques that he uses].

"Sometimes I'm walking down the street and I think of a phrase, and say to myself 'OK, that's the phrase I'm working on,' and I dissect it, to find the breathing points and to plan for the special things I want to do with the phrase."

"Put not stress, but emphasis, on the higher notes."

[She sings a wrong note, he immediately stops her] "This was supposed to be an F. You have that F, you can do it, so you need to know in your technique how you produce that F, in order to be prepared for it. You have to be able to call for it in that place. You have to lean on the notes before it, don't throw them away; lean on them, leading to the F. Your support starts not at the F, but at the C before it."

[A faculty member from the audience interrupts, and tells the singer: "You watch how Larry works that space, he makes it tall." Lawrence Brownlee, who is a very short man, immediately follows it up by retorting "There is nothing tall about me!" – the audience breaks into hysterical laughing].

[Time to end the lesson for this singer approaches, and Mr. Brownlee says] "We've been working again on just two phrases, and sometimes it takes one hour to work on one phrase, but it is worth it, because if you start the aria with a couple of well done phrases, then you continue the same way and the entire aria is successful." [He sings for her the two phrases, over-emphasizing where he breathes, and says, "ready? Let's go!"]

[The singer then repeats the piece, and when we compare what she had done half an hour earlier with what she does now, it is going from water to wine! What an effective master class! – but he is not satisfied yet.]

"I feel you are not giving yourself the best opportunity to succeed. You are sitting down on notes. You conclude them too much and make they sound heavy and they end a phrase without engaging with the next one in a flow. Lighter, lighter, lighter! You need to sing every note of the phrase but if you think too much about each one, it will sound like you are walking through mud. The idea is to keep an arc moving without getting bogged down in what you are doing. You can't sit down on your voice. [He sings and demonstrates notes in the end of a phrase being heavily concluded, and then demonstrates how they can be sung in a much lighter way that links them to the next phrase.]

"Anytime that a high voice sits and becomes heavy when it goes lower, it creates problems, because then you won't be up to the high notes that follow. Sopranos get paid for their high notes. Mezzos get paid for their high notes. I feel that none of those notes should be suffering. The tempo is now a bit too fast for you. You have to find the tempo that is right for you. Many of these composers have composed music for people whom they knew personally, and they adapted the tempi to those singers – but you are a different singer, and it doesn't quite fit for you. It may be too short or too long or too tight; then you have the license to make of it, your own."

"Any conductor or piano accompanist needs to work with the singer to allow the singer to make something special. Just remember: never be too heavy. Lightness is always more beautiful than heaviness in this role that is that of a *coquette*, so heaviness doesn't work. Don't think about this aria, 'I'll just sing it.' You need to do a whole lot of work before you even get on the stage, and perform it, because you want to go from singing it, to performing it. [applauses]

[Next, Darian Alexander Jackson, baritone from Elon, NC who is a junior vocal major at Western Carolina University – We didn't catch the name of his piece – a German Lieder piece by Richard Strauss – he sang it very well!]

[As he did with other singers, Mr. Brownlee started by asking the singer how he thought he did and what he feels was special about it, and if there was anything he felt he could improve on – the singer quoted phrasing, trying to make each line sound different].

"Yes, that's a challenge. This piece is strophy, and making it interesting can be tricky. But it was very good, very well performed. It's a tremendous opportunity to take people in a voyage. A German piece sung by an American-born singer to an American audience, we have to make sure the audience is interested in what you are doing even if they don't necessarily understand the words. We can dive into it to find those moments where you can take even more time to make each line different, since one of the lines repeats three times. Start again. [The singer does]. OK, you got to the first phrase. Where is the special moment? [The singer says, "I guess in the high notes."] Flaunt it! Take the liberty to do more! You are performing it well but you can go a step further [demonstrates it]. Bring up the words! Any challenge is an opportunity to unlock untapped potential. Reach for something inside you, because even if you think 'I'm doing well, I know this piece' there is always something to be done. You have to think, 'how can I, an American-born singer, sing this as if I were a German-born singer?' We can't ever sing it like a native speaker but we can inch closer. The way I sit on the word and take it out of the phrase can say something. I don't like to ask people 'tell me what it means' because it puts them on the spot, but I assume that you know what the words mean; you need to know, to interpret them. Give in to the words."

[The singer does it again; Mr. Brownlee stops him to encourage him to not move his hands or his body, just to give a try to acting with his voice, not his hands or body, to work on his vocal eloquence, with his hands actually tucked into his pockets]. "I want your body as quiet as possible, but say something with the voice." [The singer's voice does become more expressive, immediately]. "Now, for the second phrase, start piano, because our job is to draw the listener in. Dynamically there was not a lot of difference in the way you sang the second verse as compared to the first verse; it was fairly the same, but you can do better. "

"I had a chance to sing just this week with Cecilia Bartoli. She's been doing this for 25-30 years. I saw her in rehearsal working like crazy. I thought, 'You are Cecilia Bartoli, you barely need this.' But she is great because of the work she does every day. She doesn't go there and rest on the laurels of what she's done over all those years. She is constantly working on it. I saw that, and went to my practice room thinking 'I need to continue to work on my part because seeing her, I know that there is always something else that one can do.' I talked to a singer that has been singing a role for thirty years, but he said "If my role is today the same as it was thirty years ago, I'm not doing my job – every time I step on the stage, it's an opportunity to do something different." If you perform a role in a run of six shows, or you do a recital five times with the same songs, I believe that nobody seeing two of the performances should be able to say "he did it exactly like the last time." The only way you can make it different is when you know your piece so well that you know what you can change. "

"If you sing piano, people will adjust to you, they will lean on it and you'll pull them in. When you sing piano in the lower register, your voice can't disappear; it still needs to have your full support – it's only the dynamic level that changes. We all need to learn to do this. [demonstrates, beautifully; when Mr. Brownlee does it, it sounds magical, hypnotic]."

[The singer tries, still too loudly – Mr. Brownlee then says "I'll conduct you" and proceeds to slow down the lines in certain parts and to hush the singer a bit to lower the dynamics – now the performance improves significantly!] "You need to put colors in your singing. The best singers don't just sing; they make music."

A very funny exchange follows – Mr. Brownlee asks for the student's age, he is 20. He says "I'm 40, double your age, I still need to get used to that. Hm… you could be my son! Oh wait, I'm sure you are not!" [wild laughs from everybody].

"You have to show your strengths, not your weaknesses. If you know a part of your voice is weak for a specific song, it doesn't mean you can't sing it, but you need to make that weaker part work for you. When you have these low parts for which your voice hasn't quite developed into them yet, if you try to sing them forte when you don't have the forte, it doesn't work. But if you can say 'I'm going to take this phrase and make it work for me, in my voice,' you can still be audible, you can still sing the note, you can still support it, and no one will know that it might be forte instead, because you didn't perform it that way. That's your artistic license; you can do what you want to. I mean, you are not re-composing the Strauss notes but you make this piece work for you. It's having your own voice. I love to teach young singers, and they often ask me to teach them how to sing like such and such, and I always say, the goal is not to teach you how to sing like somebody else, but rather to be a better you. The gift that you have needs to be made special enough to set you apart from everybody else. When I go on stage, people can say that my voice is similar to some other voice, but they need to say, 'that's him, because he is doing something with his instrument that is unique to what he can do.' Hopefully we will find some new soldiers coming up, because live theater, live art, is something that hopefully is not done. When I become a voice teacher one day – something

I'll love to do – I want to get ten singers to sing the same song, and none of them will sing it exactly alike. And it is possible. There have been a thousand singers over the times and they all did something differently, and you should be one of them."

"OK, I'm usually the toughest with the last person" [laughs]. [The last singer comes up, Brett Pardue, baritone born in Elkin, NC, in his junior year at Mars Hill College as a Vocal Performance major and Piano minor. He sings a French chanson by Fauré – does it extremely well].

"I thought you did a good job. " [When asked about what he could improve on, the singer says he feels he should move more, to express emotion]. "I don't like it when people move a lot to distract listeners from what they are singing. Feel free to move, though. But vocally, what you did was wonderful. There was a lot of variation in color; there were some real ideas there, and you took it apart; one can tell you've worked a lot on the piece. Your French sounds great. I applaud you; you're very, very strong. One feels you are confident because you did good work; you've prepared, you've studied. You had a whole bunch of things in your arsenal. I tell people to do what you apparently did – take a piece of music, understand it, and write down every single piece of emotion that is possible in that piece. It may be twenty things. It could be bitterness. It could be fatigue. It could be boredom – all in the same piece. Then, find your way to musically, artistically, express that. "

"The way you approached a couple of the high notes could have been better. Do it again, but you can move; feel free to move. Does anybody here know the name Measha Brueggergosman? She is a Canadian soprano. She comes to the stage barefoot. She is expressive with her body, but she has done so much work with the expressivity of her sound, that you are not distracted by her body. Basically what I'm saying is that she has earned the right to move because she also says something with her voice."

[With this more accomplished singer, Mr. Brownlee then proceeds to working on some punctual notes – allows him to sing through several phrases but stops him about specific notes that he wants a bit quieter or a bit lighter when the note sticks out not as beautifully as other notes the singer is delivering – for example, by saying "Right before this high note you have to give it a little less before, so that you have the spin for the high note." "Here you need a better E natural."] He adds: "This is a strong performance so I'm struggling to find little things where it can be improved upon. There is not a lot to say." [They work on finding different colors and on accelerating or slowing down some parts of the musical lines – the end result does sound more polished].

"I'm fascinated by eloquent singers. I love eloquent singers! You can sing Wagner, you can sing Mozart, you can sing anything in an eloquent way. It's possible. French chansons are the perfect scenario for singing; they are elegant. Always try to be elegant in your singing! It doesn't mean we can always do it, but the goal is to be as elegant as possible. It's like a peacock – you are stretching out and showing your beauty. It comes from knowing that you've done your work and you know the little points and the phrases and the breathing."

[Mr. Brownlee goes to the piano himself and engages in more technical teaching:] "You are putting too much weight on this word 'oublier' – you need an F scale here, and in the context of this piece you can't feel like you can't sing that F sharp that will end the line. It is a place that for you is more difficult, so how do you do it? You have to think of it a couple of steps back, to prepare for it. The F sharp that comes up needs to have the most spin, the most space. You need to breathe before it and reset the vocal mechanism, so that the tension in your body is reset to free up the energy that you will need for the F sharp. You need to take a slightly longer breath here. You can't put much weight on these notes that come before it. On this word 'aimons' you need to sing it lower and with less effort. In rehearsal you need to find the freedom of this note and sing it with all you have, but then you need to scale it back and produce the same note but in a lighter way; that's the way to do it in order to leave a bit more energy for the F sharp [and so on and so forth – they work on these details and the singer's delivery which was already impressive, does improve even more.]

Then, there was a Q&A session with Mr. Brownlee. The audience was made of middle and high school kids. Mr. David Craig Starkey, director of Asheville Lyric Opera, starts by telling the students that even if they do not aspire to be singers, they can learn from Mr. Brownlee, because to succeed in all fields – if they want to be writers, or computer programmers, or anything else – it takes this kind of attention, discipline and commitment to the work, in order to get better. It takes time and effort, and whatever age they are, it never stops. He also underlines that while both he and Mr. Brownlee grew up in the same community of Youngstown, Ohio, a community deprived of many essentials, it didn't stop them from becoming successful. A young student asks the first question:

Student – How old where you when you found your voice?

Lawrence Brownlee – Let me give you a bit of my background. I grew up in a family of six kids. My father was the Church Choir Director. I was surrounded by Gospel. In school I had School Choir. I had a diverse musical background. My voice, I guess I was seventeen or eighteen when it was discovered, when they felt I had something to offer as a classical singer. When I was very small, my mother once woke me up because I was singing in my sleep. I was singing all the time, I was involved in music. I always tell people, in which and every way you can be involved in music, or Community Theater, or chorus in school, do. I know they are taking music out of the schools, which I hate. I participated in all those genres, and it made me more open to music, and ultimately I found my voice. I still go back home and sing some Gospel. I do feel that the gift that I have is in what I'm doing now – classical music. Your voice may be found at five, but you won't know what you can really do until later. But keep involved in music and try different things. Some people may find their focus early on, but it may change.

Audience member – When you were seventeen or eighteen, did you have a musical goal, like "I want to be a Gospel singer" or "I want to be an opera singer" or a pop singer?

LB – I didn't have any goal, because I didn't know at that age what the classical music world is. I thought like most people that classical singers had horns in their heads, sang in strange languages, and broke glasses with their voices. Really, to be honest, when I entered a program in my senior high school year, I was just mocking what I thought an opera singer should sound like. Low and behold, they said "you have something." I didn't have at that time any idea of what I would become or even what I wanted to do. I actually thought somewhere in the back of my mind that I would be a lawyer. That didn't happen, obviously. [laughs] I'm glad it didn't happen, although I have a lot of respect for lawyers. But singing is a gift that I enjoy very much, and I work hard at it.

Audience member – What kind of music you listened to in your room as a teenager?

LB – I listened to everything. Even now, if you look at my iPod, I have everything. I could throw names: Steely Dan, Barbra Streisand, Sting, Kim Burrell, The Police, Steve Wonder, Fred Hammond, everything. I never thought I wouldn't like this or that type of music. I'm not a big fan of Bluegrass, though.

Audience member – Did you listen to Pavarotti?

LB – Not until later. When The Three Tenors CD came up, I thought, "Oh my God, I would like to do that, right there!" But I didn't have exposure to classical music, early on. And that's no one's fault; it's just how my life turned out.

Audience member – Is classical music more important than other genres? Should an effort be made to make it important to teenagers in America, today?

LB – I think it is. I'm not saying it's more important. It's what I do, obviously. I always try to tell people that classical music is not so far from what you hear on the radio today. Yes, the style of it, the rhythms and all these things are different, but if you listen very closely to some of these rappers and pop singers, they have the motifs of Bach, or Haydn, and they don't even know it. They don't know where their music is derived from. They can say, "oh, this is a cool melody" but if someone listens to it and has been surrounded by the classical composers, this person will be able to say "let me take you to this symphony, and this motif that you saw here, was already there. This piece came from this other one." I think that when people can make this connection and realize that it is not worlds apart, people can be more interested in classical music.

Audience member – Were the competitions you entered, important for you?

LB – Yes. I was involved in a competition called NATS, which is held around the country. I went to Ohio University to compete in it, in my freshman year. I was given instruction by Mr. Starkey [the father of the Asheville Lyric Opera director, the senior Mr. Starkey, was the one who discovered Mr. Brownlee and encouraged him to compete]. This was the first time I went in front of someone outside of my close surroundings. I didn't know these people. I remember singing a piece by Strauss and the response was overwhelming. It was one of the moments when I thought "well, maybe there is something in classical music for me." It was important for me, to realize that there were so many people working to be singers. You need to learn how to separate yourself. I had worked for a semester with Mr. Starkey to present something, and I didn't know how ready I was. Obviously it worked, but then I saw the standard, the high level there, and thought "I need to work harder, because now I have to top that." Our life is to try to do better every time. It was important for me to have that experience, and realize that I couldn't just coast.

Mr. David Craig Starkey [the director of the opera, who is also a singer] – I had the same experience in my training; I went to the NATS and won it, but I thought I had screwed up and nobody noticed, and they still gave me the first prize.

LB – Yes, it's not about being perfect. Like I said before, you can have a cold or an allergy or even a mind lapse, but it's about making it special. If you are able to have a moment when you can captivate the listeners, even if you are not perfect, you can prevail, even if you mess up. I've messed up many times, we do; we are humans. But if you take the time to do something special, a lot of times you'll come out OK.

An audience member asks a question about how to stay focused and deal with all the fame and the travel to different cultures; asks if it can derail someone, as a person.

LB – You have your foundation, your family… I was fifteen when I had a chance to go to Germany to perform music. It opened my eyes to the fact that there is a lot out here, out of Ohio [laughs]. But I feel that the foundation that I had, the person that my parents raised me to be, was plenty. I feel that I am still that same person from Youngstown, Ohio. Humility is important. That's what my parents taught me. When I look at all the things I've been blessed to have done in my life, I don't need to say "Oh, I'm great." My humility is part of me. When I am out in the world, I'm still anchored by my roots, because that's who I am. The singing is what I do, it's not who I am. I was just given an opportunity to share my gift with the world. That's how I think of it.

Audience member – Why is music important to human nature?

LB – Music connects to people in a way other things can't. Music and the words together do accomplish a lot. Think for instance of a lullaby your mother may have sung to you. She may have told you many other wonderful things in life, but often that lullaby is one of the most notable things that stick to your memory – that song with the tensions behind it, with the way you can touch people adding music to words. It touches you in a level that nothing else can. Most people don't live a life without music. They have a favorite CD, or a favorite singer that puts them in a place that nothing else can. When someone is feeling bad, at times the person will say "you know what? I want to raise my spirit" and it is often done through music. If you think about it, in most ceremonies, in church, in government functions or anything, music is always a part of it, and it should be. I'm a musician so I'm a big fan! [laughs]

Mr. Starkey – It's a real addiction, but not one you need to get rid of! [everybody laughs]

LB – Thank you very much for coming!

Frederica von Stade and pianist James Meredith

The Master Class with Frederica von Stade, mezzo-soprano, and James Meredith, pianist, at the University of North Carolina at Chapel Hill, College of Arts and Sciences, Department of Music, was covered by Opera Lively on March 6, 2013

Again, we can't render here the full impact of these lessons given that we are not listening to the voices of the singers and to the vocal demonstrations Ms. von Stade does, or to Mr. Meredith's piano playing, but the readers will nevertheless be able to have an idea of this fascinating process of a master class, using a bit of imagination, and will learn a thing or two about some of the famous arias of the repertoire and their emotional context. You will also laugh a bit, given that Ms. von Stade is gifted with an extraordinary sense of humor! An interesting Q&A session happens at the end.

An opera living legend like Frederica von Stade dispenses introduction. Our readers might know less well Mr. James Meredith, who is one of San Francisco Bay Area's most well rounded musicians. He conducts the acclaimed Sonos Handbell Ensemble. He has recently been featured on Garrison Keillor's "A Prairie Home Companion," He is a frequent musical partner whit Frederica von Stade and with dramatic soprano Olivia Strapp. He has taught courses and master classes in various colleges and conservatories, and is currently on the voice/piano faculty at UC-Berkeley with the award-winning Young Musicians Program, which regularly sends students to major universities and conservatories.

Frederica von Stade – Great, we are here with all these young singers. I can tell who will sing by their hairdos. [Everybody laughs]. I just want to say this, I feel that master classes is a misnomer at least where I'm concerned. I love to just tell you what I know, tell what paths I might have gone down that I hope you don't have to go down and share any experiences and maybe a couple of tips, if that. But all the real work that you are doing, you are very well taken care of, with this amazing group of teachers you have.

The reason I do master classes, really, is that I love to hear you all sing. It's totally selfish.

Will Kelley, Diana Yodzis, Taylor McLean, Laura Buff, Allison Thomas, Frederica von Stade and James Meredith - photo credit Opera Lively

James Meredith – Yes, we are just going to hear you sing and tell you what we think, and you may take it for what value it might be for you. Discuss it with your teacher. If your teacher says "never in a hundred years," that's fine. But we'll tell you things that we've done and heard from other artists.

One thing I will say is, I'm a vocal teacher myself and I have sat in the audience with many of my students who sung in master classes, and I thought "Oh my God!" They've been asked by this person "do you know what this means?" and they looked like a deer in the headlights. How many times have we discussed this with them? Countless times. They ask them a question about something which we know they know the answer to, but the question was asked in a way that maybe they can't quite relate to those same terms… and we think "oh my God, what will this master class teacher think of me?" Right? [He and Frederica and some of the teachers in the audience laugh]. How many teachers do we have here? Have you all been through that experience? [Teachers nod and say yes!]. OK! So please be advised that I'm fully aware of that, and that we think you are great teachers already!

[The first student singer is Ms. Allison Thomas, mezzo-soprano from UNC-CH, accompanied by pianist Deborah Hollis, singing "Parto, Parto" from Mozart's *La Clemenza di Tito*.]

Stade – Brava! I thought you did decide what was going on in each part of the aria. Does everybody know what this aria is about? So you tell them!

Thomas – I'm Sesto and I'm in love with Vitelia who has just convinced me that I need to go kill the emperor. I've been very conflicted about this, the entire opera. I finally give in to what she wants, because I love her so much, I can't say 'no' to her, and this is a song where I try to leave but she is also ignoring me, implying 'if you don't do what I want I won't love you anymore' so I'm begging her, 'please stay with me.'

Meredith – This is a pants role, in case you don't know it. [people laugh]

Stade – The lady she is in love with is a real bitch, that's what she is! [the audience laughs] In every way. Manipulative, not a nice person. [To the singer:] So why did you fall in love with her? That's crazy! [laughs] It's a hard part to do, I think, because he is a little bit of a wimp, and you [the interpreter] want to fight against that all the time. So when you have a chance to be strong, you want to really be strong.

And I got this itch… this section where you had a very specific idea about it, that you couldn't go further. Right at the beginning. You don't know where you want to go. That's the big deal. He says 'parto' [I'm leaving] how many times? I don't know, twenty-five? Plus, it's an aria where he is very much concerned about Vidalia, so it's really a duet. So anytime you have a chance to be really strong and show the confusion that is written in, in different sections of it, you need to keep the thrill going. I know it is very slow sometimes, but you need to keep it going.

"Parto" [she sings the word a few times, always impacting a different twist on it, and a sense of urgency]. You are thinking about it, you are considering it. It's not an emotion yet, but it is a consideration. So it becomes a little higher, a little more incisive, and then she spurns you and uses her appeal to manipulate you. Then, in the middle of the section, you need to make it very private. Then at the end you have convinced yourself, you've smoked crack [everybody laughs] and you are ready to go!

But also, there are parts when you need to be very still. It's sort of a contemplative aria. There is some of it that concerns her, but a lot of it concerns you and all that is going through your mind with this extraordinary devotion to Tito. It's beyond a friendship. It's such a gripping, powerful relationship between Sesto and Tito, that he is completely forgiven at the end. So it's not very operatic, he isn't beheaded or anything [people laugh]; nothing terrible happens to him. There is this beautiful other aria where he is begging for forgiveness. So just try it. The main tricky thing is the rhythm. I wouldn't wait to sing the first part. [She sings it relatively fast and in a saccadic, marked way, until the first word 'Parto!']. That's what I have. Jimmy? Don't torture her. [laughs]

Meredith – No, I won't torture her. [To the pianist] Beautiful playing, by the way. This is not an easy aria to play, because she needs to be the clarinet and the orchestra at the same time. In the opening, make sure that you insert these rests [hums it, rests, hums it, rests], because that shows the hesitation.

Stade – Yes!

Meredith – And then you set the singer up, you let her take a breath in each rest. The other thing is, don't peddle the clarinet arpeggios, since clarinets don't have peddles.

Stade – They don't??? [everybody laughs]

Meredith – No. And make sure it sounds like the clarinet is upside down! [general laughs]

Stade to the pianist – Can you handle that? [laughs] So here is an idea – pam pa-pam, rest. Pam pa-pam, rest. Pam pa-pam, rest. So you are asked to do – what? You need to show what you are thinking. The first one, you think of Vidalia. The second one, you think of Tito – 'Oh my God!' The third one could be, 'oh, OK' but not convinced. If it's right on the line, it comes out as a contemplation.

I really think that one of the most helpful things in the world for any song you are singing, for any aria, is to put it in your own words, put in what you are thinking. Write it down because then you will remember what your intention is. What exactly is the nut of what you are singing? What do you mean? This 'Parto' will be this, and that's a complicated one, because you have twenty-five to go! So try that, but keep it moving. You have places to rest, so take your time.

Thomas – Do I need to express a different emotion each time?

Stade – You decide. You can put in some variation but not with too much emotion, because he is a nobleman. He acts like one.

Thomas – OK.

Stade – Sing it again so that we can really torture you. [laughs]

[Ms. Thomas sings it again, and is indeed a lot more expressive this time. Ms. Stade stops her at a certain point].

Stade – In this part, in your mind there is something going on. You need to have a physical image in your mind. Have you done it on stage?

Thomas – I've been rehearsing the role for our Spring production.

Stade – Oh, you are! Fantastic. So in this part you are trying to convince her. She is walking away because she is not convinced that you are going to do it. So you need to adjust and the next time you need to sing it a little more like 'yes I will do it!' So you need to look convincing there. Another thing, people always think that the opening needs to be 'PARTO!" [sings it very loudly and abruptly]. I don't think it is. It's not a heroic moment. I think it's a confused moment. Don't be afraid of that. It doesn't have to be the biggest note you've ever sung.

[The student sings some more, and starts the first 'Parto' more softly, becomes even more expressive in terms of conveying confusion. It becomes indeed very beautiful. Ms. von Stade stops her again].

Stade – I didn't like this 'Parto' here. You should employ a different volume here. It's a different idea. It goes from confused to polite to decided to proud. It's all of that. So when you get to this part, think about it, make it really proud. Don't be afraid to go that far. That's what opera is: excess!

Meredith – I have a suggestion. Would you consider doing an ornament in this part here? [Hums it].

Stade – Yes, it's beautiful when we do it, in this section. [Sings it]

[Ms. Thomas does as told. Wow! Big improvement!]

Stade – In this coloratura here, you are in love, so take it really, really slowly. [Demonstrates it]. Do it like this in different places, learn it, and then it comes naturally when you need to do it here. What's exciting is when it is really well thought of; and when it is, you won't be out of breath, I promise.

[The student tries it].

Stade – OK, it was wonderful! Thank you for that. [Applauses, and the student leaves the stage].

[Next we have Turner Davis, bass-baritone from UNC-CH, still with Deborah Hollis at the piano, and he sings, from Ravel's *Don Quichotte à Dulcinée*, "Chanson à boire." (Drinking song)]

Deborah Hollis and Turner Davis – photo credit Opera Lively

Stade – Are you drunk?

Davis – No. But yes, yes! [Everybody laughs]

Stade – It was great! Can you all hear me without the mike? Yes? Come up, Jimmy, on stage! OK, you are singing about 'joie' – you are happy. And you have a smile, a big smile! Hahaha! [People laugh] It's all you need. You don't have to do anything else. That's it: "Look, I'm on stage!" [acts goofy, people laugh]. It's such an usual laugh [hums the song].

Davis – It's sort of a controlled singing laugh!

Stade [to Meredith] – You've done it many times.

Meredith – Yes. It was commissioned by a movie production company, they were doing a movie on Don Quichotte and they asked Ravel to write songs for the movie. Little did Ravel know that they had asked several composers to write songs for the movie. He thought he was being commissioned. Among them was Jacques Ibert. Ravel wrote these songs, but Ibert's were chosen. The movie was to star Chaliapin, the great Russian bass.

So Ibert's songs were chosen for the movie, but Ravel's were the ones that lasted. Ravel's were much more sophisticated. Ibert's sound more Spanish. But this is a Spanish dance, the Jota, and the Jota uses castanets. By the way, beautifully played! How many pianists do we have in the audience? How many of you have played this? [no hands go up]. Yes, it's fiendish. There are these ta-ta-tas and one is different from the other. Every time I have to play this, I have to practice for days, just on those few chords. The rest of it is not that hard. You can push those a little bit, it's the whole point. [He gives more technical advice to the pianist about how to reproduce the castanets rhythm].

There is a bit of controversy about how to act this piece. Dom Quichotte is an aristocrat, but he is drunk. Many people go overboard. They act too drunk. But I think you [talks to the student singer] need to act a little more drunk. Did you see the concert last night? [Fredericka von Stade's] Not as drunk as she acted in one of those songs! [everybody laughs]. It's French drunk. They are sophisticated, they don't get overboard drunk like in other countries. But I think you need to do a little more of that. I think some of your vowels are a little too closed, so you are not allowing the resonance that you naturally have in your voice. Don't worry about doing it perfectly right now, that's something you have to train overtime. But this is a short piece – do it again, act a little more, and just try to open up those vowels a bit.

Stade – I know a lot of sophisticated drunks [laughs]. They are not sloppy, they make it clear that there is nobility there. They are very straight. Don't forget that!

Davis – OK! [Sings it again]

Stade – Great. Good. Believe in what you are saying.

Meredith – But hold off on those notes when you say it, because your top is good but we are not hearing the same thing here.

Stade – I think you are giving too much voice, all the time. You need to vary the dynamics. [demonstrates it]. You are giving full voice too often. You don't have to. You don't need to think you are not getting your money for it, because it makes you sound hoarse. Try it again with more delicacy and volume variation.

Davis – [Sings it again].

Meredith – You need to work on this staccato. You are making it difficult for the pianist to follow. You need to maintain the beat a little more – 1, 2; 1, 2; 1, 2.

Davis – [repeats it]

Stade – Now, that was perfect! [Applauses] Wonderful!

Meredith – Yes. Now you did "wha, wha, wha" without sounding like a duck. [laughs] Regardless of what the vowel is, you have to let out your natural voice. Are there composers here? Composers should always know how to sing, then maybe they wouldn't write some of this stuff they write. [Everybody laughs]. Whatever vowel Mozart wrote, Don Giovanni needs to still sing it.

David – [sings it one last time].

Stade – Wonderful voice, thank you. [general applause]

[Next Laura Buff, mezzo-soprano from UNC-CH sings "Que fais-tu, blance tourterelle?" from Gounod's *Roméo et Juliette*, with Deborah Hollis at the piano]

Stade – I just want to tell you a funny story. This was one of the first big roles I got to do at the Met, and it was with Franco Corelli, the famous tenor. I had a duel with him and I got so into it that I almost cut off his finger. I thought 'Oh Lord, oh Lord!' [everybody laughs]. I think on that second verse [sings it] you need to make it longer, like you are in a completely different place. Try it like this [demonstrates it], just try that.

Buff – OK. [Sings it]

Stade – You just take your time there. Yes, that's what I always notice, with all the pants roles you are going to be doing, the key is not how you stand, how you look, all that, necessarily; it's that young people that age cannot contain all the energy that they got. So the minute they make a move, they move really fast. I see it in my nephews who are that age. But when you are singing, you need to hold it. So take it a little slower.

Buff – [Sings it in a slower tempo]

Stade – Good, that's good. I think you can do it. The conductors won't let you, but try it anyway. [everybody laughs] When you are singing it you need to convey "you guys don't know how great I am" and then you go into action mode. [Demonstrates it].

Buff – [Sings one line, Stade interrupts her immediately].

Stade – You don't need that breath. [Sings it without pausing to breathe]. Sometimes a kick breath like that doesn't do what you need it to do. You don't need it.

Buff – [Repeats it without pausing].

Stade – In this part you need to put the dots at the end of the phrases a little more; exaggerate it a bit. [Sings it in a more forceful, staccato way].

Buff – OK, got it. [sings it]

Meredith – These vowels can't be lackluster; they need to come more in line with the vowels that come before.

Stade – It's not a big deal but yes, they need to be more flamboyant, more show-offish. It sounds like you may be slowing up here. Keep it going.

Buff – [sings it]

Stade – Brava, that was better. But then, this part that follows needs to be softer than you're doing. Try it like this: [sings it].

Buff – [does it]

Stade – Great, you can do it! Beautiful voice!

Meredith – My only comment would be that a breathing problem happens occasionally because there is a physical reason for it. When you get ready to take a breath, what tends to happen, dynamically? It tends to be louder, if you are not careful, and then it sounds unnatural. Most of the time you are OK, but you need to be careful with that. [demonstrates a couple of passages where that might happen].

Buff – OK.

Meredith – It's just a little nitpicking point, because you are doing so beautifully.

Stade – Yes, there wasn't much for us to say because you did very well. Wonderful. Thank you. [general applause].

Meredith – Rosina, come right up!

[Next, Diana Yodzis, mezzo-soprano from UNC-Greensboro, with Will Kelley at the piano, sings "Una voce poco fa," from Rossini's *Il Barbiere di Siviglia*] [She sings it and is met with prolonged applause, as she does very well]

Stade – There won't be much for me to say to you, either. I love your ornaments. The only thing I'd say, is for you to be mindful of the diction right at the beginning. I met a wonderful Italian diction coach named Ubaldo Gardini, and I made a mistake of saying "Bongiorno, Maestro!" when I first met him, and we spent the entire hour on "Bongiorno!" [everybody laughs]. So, do it like this: [she sings with very musical and clear Italianate diction – "una voce poco fa… etc.]

Yodzis – OK. [Repeats it, and is immediately stopped by Stade].

Stade – That's what I mean, you are saying "una voce" [makes it sound like an American would say the phonemes] instead of "una voce" [makes it sound very Italianate with emphasis on the sounds of the letter N, open A vowel, strong sounding O and explosive C]. Then you need to keep the musicality flowing; don't breath, do it more legato like this, with emphasis on the open vowels [sings the continuation – so beautifully!].

Yodzis – [Repeats it]

Stade – Give it less voice. Don't worry about the breathing here. The secret with opera is that you don't give it all at the first break. You have a lot of other notes to burn in this coloratura; you have a lot to show them; make them wait for it, OK?

Yodzis – All right. [sings it, until the first "vincerò"]

Stade – The coloratura needs to be more sophisticated. You start more doubtful, before you are so certain. [demonstrates it] You are not so sure that you will get Lindoro at this point. You are still thinking about it, then you get more certain as you go. The real joy of Rossini is that there really are very tender moments. You have a beautiful voice. Play with that more.

Your first Lindoro should be tender [demonstrates it] then your second one should be wilder [demonstrates it] because you are running with it, you are getting excited.

Meredith, to the pianist – It was very well played. This is a difficult piece to play. When you are looking at an orchestral score and doing it on the piano, you need to know what the orchestra is doing. But all those first chords when it's pizzicato, I suggest you soften that, because right now we are getting a little too much of overtones. You can't spike them as much on the piano.

[Yodzis and the pianist play/sing it again – Meredith goes to the piano and demonstrates some passages]

Meredith – These, you play a little harder, then later you play like this: [plays it]. This is the spot that kills everybody because the violin can make it continuous like this but the piano cannot. So, you have several options to play this, for example doubling these notes [he demonstrates and gives some other technical advice]. There is a wonderful German edition of Rossini's own reduction for the piano; it's neat to see how he did it. There is that famous quote, of someone playing on the piano one of his arias to him, and he said, "who wrote that aria?" [laughs]

Stade – Oh, I thought of something else, about the way you stopped before this note [sings it]

Meredith – Yes, there is this tradition that people need to stop there and not sing what is written; I don't know, maybe it was because of someone who couldn't sing it.

Stade – That was me! [everybody laughs]

Meredith – Mostly everybody does it, but Rossini wrote the part there to be sung, so… With your voice, you could sing it. Toscanini said that tradition is the last bad performance. [laughs]

Stade – I agree. People give too much importance to tradition. Wonderful, brava! [applauses]

[Next, Jessica Johnson, mezzo-soprano from UNC-Greensboro, with Will Kelley at the piano, sings Samira's Aria from Corigliano's *The Ghosts of Versailles* - also wildly applauded]

Kelley, Meredith, and Johnson – Photo credit Opera Lively

Stade – I will say that this was a fabulous performance, and a fabulous voice, really.

Meredith – Tell us what this was about.

Johnson – *The Ghosts of Versailles* is an opera within an opera. This ends the second act, and what happens is that this is about the Figaro characters, and Beaumarchais' ghost is writing it for Marie Antoinette, and she is sad because she is dead. [laughs] Beaumarchais goes into the opera to try to save Marie Antoinette, and get her cool back. They are at a Paris embassy, at a party hosted by the English ambassador who invited the Turkish ambassador and Samira is a gift that the Turkish ambassador has brought.

Meredith – The interesting thing is that she comes and sings this aria; she has nothing to do with the rest of the opera. So, in this opera, she doesn't really need to know anything about the opera, whereas when you do a role in opera you need to know what everybody else is doing. This is difficult to play, and this student pianist has only had this part for two days.

Stade – Wonderful! [applauses]

Meredith – Not that I'm encouraging this to happen. [laughs]

Stade – You have a wonderful voice, and I want you to take really good care of it. I want guardian angels on your shoulders, OK? So that you don't absolutely go to the end of it, no matter how strongly you feel. There's something about Humanity, when they hear big sounds, they want them even bigger, and what happens is that you blow it out. And you are a wonderful performer too! I was scared! [everybody laughs]. You are terrific. What have you been doing?

Johnson – Right now I'm working on Madame de la Haltière.

Stade – Ah, *Cendrillon*. I don't know. How old are you?

Johnson – I'm 23.

Stade – Oh, Lord! Be careful. You can do it; of course you can do it, but you want to be able to do it for twenty years. Madame de la Haltière is really low. I don't know, in your place I'd explore all the light roles until you are 30, OK? Just be careful. Whenever you have this much talent, and with all the emotion involved, you will go all the way. So, don't overuse it. Don't even sing it again today… go home! [laughs]. No, seriously. You gave us a complete kernel of song; I thought it was terrific. There isn't anything to criticize in your performance. Thank you, thank you! [General applause]

[The last singer is Taylor McLean, mezzo-soprano from UNC-CH, with Deborah Hollis at the piano, singing "Printemps qui commence" from Saint-Saëns' *Samson et Dalila*]

Stade – This was beautiful, but there are a couple of things to work on. You have so many colors in your voice, but because this is an aria that has the same tune coming back so many times, each time needs to be very specific, to convey what exactly you are expressing in each part. And then, just more dynamics. It's your decision, in terms of what dynamics to use, especially in the middle part.

Meredith – I agree. She had me, at the beginning. Do you all know what is going on in this aria? It's the first time she sees Samson, and she was sent there to seduce him, basically, and she is preparing for all that comes up. So, she has that look from the very beginning. She is there for business. But you lost me a few times in the middle. So, in the middle you have to be more specific and know what you are doing. Samson is a guy, you have him.

There's another thing. You had one gesture here, but then in the end you came out without it. So you have to practice this body language in front of a mirror. The thing to watch is that wonderful concert by Callas in Paris. The conductor was a very young Georges Prêtre and he was very bad, all over the place. [laughs]. She sings a Bellini aria, "A non credea mirarti" from *La Sonnambula.* It's a long recitative, and aria, and she has basically two gestures.

She moves her hand up here, and then she moves it here. That's all, the whole aria. It's all that it takes. I mean, you could do more, but just look at that, to see how little you have to do, and let your voice out.

Stade – It's also a question of knowing what doing nothing, physically, can do – how strong that is. It's just like noticing how strong your back is. What we do beautifully, is that to be ourselves and express ourselves and be accepted by the public, we have to keep our face in the light. Marilyn Horne was doing a concert with her husband Henry Lewis, doing *Cendrillon,* and I was sitting there kind of fidgeting, and she said to me "Flicka, stop moving and keep your face in the light." It was some of the best advice I got. [laughs]. It's so easy to do. You have a beautiful, statuesque, honest delivery; just play around with the dynamics. It's a long aria, the way it is divided, with two beats at the end of the measure, that are not quite the beat at the onset.

Meredith – You are looking at Samson and you are thinking how you are going to respond to that. Speaking of Marilyn Horne, she was the Samira at the *Ghosts of Versailles* premiere at the Met. Flicka tried to get a hold of her just to see if there were any comments she could give, and pass on. She said she would call later.

Stade – We tried. [laughs] You are just beautiful, but try this one phrase with different dynamics [demonstrates it] – naturally it grows bigger at the end, but try it differently, lowering the volume there, with the idea that you don't need to give all your voice there. You have to find a way to do a vocal transformation of it every time it repeats.

McLean – [sings that stretch, Stade interrupts her soon]

Stade – You are trying it too dramatic. Try it dolce, like you don't know what you are going to do.

[McLean repeats]

Stade – It's not over until it is over. Keep what you have, there, and keep going like this. OK, that's it, beautiful, thank you. [Addressing the faculty:] You have some great singers, here! [applause] We have time for a couple of questions from the audience.

[Audience member] Rossini composed some of your signature roles which Callas used to sing. I wonder if you listened to other singers who sang the roles before you.

Stade – Oh yes. I find it enormously useful to listen to your predecessors. These days there is no excuse not to listen, because of YouTube and everything. I remember singing a Mozart aria way too heavily, then I listened to a recording with Berganza and thought, "ah, that's the way it should be." That can always help. It's not like you are trying to imitate, by any means. Someone like Callas had such a personal style that you cannot try to imitate anything that she did, but you can learn from her. It's essential now, because we are entering a period where singing is becoming very sick, too heavy at times, and we have to go back and find the clear, light, slim singing that had been so special for so many years, by those senior singers who are dead. It's very helpful.

And for French diction, I have a recommendation. There is a YouTube of a little girl telling stories, and she is three, and everything you need to know about French is there; she says "il y avait une giraffe et un lion, et on avait peur!" ["there was a giraffe and a lion, and we were afraid" - she says it with very emphatic and emotional voice] – you get all those phonemes that the French do with the closed E, it's wonderful.

[Audience member] How do you keep your stamina while singing a very long opera? Do you get tired or bored?

Stade – We wear comfortable shoes! [Everybody laughs] It's not tedious. It's like playing your favorite sport. And it's never the same, because even though we are singing the same arias, the cast, the conductor and the sets are different. I get excited every time. That's the bad thing about Broadway – you are doing the same show for three years. But opera is never boring. There is an athletic aspect to it, and it is really fun. And it is a nice pretend. You know, I've spent way beyond the age of decency playing 14-year-old boys! [laughs]

Meredith – I'd say that the 14-year-olds are the ones who are way beyond decency! [everybody laughs].

Stade – Look at the characters. They are larger than life.

Meredith – You could ask the same question about song repertoire, which is an interesting question because when you are on stage for an opera you got the make-up, the costumes, you have other people to relate to and you look at the conductor. When you are singing a song recital you have to put all of that in your face and make a few gestures, and you are standing in front of your audience, alone. That's what most instrumentalists do not understand about singers. To do what the singers have to do is terrifying. You have to put so much research and experience into one 3-minute song, in a language that you do not speak, normally.

You know Medici.TV, a wonderful 24-hour classical music web TV, very high level. There is a wonderful documentary about Thomas Quasthoff, the German bass-baritone who just retired, unfortunately; one of the greatest Lieder singers. He teaches at the Hanns Eisler School of Music in Berlin, and he has a song competition. This is a 90-minute documentary on the competition, just German Lieder, and it is very revealing because they have a distinguished panel and they make comments not only about the singers, but about the pianists and conductors as well. It's very well balanced. What you have to learn and know to sing well these very short songs is immense.

You got now so many resources that I didn't have when I was in school! At the flick of your finger you have everything you got to know about these songs, that somebody has written or had the experience. Then you have to add your own to that. So, there is no excuse for not knowing all this stuff. It's so easy to know!

On this very stage when I was an undergraduate Gerald Moore gave a one-man show and then the next day a master class. Gerald Moore was the premier collaborative pianist of his era. He gave his one-man show and it was phenomenal. He wrote two books, *The Unashamed Accompanist*, and *Am I Too Loud?* He was brilliant, and I was able to play for him and listen to him here on this very stage. So take all your opportunities and listen to all those great singers and pianists. There are master classes you can watch online. Not that you don't have to take some of what they say with a grain of salt, but just listen. It's so much information, but it is so valuable!

[Audience member] I want to ask how you feel about the future of opera. I know it's a loaded question, but we are lucky to have great opera companies in our state right here in our yard, but many opera companies are closing down and it is discouraging when we have so much young talent willing to come out and find places to sing. You've done so much outreach with children, obviously, in California. What is your sense of the landscape?

Stade – I think in some ways it's an exciting time for opera, because there are more operas being written in English than in any other time. There are great composers out there right now, and they are really celebrating the voice. They are not doing yeeeh-yeaaaahhh [sings all over the range of the scale, people laugh], they are composing wonderful operas that the public responds to, so beautifully.

As singers, we have one task, and is a big one: to sing. And the rest you can't control. You can't control your career, you can't control who likes you and who doesn't like you. For the fifty people who love you on stage there will be fifty people who don't. All you can do is do what you do, and be open to what is happening because there are very innovative and exciting things happening. Just keep singing. Don't let the economy stop you. It may be one of the best things happening to opera, because we are having to turn to innovation. We are having to work harder to go out there and be available as entertainers.

Meredith – The kids that I work with, I take them all to the opera. I have eighteen students between the ages of eleven and seventeen. We get to the opera, the companies are very generous in giving us tickets, and they love it; they really love it. I never had that opportunity at that age. I'd see an opera singer on TV if I was lucky, and my dad's response to it was "shoot her and put her out of her misery." [everybody laughs] I never saw an opera until I came to school here and sang at the chorus; that's what got me hooked. Those operas we did are the operas that I adore, to this day. So, the kids love it. They get wrapped up in all the drama. We have three major companies and several smaller companies that do all sorts of things for the kids.

Stade – And I take even younger children to the opera, from the elementary school where I teach, and I took them even to heavy and hard operas like *Die tote Stadt*, and *The Rake's Progress*, where even I don't know what is going on… [laughs]. They never, even in a five-hour *Don Giovanni*, have wanted to leave. They are fascinated by the stage, by the singing, by the orchestra, they have a million questions, some of them have never been to San Francisco, or to an opera house…

Meredith – Or never heard any classical music in their lives.

Stade – They never heard anything beautiful. Something beautiful. I mean, I love pop music, but some of it is not "beautiful." [laughs] Thank you! [applause]

DIVISION SIX – THE COMPOSERS

CHAPTER TEN - CONTEMPORARY OPERA COMPOSERS

George Benjamin

In one of our most interesting interviews to date - and fittingly, Professor Benjamin was our 100th interviewee - Opera Lively talked in July 2013 with the incredibly talented composer in anticipation of the US Premiere of his outstanding opera *Written on Skin.*

Luiz Gazzola and George Benjamin – Photo credit Opera Lively

Written on Skin has been deemed by the influential French newspaper Le Monde the best opera written in the last twenty years, and has been heralded by many as the quintessential masterpiece of this first part of the 21st century. It has not only phenomenal dramatic impact from the text of famed English playwright Martin Crimp, but its music is exquisitely beautiful. Opera Lively will be publishing soon a guide book to it, containing the full libretto (duly authorized by its publishers).

Opera Lively - I congratulate you on the incredible success of *Written on Skin* which has taken the opera world by storm. I confess that it is in my opinion one of the three best contemporary operas I know, and one of the top twenty overall of all time, in my preference. So, we'll be soon talking extensively about *Written on Skin*, but I'd like to start by asking you about your music, in general. I see its style as something that is a bit hard to pinpoint – you do seem to employ chromatic scales and pentatonic scales, and in the past you've used microtones [intervals smaller than a semitone], but sometimes you also seem to zoom into a note and sustain it for long periods. Please clarify for our readers what is your musical style, and whether or not you affiliate yourself with any sort of school or movement.

George Benjamin - I have used microtones in some of my pieces – quite a long time ago – but they are not a regular part of my technique. My music is not conventionally tonal or atonal, and indeed frequently poly-harmonic, and I'm afraid I don't have a simple label to describe it. I have never been a member of a movement or group, and have always valued independence above all things.

OL - I think that what is admirable in your music is that you are very clear, very transparent. There is an incredible purity of sound. You employ sometimes a large orchestra – like in your *Written on Skin* with 60 instruments – but you seem to use each section of the orchestra sparsely and not simultaneously, so that while there is polyphony and lots of colorful texture, there are also moments of crystalline focus on one instrument, or of course when it's opera, on the voice, which seems to drive the harmonies and be the strongest core of the piece (which we, opera lovers, very much appreciate!). I believe that this is very efficient to tone-paint dramatic, strong, conflicting emotions. I know that this is too broad a question to ask, but maybe not. What would you say you try to express with your music?

GB - Quite simply I try to express or represent what the text demands – its narrative as well as its form. Transparency is frequently a major priority for me – I love the idea of a multi-faceted musical fabric where all elements are simultaneously perceptible, individually as well as in combination. In Written on Skin it was essential to me that the voices could sing softly and yet their lines – and the text – could be heard. And the way to achieve contrasts in colour across a large structure is through omission – leaving an aural "vacuum" in the texture, and then filling it while preparing another one... So, just in terms of orchestration, the first loud high trumpet note in the opera appears 40 minutes into the structure; the glockenspiel has only one note in Part One; the glass harmonica is only used in two scenes in the whole work; high soft flutes are only used once, etc. And the same approach applies to below the musical surface and to the formal (and above all harmonic) elements.

OL - I listened to your *Dance Figures* and simply loved it. *Sometime Voices* was also very nice. I am eager to get to know more of your output. If a classical music consumer wanted to get acquainted with the very best pieces of George Benjamin, what would the man himself – you - advise him or her to get?

GB - Probably, I think, start with my two operas – *Written on Skin* and *Into the Little Hill. Dance Figures* is more accessible than some of my other works, and much simpler in form and expression; alternatively perhaps I might mention *Upon Silence, Three Inventions for chamber orchestra, Palimpsests* or *Shadowlines.*

OL - As we the Opera Lively staff listened to *Written on Skin*, one of us heard influences of Britten, Debussy, and Berg. I heard Sciarrino especially in the way that you elongate the vowels, and Debussy in terms of dreamy, hypnotic sounds from the orchestra – *Pelléas et Mélisande* comes to mind (not to forget that Mr. Crimp's libretto touches on relatively similar themes to those of Debussy's masterpiece). If not, who were the greatest influences on you? I know that you studied with Peter Gellhorn, Alexander Goehr, Robin Holloway, the great Olivier Messiaen, and Yvonne Loriod – and did you study with Pierre Boulez?

GB - He has been extemely important to me, though he wasn't my teacher.

OL - I know you are a fan of Ligeti. You have also mentioned at one point that Purcell and Webern were divisors of waters in your musical growth, and you've quoted Indian music as influential as well. So please tell us about the synthesis of these multiple influences you might perhaps feel your music has evolved into.

GB - The most important influences? Indeed, most of the composers you mention above (though not all!). Though there are probably some others as well.

OL - Every composer has their own process that works for them. Sometimes it is an earwig that catches in the mind from which major parts of the score are spun. What can you tell us about your own composition process? From where does it come?

GB - I have techniques though no fixed method. Composing always remains a challenge for me; every passage seems almost impossible at first, and somehow I find a way of realising what is required. All I can say is that I sketch copiously and throw out 30 times more than I keep – and there is a lot more going on behind the scenes than sometimes seems the case.

OL - At the very young age of 16, you took lessons from Messiaen. Apparently, he compared your musical talents to those of Mozart. How did that come about, and how did you receive this evaluation from the great master? Did it place a burden on your shoulders?

GB - He was the most wonderful, devoted, enthusiastic, and inspiring teacher; I loved and revered him and I owe him more than I can ever express. Sometimes his enthusiasm, however, got carried away, and I never took that comparison to Mozart at all seriously...

OL - After a number of very well received instrumental pieces, you took upon yourself to compose a short opera, and then a full length opera. What brought you to the operatic art form? Can you please describe to us what is your relationship with opera, and how did it evolve over the years, from childhood into adulthood?

GB - I already wanted to write opera, even when a young child. I had a wonderful illustrated book of myths and fables, and would improvise operas to them in my head for hours on end. Then I sometimes accompanied silent movies on the piano as a student, and that taught me something about controlling large stretches of time as well as narrative pacing and intention. But the crucial element was, for me, the meeting with Martin Crimp – his style and his language inspired me and, quite simply, opened the curtains of musical theatre to me...

OL - Let's address your fist opera, *Into the Little Hill.* It is really surprising, how you and Mr. Crimp got a traditional story like that of the Pied Piper of Hamelin, and packed so much in 37 minutes. How did the idea of setting this to music come about?

GB - It was one of the 50 subjects I suggested to Martin when we first agreed to collaborate – a list that I had been preparing for decades. The Pied Piper was there because I had already started an opera on that subject when about 14, with text by a school friend. (It was terrible, by the way, and fortunately never got beyond the first appearance of the rats...)

OL - The Stranger – the Pied Piper character in your opera - says that music opens the door to the heart, and that music stops death. One would say it's a direct quote of how powerful music is. Was this a particular intention of this piece?

GB - Yes absolutely, one of its main themes.

OL - Why did you employ two female voices – a soprano and a contralto – to sing each, multiple characters?

GB - Economy of means above all; though I perhaps also have a slight preference for high voices. And the wonderful singers for whom I conceived the work – Anu Komsi and Hilary Summers - inspired me.

OL - Any particular reason for not having an overture, and starting the first bars with the piercing shouts "kill, kill"?

GB - Yes, immersing the audience into the drama immediately, without any comfortable or engaging instrumental preparation.

OL - *Into the Little Hill* was very well received. Did the motivation to write a full-length opera come from its success?

GB - Yes, of course, though it had been an ambition, as I mentioned before, since my beginnings as a composer.

OL - Did you expect when you composed *Written on Skin* that it would be so well received by critics and audiences alike?

GB - I never began to imagine the response it has received...

OL - How did you get to collaborate with Martin Crimp? I know you met him in 2005 after looking extensively for someone to write for you an opera libretto. Other than being an incredibly talented playwright, he is also a pianist – did this latter aspect help in terms of your operatic collaboration?

GB - A mutual friend – the distinguished American violist and scholar, Laurence Dreyfus – introduced us. Martin is an extraordinary writer and yes, his intense musicality is also immensely helpful for our work together.

OL - Who picked the story that was the source for Written on Skin, you or Mr. Crimp? How was the process of selecting the theme for the opera?

GB - Martin's eldest daughter Catherine was responsible for finding the precise Occitane story on which the opera is based – though it was the director of the Aix festival, Bernard Foccroulle, who encouraged us to look in that direction. The work, indeed, owes an untold amount to him.

OL - What aspects of this 13th century story inspired you to compose an opera? Some will say it's a feminist theme with this strong heroine Agnès.

GB - The story is simple, strong and dramatic. It deals with big, universal themes. But it was Agnes' response to her husband's gruesome crime which was the deciding factor – her defiance is in the original text, and I believe it remains powerful and startling even today.

OL - Did Martin Crimp write the entire libretto before you started on the musical composition, or was it a collaborative effort?

GB - We met and talked endlessly before he wrote the text, though I didn't start composing till Martin's task was complete.

OL - Your music is incredibly atmospheric, at times sensual, even erotic, at other times urgent and powerful complementing the dark actions and words of the libretto. The ups and downs of this powerful story are admirably rendered by your music, employing for instances static periods of tension, then shocking, furious orchestration when things get hectic. How did you proceed to create this incredible match? Line by line with, or in broader painting strokes?

GB - Both, at the same time! I had to be aware of the sonorous implications of every word in the text, while constantly trying to shape and control musical construction on the largest scale. Both are essential, I believe – though the fusion is far from easy. It's like simultaneously looking through a microscope and at a distant alpine landscape, if that's not too picturesque or banal an analogy...

OL - Let's address a little bit your use of two great instruments that are rarely seen in opera: the viol or viola da gamba, and the glass harmonica.

First, the viola da gamba, which you contrast with cellos and basses and low trumpets, trombones and horns. What did you want to express with this arrangement?

GB - The viol is only used in scenes 6 and 15, two moments of great importance in the story. Its melancholy and sensual tones add, I hope, a new timbral dimension to the work at these junctures. I also wanted to coat the instrument's sound in unusual timbres, in particular medium-low brass played fortissimo with practice mutes – mutes by which very strong playing becomes soft and seems apparently distant. A by-product of these mutes played loudly (the force employed is still clearly audible) is an expansion of harmonics, in a way not too far from the viol's own generous spectrum – hence I believe they combine well, creating a spangled overall sonority.

OL - Now, the glass harmonica. I simply love it. One of my favorite operas is *Die Frau ohne Schatten*, and it uses it. I also feel that the productions of *Lucia di Lammermoor* that do use it in the mad scene like Donizetti intended, get to be much more haunting and beautiful than those that use a flute, instead. So please tell us about how you utilized this fabulous instrument in *Written on Skin.*

GB - The instrument has fascinated me for years, though I never used it before. I love the way one can hear the friction between the fingers and the glass; the resultant sound is simultaneously extremely resonant and yet highly fragile. It's also a wonderful harmonic resource and I have written some pretty complex chords for it (up to 10 notes!). It's also used in only scenes 6 and 15, like the viol, so it's reserved exclusively for these two important moments. The Boy is an illuminator, and I imagined these instruments as the most special hues he could use...

OL - The narrative technique in the third person – where the characters talk about the action before they perform it, and refer to themselves as The Protector, The Boy, and The Woman, is very powerful, besides functioning like a sort of meta-language about the operatic art form itself, with its artificiality – people don't talk to each other by singing while in opera they do, so this narrative form introduces an element of theatre within the theatre that is very interesting for opera. This is Mr. Crimp's hallmark style, since his play *Attempts on Her Life*. This, coupled with the role of the Angels in moving events along, made me feel that the opera addresses the inevitable destiny of the characters, like a train wreck in the making that can't be stopped, given the human condition. Would you agree? If not, how would you define the function of this particular narrative structure?

GB - You have expressed it very well, thank you. The place of opera in our culture has changed – a lot – since the 19th century and both Martin and I felt impelled to address the challenge of how to make the form feel natural in the 21st century. The auto-narration we have used is one response to that crucial issue. This very simple convention, paradoxically, allows me to be more spontaneous and direct than would have been the case with a more conventional text. Plus, for me, it also provides moments of strange poetry which lift the work into the realm of dreams.

OL - This might be more a question for Mr. Crimp but I guess you're also fully equipped to address it. Some of the libretto evokes downright macabre imagery. For example, the Protector's line, "Take his hair in your fist - says the third - pull his head back for a kiss: and as you are cutting one long clean incision through the bone, examine your own portrait in the glass-black mirror of his eyes." This is also a great example of the juxtaposition of sensuality and death imagery in this opera--for example here, of one man sensually kissing another as he draws the knife through the other's abdomen, looking in his eyes. Any comments on Mr. Crimp's powerful text, and its imaginative and concise use of language?

GB - Quite simply his language, as well as his unique sense of structure, inspires me; it's as simple as that! Plus he is the most generous of collaborators, and I do feel that he plants his texts with the specific words and imagery that will most directly provoke my music.

OL - In both *Into the Little Hill* and *Written on Skin*, there are anachronistic elements – the limousines in the first one; the references to an international airport in the second one, etc. The interplay of past and present is very interesting in the libretto. For example, when The Boy is talking about the future and says, "I'm thinking that when, when this wood and this light are cut through by eight lanes of poured concrete, I'm thinking that the two of us and everyone we love, everyone, will have been dead for a thousand years." This particular staging by Ms. Katie Mitchell is definitely looking back at this medieval story from contemporary times. Were you trying to get at how perennial these human dramas are?

GB - Yes, absolutely- plus the alluring strangeness of juxtaposing distant history with today.

OL - The opera seems to progress at a hectic pace through the setting up of the situation in Part One, with growing tension and an explosion of eroticism to end it; then, a very disrupted and fragmented Part Two where all the emotions are in turmoil; then we get to the lyric, ponderous, almost serene Part Three where the damage has been done and now it's a question of letting it all take its course (well rendered by Katie Mitchell in the slow-motion final scene). One would say that an essential characteristic of *Written in Skin* is it harmonic motion. It also doesn't seem to employ leitmotifs – there is always novelty as it goes on, making for a very rich score. How do you describe the musical structure of your opera?

GB - There is definitely something in what you say; in particular the scene after The Boy's murder in Part Three where – before Agnes's final aria - the music does somewhat retreat from the heat of the narrative in order to let the drama take its inexorable course.

There are no conventional leitmotifs, though there are leit-harmonies and leit-timbres, if you will allow me to employ those terms! And yes, harmonic motion is extremely important, an absolutely crucial resource in the construction of form on this scale.

You say "always novelty"? Yes, exactly – I wanted, until the last bar, to continuously introduce fresh and unexpected elements into the work's sound-field, in tandem with the drama and its evolution.

OL - Those that have seen the world premiere will by now have tied the three main roles to Bejun Mehta, Barbara Hannigan, and Christopher Purvis, not to forget the excellent complimarios Victoria Simmonds and Alan Clayton. You worked very closely with them during the composition and it can be said that they created the roles. Tell us about the collaborative process with the singers.

GB - All five of the singers came to my home, and I accompanied them in lieder and took copious and detailed notes of their precise vocal capacities. I had their voices in mind throughout the process of composing, and their vocal idiosyncrasies directly shaped the vocal lines I wrote.

OL - How much input did they have to give regarding the vocal lines?

GB - Nothing regarding the precise notes themselves; but the lines were conceived directly into their voices, which are therefore – in a way – present in every single bar of the score.

OL - How has it been to work with other singers on the roles which you created for your original singers? Have you had to modify the score or vocal lines in any way to accommodate different singers?

GB - No accommodations have been necessary – and, of course, it's fascinating for me to hear others perform the roles, though nothing will ever erase my memories of the original cast and their extraordinary performances.

OL - The Aix-en-Provence Festival production was extremely powerful. For example, when Purvis embraces Mehta and sings of telling Agnes of The Boy's betrayal with Marie. Was it as you had envisioned in your mind's eye as you composed the work or where there new elements which Katie Mitchell surprised you with? How closely did you work with Katie on the world premiere staging? We've interviewed stage directors before, and they said that when they are staging a work by a living composer, some of them feel it's the composer's baby, and they feel that they must respect the composer's artistic vision. Some others said the composers stepped back and let them develop their own vision. Who had artistic control over the world premiere?

GB - Katie's work was superb and yes, she surprised me with many things – it's an authentic production of the work after all, something I'm not really sufficiently skilled or experienced to envisage myself. And yet Martin and I worked very closely with her before and throughout rehearsals, and she remained absolutely loyal to our vision for the piece.

OL - Now that you have seen *Written on Skin* staged, are you satisfied that it succeeds dramatically as you imagined while you were composing it? Is there anything you would change?

GB - Probably not, though I'm too close to judge... But the work is complete, out in print (my excellent publisher has already produced the vocal and full scores) so even if I wanted to change it now it's not possible.

OL - We are about to have the US premiere of *Written on Skin*, conducted by yourself, at the Tanglewood Festival on August 12. What are your expectations for this performance?

GB - I love Tanglewood – I think this is my sixth visit since 1999 – and I hugely look forward to working with the gifted young musicians there in the wonderful Ozawa Hall, in that exceptionally beautiful landscape.

OL - Are you at a liberty to tell us about future plans for having the opera fully staged in America? We do know of the upcoming European runs up to this 2013-2014 season – your opera has achieved runs by 8 different companies in 13 months which is utterly remarkable for contemporary opera – so, you don't need to tell us about what is already happening, but we'd be curious to know about the future. What else is in the horizon?

GB - There are several more new productions confirmed over the next few years, plus continuing revivals of the original one. There are also advanced plans for fully staged performances in the USA, though it's too early for me to be specific.

OL - You have quite a talent for dramatic tone painting. Would you like to explore other genres, such as lighter, comedic opera?

GB - I love comedy, but am not entirely convinced by the comic potential of music – at least my own music. Though I do love *Gianni Schicchi*; let's see in due course...

OL - Your next commission is scheduled for 2018, which is five years out. How did you schedule this? Are there other projects you will be working on in the meantime, or it's just because opera houses these days are all booked up for the next several years? Are you at a liberty to tell us a bit about this commission? Have you already thought of a theme?

GB - Sorry, both Martin and I are highly secretive about our work, so my lips have to remain sealed. Though neither of us work fast, so five years isn't excessive...

OL - Sometimes contemporary opera with its emphasis on drama and, for the non-initiated, its less melodic, more fragmented music, has an uphill battle to win the hearts and minds of traditional opera lovers. But how would you go about this uphill battle, in terms of conquering an audience? I mean, you've done it already, given that the Royal Opera House shows of *Written on Skin* sold out, so you may have some insight to share with us in terms of getting other pieces to be as successful – besides, obviously, having talented composers like yourself at the helm. Is there something that can be done to better familiarize the public with the language of contemporary opera? I feel that in mainstream media classical pieces of other eras are given a lot of exposure, but contemporary music is not.

GB - Write from the heart, try to understand theatre, take risks with the form and take nothing for granted, and above all love the human voice and its interface with instruments – that would be my immediate advice.

But I am encouraged, it has to be said, in the seemingly huge interest in modern opera that has emerged in recent years here in the UK and across

Europe.

OL - I'd say, in America as well, there is strong interest in contemporary opera, and we at Opera Lively do our best to cover it. Do you follow the work of other contemporary composers?

GB - Yes, a lot – in particular for my conducting and teaching work.

OL - What colleagues of yours do you admire?

GB - From approximately my own generation: Oliver Knussen, Tristan Murail, Hans Abrahamsen, Unsuk Chin, Simon Holt, Julian Anderson... And amongst young composers that really interest me (including some of my own students) I might mention names like Luke Bedford, Sean Shepherd, Saed Haddad, Vasco Mendonca, Dai Fujikura, Martin Suckling, Christian Mason...

OL - Teaching seems to be one of your passions. Tell us about today's students of composition, especially those who want to focus on opera. In this day and age of worldwide economic crisis and budget constraints for the high arts, what advice do you give to your young students who want to embrace a career in composition?

GB - I can't usually advise them about their careers, but I can try to help with their compositional technique and clarity of vision. There is much interest in new opera here in the UK, and, though limited, there are resources which young composers can approach for experiment and research in this field.

OL - Your partner Michael Waldman is a filmmaker. Are there plans to get into scores for the movies?

GB - No plans for movie music! Though I do love film as a medium its musical potential, alas, usually seems distinctly limited.

OL - Let's end if you don't mind by asking you about the person underneath the artist. What are some of your extra-musical interests?

GB - Literature, art, cinema, landscape, my extended family and friends, tennis...

OL - What kind of person are you, in terms of personality?

GB - For that, you would need to ask Michael!

OL – Thank you for a great interview!

GB – Thank you!

Kevin Puts

Kevin Puts' first opera *Silent Night* premiered in 2012 at Minnesota Opera to smashing public and critic acclaim, and won the 2012 Pulitzer Prize for Music. It got a second run at Opera Philadelphia. We interviewed the composer in January 2013. He beautifully transmitted to us his new-found passion for the operatic genre, and his visceral relationship with music. Mr. Puts expressed to our readers the ins and outs of the creative process of a new opera, and his exhilaration in being part of this phenomenon.

Opera Lively – I've just listened to your opera; congratulations, it is very beautiful.

Kevin Puts – Thank you.

OL - This is your first experience writing opera, after significant symphonic work (four symphonies, several concertos, and one vocal piece for baritone and chamber ensemble called *Einstein on Mercer Street.* Let's first talk about your music. Do you identify yourself with a specific movement? Who are the contemporary composers you admire?

KP – I don't identify myself with a specific movement by any means. I have very broad tastes and I think perhaps the fact that I have such wide-ranging musical interests is why I enjoyed writing opera so much. Certain composers define their style and then they need to find a subject that will suit it. I don't feel that way, I feel interested in a lot of subjects for opera. The interesting thing for me is to approach each of those projects in a different way, and to do whatever I need to do, musically, to fit the story. I like a lot of different music these days. I like the post-minimalist composers like John Adams and Steve Reich, I like Christopher Rouse very much, Thomas Adès…

People assign certain labels to my music but I never found any of them absolutely accurate. There is a lot of variety in my style. It is really pretty hard to define it. I've never really tried to define it or to limit myself to certain stylistic traits that would be easily definable.

OL - I understand that William Bolcom was your teacher. We like his eclectic style and love some of his pieces like his operas *A Wedding* and *A View From the Bridge*. Was he a major influence for you? Or were any of your other teachers also major influences?

KP – That's right. William Bolcom is someone whose music I admire very much because he is so adept at so many different styles and techniques! More than influencing my music, I'm philosophically influenced by his approach and his belief in what music can be. His style and approach lend themselves very well to a lifetime of composing. You never get tired of writing music because you are always trying something new and it all feels personal. I believe he is a great opera composer because he is so flexible!

A lot of my teachers were influences in different ways. Christopher Rouse remains a big influence because his orchestration, his use of the instruments in the orchestra is so meticulous! Long ago we entered in an age in which anything goes and value judgments are often to be put aside or at least aggressively relaxed, and we are supposed to accept anything that a composer throws at us, but I think that Christopher Rouse's music works on a very objective level, and that's the way I try to make my music work as well for it to be right. There is a right and a wrong, the way I approach music. Something either works, or it doesn't. I think Rouse approaches music in the same way.

OL - You've mentioned that in your opera, there is "music that is atonal, strictly tonal, minimalist, and unashamedly emotional." Indeed, for example, in lieutenant Audebert's first act aria, we can hear an insisting accompaniment with repetitive structures that is very evocative of Philip Glass' music. Other moments seem neo-Romantic, with melodies inspired by 19th and 20th century composers. Battle scenes tend to be atonal. How did you go about melding it all together?

KP – I was aware that I was going to use a lot of different styles. Early in the opera after this pseudo-Mozart opera moment occurs, a theme is developed, which is based on one of the motives in the Mozart-sounding music – a falling fifth motif, and that becomes the battle theme, or the war theme for lack of a better term. I used that theme to tie everything together. It keeps coming back; it is always clothed in different harmony. Even if it is subconscious, my hope is that it connects the various styles that you hear in the piece.

Of course, transition is crucial. You got to find a way to deftly move from one style of music to the other. It has to be done in a very crafty way that feels organic. I could go into that in more theoretical detail, but it might be of not much interest to do that.

What I love about opera is that it demands the broadest range of emotion. You have to go – for me in this piece anyway – in the direction of atonality and challenging, dissonant music, and in the opposite direction of absolute simplicity. It needs that kind of range.

OL - Are there opera composers that inspired you? Were you an opera aficionado before writing this piece?

KP – I'm not an opera aficionado by any means. I'm not an opera buff. I don't know opera very well. I'm learning opera. Composers whose operas I love would be Mozart, Puccini, and I'm only now getting to know Verdi. I never knew Verdi very well. I knew Wagner a little bit and of course I've studied his music. I'm interested in Alban Berg. I like *Lulu* and *Wozzeck*. For me his style is very strict and limited, but I don't mean it in a pejorative sense. I like John Adams' operas; I like *Nixon in China* very much. I think Benjamin Britten is fantastic. His operas affected me the most, and taught me what I need to do, the most. They come the closest to this expression that I am interested in, the balance between aria and dialogue. That's a challenge, for me. I want the dialogue to sound convincing as dialogue, but I also want it to be musically interesting and singable, and I think that Britten solved that very well. And also, his pacing is impeccable, especially in his big operas *Peter Grimes* and *Billy Budd*; I just love them.

OL - Some people say that there is these days almost an American genre of writing new opera, since after a belated start from the great European masters (necessarily so, of course, since we are a younger country), opera is actually getting a strong foothold in the United States and we've been premiering many new works. Our pieces usually are strongly dramatic, and often include some spicy orchestration. Do you see your opera as part of an American style, or do you see yourself as influenced by other perspectives?

KP – I don't really exactly know whether my music fits into an American style or into the tradition of the European masters. No matter what, my music is often referred to as American. It could be that the people hear a kind of American romanticism – Samuel Barber and Copland – and they also hear overtones and echoes of minimalism in various places. Those things are there in *Silent Night*. So, either consciously or subconsciously – I actually don't remember how conscious it was [laughs] – I made some attempt at making the French music sound French, the German music sound German to some degree. I don't think it was very conscious but it comes off that way. People hear Debussy when they hear the French music. They hear Webern or Strauss when they hear the German music.

I know that this is a very exciting time for American opera. It seems that orchestras and symphonic organizations are having a hard time right now financially, but opera companies seem to be doing better. I'm not sure of this exactly, but I think a lot of it has to do with commissioning. A lot of opera houses are not really afraid of commissioning. They see that as a vital and exciting part of what they do. They are still able to get audiences for it.

OL - Much is said of contemporary opera that many of its pieces are based on strong dramaturgical values but less accomplished vocal writing. I've heard from singers the accusation that many contemporary opera composers don't understand the voice. The public often craves melodies, while often composers these days favor music that is not immediately pleasing to the ears of an operatic public accustomed to the great melodies of the Baroque, Classical, and Romantic periods. In caving in to the public's craving, however, composers don't want to be called sentimentalists and to churn out music that has colors that could be described as "been there, done that" – so, finding the right musical language for contemporary opera must be difficult. How do you position yourself in this controversy?

KP – This is a really challenging question [pauses, thinks]. This is what I was alluding to, before. In fact, one of the reviews of *Silent Night* recently discusses this to some extent, that most of the melodies were in the orchestra [laughs]. It may be true, but I still try to make the vocal lines melodic and lyrical and something that the singers can do something with. Mostly what people mean by melody is a memorable tune, like Mozart or Gershwin or John Williams or Puccini. You know, it is very difficult to do that and be convincing, especially when you are in the middle of theater and drama, making the opera feel like a story, to suddenly stop and have something which is a melody in the traditional sense and is formally designed like a song. Usually you need repetition, so there needs to be strophic structure to it. It is difficult to do that and remain convincing as a storyteller, and not to feel that it is derivative of music that is 200, or 100, or 150 years old. It is something that I struggle with, and I'm... [sighs]... still working out this issue.

How do I give singers melodies that they can really do something with and that are memorable, but are not sentimental? I guess sentimentalism is the right word. Honestly, it can just sound foolish [laughs], like this big soaring melody. It could be a soaring line. It could be a line but not something that people can define or remember.

Actually harmony is more important than anybody realizes. In fact, people say "I love the melodies in your piece" but I think that really what they mean is a harmony. Harmonies give the music a satisfying structure and a sense of growth and beauty. I think most of the beauty comes off not just in the shape of the melody, but in the harmony that supports it. So, you can use a beautiful series of harmonies, and the singer can float on top of that and sing things that are lyrical, but not absolutely memorable in the way you remember a children's song or a Mozart aria. I'm not sure I answered that well.

OL – You did, it was a very interesting answer.

KP – OK. [laughs]

OL - With such complex characters in three different cultural contexts – Germans, Scots, French – have you made use of leitmotifs to musically differentiate them? If yes, can you give us some examples? What ideas or characters have you underlined with recurrent themes?

KP – I didn't use leitmotifs for the different characters, but I think I associated emotions and situations with the type of music rather than a leitmotif as in a series of notes or rhythms. For example, Lieutenant Audebert and his father, when they speak, they converse in a sort of recitative style, but the underlying music is a pattern of string passages that returns in various places. There is actually a motif, this [hums it], this turn that you associate with these two characters. Lieutenant Sprink when he is communicating this battle-torn self, there is a certain style that he sings in, that is pretty atonal, actually, but usually there is a referential pitch, like a sustained pitch that he sings against, so that style is there when he is trying to overcome the fact that he has been so traumatized by the war.

There aren't so much leitmotifs to differentiate the characters. Maybe it's naïve but I try to paint exactly the emotional picture, to reflect the emotion of each scene with the music, to get exactly the kind of flavor of each scene through the harmony and the type of music. It comes from the fact that this is my first opera and I spent so much time writing symphonies and pieces where you don't have any story; you don't have any visual element; the music has to say everything. So I took that philosophy to this piece, with the understanding that you can only rely on the music to tell the story, which is not true in opera, of course – you have actors, and you have scenery, and the script, which is the libretto that tells you a lot. For my next opera I may do a little more of that, associating various materials with characters.

OL - In this piece, a central musical role is played by the bagpipes, an unusual instrument for opera orchestras, to say the least. Please tell us about it.

KP – Oh yes, it is an unusual instrument. The bagpipes were not in the orchestra – they proved to be so loud that I had to put them backstage, so there is someone on the stage that is miming and making it look like he is playing, but the bagpipe is way backstage, in a box [laughs] because outside the box, it is too loud. We experimented with that, but we definitely wanted to have a real bagpipe, playing.

OL - There are short moments of quasi-spoken dialogue, and some moments where silence is used to build up the emotional tension. Can you please tell us about some of the devices you've used to keep the narrative going and to convey the theatrical elements in your music?

KP – I think I just kind of use my instincts for that, but there are moments when very little happens that are much more dramatic than when a lot happens. Silence or minimal accompaniment can be very powerful. I tried to not keep things so busy all the time that it is tiring to hear. Certainly you can be very powerful when all that the audience is hearing is a single sustained pitch.

OL - Have you or Mr. Campbell had any interaction with the creator of the movie, Christian Carion?

KP – We did not have any interaction with him, to my knowledge. Mr. Carion approved the libretto and he gave us his permission to continue, and I hope that he gets to hear the piece at some point.

OL - Obviously a central idea behind the movie *Joyeux Noël* – and actually the real-life events that inspired it were a real demonstration of the same principle – is music being able to establish bridges between human beings and communicate common emotions as a way of bringing peace in the middle of conflict. Please tell us about how you describe your relationship with music and the value of music in today's world.

KP – Honestly, my relationship with music is almost a religious one. I am not a religious person, so for me music is the evidence that there may be something greater than myself, something that I can't really understand. A wonderful concert and beautiful music can unite people and can provide a sense of community. For me music is the best example and the best evidence that our humanity means something and is important.

OL - Let's talk about the creative process for this piece. It was commissioned by Minnesota Opera, and they offered you and your librettist Mr. Campbell, workshops and other expert resources, such as translators to work on the opera's different languages (German, French, English, Latin, and Italian). How long did it take to compose it? What use did you make of the resources at your disposition? What changes did you make that came from input you got from Minnesota Opera's seasoned operatic professionals? Can you give us specific examples of input received and change made?

KP – It took about one year to compose the first and second acts in a piano vocal score, but I made very clear notes to myself, because I heard the piece orchestrally in my mind, and the piano parts are very awkward and difficult to play. I made so much effort to revise it and make it easier! But I made very detailed notes to myself so that when I orchestrated it, it would be easier to do it. The orchestration still took about a year. So the entire process took two years.

We had three workshops at Minnesota Opera, and it was a terrific process. One workshop that I directed had the young artists of the Minnesota program who were there in residence, and they sang the entire first act for us, and some of them were actually in the premiere as well. Everybody gave good advice and I appreciated it. I'm used to composition being a very lonely endeavor. It's all me by myself in a room with a computer and a keyboard, and here you have lots of people to talk about things with. I'd ask, "Will this piece work? Do you think this is clear? Do you think this aria needs to be more lyrical?" and everybody would give great advice. I found it to be a very satisfying environment.

Most of the changes made were in terms of pacing – "we need more time here, or less time there." Some scene changes need to happen – it's a pretty complicated set, on a revolving disc, and set pieces which move around it, so... Some things need to be in place for the set pieces to move around. And then there was one moment when actually someone from the opera company said "you know, I don't think you did well here, I think you could do better with this aria; it could be more singable, more lyrical, and more triumphant." And I took it seriously, and worked on it until everybody agreed with it.

OL - One of the advantages of creating new opera, for singers and conductors, is obviously the fact that the composer is alive and things can be worked out in real time. First of all, singers are there in flesh and bone. Have you adapted your vocal writing to the specific singers that were creating the roles?

KP – Yes, in fact I adapted the last aria that William Burden sings for his character Nikolaus Sprink. His last aria was written when I found out that Bill Burden was going to be cast as Sprink. I rewrote that aria and actually asked Mark Campbell for some more text so that I could make something more expanded for him so that he could have a real aria kind of moment.

OL - What about the conductor maestro Michael Christie? How were your interactions with him? Did you make musical changes based on his input?

KP – Michael Christie is wonderful. Yes, Michael suggested a couple of things, but in general he is very interested in bringing the piece to life the way that I imagined it. He was just so open to ideas I had! Tempo, and style, and style that players play in… He has a lot of experience with new music, and it shows. He really knows how to work with the composer and to work with the orchestra and teach them the vocabulary of this new piece. He is very patient but also very demanding. In a friendly way, he is very demanding with his orchestra, so, he is the perfect collaborator.

OL - We've asked questions of a stage director – German director Ms. Yvonne Fontane [Volume 1]- who was working on a new opera in England, with the composer present. Now we're interviewing you and taking it the other way around (different pieces, of course, but the same situation). So, from that director, we wanted to know if there was some restraint placed on her creative freedom, because of the, maybe, intimidating presence of the live composer, since after all it was his opera, and she needed to try to fulfill his vision – something very different from the leeway and liberties some directors sometimes take when re-working pieces of the existing repertoire, such as what is done in the movement known as Regietheater. However, she said, the piece started to take a flight of its own and at some point the composer sort of backed off and just watched her work her magic, and seemed very pleased with the result. We've had on the other hand indirect account that Ms. Saariaho was very polite about the first staging of one of her operas, but didn't seem – granted, it's our guess – too pleased or too enthusiastic about the result.

So, back to you, and your work with Mr. Eric Simonson, the stage director. Did the two of you, or the three of you including Mr. Campbell, get together to discuss specific scenes? Where there any conflicts so to speak (a strong word, but I mean it in the good sense), about different visions for certain scenes, and if yes, how did they get resolved? Would you want to change anything, in future runs? Are you pleased with the way your work has been staged?

KP – I was told before I wrote this, by other composers: "Oh, you know, don't write an opera, because you will have to work with some director who will destroy the piece and will have a totally different vision for what the piece should be," etc., and I just didn't find that to be the case at all. I found Eric Simonson very respectful of what we envisioned for the piece. Honestly, it was just a very friendly relationship. I wish I had better stories to tell you, but I really don't. For me, I didn't have an incredibly precise picture of how I wanted everything to look, or the staging, etc. I just knew and was mainly worried about the music, the rhythm of the music and the pace of things being exactly right, and sounding exactly right and evoking the nature and the emotion of the scenes to my satisfaction, and once that happened – and of course it took three workshops and the rehearsal period of the opera itself for it to happen, to get that in place – once that was there, I was pretty happy, I was sort of just dazzled by the whole thing. It was my first experience so I was just interested in watching it all happen. They did more than what I imagined they could do, and of course the costumes and scenery came into play, and it was all fascinating for me.

OL - Your opera was very well received by critics and public. You must be well-deservedly pleased. This may sound silly to ask, but I will, anyway: do you see a difference in, maybe, warmth of reception, between the operatic public and the symphonic public?

KP – It's an interesting question. [pauses] Hm… I don't necessarily see a difference in the kind of public. I think that we all basically like the same things in music. You can talk about more or less sophisticated audiences. There are very sophisticated people who are better read and more articulate than I am, but we all appreciate the same music. I think this is true of both the symphonic and the operatic audiences. We all know when something feels phony, when it doesn't feel genuine, when it feels forced, when something just doesn't work, when something is disappointing, and I think that maybe it is true that more of the weight of the piece is carried by the story, in opera. If the story carries the piece pretty well then the audience will be much more lenient in their estimation of the music. I think this may be true.

When I had symphonic pieces played I got both very good responses and lukewarm responses. I often find, though, with symphonic audiences that when there is something in the piece that is outside of the abstract, when there is something real, something they can think about, some kind of story or program to the piece, they are always much more receptive. I don't know why that is, exactly. Of course in opera we always have something for the message, so it makes it easier.

OL - Then, you won the Pulitzer Prize. Can you describe for us the circumstances and your thoughts when you learned that you had won the Pulitzer?

KP – I was totally shocked when I heard about the Pulitzer Prize. I was sitting home with my family, and the phone rang, and it was the Associated Press. I didn't even pick it up because I wasn't by the phone. [laughs] I didn't even realize I was a finalist. Instantly, everything changed. It was kind of shocking, how that day went, from being very ordinary, to just a complete barrage of phone calls – from everybody I know, and from every newspaper and radio station in the area and the country. You know, a couple of weeks go by and it kind of calms down, but it really never goes away entirely. I think that for some reason, once you have the name of the award associated with you, in the eyes of a lot of people it places more value on your work, so I got a lot busier with requests for various things, so I think it definitely does change things for me in terms of my life as a composer.

OL - Your opera is having its second outing at Opera Philadelphia. How is for you the experience of seeing it on stage for another run? Many members of the team are the same but there are a few changes. Are there significant differences for you, between the two runs? And any different emotions for you, as a composer?

KP – It's been very good at Opera Philadelphia; very good, actually. Many of the members are the same. Karin Wolverton who sang Anna, and Kelly Kaduce who is singing Anna now are very different, and they bring different things to the role, but I think they are both doing great things; what they do work for different reasons.

OL – Can you elaborate on this, a little?

KP – They have very different voices. But let me tell you what the experience of a different run is. I'm much more comfortable with the piece. Everyone in the cast is much more comfortable as well. You just feel them delivering their roles with confidence. The interaction is much more electric. And I'm learning more as I am sort of relaxed, I'm not worrying about "oh, is this going to go well, is this going to go well?" Composers worry about every event working. Now I can sit back and trust that it will work, and think about, next time, what I will do differently - what is really working here in terms of vocal writing, for one thing, and what I will try differently with my next opera.

OL – Did you participate a lot more in the rehearsal process in Minnesota as compared to Philadelphia?

KP – Yes. Much more for Minnesota; I was there for about five week;, we did a lot of work, I was there for almost all the staging rehearsals. Here in Philadelphia I was there for only about four rehearsals. I found that they really just didn't need me. [laughs]

OL – Are there other planned runs in other opera companies? Do you think of taking the opera abroad, and have had any propositions, if you're at a liberty to say?

KP - There are others. The ones I am pretty sure of are Fort Worth Opera, Cincinnati Opera, Kansas City Lyric, and Calgary Opera.

OL – I'm glad to learn that it is going forward.

KP – I'm happy to see that there is more, because you know, once you do a big opera, it's a big project and of course you want people to do it.

OL - Now, with this smashing success, what are your thoughts about continuing your career as an opera composer? How pleased are you with the genre? Any plans for new works we may look forward to, if you are at a liberty to say?

KP – Oh yes, you know, now I'm completely addicted to opera. *The Manchurian Candidate*, I don't know if you heard about that; do you know that story?

OL – Oh yes, I do, it's the film in the early sixties about a conspiracy to prepare a man to become the president of the United States.

KP – Exactly. So, we are doing that for Minnesota Opera; I'm working with Mark Campbell again.

OL – Oh, wow!

KP – Yes, so, we are already working on that. I've got some other projects that are non-operatic that I'm working on, but it is hard for me to get away from this libretto, because I want to get started. It just does something for me, to tell a story with music, you know? I grew up loving film and film scores; I'm always imagining something. When I write music I often think of something non-musical, something real, like I'm telling a story, even if I'm not telling a literal story. Then, for me, to see on page one "this is what is supposed to happen on the stage," it just excites me creatively in a way that I hadn't experienced before. So writing opera is just something I'm now completely addicted to.

OL - What pieces of literature or cinema do you believe deserve operatic treatment that haven't been done yet? Any big sleepers out there that are just waiting for an adventurous composer to make them into an opera? Now that you've been through this, does it happen to you to read a novel, watch a stage play or a movie, for example, and think, "huh, I could make a good opera out of this"? Any specific examples?

KP – [laughs] Interesting! I don't know, I'm really bad at finding things that will work on the operatic stage. Of course, I'd love to write *To Kill a Mockingbird*, it's a wonderful novel, one of my favorite novels, but my librettist told me that it would be very difficult to do on stage, it would be hard to get it right. I'm actually in the process now of thinking of some more subjects. But I have a hard time with this for some reason, I always find it more interesting when somebody else finds something for me, then I think, "Oh, I could do that!" So, I don't have a lot of ideas at the moment, but once I do, I'll probably try to approach some companies.

OL - Of everything that you've composed – symphonies, concertos – what would be your favorite piece, and would *Silent Night* be good competition there? Do you feel better about the opera than about other pieces you wrote?

KP – Yes. I have to say, and I think a lot of it is the fact that like I described earlier, there was so much time to get Silent Night right. To get it the way I wanted it through all these workshops, re-writing and re-orchestrating, I really do feel that it probably is my best piece. I really feel very happy with it. Yes, I feel that this moment here, that moment there, that was exactly the expression that I intended, and I got it, the best that I could do. And sometimes it is difficult to do that, with say, orchestral pieces, where there is so little time… Once I hear the piece the premiere will be three or four days later! [laughs] It's very difficult. There is a certain surprise that occurs, no matter how clearly you can hear a piece in your inner ear. You imagine that, and it is just different when you get real players to play it. For me it's kind of a shock, sometimes, to adjust to that. And often the dynamics of the performance are very different from private listening on your own. I need to have a concert happen, I need to have a performance, then I can make adjustments. I just don't often have those opportunities with orchestral pieces.

My string quartet, the one I called *Credo*, I think is one of my best. I think my Symphony No. 4 is strong. Actually, if you ask a composer, it's always their latest pieces that they like the best. I wrote two new pieces for chorus, which I think are pretty strong. [laughs]

OL - May we, if you don't mind, finish by giving our readers a flavor of the man Mr. Kevin Puts underneath the composer (we do understand that one can't be separated from the other)? What are some of the ideas, causes, or activities that you praise and like in your non-musical life? How do you define your personality and your take on life, in general? Do you aim at expressing anything in particular, with your music? Do you see a social impact you may be able to accomplish through your music?

KP – I'm not sure how interesting my personal life is. My music is something separate from the person I am. I don't know if my personality reflects the style of my music or the nature of my music. When I write music I go to a certain kind of place, emotionally and intellectually, and I know when I'm there that it is a great place to be, but I'm not there all day long.

I have a family, my wife plays violin at the New York Philharmonic. I have a 3-year-old son. I'm not a guy who surrounds himself constantly with arts. I like being with my family, I like being with friends, I like watching movies and sports, [laughs], I don't spend all day long in art museums, I don't go to very many concerts; to be honest; I listen to music by myself.

I like being funny. My music always comes off as serious, but I don't come off that way as a person. Those who know me could be led to wonder whether my music is sincere. It is sincere, I just don't feel… I avoid pretense as a person as much as possible [laughs], I don't feel I need to perform the role of a composer in my persona, in my daily life. My hope is that the music speaks for itself and works on its own.

OL - How did your relationship with music begin? In your childhood, or as a teenager? Can you tell us a bit about your path into music?

KP – When I heard music as a kid, I was hooked. My parents played recordings for me. My parents are not musicians but they love music, they played Beethoven symphonies for me, and I was into Dvořák's music. I was just hooked, I wanted nothing more, I just wanted to listen to music in my head. Kids came over to the house, I was very young, and I would try to play them these recordings, and they would just kind of walk out of the room, you know? [laughs] It's that connection that you have when you are very young. It is not a choice, it's just a kind of obsession, really. It's just something that is deeply part of me and has always been. I played the piano very seriously through the end of college. I played concertos and recitals and that kind of thing. And I composed all the way through. I just decided eventually that composing was far more interesting to me than performing.

I just love the whole phenomenon of the musical score being communicated through a performance. The kind of coldness of the score, the black and white dots and lines and how simple it is – it can be complex, but how it doesn't make any noise, but contains the recipe for something amazing! I was always fascinated by scores and by creating them, something that has all the information that I intend embedded into it, and all that has to be done is that it has to be read with respect and taken seriously by the musicians. Of course there is flexibility within that; great musicians will take license when they need to, but I just love the idea of saying everything I need to say with the score, and here is this document and it will always be that way. Composing is just a fascinating thing for me. I thing notation is a fascinating thing, and of course, the unknown of not knowing what I will do is incredibly scary.

The libretto for *The Manchurian Candidate*, you open it up and it doesn't make any noise, it's just words and stage directions and lines. It's exciting and also scary, to think about what I'm going to do with it. It's exhilarating for me.

OL – Interesting! You are a professor of composition at Peabody. Is teaching one your passions?

KP – Yes. What is really fascinating is how you learn that every composer operates in a completely different way. The way each composer approaches music varies so much from one student to the next, so they all need different things, and you have to feel out what they need, and what - kind of psychologically - composition is for them, before you can really help them out. So, it's very interesting from that perspective. You have to understand and really get to know them and what they need, so it feels more like therapy than music lessons [laughs].

OL - What are some of the ideas about this *métier* you'd like to transmit to young composers?
KP - I don't know what I want to transmit to them. The reason I think *Silent Night* works – if it does work – is because I am able to get out of the way as a composer, and do what the story dictates. A lot of composers are so worried about their own agenda, putting themselves forward, so that the story can become convoluted or miscommunicated. Maybe it's because I haven't tried so rigorously to define my style. But I'm able to just say, "OK, what does this scene need?" And it may not be that interesting, from the point of view of the composer; it may not be that sophisticated or technically difficult to accomplish, but this is what needs to happen to transmit the story. I think it's something I can do; I can do it well, and it's probably what helped me with this opera.

OL - In this day and age of economic crisis and tight budgets for the arts, how do you see the young people getting into the business, these days? Do you talk to them about hardships?

KP – I don't know what will happen. I feel very lucky to have had these opportunities to write opera. It's very expensive to commission a new opera and to produce it, and it is very unpredictable; it's a scary venture for these companies, but there are those who are doing it. Minnesota Opera is amazing in that way, as is Opera Philadelphia. I'm going to be doing a new opera for Minnesota Opera, and also a new one for Opera Philadelphia in a few years. There are just companies that believe that commissioning is important, and they are willing to take the risk. Honestly, I'm in awe of these companies. I don't exactly know how they raise this money to produce these new pieces, but they do. I don't know exactly how it still happens, when everybody is trying to save money and we are still in an economic crisis. I don't know how it happens but I feel very fortunate that at least at this moment I'm part of it.

OL – Thank you so much for your time and your thoughtful answers.

GENERAL INDEX

In the next few pages the reader will find a general index.

It includes opera titles (and rarely other musical works), italicized and usually in original language, but sometimes in English when it is the common usage, such as *The Bartered Bride* rather than *Prodaná nevěsta.* Articles in opera titles are taken into account for alphabetization. This is true for both English titles and foreign language titles, therefore *A Midsummer Night's Dream* comes under A rather than M, and *La Bohème* or *Il Trovatore* come respectively under L and I rather than B or T.

The index also includes composers, and those are mostly listed and alphabetized by last name only in Anglicized form when it's the common form of reference (people usually simply say Handel instead of Georg Frideric Händel), unless a more obscure composer or one with a relatively common last name are best known by their full name. Sometimes the composer's first name is needed for differentiation – the case for instance of Richard Strauss since his last name could be confused with the Viennese waltz composers of the same name. Richard Wagner on the other hand is simply listed as Wagner. Only major composers have systematic multiple entries.

Any time a name has a first name attached to it, the first name takes priority for alphabetization, so Richard Strauss comes under R rather than under S.

Opera singers are generally represented by full name and alphabetized by first name. So, look for Luciano Pavarotti under L rather than P. Conductors and stage directors are also listed, usually with full names and alphabetized by first name. Orchestras are listed by the first letter of their names. We listed some Opera Houses / Companies but did not list names of arias, or names of opera characters).

Given the variability inherent to the method we chose to use (the common form of reference), we encourage the reader, when not finding what he or she is looking for, to try to look up specific names by both first and last name, or opera titles by both original language and English.

ABOUT THE AUTHOR

Tenor Matthew Polenzani and Luiz Gazzola © Opera Lively Press

Luiz Gazzola, MD, PhD, has loved opera since a lucky encounter with *Carmen* decades ago. Over the years, he has explored the opera repertory from Monteverdi to Unsuk Chin, taking in hundreds of recorded and live performances (he used to live two blocks from the Metropolitan Opera House), as well as reading widely on the subject. Opera is in Dr. Gazzola's blood, given that he is a dual citizen of Italy and the United States who speaks five languages. He holds the position of Senior Editor at Opera Lively, and is the author of "The Opera Lively Guides – Les Troyens," also published by Opera Lively Press.

His passion for this fascinating art form drove him to embrace a second career as a registered opera journalist, while remaining active as a Board Certified Psychiatrist. Dr. Gazzola, who authored a book on Obsessive-Compulsive Personality Disorder, is a graduate of Columbia University, with a doctoral degree in Psychoanalysis from the University of Paris, France. He has written articles for cultural magazines, and led a seminar on Cinema and Psychoanalysis at Columbia University. Opera, cinema, and literature join fine wines as his main interests outside of his family and profession. He currently lives with his wife Marta in North Carolina, where he teaches students from Duke University. In between Psychiatry lessons, he always makes a point of introducing opera to his students, refusing to be discouraged by a dismal 6% conversion rate for new opera fans among them!

www.ingramcontent.com/pod-product-compliance
Lightning Source LLC
Chambersburg PA
CBHW021350090426
42742CB00009B/803

* 9 7 8 0 6 9 2 2 8 5 1 2 1 *